AMERICA'S BEST HISTORIC SITES

America's Best Historic Sites

101 Terrific Places to Take the Family

B. J. Welborn

Cover photos by Photodisc.
Top photo of the Statue of Liberty and the Manhattan skyline;
bottom photo of the White House Ruins, Canyon de Chelly, in Chinle, Arizona.

The author encourages correspondence.
Her e-mail address is BJWELBORN@aol.com.

First edition
Published by Chicago Review Press, Incorporated
814 North Franklin Street
Chicago, Illinois 60610
ISBN 0-7394-0050-9
Printed in the United States of America

To my father, the late Ed Welborn, and my mother, Lucille Welborn. Thanks for the childhood pilgrimages to colonial settlements, Civil War battlefields, and historic outdoor dramas.

As the twig is bent, so grows the tree.

Contents

Colorado

Montana

New Mexico

Utah

Wyoming

Geographical Regions Map

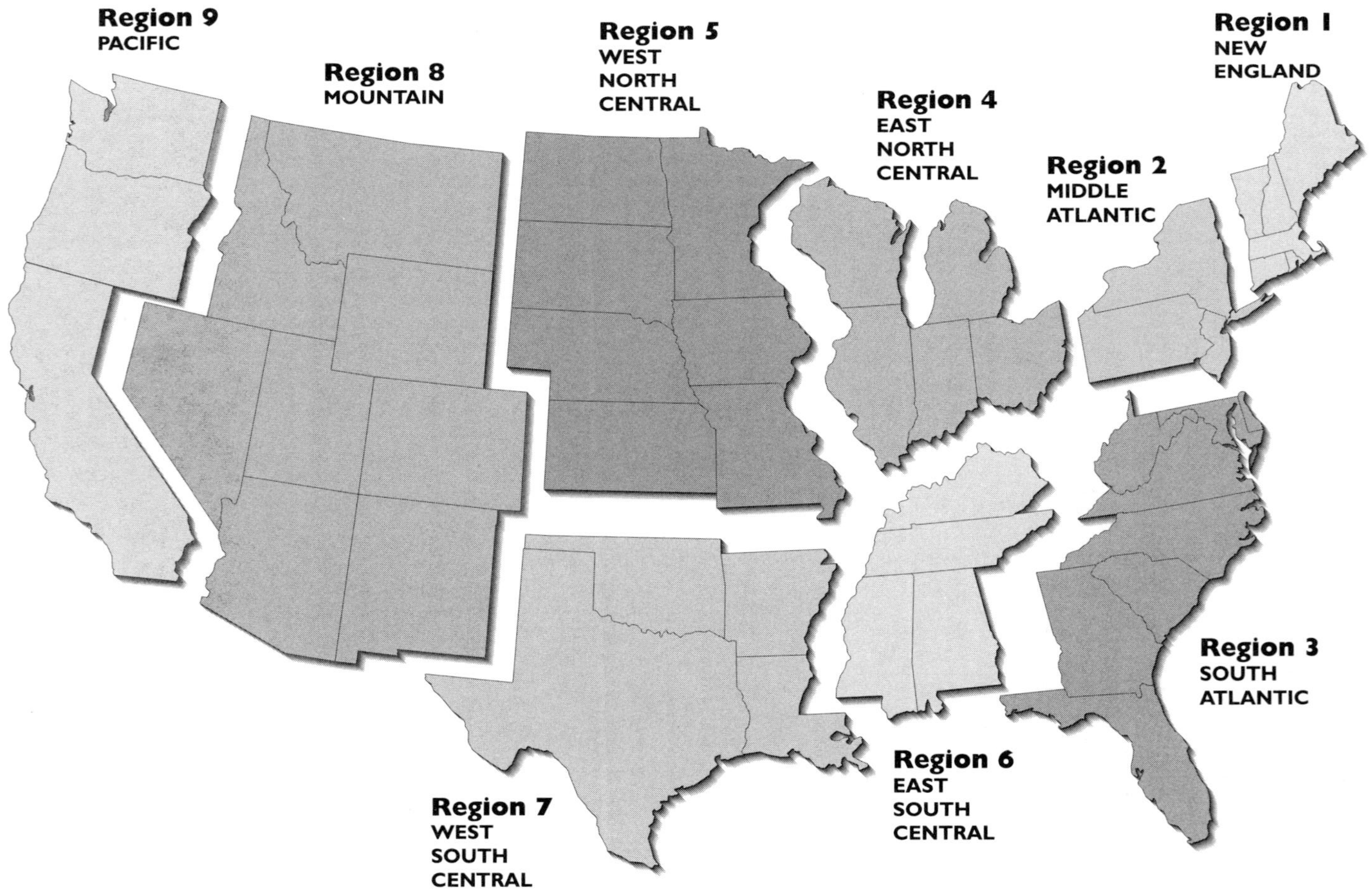

Region 9
PACIFIC

Region 8
MOUNTAIN

Region 5
WEST
NORTH
CENTRAL

Region 4
EAST
NORTH
CENTRAL

Region 2
MIDDLE
ATLANTIC

Region 1
NEW
ENGLAND

Region 3
SOUTH
ATLANTIC

Region 6
EAST
SOUTH
CENTRAL

Region 7
WEST
SOUTH
CENTRAL

National Trails System Map

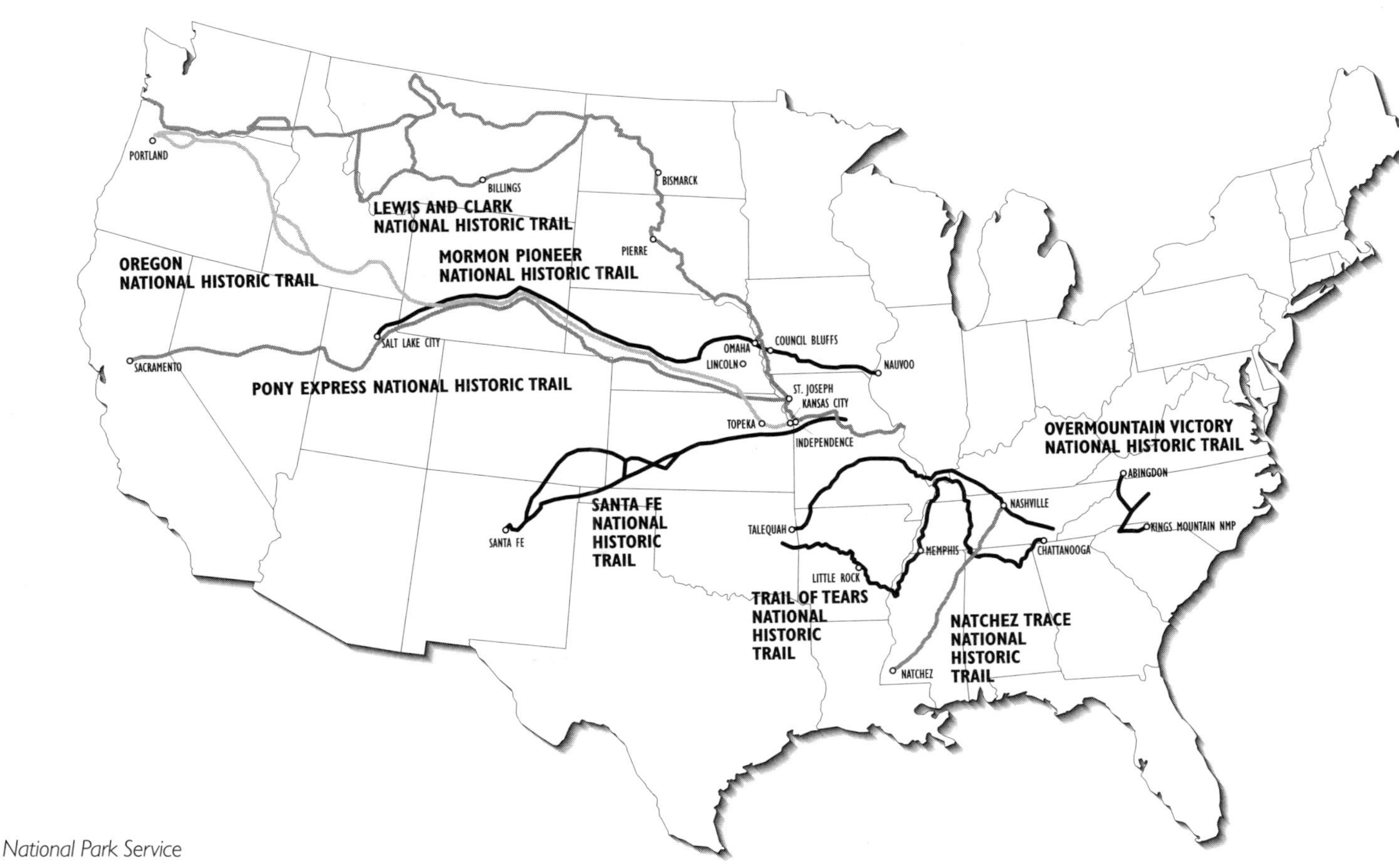

National Park Service

Introduction

Did you know that you can see Thomas Edison's lab just as the great inventor left it; smell the gunpowder on Lexington Green just as minutemen did in 1775; walk the Montana ground where General George Custer met his fate; touch the wagon ruts made by pioneers on the Oregon Trail; and examine 1,000-year-old fingerprints left by prehistoric Indian masons in Arizona?

America's historic sites are more than roadside markers, empty forts, and monuments to the dead. The best sites help you relive history-altering moments and get to know the people—both famous and ordinary—who made a difference.

Like no other travel guide, this book opens the treasure chest of American history. Inside you'll find details on the who, what, when, where, and why of America's best historic sites, boiled down into an easy-to-use guide format.

As this millennium ends and another begins, interest in history reaches a natural crescendo. Parents and other travelers who love history can take advantage of the times. Visiting historic—and prehistoric—sites can be a fun and entertaining treat for the family, and it's the best way to truly understand history.

The theory behind this book is a Chinese proverb:

> ***Tell me and I'll forget;***
> ***show me and I may remember;***
> ***involve me and I'll understand.***

Hands-on history lessons take preparation. Otherwise trips to the places where history unfolded can be, at best, hit-or-miss propositions. At worst they can turn into miserable, tiring, best-forgotten experiences for everyone. This book is designed to help parents enable their kids to understand American history.

My interest in American history began in childhood with Sunday picnics at Civil War battlefields. My father would have us four kids comb the site looking for Confederate bullets. Were we ever excited to find a pointed rock, certain it was a handcarved remnant of the war. As an adult and mother of two, I wanted to cultivate the same love of history in my children that my father cultivated in me.

So I took it upon myself to travel the country, visiting historic sites and finding the best places for families to visit. I flew 35,000 miles, drove 25,000 miles, and walked 300 miles—all in one year. I entered a parallel universe where people wear the garb of yesteryear, act as if they've never heard of a computer, and daily celebrate our diverse national heritage.

I've come back to create a book that gives parents all the information they need for pleasant, memorable visits to America's best historic sites.

This guide is unique. In it you'll find:

- **A comprehensive alphabetical listing of the best** federal, state, local, and privately operated historic sites across America.
- **An unusual mix** of sites, some well known and some obscure, but all places where important and exciting events unfolded—events that changed the course of American history. Details of national historic trails, such as the Oregon Trail and Lewis and Clark Trail, are included, too.
- **Unique information for parents**: where to find a site's attention-grabbers, the things that will generate excitement in kids that leads to the kind of emotional involvement that cements memories—and history lessons.
- **Helpful information** including on-site locations, hours, days of operation, fees, parking, web sites, and where to get additional information.
- **A historic frame of reference** putting the events that unfolded at each site into historical context. (This could take you hours of research and is rarely included in park literature.)
- **Hot tips** to make a family visit more pleasant: what to take, age appropriateness, locations of food and accommodations, and suggestions for advance reading and video viewing.
- Background information, both **then and now,** gives compelling details linking historic events to present-day visits. This'll give you stories to tell the kids while touring a site.
- Information on sites **elsewhere in the area** so you can plan an extended visit.
- **The best stuff** each site offers—a brief description of the most interesting things that afford hands-on excitement.
- Finally, an appendix that contains my list of **top ten sites,** both historic and prehistoric, for families. No matter where you live, it's worth a trip just to see these sites. Another appendix contains my list of **ten hidden jewels,** sites worthy of a look if you're in the area. These distinctions are also noted in the listings themselves.

Here are a few details that will also prove helpful.

All sites have restrooms.

All sites are wheelchair accessible, except where noted.

Group reservations are encouraged everywhere.

Site fees are indicated with the following code:

$ The entrance fee is less than $10 per person.

$$ The entrance fee is between $10 and $25 per person.

$$$ The entrance fee is more than $25 per person.

Entrance fee as well as hours of operation are current as of publication date. These are subject to change, however, and may differ at the time of your visit. Note that sites listed under "Elsewhere in the Area" may have entrance fees, but these are not included throughout.

A couple of caveats: Parents should think twice before taking children under the age of seven or eight to historic sites, that is, if you want to teach them history. Until the ability to reason abstractly kicks in, children can't understand the historic relevance of a site. Dr. Bart Wendell, a Boston-area psychologist, puts it this way: "Young children appreciate the concrete elements of a site, what they can see, touch, taste, and smell. The historic significance probably will be lost on them. Without concrete elements, young children most likely will be bored. Parents should be flexible."

Visitors to America's historical parks often find signs with these words: "Take only photographs, leave only footprints." This means don't pick up artifacts, deface natural features, or disturb wildlife. Such actions are illegal and punishable by fines. Vandalism threatens to destroy much of our collective history. Take a moment to remind children that people who care won't damage these irreplaceable treasures.

America's Best Historic Sites opens the door to terrific experiences in history for the entire family. Happy trails!

1

NEW ENGLAND

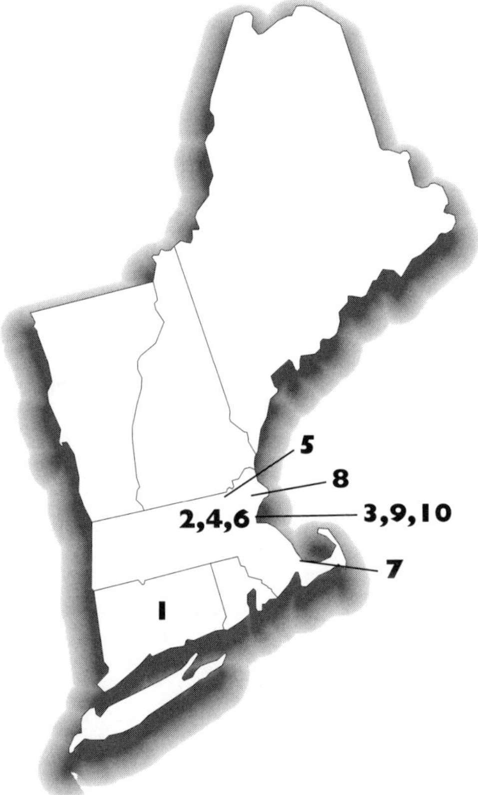

Key

Numbers correspond to site numbers on the map.

Connecticut
1. Mark Twain House

Massachusetts
2. Battle Road
3. Freedom Trail
4. Lexington Green
5. Lowell
6. North Bridge
7. Plymouth Rock
8. Salem
9. Tea Party Ship
10. U.S.S. *Constitution*

Freedom Trail

Boston's Path to American Independence

Location Downtown and North End of Boston, Massachusetts, and adjacent Charlestown.

Boston National Historical Park distributes information about the Freedom Trail, a 2½-mile walking tour of 16 historic sites. Sites are operated by various entities with individual days and hours of operation. Some charge an admittance fee ($). You can reach all of the sites by public transportation. For more information contact Superintendent, Boston National Historical Park, Charlestown Navy Yard, Boston, MA 02129. Tel. (617) 242-5644.

Frame of Reference In the early to late 18th century, Boston was a stormy incubator for the American Revolution (1775–81) and site of early Revolutionary War fighting.

Significance Colonial Boston played an active and important role in pre-Revolutionary America and was the site of the first major battle of the Revolution, the Battle of Bunker Hill, soon after the outbreak of fighting in nearby Lexington and Concord. The famous historic sites along the Freedom Trail tell Boston's story of that time, as well as other tales of the city's role in the political, cultural, and intellectual development of America.

The Woman Rider

The Revolution was underway on the night of April 26, 1777, when Sybil Ludington made her not-so-well-known ride. The 16-year-old patriot rode from town to town in Connecticut and New York to warn the colonists that the British were raiding Danbury, Connecticut. Her horseback ride produced enough volunteers to thwart the redcoats the next day. Sybil's New York hometown was renamed after her. Her ride covered twice the ground of Paul Revere's.

About the Site The Boston National Historical Park includes the 2½-mile Freedom Trail connecting the historic sites, with several interesting neighborhoods along the way. A wide, red-painted line marks the walking trail. The trail begins on Boston Common, America's oldest public park, purchased by Puritans in 1634.

The trail includes these sites: the 1795 State House (Paul Revere's company made the copper dome); the 1809 Park Street Church (gunpowder was stored here in the War of 1812); the 1660 Granary Burying Ground (final resting place of the victims of the Boston Massacre, Paul Revere, John Hancock, and Sam Adams); Kings Chapel and Kings Chapel Burying Ground (burial place of William Dawes, also on the midnight ride, and Mary Chilton, the first Pilgrim to touch Plymouth Rock); site of the country's first public school, Boston Latin, 1635); 1729 Old South Meeting House (where the Boston Tea Party began);

1718 Old Corner Bookstore (center of 19th-century literary America); 1713 Old State House (seat of colonial government); Boston Massacre Site (where British soldiers killed five colonists on March 5, 1770); 1742 Faneuil Hall (dubbed "the Cradle of Liberty" because of the public protests against British policy voiced here) and marketplace; 1680 Paul Revere House (where the famous silversmith lived at the time of his midnight ride and Boston's oldest wooden structure); 1723 Old North Church (where Revere saw the two lanterns that started his famous ride); 1659 Copp's Hill Burying Ground, burial site of Cotton Mather, the Puritan minister who fueled the Salem witch hysteria; 1797 U.S.S. *Constitution* (famous War of 1812 "Old Ironsides" and world's oldest commissioned warship afloat); and the Bunker Hill Monument commemorating the first major battle of the American Revolution, fought on June 17, 1775.

Costumed guides abound along the trail and at each site, offering talks and answering questions. The sites all are owned and managed individually by federal, state, and city governments and private organizations.

Hot Tips Whew! Walking the Freedom Trail in bustling downtown Boston with its maze of narrow, one-way streets and heavy traffic is a challenge, but it's the best way to experience the historic sites. Do not attempt to drive the trail! That's a path to frustration. Lack of on-street parking at the sites and unmarked streets can spoil the visit. Also, trolley tours are available throughout the city ($). This is the best way to tour if you're short on time or energy.

Allow at least 1½ hours to walk the trail nonstop. It's more realistic, however, to plan a three- to four-hour stroll, and if you plan to actually go inside the landmarks, it's smarter to take an entire day—or two.

There are a number of ways to walk the trail—self-guided or guided, free or for a fee. To begin your free tour, find a parking garage or take public transportation to the National Park Service Visitor Center at 15 State Street beside the Old State House. You can walk the trail beginning at the other end at "Old Ironsides" in Charlestown.

Paul Revere Capture Site

In Concord, 16 miles west of Boston and about ⅜ mile west of where Nelson Road meets Route 2A stands another boulder and plaque marking the Paul Revere Capture Site. (If you walk there, watch out for speeding drivers.) Here, at the historically described curve in the road, British soldiers captured the famous Alarm Rider. Revere was one of 30 patriots who organized to watch the movements of the British and gather intelligence on the Tories. A British patrol halted Revere and two other riders, William Dawes of Boston and Dr. Samuel Prescott of Concord. Dawes escaped and Prescott cleared a stone wall, carrying the alarm to Concord. Revere tried to escape but was quickly intercepted by the British and carried back to Lexington. Upon release, he warned John Hancock and Sam Adams, who were at the Hancock-Clarke House in Lexington.

As of publication, a new monument marking the capture site is scheduled for opening in Spring 1998. A parking lot will be located next to the monument. Plans call for a boulder with a plaque to be housed in a granite canopy. The plaque reads "At this point, on the Old Concord Road as it then was, ended the Midnight Ride of Paul Revere."

Hot Tip for those with precious little time and/or absolutely no interest in walking Seek out the John Hancock Tower (it's the 60-story shiny black building—the tallest in New England—at Copley Square), entrance at St. James Avenue and Clarendon Street, and take the elevator to the observatory at the top ($). You'll get a 360-degree view that takes in all the sites for miles. The observatory is open daily, except Thanksgiving and December 25, Monday through Saturday, 9 A.M.–11 P.M., and Sunday, 10 A.M.–11 P.M. Last tickets are sold at 10 P.M. For information call (617) 572-6429. The downtown Prudential Center's 50th-floor Skywalk also offers the view. Tel. (617) 236-3744.

There are plenty of wonderful places to eat in Boston, many alfresco in the warm months. Accommodations are available throughout the city.

The Best Stuff It's tough to choose, but the Revolutionary sites you probably learned about in grade school are the best part of the trail. Topping the list: the Old North Church, U.S.S. *Constitution*, and Bunker Hill Monument. Add Faneuil Hall for its fiery history and marketplace ambiance and the Old State House for its fascinating museum ($). Here's what you must take time to see:

Old State House and Museum. Inside this meeting house of the Massachusetts Assembly the ordinary public was allowed for the first time in modern history to view government at work. During a debate on the Stamp Act in 1766, spectators in the gallery heckled defenders of the Crown. Boston agitators consistently incurred England's wrath in speeches here. When the new State House on Beacon Hill was completed in 1798, this small, two-story brick building was rented out for stores and offices. In 1882 the Bostonian Society opened a museum here.

Now, upstairs over a subway station, you can enter the tranquil second-floor museum and see these treasures: 1) A vial of tea from the Boston Tea Party. The tea leaves came from the boots of a party participant and were saved in a 3½-inch vial of late-18th-cen-

Finding Paul Revere

Overrated Hero or Minor Character in History?

Listen, my children, and you shall hear,
Of the midnight ride of Paul Revere . . .

Once upon a time, not so long ago, Paul Revere was an American legend, a folk hero immortalized by Henry Wadsworth Longfellow's 1861 poem, "Paul Revere's Ride," read in schools throughout the land.

As of late, however, Revere's reputation, once with a patina as dazzling as one of his famous silver tea sets, has been tarnished. The Boston political insider, propagandist, entrepreneur, father of 16, and trusted patriot messenger who made the ride from Boston to Concord 220 years ago to warn "the British are coming" has fallen victim to rampant cynicism. Is Revere an overrated hero or just a minor character in history?

Besides reading up on the man—and there are books aplenty—you can visit Boston and see at least ten sites directly connected to Revere and decide for yourself whether Revere deserves his good reputation or not.

Note For an especially meaningful copy of Longfellow's poem, go to Longfellow's Wayside Inn, off The Boston Post Road (Route 20) in Sudbury, 15 miles west of Boston. Here the famous poet and friends gathered to tell tales, including the story of Paul Revere.

tury green glass. 2) A cannon ball from Bunker Hill and a musket probably used in the Boston Massacre. 3) A crimson velvet suit of Boston agitator John Hancock, later Massachusetts's first governor.

The first floor served as the town's first merchants' exchange, a precursor of the stock exchange. Today the area of State Street extending from the Old State House is Boston's financial district. Outside, below the great clock, is the balcony from which the royal governors read proclamations. On July 18, 1776, Colonel Thomas Crafts read the new Declaration of Independence to the crowd.

Boston Massacre Site. The infamous 1770 Boston Massacre happened in front of the Old State House. British officers killed five Americans when the officers fired into a taunting crowd. Patriots made the most of the incident, Paul Revere's famous silver engraving of the massacre leading the way. (The engraving was copied and distributed throughout the colonies, solidifying Revere's reputation as the supreme patriot propagandist.) Today a circle of paving stones in the center of a busy intersection marks the site.

Faneuil Hall. A gift to Boston from merchant Peter Faneuil in 1742, this meeting hall and market is one of the city's most cherished landmarks. Colonists first dared to speak against British rule here at heated town meetings—still a New England tradition, though not in Boston, a city since 1822. In this four-story brick building (enlarged in 1806), angry colonists first met the night of the Boston Tea Party but, to accommodate the large crowd, moved the meeting to Old South Meeting House. The lower floor has always been a market, as it is today. The market—commonly called Quincy Market—includes three granite buildings and a bustling plaza offering food, gourmet coffee, shopping, and free speech. Faneuil Hall (pronounced Fannel), topped with its famous copper-and-gold-leaf grasshopper weathervane, still functions as a public meeting room where issues continue to be debated.

Old North Church. Boston's oldest standing church building towers over Boston Harbor in the North End, near Revere's house. Here on April 18, 1775, the church's caretaker, Robert Newman, crept up the tower steps unnoticed by British soldiers milling in the streets. One, if by land; two, if by sea were the instructions from his friend Paul Revere, a trusted patriot express rider. Two lanterns signaled to colonists Revere's intelligence that British troops were crossing the Charles River on their way to Concord to seize munitions and possibly arrest John Hancock and Sam Adams, who were hiding there. Revere took a horse in Charlestown and carried the warning of approaching British troops to Lexington and Concord. (Revere's ride—and not Dawes's nor Prescott's—became entrenched in the American psyche by Henry Wadsworth Longfellow's poem, "The Midnight Ride of Paul Revere.") The next day, the first shots of the Revolution were fired in Lexington.

Note You can see one of the original tin lanterns used in the Old North Church tower in the Concord Museum, 200 Lexington Road in Concord.

Visiting Old North Church today, you see the same 191-foot steeple with the arched windows of the belfry where the lanterns shone. (The spire was replaced after destruction by a 1954 hurricane.) The belfry houses the first church bells to peal in North America.

A costumed guide tells of the brick church's many claims to fame: Pew 62, used by royal governors including General Gage, who sent British troops to Concord; the 1,100 bodies buried under the floor, including that of Major Pitcairn, who led the British troops at Lexington and Concord and was killed at Bunker Hill; the recently uncovered window through which church caretaker Newman escaped after lighting the two lanterns; the original church organ case; and the original 1740 weathervane atop the steeple.

The white-walled interior looks the same as when the first Anglican worshipers prayed here. Even today there are no electric lights. Candles are used for services, as they have been since the church opened in 1723.

The Prado. Don't miss the poplar-lined Paul Revere Mall (locally called the Prado), displaying a towering bronze Revere on horseback and 13 bronze panels by Robert Savage Chase showing the history of the North End. A small museum and gift shop next to the church houses several important historical items, including a small bottle of Boston Tea Party tea, Major Pitcairn's sword blade, and a musket used by Colonel Robert Gould Shaw, a Bostonian who led a black regiment in the Civil War.

Hot Tip You can buy a wonderful illustrated guide for kids, *Look at the Old North Church*, at the gift shop. Pick up the eight-page pamphlet before your tour.

Bunker Hill. At the far end of the Freedom Trail, across the Charles River in predominately Irish Charlestown, stands the 221-foot granite Bunker Hill Monument. In one of those twists of history, the Battle of Bunker Hill was actually fought on nearby Breed's Hill, and at the summit of this hill amid Charlestown townhouses stands the monument. (In a last-minute change of plans, patriot forces hastily built an earthen fortification atop Breed's Hill, next to higher Bunker Hill. Breed's Hill offered a better vantage point closer to Boston. The switch in plans may have caused the name confusion, although locals also confused the names of the hills.)

The obelisk, finished in 1842–40 years before the taller Washington Monument—reminds us of the first major battle, waged between 2,200 British troops and about 1,000 New England soldiers that left the now-grassy hill slippery with blood. American troops had learned of British plans for a three-day sweep through the countryside and decided on preemptive action.

Because of a patriot shortage of gunpowder, leader Colonel William Prescott reportedly ordered colonists not to fire "until you see the whites of their eyes."

In three successive waves, the redcoats marched up the hill in 80-degree heat. The patriots mowed them down. But lack of gunpowder eventually caused a colonial retreat, and the British took the hill with a cost of 1,054 casualties. The colonists lost about 400. The British paid a high price for this "victory."

Today's Freedom Trail leads visitors up granite steps in Charlestown's 38-acre Monument Square, past the New Hampshire gate (that state supplied most of the militia force at Bunker Hill), and up granite steps to the monument and adjoining lodge, which houses a small museum. You can climb the 294 steps up the monument (no elevators) and enjoy a spectacular view.

Stone markers show the outline of the patriots' earthen fort. From the hilltop, encircled with an iron fence, you can see the spire of St. Francis de Sales Church atop the true, now highly developed, Bunker Hill to the west. Breed's Hill itself is about 1/3 the height it was on June 17, 1775. Its soil later was used for landfill to expand Boston.

Hot Tips The Raytheon Bunker Hill Pavilion, next to the Charlestown Navy Yard on Water Street, shows a must-see ½-hour, multimedia show about the battle every half hour ($). *Whites of Their Eyes* is in-the-round on 14 screens with 22 life-size costumed figures. This thunderous reenactment may scare very young children. The show airs daily, April through November, 9:30 A.M.–4 P.M., with extended summer hours. The museum is open year-round. Tel. (781) 241-7575.

Then and Now Thanks to aggressive preservation efforts, many of Boston's pre-Revolutionary and Revolutionary sites teem with millions of tourists annually. Amid the bustle of this major 20th-century city, you can find the story of the birth of a nation.

Elsewhere in the Area Find the Boston Tea Party Ship and Museum off Congress Street; Lexington and Concord, sites of the first Revolutionary War fighting; the Black Heritage Trail in the Beacon Hill area; and the Public Garden with its famous Swan Boats.

Lexington Green

Where the First Blood of the Revolution Was Shed

Location In the center of Lexington, Massachusetts, 16 miles northwest of Boston. The Lexington Green is a triangular open space formed where Bedford and Hancock streets meet Massachusetts Avenue.

Lexington Battle Green is an open public park that you can visit any time. Important historic buildings in the area are owned and operated by private entities. For information on fees and hours of operation of these sites and others contact the Lexington Visitors Center, 1875 Massachusetts Avenue, Lexington, MA 02173. Tel. (781) 862-1450. Hours are daily, except Thanksgiving, December 25, and January 1, 9 A.M.–5 P.M. A reenactment of the 1775 historic events of the Green takes place every April 19, beginning at dawn. Arrive early.

Frame of Reference Lexington Green was the location of the outbreak of the Revolutionary War (1775–81), on April 19, 1775.

Significance Here 75 Lexington minutemen—warned by Paul Revere and other patriot messengers—confronted several hundred British soldiers "secretly" marching from Boston to destroy colonial arms and ammunition stashed in Concord. Despite orders on both sides not to fire, someone fired a single shot in the early light of dawn. In response the redcoats took battle positions and, without orders, shot over the heads of the minutemen. The colonists fired back. After less than 30 minutes, seven minutemen and one unarmed colonist were dead. Ten other Americans were wounded, as well as two British soldiers. It wasn't obvious at the time, but this heated skirmish had ignited the American Revolution.

The British troops marched on to Concord, where minutemen from surrounding villages waited. The first full battle of the Revolution took place at the North Bridge in Concord later that day.

About the Site The Lexington Battle Green was once the old Village Common, the grassy common grounds of colonial times set aside for cattle. On this two-acre grassy common, the minutemen—farmers and merchants who pledged to be ready to fight on a minute's notice—gathered to face the British advancing from Boston under Paul Revere's watchful eye. In this shady triangular park you will find an inscribed boulder marking the minutemen's line of defense, the spot where the belfry stood that housed the bell that first called the patriots to the green, and the oldest Revolutionary War monument in America, erected on the green in 1799. The remains of the men killed in the Battle of Lexington are buried around this monument.

An American flag atop a giant flagpole flies over the green 24 hours a day by act of Congress. High up the flagpole a black sign with gold lettering reads "Birth Place of American Liberty."

Here also you will find the huge bronze Minuteman Statue, musket in hand, facing the east, watching for the British.

Monuments and historic homes surround the green. The Lexington Historical Society owns and operates three original buildings of great importance: the 1710 Buckman Tavern ($) next to the green, where minutemen headquartered and waited for the British; the Munroe Tavern ($), one mile east, which served as British headquarters and hospital; and the Hancock-Clarke House ($), a few blocks north, where patriots John Hancock and Samuel Adams slept when Paul Revere arrived to warn them that the redcoats were coming. It had been rumored that British troops had been ordered to arrest Hancock and Adams, who were accused of fostering rebellion in the colonies.

Hot Tips It may be tempting to drive by Lexington Battle Green, gaze at the towering memorial flag and monuments, and then drive on, as you mutter to yourself, "So that's where the Revolutionary War began." Don't do it. You'll miss out on some really fascinating places, treasured artifacts, and many great stories of American history. In fact, plan to spend at least several hours nosing around here. In addition to the historic sites, downtown Lexington offers interesting shops and fine dining, alfresco in the warm months.

Begin your visit with a stop at the Lexington Chamber of Commerce's Visitor Center next to the green. Here you can get maps and view a diorama of the battle with taped narration. (Buy a copy of the narration for 26¢.) If you have younger kids, look for *The Children's Coloring Book of Lexington, Massachusetts,* with stories of the day. It's a wonderful account.

Buy tickets to tour Buckman Tavern, Munroe Tavern, and the Hancock-Clarke House at the gift shop behind Buckman Tavern. Reservations are required for groups of 10 or more. For information contact The Lexington Historical Society, P.O. Box 514, Lexington, MA 02173. Tel. (781) 862-1703. Park on the street or in the small public parking lot off Waltham Street. Be prepared for walking. Watch out for heavy traffic. Accommodations are available in Lexington.

A good read for young people is Howard Fast's *April Morning*.

The Best Stuff Lexington Green and the area immediately around it are well preserved. A visit to this low-key historic site, surrounded by old white clapboard homes and churches, can seem like a visit back to the 18th century. You can stand exactly where the edgy minutemen waited in two lines at dawn. But the story of that April 19 more than 220 years ago is best told at Buckman Tavern. And a visit to the 1698 Hancock-Clarke House is icing on the cake. Both are open daily, mid-April through October, 10 A.M.–5 P.M., Sunday, 1 P.M.–5 P.M. Visits are by guided tour only.

The costumed guide at Buckman Tavern takes you first into the tap room. This small room with its seven-foot-wide brick fireplace and bar served as a meeting place for travelers and locals alike—all male. Women were never allowed; they met in the ladies' parlor—open to men—across the entrance hall. (Even the tavern owner's wife and daughter couldn't enter the tap room.) Today you can see two peepholes drilled into the original 1709 wall between the tap room and the kitchen. Through these holes the women watched from the kitchen to see when more food was needed.

Beneath these same wood ceiling beams of the tap room, Captain John Parker, a farmer who led the Lexington minutemen, and his men waited all night on April 18, 1775, for word that the British were near.

The most famous treasure of the 300-year-old Buckman Tavern resides in the front hall, encased in Plexiglas. This is the heavy front door that took a British musket ball during the bitter exchange of fire on the green. U.S. presidents and visitors from around the world have traveled here to stick their fingers into the 1½-inch hole the stray musket ball made in the reddish wooden door. The Plexiglas prohibits that now, but take heart in the fact that a three-foot piece of whitewashed clapboard from the tavern front has been saved and displayed in an 1813 tavern wing once used as a post office. You can stick your finger in that hole to your heart's content.

Every one of the carefully restored six rooms open for touring brims with colonial treasures and authentic glimpses into Revolutionary-era life. Guides give colorful explanations of how the tavern owners baked bread, how gossiping men quaffed home-brewed beer, and how the tavern owner, John Buckman, placed a special four-candle lantern in his window indicating a sleeping place to the nighttime traveler. But the best tale surrounds the five-foot wooden kitchen table where Buckman and his family routinely ate until the history-making day of April 19, 1775.

After the exchange of fire at dawn, the wounded were taken to the tavern kitchen where a local surgeon, Dr. Joseph Fiske, attended them. Hearing this, the British commander, Major John Pitcairn, allegedly sent his wounded there also. Dr. Fiske operated on a British soldier on this very table placed at the far end of the kitchen. The soldier later died and was buried as an unknown soldier in the nearby Old Burying Ground. A headstone marks the grave. Later Dr. Fiske sent the British a bill for his services. The war debt remains unpaid.

Treasures at the Hancock-Clarke House, Paul Revere's destination on his ride from Boston, include the very bed where patriots Sam Adams and John Hancock slept when Revere rode to the front parlor–bedroom window around 1 A.M. and warned them. (Adams and Hancock, longtime friends, fled to Woburn, Massachusetts.) A small museum at the house displays Dr. Fiske's leather saddle bags (he became a surgeon in Washington's Continental army), Major Pitcairn's pistols, and the drum on which 19-year-old William Diamond "beat out the long roll," as Captain Parker ordered, to recall the minutemen to the green at dawn.

Then and Now On April 19, 1775, Lexington was a small farming village, having been incorporated in 1713. It began as the farming area of Cambridge, and its 400 or so inhabitants were called simply "the farmers." Today's Lexington is a sophisticated, upper-middle-class Boston suburb teeming with resident professionals, teen in-line skaters, and history-loving visitors. The downtown "village area" is low-key; no building rises above the dominating American flag on the Battle Green.

The green itself serves as a local park. In understated New England style, unobtrusive boulders and monuments mark the location of the Meeting House and the belfry that housed the bell that first summoned the minutemen to the green on April 18, 1775.

The minutemen waited in surrounding houses and Buckman Tavern until William Diamond's long drum roll.

An authentic replica of the belfry now keeps watch on a hill adjacent to the green at Massachusetts Avenue and Clarke Street. Visitors toss coins at the foot of the oldest Revolutionary monument, where the remains of the "martyrs" who "nobly dared to be free!" were reburied within a wrought-iron fence. Twelve survivors of Captain Parker's minutemen helped rebury the bodies in 1835.

On the boulder marking the place where the minutemen formed their lines is an inscription of the words Captain Parker supposedly told his men that fateful morning as they faced the British: "Stand your ground. Don't fire unless fired upon. But if they mean to have a war, let it begin here."

And here is where the first military encounter that sparked the American Revolution took place.

Elsewhere in the Area The Museum of Our National Heritage, located east of downtown Lexington at the intersection of Massachusetts Avenue and Marrett Road (Route 2A) features changing exhibits on American growth and development. A permanent exhibit, "Lexington Alarm'd!," tells what life was like in the small town where the Revolution was sparked.

Lowell

America's First Great Industrial City

Location Northeastern Massachusetts, 32 miles northwest of Boston. Take I-495 or U.S. 3 to the Lowell Connector, exit 5B onto Thorndike Street. Go ½ mile to Dutton Street. Turn right on Dutton and proceed to the visitor center parking lot on the right. Commuter rail service runs from Boston's North Station to Lowell's Gallagher Terminal.

Lowell National Historic Park Visitor Center is open daily, except Thanksgiving, December 25, and January 1, 9 A.M.–5 P.M. Days and hours of operation for other park museums and exhibits vary. Some have admission fees ($). Trolley tours and barge tours of canals are seasonal. Ranger-guided tours of some exhibits require reservations. For information contact Lowell National Historic Park, 246 Market Street, Lowell, MA 01852. Tel. (978) 970-5000.

Frame of Reference The second quarter of the 19th century to the 1930s was the time of the industrial revolution and the growth of the labor movement. Lowell experienced its heyday in the years around 1850. The city's first mill began operation in 1822; its mills began closing in 1912, most heading south. By 1930 Lowell's economic boom had ground to a halt. The last of the original mills closed in the 1950s.

The Industrial Revolution: An Overview

During the colonial period, manufacturing remained largely in the home. Industry in America later came in the form of small shops, some later expanded, where articles such as shoes were manufactured by hand. But Great Britain led the way in industrial production. In cities such as Manchester the flying shuttle, the spinning jenny, and other inventions mechanized the production of textiles. Meanwhile, in America's Northeast, technology was giving rise to the factory system. Here are some highlights:

1790: First cotton mill opened in Pawtucket, Rhode Island, on the Blackstone River, owned and operated by Samuel Slater, who employed children in his factory

1793: Cottin gin invented by Eli Whitney; cotton gin and cotton production increased spectacularly

1794: Earliest New England canals constructed

1796: Pawtucket Canal built along Lowell's Merrimack River

1799: Mass production of interchangeable musket and pistol parts—the result of Americans perfecting this European idea

1800: Jefferson and Hamilton's great debate concerning the place of industrialization in America

☛

Significance Nineteenth-century Lowell—named for Francis Cabot Lowell, the Boston investor whose ideas led to the founding of the city's first mill—led America into the industrial age and became America's first great industrial city. The Lowell of 150 years ago, with its natural, 32-foot power-yield-ing falls on the Merrimack River, grand network of canals, and 140 massive brick textile factories, embodied the sweeping change that industry brought to America.

Lowell's history of success and failure reflects the roller-coaster manufacturing economy of the Northeast, where the seeds of large-scale industrial enterprise first grew. Lowell, world-famous in its golden age, best represents a young country's dramatic shift from a rural, farming society to an urbanized, industrial one. This "Spindle City," begun by a group of Boston investors, tells the story of America's industrial revolution.

About the Site Lowell National Historic Park is a combination of government and private properties ranging over several city blocks in downtown Lowell. The park includes original textile mills; an original "dormitory" for young women, who made up the main work force in the mills for a time; the Working People Exhibit; and the Boott Cotton Mills Museum ($), featuring an operating weave room and the New England Folklife Center of Lowell. These sites are open for self-guided tours. The Tsongas Industrial History Center, also at the Boott Mill, offers a variety of excellent programs for students and teachers, including a boat ride on the Merrimack River. An upstairs theater features a 24-minute audiovisual program, *The Wheels of Change, the First Century of American Industry*.

The Suffolk Mill houses a turbine exhibit in which a restored 19th-century turbine fed by water from a canal built in 1948 operates a power loom. Ranger-led limited tours are offered seasonally.

In warm months you can board a barge and tour some of the six miles of canals fed by the Merrimack River in the "Venice of America," going through old, restored locks. You can get around the park on a turn-of-the-century trolley or on foot by the canalway path bordering the canals. Exhibits and signs guide you along this path. In and around the park, a network of

1804: Manufacturing takes root with some advances, such as picking and carding machines

1807: U.S. government restricts imports anticipating the War of 1812—a boon for U.S. manufacturing; boon ended with the war when British goods returned

1810: Dozens of water-powered looms begin dotting riverbanks of southern New England, which had the advantage of many rivers for water power and transportation

1810: A prominent New England investor, Francis Cabot Lowell, goes to England and learns industrial secrets

1814: Lowell's Boston Associates build a cotton mill in Waltham, Massachusetts—a foreshadowing of the Lowell experiment

1815: Northern mills number in the hundreds

1818: Power looms installed for production; more people work long, scheduled hours in factories

1822: First mill opens in Lowell

In its golden age 140 mills thrived in Lowell, the "Manchester on the Merrimack." Striving to avoid the dark conditions of Great Britain's industrialization, the Lowell founders initiated high-minded ideas, including a system of paternal supervision for workers.

All the while, the practical bent of Americans and their penchant for daring and getting ahead produced myriad technological inventions. By the mid–19th century, there was a rush of immigrants to fill jobs in major cities.

▲

buildings, parks, and sculptures along a 90-minute self-guided downtown tour reveals treasures of 19th-century Lowell.

The visitor center, housed in a 1902 mill complex, offers exhibits, a gift shop, and a very good 20-minute multi-image slide show, *Lowell: The Industrial Revelation*.

Hot Tips Guided tours go on rain or shine, so prepare for the weather. You'll be walking mainly on sidewalks, but there are many steps and street crossings. Beware of heavy traffic in the downtown area.

For a valuable perspective on Lowell and the industrial revolution, read the National Park Services' official handbook, *Lowell: The Story of an Industrial City*. You can learn the real story of mill life in the slim book *The Lowell Mill Girls*, edited by JoAnne B. Weisman in the Perspective on History Series. Both are available at the visitor center. Accommodations and food are available in the immediate area.

The Best Stuff Everyone will get a kick out of the canal ride. And young people are sure to love the ear-throbbing noise and the heart-thumping vibration of the floor from 88 authentic looms in the long, rectangular weave room at the Boott Cotton Mill, opened in 1836 and closed in 1954. Before entering, visitors place foam earplugs in their ears and "punch in" for work. You'll leave with a clear picture of what mill workers faced during their 60-hour work week filled with ear-damaging noise, poor lighting, high heat and humidity, dangerous machinery, and air filled with cotton dust.

No wonder the "Mill Girls," young single women from New England farms who made up Lowell's earliest work force, and the later processions of immigrants that replaced them, organized for better pay and working conditions. Ironically, it was the New England mill workers' strikes—fueled by a shutdown in Lowell—that contributed to capital flight to the South.

Then and Now By 1936 the decaying factories in Lowell gave parts of the city a war-ravaged appearance. The last of the mills closed in the 1950s, and the city's tough economic conditions persisted for decades.

In the 1970s, long after its glory days were gone, Lowell undertook its own rehabilitation. Leaders decided to boast of its ethnic and industrial heritage. Congress established the national park in 1978, and the acquisition of sites and renovation work began. The Boott Cotton Mills Museum opened in 1992, and work to restore the park to its 1850s appearance continues. Today the Spindle City is home to many in the latest immigration wave of Vietnamese and Hispanic people. The city continues its cycle of economic good and bad times. Lowell is a living museum to the industrial revolution and the labor movement.

Elsewhere in the Area The New England Quilt Museum is at 18 Shattuck Street, downtown Lowell; Jack Kerouac Commemorative is in Eastern Canal Park.

North Bridge

Where the First Battle of the American Revolution Took Place

Location Concord, Massachusetts, a northwestern suburb of Boston, spanning the Concord River in a park off Monument Street. From Concord center, travel around the rotary toward the Colonial Inn, and veer north onto Monument Street. The bridge is located ½ mile on the left down a footpath, once a "colonial highway." Parking is on the right. You also can continue down Monument Street, take a left onto Liberty Street to park at the visitor center, and begin your tour there.

Old North Bridge is a part of the Minute Man National Historical Park, which also includes portions of the "Battle Road," Hartwell Tavern, the Battle Road Visitors Center in Lexington, and the Wayside ($) in Concord, home of literary stars Nathaniel Hawthorne, Louisa May Alcott, and Margaret Sidney. The North Bridge Visitors Center is open daily, except December 25 and January 1, 9 A.M.–5 P.M. For information contact Superintendent, Minute Man National Historical Park, 174 Liberty St., Concord, MA 02174. Tel. (978) 369-6993. A popular reenactment of 1775 historical events at the bridge takes place every Patriot's Day, April 19, beginning at dawn. Arrive early. Many related events in Lexington and Concord also precede the day.

Battle Road

Where Colonials Took Revenge on Fleeing British

Trouble was just beginning for the British troops as they marched out of Concord more than 220 years ago. In the last two days, they had faced colonial wrath at Lexington Green and North Bridge, but the Americans' full, furious anger at the Crown was yet to be unleashed. This would happen in the next few hours along what now is known as Battle Road.

Around noon, on Wednesday, April 19, 1775, the reassembled British force began its return to its Boston base. Colonial militiamen, their ranks swelled by more men from nearby towns, gathered around a house at Meriam's Corner east of Concord. The British crossed a small bridge and fired on them. The militiamen swarmed into the road and replied in kind. Thus began a bloody day of guerrilla warfare. As the regimented *and aghast* British marched in military formation the full, six-hour, 16 mile return to Charlestown, colonials sniped at them from behind rocks, barns, trees, houses and stone walls. At several points along the route, militiamen ambushed the British with deadly results. By the time the exhausted Redcoats reached Boston Harbor, they had suffered more than 250 casualties; the Americans, 93.

Today, you can tour the Battle Road from Meriam's Corner to Boston by car. Most of the Road is heavily trafficked highway, but a portion remains in quieter, residential areas of Lexington and Concord, called *the most historic town in America.* For a closer look, you can walk or bicycle a 5.5-mile interpretative trail that follows sec-

Frame of Reference The first organized battle of the American Revolution took place little more than one year before the 1776 signing of the Declaration of Independence, on April 19, 1775, the day the first shots of the Revolution rang out on Lexington Green. It was several days before the confrontation at Bunker Hill, now called the first major battle of the Revolution.

Significance At this arched wooden span over the Concord River, colonists were ordered for the first time to fire on British troops. The midmorning exchange of fire involved 96 British soldiers and about 400 colonial militiamen and minutemen from Concord and four surrounding towns. (Massachusetts organized a militia, as other colonies had, at the insistence of the Continental Congress. The militia formed a special unit of young, able-bodied men to be ready at a moment's notice, the minutemen.)

The red-coated British, whom New Englanders derisively called "Lobsterbacks," had marched from Boston in search of colonial munitions stores in Concord, the provincial arsenal for the Massachusetts militia. The Bennett farm near the North Bridge was a munitions storehouse. Paul Revere and other patriot messengers had sounded the alarm after learning the British had crossed the Charles River and marched west.

The colonial militia gathered on a hill overlooking the bridge and advanced. The British met them to stifle the fires of rebellion. The British fired, killing two men from nearby Acton. The colonists returned with "the shot heard round the world," a phrase later coined by Concord writer/philosopher Ralph Waldo Emerson. In the volley, two colonists were killed, four wounded; two British were

tions of the original Battle Road. The trail offers vistas of fields that have been farmed for hundreds of years, as well as new footbridges over protected wetlands. Where the trail follows the actual road taken by the British fleeing back to Boston, the trail is the size of the historic road *about 20 feet wide* and is packed with dirt as it was in 1775.

Twenty-four interpretative panels, to be installed in 1998 and 1999, will mark the trail. Granite markers currently point out important historic sites, such as the 1754 Hartwell Tavern, the restored 18th-century Captain William Smith House and the Paul Revere Capture site. Visitors can begin the trail at Meriam's Corner, the Visitor Center or at several places in between. Parking lots are located at both ends of the trail and at the Revere Capture site.

The heart of the road lies next to the newly renovated Minute Man National Historical Park Visitor Center on Route 2A (Massachusetts Avenue) just west of I-95 in Lexington. Here, a ⅛-mile trail along a section of the 18th-century Bay Road, linking Boston with Fort Ticonderoga in New York, is fully restored. This section, then called Nelson Road, still has original stone walls at its edges that the colonials hid behind to fire on the British. (Colonial farmers piled the stones at the edge of their rocky New England property as they plowed their fields. The low stone walls had the serendipitous effect of clearly marking property boundaries and roads.) Walls along Battle Road sections have been reconstructed.

A stroll down Nelson Road today reveals the stone foundations of Concord homes and various landmarks documenting skirmishes. It's exciting to come across the Minute Man Boulder about 10 feet back from the clay road. The silent stone, now not far from Boston commuter traffic and a playground, stood sentinel as Paul Revere rode past on his famous midnight ride.

killed, and nine—mostly officers—were wounded. The North Bridge battle is an important part of the events surrounding April 19, 1775, including the skirmish at Lexington and the 18-mile British retreat down Battle Road to the safety of British-held Boston. These events signaled the start of the American Revolution.

About the Site The original 1654 North Bridge was removed in 1793. The wooden one you walk across today, built in 1956, connects the ground where British troops stood on one side and the colonists on the other as the shot heard around the world was fired. You can start your visit at the bridge or the visitor center at the other end of a self-guided 1/4-mile walking tour. The visitor center, situated on a high bluff overlooking the river, is part of a brick mansion that belonged to an old Concord family. It houses a small museum, gift shop, and theater where you can see a 12-minute video on the North Bridge battle and events leading up to it.

Beginning on Monument Street, your tour takes you down a maple-lined dirt path dotted with informational markers. To the left stands the Old Manse, home to Emerson and Hawthorne. In addition to the bridge, three major monuments dominate the site: the bronze Minute Man statue (where the colonists stood their ground), the granite obelisk Battle Monument (on the opposite shore where the British gathered), and the grave of the British soldiers who died here.

Exhibits in the visitor center tell the story of April 19, 1775 and its aftermath. The centerpiece is a spectacular 40 by 15-foot mural of the fighting on April 9, 1775, Return to Boston under Fire. The Center also houses a small gift shop and two theaters. The larger theater features a riveting multimedia show The Road to Revolution; the smaller theater runs a 22-minute orientation film, The Key to Our Liberty.

The Minute Man National Historical Park Visitors Center is open daily 9 A.M.–5 P.M. from the third week in April to the end of October. Call for exact schedule. Tel. (781) 862-7753. Park rangers offer 1½-hour interpretative walks, In the Footsteps of the Minute Men, on Saturdays and Sundays during the summer.

Hot Tips You can buy a self-guiding trail booklet, *Battle Road Heroes* for 50 cents at the Visitor Center.

The Visitor Center on Battle Road is the best place to begin your tour of both the Minuteman National Park and Lexington Green in season when the Visitor Center is open. Plan to spend about two hours at the Visitor Center and the Battle Road interpretative trail. Allow at least a day for a cursory tour from North Bridge in Concord, through Lexington and other Boston suburbs, to Bunker Hill in Charlestown and the Freedom Trail in Boston.

In the immediate area Punkatasset Hill, where the colonists gathered, is the home of Major John Buttrick, who helped lead the colonists at North Bridge, as well as the homes of others involved in this battle. There's also the "bullet hole house," where its owner Elisha Jones—who was hiding military supplies—barely avoided the British soldier's shot that landed in the door frame. (Glass encases the hole today.) The site begins the Battle Road, along which the British retreated to Boston under angry colonial fire. Costumed guides give talks about the battle and answer questions from mid-April to November.

Hot Tips Allow 1½ hours for your visit, more if you visit the Old Manse and other homes. This is a site to savor. You should incorporate your visit with a leisurely stroll through downtown Concord, where there are additional historic sites and interesting places to eat and shop. (If your visit here is part of a tour of the entire Battle Road, you're already spending a day or two in the area.) Maps and a full schedule of park events are available at both the North Bridge and Battle Road visitor centers.

For a special family treat, rent a canoe or boat at South Bridge Boat House, 496 Main Street in Concord. Paddle downstream about half a mile to North Bridge, drag the boat ashore, and picnic on the rocks. Food and accommodations are available in Concord.

The Best Stuff The monuments marking the soil on each side of the bridge where the colonists, mostly farmers, and the highly trained and uniformed British faced off epitomize the emotional events of April 19, 1775.

Battle Monument. The first monument you see, a granite obelisk at the foot of the bridge on the north side, was erected in 1836 where the British had stood. Designed by Solomon Willard of Bunker Hill Monument fame, the Battle Monument dedication of July 4, 1837, was lavish and attended by famous Concordians, including Emerson and Reverend Ezra Ripley. Emerson wrote the "Concord Hymn" sung during the dedication, and Ripley wrote the inscription found on the obelisk base:

> ***Here on the 19 of April 1775 was made the first forcible resistance to British aggression. On the opposite bank stood the American Militia. Here stood the Invading Army and on this spot, the first of the Enemy fell in the War of that Revolution which gave Independence to the United States.***

Minute Man Statue. Because the Battle Monument stood on the British side of the bridge, controversy naturally ensued. Adding fuel to the fire was the fact that the famous bridge itself had been removed and replaced by two others in less flood-prone areas. Finally, 37 years later, the bridge was rebuilt in its exact 1775 location (the old bridge location), and another monument—the Minute Man statue—went up on the south side of the wooden span. Daniel Chester French, a young unknown Concord sculptor (who went on to sculpt the Lincoln Memorial in Washington, D.C.), created the bronze statue of a young minuteman, his left hand resting on a plow and his right hand clutching a musket. President Ulysses Grant, the Union Civil War general, and 4,000 others attended the 1885 dedication ceremony. (Many of the colonists who had fought side by side in the French and Indian War also fought together at this bridge 110 years before this ceremony.) Inscribed on the granite pedestal of the Minute Man are lines from the first verse of Emerson's "Concord Hymn":

> ***Here once the embattled farmers stood,***
> ***And fired the shot heard round the world.***

Grave of British Soldiers. Two British privates died and, after the battle, were hastily buried beside a stone wall at the bridge by Concord residents. One of these deaths sparked a hot rumor among the British—highly trained in formal European warfare—that the colonists had taken up the savage ways of the Native North American. A militiaman, seeing that one downed soldier was not yet dead, whacked him in the head with a hatchet, finishing the job. The British thought their fallen comrade had been scalped.

A boulder bearing a bronze plaque marks the grave of the British soldiers at the bridge. Beneath a towering maple, you'll see this inscription amid the hostas and impatiens planted on the grave: "They came three thousands miles and died to keep the past upon its throne; Unheard beyond the ocean tide, their English mother made her moan."

Then and Now The exchange of fire at North Bridge lasted but a few minutes, the culmination of fear and anger following American deaths at Lexington Green and the relentless search for colonial munitions in Concord. The British were going door-to-door in Concord seizing supplies and burning them. The militiamen gathered on Punkatasset Hill not far from the bridge, and, marching lower, they could see smoke rising over the town. British troops moved toward the bridge, and militiamen, fearing homes had been set ablaze, met them there. In a hurried council of American officers, Concord Adjutant Joseph Hosmer asked, "Will you let them burn the town down?"

The militia decided to march into town. As they arrived at the bridge, they saw British regulars removing loose planks in a flimsy effort to halt the militia's advance. Colonial leader John Buttrick ordered them to stop; the British formed ranks at the foot of the bridge and answered with a round of fire.

The first three rounds fell into the river. But a full volley followed, cutting down Issac Davis, whose Acton company led the march at the bridge. Abner Hosmer of Acton also was killed. Buttrick leaped into the air and shouted the words that changed the course of history: "Fire, fellow soldiers, for God's sake, fire!" The minutemen marched over the bridge, and the British scattered.

After the battle the King's troops retreated to the center of town, regrouped, and rested. Then they began an all-day march toward Boston Harbor down a 16-mile stretch known now as "Battle Road." By the end of the day British casualties totaled 273. American casualties stood at 95.

Today's parklike setting at the bridge looks quite different from the open landscape of cleared farms, pastures, orchards, and meadows of 1775. Many homes of the men who fought at the bridge, however, as well as many other period buildings still stand. The homes of Isaac Davis and Abner Hosmer are important landmarks in Acton, eight miles west of Concord. A granite monument to Davis dominates Acton's town square. Modern minutemen in tricornered hats and period dress lead parades and fire their muskets at public ceremonies throughout the area.

Elsewhere in the Area Explore what locals call "the other revolution," the literary revolution that centered on Concord. Begin with the Old Manse, next to the North Bridge, then move on to the Wayside, Walden Pond (where Thoreau wrote), Sleepy Hollow cemetery (resting place of many literary luminaries), Emerson House, and the Concord Museum, which teems with Emerson and Thoreau memorabilia.

Note The 1718 Old Corner Bookstore, publisher of Emerson, Thoreau, Hawthorne, Longfellow, and others, is part of the Freedom Trail in downtown Boston.

Plymouth Rock

Where the Pilgrims Landed

Location Southeastern Massachusetts, in the present-day town of Plymouth, 40 miles southeast of Boston via Route 3. Follow signs to Plymouth Rock and the *Mayflower II* on the waterfront of Cape Cod Bay. Plimoth Plantation (spelled as then-governor William Bradford spelled it in his journal), is located 2½ miles south of the town on Route 3A.

Plymouth Rock itself is outdoors and can be viewed any time. Plimoth Plantation ($) and the *Mayflower II* ($) are open April through November, 9 A.M.–5 P.M., with extended summer hours. The museum and gift shop remain open in December. You can experience a traditional feast ($) at Plimoth Plantation on Thanksgiving Day with reservations. For information contact Plimoth Plantation, P.O. Box 1620, Plymouth, MA 02362. Tel. (508) 746-1622. Hours and days of operation for other Pilgrim-related, privately operated sites vary. Contact the Plymouth Area Chamber of Commerce at (508) 830-1620 or Plymouth County Development Council, P.O. Box 1620, Pembroke, MA 02359.

Frame of Reference Nearly 400 years ago in the 17th century English colonists began putting down roots in the New World. The Plymouth colony years were 1620 to 1691.

Significance Tradition has it that on this glacial boulder a group of extremist Puritans, now referred to simply as Pilgrims, first set foot in the New World in December 1620. The rock is one of America's earliest patriotic symbols and among the most enduring. After debarking the ship *Mayflower*, the Pilgrims endured enormous hardships to establish the Plymouth colony, one of the earliest English settlements in America and the first founded by people seeking religious freedom.

After their first successful harvest in 1621 the Pilgrims celebrated, along with 90 Native North Americans, the first "harvest feast," which President Abraham Lincoln recognized in 1863 as the first Thanksgiving. The Plymouth colony also gave America one of its earliest documents for self-government in the Mayflower Compact, signed by 41 of the Pilgrim leaders aboard their ship before they began building their settlement.

Plymouth Rock has come to symbolize the ideals associated with the Pilgrims, ideals that also represent popular American virtues: faith, courage, patience, love of self-government, and freedom. Plymouth Rock is often called "America's Cornerstone."

About the Site The small harbor district of Plymouth functions as a living memorial to the Pilgrims. The centerpiece is Plymouth Rock, protected by a templelike, granite canopy in Pilgrim Memorial State Park at the shore of Plymouth Harbor along Water Street. Moored at adjacent State Pier, the *Mayflower II*, a brightly painted replica of the famous *Mayflower*, welcomes you aboard. Costumed interpreters portray actual passengers and crew, inviting visitors to ask questions about their voyage on the 90-foot merchant vessel.

Other sites along the town's Pilgrim path include these:

- **Pilgrim Hall,** 75 Court Street, the nation's oldest museum. The hall, erected by the Pilgrim Society in 1824, exhibits authentic Pilgrim possessions, including the Bible of Plymouth colony's second governor, William Bradford; the sword of military leader Miles Standish; and the cradle of the first white child born in New England.
- **Burial Hill,** entrance at First Church near Leyden Street. This was the site of the Pilgrims' first meeting house and fort.
- **Site of the original settlement,** on Leyden Street near the waterfront.
- **Cole's Hill,** across from Plymouth Rock on Water Street. This was where the Pilgrims secretly buried their dead at night the first bitter winter so that Native North Americans could not detect how much the colony's numbers had diminished. (Half the *Mayflower* passengers died.) Colonists planted corn over the unmarked graves.
- **Plymouth National Wax Museum,** atop Cole's Hill. This is the nation's only museum dedicated solely to the Pilgrim story. It features 180 figures in 26 life-size scenes.
- **National Monument to the Forefathers,** Allerton Street. The largest solid granite monument in America, built in 1889, is 216 times life-size.
- **Mayflower Society House Museum,** 4 Winslow Street. This museum houses artifacts of *Mayflower* descendants.
- **1749 Court House.** The oldest wooden court house in America is in Town Square.

Statues include one of Governor Bradford. There are also a gristmill (a mill for grinding grain) and several historic homes, including the 1677 Harlow Old Fort House built with timbers from the Plymouth fort, 119 Sandwich Street.

Gift shops and restaurants crowd the waterfront area. There's an information center on North Park Avenue near Water Street. Except for Plymouth Rock, which is maintained by the commonwealth of Massachusetts, sites are private ventures.

Hot Tips You'll find several ways to tour historic Plymouth: by trolley ($), land and water vehicles ($), and a nighttime guided "lantern tour" ($). You also can take a seasonal harbor tour by ferry, which will take you to Provincetown at the tip of Cape Cod. Here's where the Pilgrims first checked out the countryside after being blown off course from Holland. They decided the area was too harsh, reboarded the *Mayflower*, and ended up in Plymouth.

It's best to write for maps and information in advance, but you can pick them up at Plimoth Plantation Visitor Center or at the Information Center downtown. On-street parking is limited in Plymouth, so check the map for the eight public parking lots. At Plimoth, park at the visitor center.

Because most sites are outdoors, you should dress for the weather, which often is damp in New England. Walking trails at Plimoth Plantation are dirt and gravel and can be muddy. Some parts are steep. Wear comfortable shoes. Be prepared for insects in warm months, and watch for ice in cold ones. Food and a picnic site are available at Plimoth Plantation. Food and accommodations are available in Plymouth.

Many books for youth are out there about the Plymouth colony. A good one is Marcia Sewall's *The Pilgrims of Plimoth*. Check out *The Thanksgiving Primer* offered in the Plimoth Plantation Museum Shop. This is a guide to recreating the First Harvest Feast.

The Best Stuff A rock, a boat, a village: these are the things embedded in our memories since childhood, and these are the things that will grab you now. (And your kids will like them, too.)

Your first reaction at seeing Plymouth Rock for the first time may be the same one many tourists from around the world have. "It's so small," they gasp, snapping a photograph. However, some of The Rock lies under the sand. It's easy, considering the impact the rock has on our national psyche, to picture this gray boulder—measuring about 4 by 5½ feet—in the same category as the Rock of Gibraltar. What's more, the rock has a crack running diagonally across it, the result of one of several ceremonious relocations since the rock's historical importance was first identified in 1741.

The year "1620" was carved on the rock in 1880, the year the peripatetic boulder was returned to the waterfront and reunited with its lower half (which had been split off in yet another move in 1774). Although the rock was not mentioned in the two written accounts by Pilgrims, some historians assert that the boulder might have supported a boardwalk of sorts for the *Mayflower's* crew of Pilgrim "saints" and the "strangers" they recruited for the voyage. The iron grate of the harbor-facing side of the granite canopy, built in 1920, allows seawater to swirl around the boulder at high tide.

You can tour several decks of the colorful *Mayflower II*, complete with seaworthy sails and the trappings of crammed, dank, and treacherous sea life. Interpreters tell stories in dialect of the transatlantic voyage centuries ago when the original vessel transported 102 passengers and 26 crewmen to the New World.

At Plimoth Plantation, stop first at the visitor center and view the 12-minute orientation slide show and exhibits. Walk the broad dirt "first street" of the stockaded village on a hill and meet Governor Bradford, Hester Cooke, and "strangers" John Alden and Miles Standish. Converse with them as they go about their daily chores in their clapboard homes with thatched roofs of water reeds. Don't expect them to know anything beyond the year 1627, and don't think you're going to see the tall black hats and silver-buckled velveteen shoes of folklore. The men wear woven woolen caps and practical leather boots.

The farm animals, outdoor ovens, raised herb gardens, and meetinghouse (with an armed fort upstairs) add to the ambiance and fun of the visit. Also at the site: Carriage House Crafts Center, Eel River Nature Walk, Nye Barn, and the re-created homesite of Wampanoag Indian Hobbamock.

Then and Now The term *pilgrim* refers to people journeying to a holy site. *Mayflower* leader William Bradford referred to his fellow travelers as "Pilgrims" in 1620. The term was popularized after an ode written for the 1792 Forefathers' Day celebration, begun in 1769 by the Old Colony Club.

Although President Lincoln popularized the First Harvest Feast as the national holiday Thanksgiving, America's true first "Thanksgiving Day" was celebrated on November 26, 1789. President George Washington proclaimed the national holiday as a day of thanksgiving for the Constitution.

The Pilgrims undertook their voyage across the Atlantic after 10 unhappy years in the Netherlands, where they escaped from England to avoid persecution after they severed all ties with the Church of England. The Leyden group secured a land patent from the Virginia Company and promised to pay back financing for the trip to the New World by sending back items, such as beaver furs, to be sold in England. Many Pilgrims already had left the Plymouth Village seeking more land and opportunity when the colony united with the fast-growing Massachusetts Bay Colony in 1691.

Today visitors roam the land where the Pilgrims settled. Town Brook, its fresh water an important reason the Pilgrims chose this place for their settlement, still winds its way from Jenny Pond to the Plymouth waterfront. Local motels have names like the Governor Bradford Motor Inn, and the harborfront of the ascetic religious separatists now sports a yacht club and public beach.

Elsewhere in the Area Cranberry World is at 225 Water Street.

Salem

Where 20 "Witches" Were Put to Death

Location Northeastern Massachusetts, 16 miles north of Boston. Take Highway 128 north to Route 114 east, or take Route 1A from the south.

Most of the sites in Salem are privately owned and operated. For visitor information contact the Salem Office of Tourism and Cultural Affairs, Salem City Hall, 93 Washington Street, Salem, MA 01970. Tel. 1-800-777-6848. Or contact the Salem Chamber of Commerce, Old Town Hall, 32 Derby Square, Salem, MA 01970. Tel. (978) 745-3855. Days and hours of operation vary from site to site. For information on the Salem Maritime National Historic Site contact Superintendent, Salem Maritime National Historic Site, Custom House, 174 Derby Street, Salem, MA 01970. Tel. (978) 740-1660.

Frame of Reference The Salem Witch Trials took place during a brief period of religious frenzy in the 1690s.

Significance Although Salem, Massachusetts, is known historically as the center of commercial shipping in early America, with its 18th-century wharves preserved in the Salem Maritime National Historic Site, it's best remembered for the outburst of witch persecutions in 1692 when 20 people accused of witchcraft were put to death.

About the Site The Salem tourist industry has dubbed the city "the bewitching seaport," combining the area's two big crowd pleasers, the historic waterfront and the witch-related sites. Salem is a walkable city, one where you can park your car for the day and easily take in the historic sites on and around the red-painted Heritage Trail. There are plenty of eating and shopping outlets along the main streets and in the pedestrian malls. Salem also is the site of American writer Nathaniel Hawthorne's House of Seven Gables, which is open for tours.

If you're interested in the witch persecution aspect of the city, put these stops on your list: the Salem Witch Museum, the Witch Dungeon Museum, the Salem Wax Museum of Witches and Seafarers, and the Salem Witch Trials Memorial. This list is by no means complete, but you'll more than get the point about the persecutions at these sites.

A tour of the historic waterfront can include visits to wharves, warehouses, the Custom House, and important homes and shops. The best place to start is at the National Park Service Visitor Center at 2 Liberty Street. Here you can pick up maps; find exhibits on early settlement, maritime era, and the leather and textile industry; and view an orientation film on historic Essex County. The city teems with historic homes and museums, including the Peabody Museum, which displays maritime artifacts and exotic mementos of voyages around the world.

Hot Tips It's worthwhile to set aside a whole day to visit Salem.

If driving, you can find on-street parking, but it may be wiser to look for one of several downtown parking garages. Blue signs note the way. You can take a bus or commuter train from Boston's North Station (commuter train and bus information, 1-800-392-6100). Private companies in Salem offer tours by trolley or limousine, as well as whale-watching excursions. A Tour Mate package available at some sites offers auto-tour cassette rentals.

Recommended previsit reading includes Arthur Miller's *The Crucible*. The latest movie version of the book, starring Daniel Day-Lewis, hit screens in 1996. Video stores also may have the 55-minute video *The Witches of Salem: The Horror and the Hope*.

The Best Stuff Historic seaports are interesting, and Salem by some measures surpasses Mystic, Connecticut; Rockport, Massachusetts; Baltimore, Maryland; and San Francisco, California. But chances are you'll be coming to Salem to learn about the infamous 17th-century witch persecutions. If so, make a beeline to the Salem Witch Museum ($) in Washington Square across from the Salem Common. A towering stone Romanesque-style building houses the museum, where you experience a ½-hour presentation about the witch hysteria and persecutions of 1692—in the dark. No wonder the museum is such a popular Halloween destination!

The in-the-round presentation features wax figures, eerie music, and dialogue based on historical research. Lobby exhibits further tell the story. There's also a gift shop. (Some of the souvenirs here and around town are a real scream.) The museum is open daily, except Thanksgiving, December 25, and January 1, 10 A.M.–5 P.M., and in July and August, 10 A.M.–7 P.M. For information contact the Salem Witch Museum, Washington Square, Salem, MA 01970. Tel. (978) 744-1692.

Another must-see stop is the Witch Dungeon Museum ($) at 15 Lynde Street. First you enter a theater and see a professional reenactment of a witch trial. Then you descend into a re-created dungeon where the poor unfortunate souls accused of practicing witchcraft were imprisoned—at their own expense. (Pity the poverty-stricken prisoner, whose confines were so small that he was forced to pass the hours in a sitting position.) For information contact Witch Dungeon Museum, 16 Lynde Street, Salem, MA 01970. Tel. (978) 741-3570.

A drama titled *Cry Innocent: The People vs. Bridget Bishop* plays June through October at the Old Town Hall. Call (978) 927-2300, ext. 4747, for information.

Beyond the theatrics, the Salem Witch Trials Memorial off Charter Street relays the true horror of the persecutions of innocent people more powerfully than anything else in town. The grassy plot's understated design incorporates stone benches etched with the names of the persecuted, protected by trees and surrounded with a low stone wall deliberately unfinished. It's a monument to the work for tolerance and human rights, never a finished task.

Then and Now The outburst of witch persecutions in Salem (another name for Jerusalem) and nearby Salem Village (now Danvers) came on the heels of similar persecutions in France, Germany, and England. The zeal to hunt down agents of the devil had been incorporated into Christian religion, both Catholic and Protestant. Some New England Puritans were unrelenting in the search for witches.

The Salem story begins with a black servant named Tituba who practiced voodoo and a handful of bored adolescent girls who listened to her stories. Townspeople began to think Tituba practiced witchcraft, and the girls—twitching and speaking in tongues—started making accusations. Trials were held, people were imprisoned, 19 were hanged, and one unrepentant man, Giles Corey, was pressed to death with heavy stones.

Today the museums and dramas give a visitor a fairly accurate account of that dark period in the 1690s. A walk to the hill where the 19 witches were hanged and a few quiet moments at the Witch Trials Memorial will bring home this story of prejudice and fear.

Elsewhere in the Area Gloucester, America's first seaport and the Pilgrims' second settlement, is 16 miles north of Salem. For information contact the Gloucester Tourism Commission, 22 Poplar Street, Gloucester, MA 01930. Tel. 1-800-649-6839.

Tea Party Ship

Remembering Boston's Famous Tea Dumping

Location Downtown Boston, Massachusetts, in Fort Point Channel of Boston Harbor, near the corner of Atlantic Avenue and Congress Street. From the north take I-93 south to High Street/Congress Street exit. Take the first left at Congress. From the south take I-93 north to Downtown/Chinatown exit. Go right at Kneeland Street, left at Atlantic, second right at Congress. From the west take Mass Pike (I-90) to Downtown/South Station exit. Go to Atlantic and right at Congress.

The Boston Tea Party Ship and Museum ($) is open daily, except Thanksgiving, from March through November, 9 A.M.–5 P.M., and in summer, 9 A.M.–6 P.M. For information contact the Boston Tea Party Ship and Museum, Congress Street Bridge, Boston, MA 02210. Tel. (617) 338-1773.

Frame of Reference The Boston Tea Party took place during the tumultuous years leading up to the Revolutionary War, on December 16, 1773.

Significance This is the approximate site where a band of 60 to 150 Bostonians disguised as Mohawk Indians protested England's odious Tea Act of 1772 by dumping 342 chests of East India Company tea from three ships into Boston Harbor. The Tea Act allowed the East India Tea Company a monopoly on shipping tea to America. Parliament also said that the tea business would be funneled only through certain loyalist merchants, thereby undercutting American free trade already hindered by the tax on tea. Many American merchants faced financial ruin.

The Tea Act was one in a long series of issues that angered patriots and served to galvanize anti-British sentiments. Boston's daring nighttime protest prompted other "tea parties" in the colonies, stoking the fires of rebellion and provoking more British retribution. The colonies moved further down the road to revolution.

About the Site The site features an authentic reconstruction of the type of ship used in 1773 and represents what historians think one of the three tea-loaded ships docked in Boston Harbor on the night of December 16 looked like. That ship was the Danish brig *Beaver II*, the smallest of the three merchant ships at Griffin's Wharf in December 1773. (The actual site of Griffin's Wharf and the Tea Party are lost due to Boston's practice of filling in Boston Harbor for city expansion. A towering building now occupies the original spot at 470 Atlantic Avenue, several blocks from today's Tea Party Ship.)

A small museum, featuring a 15-minute slide show, "Paul Revere Remembers the Boston Tea Party," and a gift shop are part of the site where the 110-foot *Beaver II* floats. Costumed interpreters lead visitors in a rousing "New England town meeting" led by patriot Sam

Adams. The crowd, wearing yellow "Mohawk" feathers, then swarms the *Beaver II*. On board you'll hear about the historic night from none other than famous Bostonian Paul Revere, who raided a ship during the Tea Party.

As a final act of defiance, visitors can toss a bale of tea over the ship's side. Mr. Revere then hauls the dripping tea bale, attached to a rope, back on board for later acts of defiance.

Hot Tips Space is tight aboard the *Beaver II*, as well as on Griffin's Wharf. It is best to arrive early and beat the crowds, some spilling over from the Boston Children's Museum, a short walk down Congress Street. About 127,000 visitors board the *Beaver II* yearly. The ship can be reached by subway, called the "T," or on foot by following the Freedom Trail. Accommodations and food are available in the immediate area of downtown Boston.

The Best Stuff What makes a visit to the Tea Party site special is the hands-on nature of the place. Just inside the gate an exhibit asking "Do you have what it takes to be a revolutionary?" allows visitors to lift a 100-pound tea chest by block and tackle as the Sons of Liberty did from the hold of the *Beaver II* more than 220 years ago. (Of course, the actual East India Tea Company chests weighed about 350 pounds each and had to be hauled 10 feet up to the deck.) More hands-on exhibits are sprinkled about the site.

Kids will enjoy Sam Adams's town meeting (a tradition that still survives in many New England towns) on the wharf and Paul Revere's tale of the history-making night on board the ship. But it's fun for everyone to roam the deck and hold of the 130-ton *Beaver II*. Down the ship's hatch you can see the dark, damp place where the tea chests would have been stacked—112 fit on this ship—and hear the taped voice of a sailor decrying the harsh conditions of sea life: rancid horsemeat to eat, a narrow bunk for sleeping, and dangerous, confined quarters. "A prison would be better," he laments.

Then and Now Boston in the years before the Revolution already was a town of great education and culture—and a hotbed of rebellion. In both private and public meetings, anger at British taxation without representation was a constant topic. The Sons of Liberty kept things stirred up, with patriot Sam Adams in the forefront. As Americans protested, British response sharpened. Finally, in the winter of 1773, after several heated town meetings of overflow crowds and colonists' demands that England allow its tea ships to return without unloading their cargo, anger culminated in a single act of defiance.

Tea Party participants disguised themselves with blankets, capes, and shawls. They did not want to be recognized for fear of British reprisals on their families, although historians debate whether anyone actually wore feathers. The "Indians" boarded the three ships moored at Griffin's Wharf—the *Dartmouth*, *Eleanor*, and *Beaver*. It took three hours of backbreaking labor to lift the lead-lined tea chests, open them, and dump the 10,000 pounds of tea into the harbor. It's estimated that the tea was worth about $1.5 million in U.S. mid-1990s dollars.

Word of the carefully planned Tea Party had spread around town, and a crowd cheered as tea splashed into the cold water. Afterward Paul Revere rode out on horseback to spread word of the deed. Great Britain later launched a series of harsh reprisals, including the closure of Boston's harbor. American reaction was swift. The First Continental Congress met, and British and colonial fighting broke out in Lexington and Concord. Then the Second Continental Congress formally adopted the Declaration of Independence on July 4, 1776.

With a little imagination, today's visitors can relive the December night in 1773 that helped set these events in motion.

U.S.S. *Constitution*

World's Oldest Active Battleship

Location Charlestown, Massachusetts, over the Charles River west of Boston. The ship is moored in the Charles River in Boston Inner Harbor's Charlestown Navy Yard, where she was launched in 1797. The ship is one of the historic sites on Boston's Freedom Trail.

The U.S.S. *Constitution* is open daily, 9:30 A.M.–sunset. The U.S.S. *Constitution* Museum ($) is open daily, except Thanksgiving, December 25, and January 1, from June 1 through Labor Day, 9 A.M.–6 P.M., spring and fall, 10 A.M.–5 P.M., and December 1 through February 28, 10 A.M.–5 P.M. For more information contact U.S.S. *Constitution* Museum, P.O. Box 1812, Boston, MA 02129. Tel. (617) 426-1812. Children under six and active military personnel are admitted free.

Frame of Reference The U.S.S. *Constitution* was commissioned in 1797, at the end of the 18th century, at the beginning of the new nation, when Congress saw the need for a navy to protect American foreign trade. During the War of 1812 the wooden warship with a 21-inch-thick hull—dubbed "Old Ironsides" by the British—embarked on her major exploits. The frigate is on active duty today.

Significance The 200 colorful years of this ship's history make it one of the most significant symbols of freedom in America. George Washington named her the *Constitution* after the document that the 204-foot, heavily armed yet swift frigate was to defend. This "Eagle of the Sea," with its masts towering 20 stories into the salty air, is the oldest commissioned warship afloat in the world.

About the Site The U.S.S. *Constitution* welcomes visitors from its berth in the Charlestown Navy Yard (1800–1974), also a unit of the Boston National Historical Park. She floats across the Charles River from the shipyard in Boston's North End where she was built as the third of six vessels commissioned for the country's new navy. Today only about 15 to 18 percent of the venerable ship is original—the live oak center section below the water line. The remainder has been faithfully restored in several major overhauls, allowing the ship that never met defeat in its 42 battles or even had an enemy step aboard (except as a prisoner of war) to escape peacetime destruction.

Authentically costumed guides—active-duty enlisted men—escort you across the ship's deck. You then descend a ladder to lower decks. Watch your head: the ceiling is only 5½ feet high. (Renovations for the *Constitution*'s bicentennial celebrations, completed in July 1997, allow visitors to tour all lower decks.) Garrulous sailors tell what life was like for the 450 men and boys who lived for months and years aboard this vessel outfitted with 52 mighty guns, now replicas.

The museum across the paved navy yard (about the length of a football field) offers ship artifacts as well as displays about the *Constitution's* exploits against Barbary pirates and foreign warships, her diplomatic missions, and life at sea. There are also terrific hands-on exhibits targeted at kids. The Figgie Theatre regularly shows a 10-minute film on the frigate.

Hot Tips Don't miss the museum gift shop (in Building 22), where you can buy a sample of original wood from Old Ironsides's hull. Plan to spend two hours visiting the ship and museum. If you want to visit the other immediate sites—the Bunker Hill Monument and Pavilion and the Charlestown Navy Yard—allow two more hours. The navy yard has a separate visitor center in Building 5, near the *Constitution*. Pick up a brochure there, and see slide shows about the yard (38 acres of the original 130-acre site are preserved) and its famous ships on request.

The Raytheon Bunker Hill Pavilion stands behind Building 5 on Water Street. Follow the red-painted Freedom Trail northeast to the Bunker Hill Monument, a 10-minute walk. You can get a light lunch or snacks at the Shipyard Galley in Building 10, across Pier 1 from the *Constitution*. It's fun to eat at an outside table with the ship's cannon bearing down on you. With a slight turn of the head, you can see the Boston skyline, the Bunker Hill Monument, and the World War II destroyer *Cassin Young*, target of several Japanese kamikaze attacks.

Watch for uneven pavement and rail tracks in the shipyard. Food and accommodations are available throughout the Boston area.

The Best Stuff It's the ship, of course. Walk up the steep boarding plank and into the year 1812, when Old Ironsides lifted sagging American morale with the defeat and sinking of the British warship *Guerrier*. (The museum houses a walk-through exhibit of this famous battle.) You see and hear about the scuttlebutt (water barrel where sailors gossiped), the grod barrel (from which men were rationed two pints of 198-proof rum daily), the barber's chair (where sailors experienced a monthly hair cut and any necessary tooth extractions or other minor surgery), the raising of the 5,300-pound anchors, noisy and dangerous cannon firings (after a half hour, ears were bleeding), hot-racking (sleeping in shifts, thus keeping the hammocks warm), and powder monkeys.

Powder monkeys were small boys, 8 to 12 years old, who scurried up and down the ladders fetching gunpowder stored in the lowest ship deck. Learn of their story in a hands-on museum exhibit. Upstairs, a new exhibit tells about the *Constitution's* latest restoration, showing how the original 34 diagonal oak riders that gave her legendary strength have been replaced by square laminated stiffeners. Paul Revere manufactured the ship's original copper bolts and brass bell.

Then and Now It's awesome to gaze at the towering ship from dockside. An 1812 15-star flag waves above the ship with the black-painted, white-trimmed frigate is framed by Boston's skyline. As you look up, you'll see three platforms high on the masts—called fighting tops—where sharpshooters targeted enemies at close range. (You'll find an 1814 Blunderbuss used from these fighting tops in the museum.) The ship today sports some 20th-century amenities including fluorescent lights, a sprinkler system, and a protective canvas canopy. Below portholes and hatches still supply the only fresh air, but breathing is better thanks to tour limitations. Be prepared to wait your turn.

On July 21 1997, on the 200th anniversary of her commissioning, the ship sailed on her own for the first time since 1881. After a third overhaul, financed mainly by pennies raised by schoolchildren, the venerable old ship sailed off the Massachusetts coast with great fanfare. She sported six new, billowing sails mounted on strengthened masts with new rigging. Eventually, as fund-raising permits, the frigate will have a full complement of 36 sails. On the ground, they'd cover one acre.

You can join thousands of celebrants who line the shores of Boston Harbor every July 4 when tugboats turn Old Ironsides around, thus allowing her to weather evenly in port. There she serenely reminds visitors of the document for which she was named.

Elsewhere in the Area For information on the Charlestown Navy Yard contact Superintendent, Boston National Historic Park, 15 State Street, Boston, MA 02109. Tel. (617) 242-5644.

2

MIDDLE ATLANTIC

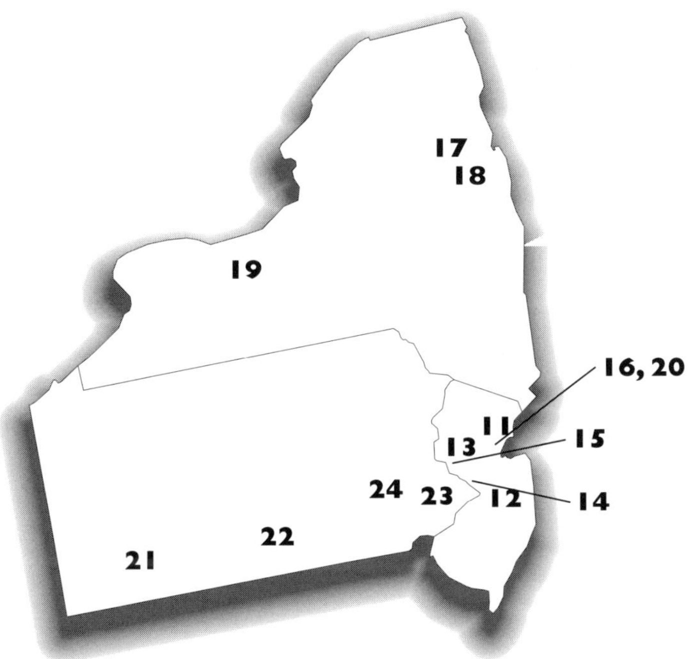

Key

Numbers correspond to site numbers on the map.

New Jersey

11. Edison's Laboratory
12. Monmouth Battlefield and Molly Pitcher's Well
13. Morristown
14. The Old Barracks
15. Washington's Crossing (also in Pennsylvania)

New York

16. Ellis Island
17. Fort William Henry
18. Saratoga Battlefield
19. Seneca Falls
20. Statue of Liberty

Pennsylvania

21. Fort Necessity
22. Gettysburg
23. Independence Hall
24. Valley Forge

Edison's Laboratory

Where the Famous Inventor Worked

Location West Orange, New Jersey, in metropolitan New York City, ten miles northwest of Manhattan, at Main Street and Lakeside Avenue. Take exit 145 from the Garden State Parkway to U.S. 280. Take exit 10 north onto Main Street.

Edison National Historic Site Visitor Center ($, ages 17 and up) is open daily, except Thanksgiving, December 25, and January 1, 9 A.M.–5 P.M. Parking is limited. Lab visits are by guided tour only at 10:30 A.M. and 3:30 P.M., daily. Entrance also covers a tour of Edison's nearby estate, Glenmont, open Wednesday through Sunday, 11 A.M.–4 P.M., except holidays. Educational events are scheduled year-round. Group reservations are required. For information contact Edison National Historic Site, Main Street and Lakeside Avenue, West Orange, NJ 07052. Tel. (201) 736-0550.

Frame of Reference Edison worked here during the most productive years of his lifetime from 1887 until his death in 1931.

Edison's Birthplace

Edison's birthplace in Milan, Ohio, is open to the public. The three-story brick home and the Edison Museum are located near the Ohio Turnpike on Route 113. Contact Edison Birthplace Association, Inc. Tel. (419) 499-2135. There's also a memorial tower in Menlo Park, New Jersey, at the site of the laboratory where Edison invented the first practical light bulb.

Significance This is the site where the famous American inventor Thomas Alva Edison, who was awarded a record 1,093 patents in his lifetime, conducted research for 44 years. Edison and his teams of scientists and technicians developed and perfected numerous inventions here, then placed them into mass production at a complex of factory buildings surrounding the research laboratories.

About the Site The site encompasses the original red-brick, three-story, 250-foot-long main laboratory, which remains much as Edison's staff left it in the years after his death; and four one-story specialized labs at 90-degree angles to the main lab, all clustered in several acres. The main lab functioned as the heart of the massive complex. The lab has machine shops, an engine room, glass blowing and pumping rooms, a chemical and photographic department, a unique stockroom, testing rooms, and Edison's 10,000-volume library.

Across Lakeside Avenue a four-story concrete building, once an Edison factory, runs a city block deep. The factory now houses upscale shops and offices. It remains the sole survivor of a once-extensive complex of factories that encompassed many city blocks.

Enter through the visitor center on Lakeside Avenue, located in the former powerhouse of the main lab. (In Edison's day, employees entered through a front brick arch on Main Street.) Here you can view Edison memorabilia and major inventions—including the first practical incandescent lamp, the phonograph, the kinescope, and the iron-alkaline storage battery. There's a small bookstore here.

You can take a guided tour of Glenmont, the estate where Edison and his second wife, Mini, moved into in 1886, at regularly scheduled times. The red, 29-room, stone-and-brick mansion now occupies a plot in private residential Llewellyn Park, the first planned residential park in America. The home still contains original furniture, paintings, books, and gifts to the Edisons and their three children. You must get a pass for the tour at the visitor center for admission past the gatehouse. Edison died in the master bedroom on October 18, 1931, at age eighty-four. He and Mini are buried in a simple plot behind the home.

Hot Tips The lab tour is geared toward kids in fourth grade and older. The lab is crowded, and breakables are within reach. Do not take very young children on this tour! Touch nothing! (Park rangers wear white cotton gloves when pointing out treasures.) No food, beverages, or smoking are allowed. Heat and humidity may force closing of some portions of the lab. Tours go from building to building, so dress for the weather. Food and accommodations are available in West Orange. Allow two hours for your visit. Advance reading enhances the tour.

The Best Stuff Edison's office/library, where tours begin and where the famed inventor began his day, is the heart of the laboratory complex and the heady highlight of the visit. Step inside the massive doors into the dark, wood-paneled "think tank," a large rectangular room lined with two tiers of study carrels (open-front offices) for staff. From his huge, rolltop desk in front of a conference table and fireplace at one end of the three-story room Edison could see and converse with researchers as they worked. For quick reference Edison amassed 10,000 volumes in the library. He and his staff left 35,000 notebooks, now housed in a vault at the site.

The thing that really grabs you about the office, with its green-shaded electric lamps, gifts, accolades—including Edison's Congressional Medal of Honor—and memorabilia, is Edison's bed. Tucked among the books in one corner is the sleeping cot Mini gave him. She worried about Edison's long working hours (16 to 20 hours a day) and his tendency to fall asleep late at night on the floor of his lab. A chest for personal belongings sits at the foot of the cot. Here are some other eye-openers:

- **Stockroom.** Down a short hall from the library is the inventor's version of a stockroom, where you can still see, as Edison put it, "everything from an elephant's hide to the eyeballs of a U.S. senator." (The eye was petrified and willed unsolicited to Edison. It's not actually in the stockroom.) In other words, anything that might be of use in inventing is here. When you peer into the wire mesh screen surrounding the stockroom, you can see a pile of human hair in different colors and textures (in case those factors might make a difference in an experiment). There's a hippo tooth, a huge tortoise shell, pipes, coils of wire, and hog bristles. Researchers would request materials from a clerk at the gate and leave an identifying tag showing who had what tool or material. A calendar showing August 1932 hangs inside.

Black Maria. A replica of the "Black Maria," the world's first motion picture studio, is worth the trip to the site. The black house (1893–1903) revolved on a circular track to capture sunlight for filming the first movies using Edison's "kinetophone," Edison's name for his motion picture projector with sound.

Chem Lab. The freestanding chemistry lab preserving Edison's last great experiment comes at the end of the tour. Though he was 80, Edison realized the need for the United States to produce its own rubber. During World War I the country depended on foreign sources for this vital material, but, true to his proclaimed desire to "create the largest possible measure of happiness and prosperity," Edison set about deriving rubber from plants.

Bales of various plants were shipped to the lab. Researchers crushed and tested leaves. Edison chose simple, abundant goldenrod as the source of the raw material needed to produce rubber. But he needed big goldenrod. Consulting with other scientists, Edison grew a 15-foot variety of goldenrod in his experimental gardens in Florida. Leaning against a wall in the lab in a 15-foot wooden case is one of the giant, now-dried, goldenrod plants shipped to the lab.

The lab's 10 workstations host nearly 70-year-old vials, apparatus, and bottles, many bearing Edison's handwritten labels. On a hook off to the side, the now-yellowing white lab coat that Edison wore on his last day at work hangs where he left it.

Then and Now At the height of production from 1919 through 1920, 10,000 employees worked in the factories, and a staff of 200 worked with Edison in the main lab. Edison's employees ran the complex for a while after his death in 1931. The site became a private museum in 1947 and a national historic site in 1955.

Today Edison's Lab is a quiet enclave frozen in time amid a busy downtown business district. The rows of machines in the machine room stand idle as they were left, though they are cranked up for special events. Edison's desk remains a study of organized clutter: small, corked bottles of Listerine for smoker's breath; antacids for his ulcer; paper clips; and stacks of papers sit on the green blotter.

Think, think, think. Work, work, work. Edison's formula for success and his lab linking technology and business remain the blueprint for modern private research and development. His pioneering industrial research lab is a monument to creativity, perseverance, organization, and practical application. It is among Edison's greatest inventions.

Thomas Edison's West Orange, New Jersey laboratory was a prototype for today's industrial research and development laboratory. Edison worked here from 1887 until his death in 1931.
Edison National Historic Site

The Old Barracks

Where the Hessians Were Quartered in Trenton

Location Downtown Trenton, New Jersey, on Barracks Street, adjacent to the New Jersey State Capitol on West State Street. From Route 29 take the Willow Street exit to Barracks Street.

The Old Barracks Museum ($) is open daily, except Thanksgiving, December 24 and 25, January 1, and Easter, 10 A.M.–5 P.M. Groups should make an appointment. For information on educational programs, including A Call to Arms Summer History Day Camp for children ages 9 through 12 and visits by George Washington, contact the Old Barracks Museum, Barracks Street, Trenton, NJ 08608. Tel. (609) 396-1776.

Frame of Reference The Battle of Trenton took place on December 26, 1776, during the Revolutionary War (1775–81).

Significance Built in 1758, the Old Barracks is the only freestanding British barracks from the French and Indian War remaining in the United States. But the Barracks is best known as quarters for the Hessians (German mercenaries) during the Battle of Trenton. Hessians made up about ⅓ of the British forces in the colonies during the Revolution. They were highly trained, fierce, and feared.

General George Washington's surprise early-morning attack and victory at Trenton—the first significant win for the Continental army during the Revolution—prevented a possible British move against Philadelphia. The battle established Washington's morally and physically drained army as a force the British must take seriously.

The Battle of Trenton took place after Washington crossed the icy Delaware River on Christmas night.

About the Site The three-story, stone Old Barracks has the shape of a reclining letter **C** and occupies half a city block, a time capsule amid the gray buildings of downtown Trenton. You enter through the furnished Officers House at the right of the courtyard, where costumed interpreters begin guided tours. You go through period rooms and gallery spaces displaying artifacts from the 18th and 19th centuries, as the guides weave colorful accounts of colonial life, the Revolution, and the two battles of Trenton. (The second battle, which also resulted in a Continental army victory, occurred 10 days later.) A corner room that served as a Continental army hospital later in the Revolution also is furnished.

On the left from Barrack Street, at the shorter end of the **C**, the Quarter Master's Store offers many delights for kids.

Hot Tips Parking is tight downtown during the week. Weekend parking is best found next to the barracks, behind the State House. A nearby pedestrian mall offers restaurants and shops. Accommodations are available in and around the city. Ask guides for a copy of the picture story of the museum, designed for young readers. Allow 1½ hours for the guided tour.

The Best Stuff The costumed history teachers who take you around the officers' quarters and barracks brim with enthusiasm and plenty of educational stories about the site and the Revolutionary War. A tour of the site reveals obscure facts regarding officers' eating and drinking habits (drinking alcoholic beverages was the favorite form of recreation), the significance of uniform decorations, how military letters were mailed, why the rope bedsteads (the "bed" was the mattress; the "bedstead" was the frame) had curtains, and why the officers' foyer was painted green. (It was an expensive color and helped distinguish the habitat of gentlemen.) Take some time in the Revolutionary-era hospital room where thousands of smallpox inoculations were given and soldiers were bedded while the vaccine had a chance to take effect. Smallpox was the number one killer disease of the 18th century.

Then and Now On December 26, 1776, after crossing the Delaware River on Christmas night, Washington and his troops arrived in Trenton around 8 A.M. The Continental army was hungry, exhausted, and ill equipped; the Hessians quartered at the Trenton Barracks were well-fed, highly trained, and confident. They also were asleep when Washington arrived, just as the desperate general had calculated. For more than two hours in rain, snow, sleet, and hail, the Hessians and the Continentals fought outside the barracks and all over town. The barracks exterior today has been restored to look as historians think it looked at the time of battle. (Full interior restoration is slated to continue through 1998.) The barracks resembles a small, stone hotel with a slate roof and a whitewashed, second-floor balcony.

Finally the tide of victory rolled toward the Continentals, as the Hessian leader was killed, a command was misunderstood, and key enemy cannons became mired in mud. Few Americans were hurt; none died in action. Americans captured 918 Hessians and killed 30. It was a time of celebration for Washington and his courageous army.

Through the years the barracks has undergone numerous changes and uses: housing for soldiers and officers (from both sides of the Revolutionary War), a hospital, apartments, private homes, a school, and finally a museum. At one point a new road to the State House halved the building. Today architects and historians continue to study the empty soldiers' barracks (the back of the **C**), and careful restoration to its original appearance continues. Eventually the entire building will be furnished with period furniture and open for touring.

Elsewhere in the Area Washington's Crossing is 8 miles north, Princeton is 12 miles northeast, and historic Camden is 37 miles south. Trenton itself is a historic treat. Pick up information at the Convention and Visitor's Bureau at the corner of Lafayette and Barracks streets. Tel. (609) 777-1771. The state capitol, second oldest in the country, offers guided tours. (The oldest capitol is Santa Fe.)

◆Hidden Jewel◆

Washington's Crossing

Where General George Washington Crossed the Delaware

Location Straddling the Delaware River in both Pennsylvania and New Jersey, about eight miles northwest of Trenton, New Jersey. From Trenton take U.S. 195 north to Route 29. The entrance to the Pennsylvania state park is just off Route 29. The entrance to the New Jersey state park is on Route 546, which intersects Route 29. Follow the signs.

Washington's Crossing Historic Site is actually two separate state parks, one in Pennsylvania and one in New Jersey (3½ miles apart). One admission ($) is good for both parks. The site is open Monday through Saturday, 9 A.M.–5 P.M., Sunday, noon–5 P.M.; but hours may vary, so call ahead. Every December 25 there's a reenactment of Washington's famous crossing using authentic Durham boat replicas. For information contact Washington Crossing Historic Park, P.O. Box 103, Washington Crossing, PA 18977. Tel. (215) 493-4076. Or contact Washington Crossing Association of New Jersey, P.O. Box 1776, Titusville, NJ 08650. Tel. (609) 737-9303.

Morristown: The Worst Winter

The main body of George Washington's Continental army also spent two winters during the Revolution encamped at Morristown, New Jersey. Morristown, chosen for its strategic location, natural protection, and sympathetic citizenry, was the site of Continental army encampments for the late winter of 1777 and the winter of 1779 to 1780. Troops encamped at Valley Forge in the winter between those years.

Washington's first Morristown encampment began on January 6, 1777, following victories at Trenton and Princeton, New Jersey. At the second encampment, beginning December 1, 1779, soldiers endured far worse conditions and more suffering than they did at Valley Forge. Between November and April, 28 snowfalls up to four feet deep blanketed the area. The Hudson and Delaware rivers froze solid. Except for one day, temperatures remained below freezing for all of January. Mutiny and severe punishment multiplied the misery of hunger, disease, and nakedness.

When you visit Morristown today, you can see several reconstructed log huts that housed troops on Jockey Ridge; the Wick Farm, where commanders lodged; and the Ford Mansion, which served as Washington's headquarters. An orientation film and museum at the visitor center explain Morristown's role in the Revolution. There's also a small gift shop.

For more information contact the National Park Service, Morristown National Historical Park, Washington Place, Morristown, NJ 07960. Tel. (201) 539-2085.

Frame of Reference General George Washington crossed the Delaware during the Revolutionary War (1775–81), on Christmas night, December 25, 1776.

Significance Here General George Washington led a ragged, filthy, and starving army of 6,000 men across the icy Delaware River from Pennsylvania into New Jersey en route to a battle with Hessian mercenaries at Trenton. Depictions of Washington bravely crossing the Delaware are among the most familiar and admired historical artworks in America.

Washington's army earned its first significant Revolutionary victory at Trenton on Christmas night, then went on to repel British redcoats at Princeton on January 3. Though relatively minor, these improbable and morale-boosting victories proved to be a turning point in the war for America's independence from Great Britain.

About the Site The parks are run by separate entities. Historical markers distinguish the points where Washington's boats most likely departed the Pennsylvania shore and where they landed in New Jersey. The riverfront sites are connected by a one-lane bridge.

The Pennsylvania side of the park has 18 historic buildings buzzing with costumed interpreters and regularly scheduled Revolutionary "encampments." Here you can touch replicas of the big Durham boats Washington and his troops used that Christmas night, and you can see an exact copy of Leutze's famous painting *Washington Crossing the Delaware*. There are museums, exhibits, and plenty of 19th-century homes lining the streets of re-created Taylorsville, a Quaker village that grew around the ferry site long after the famous crossing.

On the New Jersey waterfront, a replica of a flatbed ferry, much like the one built on the site in 1848, sits beside a small 18th-century ferryhouse. The ferry is much like the one Washington used to transport his artillery in 1776. East of the river the visitor center in the 807-acre New Jersey park houses the Swan Collection of the American Revolution. Browsing this small museum is a treat for Revolutionary War buffs as well as for those with only a passing interest.

Hot Tips The best way to start your tour is at the visitor center in Titusville. Park at the visitor center and allow an hour to see the museum. Here you can find picnicking facilities, a playground, and hiking trails. Pick up a map to guide you to the river and Pennsylvania side of the site. Park at the riverfront, see the ferryhouse, ferry, and markers, and then walk over the bridge into Pennsylvania. Walking the narrow bridge is definitely preferable to driving across—it's a tight squeeze.

Come prepared for the weather. Walking is mostly on gravel paths. Walking paths and bicycle trails crisscross the New Jersey park.

Food is available in Taylorsville. A less-crowded bet is to eat in Trenton 8 miles south of the park. Accommodations are available in Trenton, Princeton, or the Philadelphia area.

The Best Stuff It's thrilling to stand in the place where the future first president and his ragtag army actually crossed the Delaware. Check out these items in the museum at Titusville, and find out how truly difficult and circuitous the march toward American independence was.

- **Washington's Orders.** This is the original letter from General Washington's secretary, dated December 1, 1776, ordering a colonist to secure the boats to cross the Delaware. Lack of local support for the Continental army meant the crafts were confiscated for the four river crossings. The letter, part of the Swan Collection, bears Washington's signature.
- **Real Revolutionary Money.** The museum displays a large collection of authentic continental coins and currency, including the first continental dollar made. Curator Harry Kels Swan is fond of placing the plastic-encased dollar in children's hands. Among the swords, weaponry, and tools, you also can see a rare, bright-red German officer's coat. The coat was America's first military recruiting tool. After the coat was presented to Washington upon his Trenton victory, the General gave it to his commander-in-chief, who displayed it around New Jersey as he persuaded reluctant youths to join the army.
- **Boat Replicas.** On the Pennsylvania side kids will love to touch and peer into the four replicas of the shoulder-deep Durham boats Washington used to transport 2,400 men. (The boats are big, not like in the famous paintings.) About 200 horses and 18 big guns also crossed the river in boats and ferries.
- **Tower at Washington's Lookout:** Drive north several miles on Highway 32 to Bowman's Hill Tower. The 110-foot stone tower marks the spot on the 308-foot hill where Washington stationed a lookout to watch enemy movement in New Jersey. A climb to the top offers a panoramic view of the area. A bronze plaque inside, quoting Trevelyan, an English historian (1838–1928) reads:

Monmouth Battlefield and Molly Pitcher's Well

June 18, 1778, was a scorchingly hot day in central New Jersey. It also was the day one of the biggest battles of the American Revolution raged. The Battle of Monmouth was the last major confrontation in the north and the fight that made a young scrubwoman named Mary Ludwig Hayes—whom we know as Molly Pitcher—a legend.

An exhibit in the visitor center at Monmouth Battlefield State Park in Manalapan and Freehold Townships explains that Hayes, age 24, "chewed tobacco and swore like a good trooper." Her husband, who manned a cannon during the battle, either was wounded or overcome by the horrible heat. A witness, James Sullivan Martin, saw Mary pour water on the cannon to cool it, then take over the firing. Supposedly a bullet tore through her dress right between her legs. Legend has it that Mary went on to collect buckets of water from a nearby well or stream and took the life-giving liquid around to the thirsty soldiers, possibly in a pitcher. The grateful men affectionately called her Molly Pitcher.

After the battle—a colonial victory—an officer presented Mary to General George Washington, who made her a sergeant with half pay. Hayes lived 50 more years and died in poverty. She was buried in an unmarked grave. Today, with some effort, you can find a concrete block that inconspicuously marks Molly Pitcher's Stream, still gurgling near an orchard on the battlefield.

Monmouth Battlefield is open daily, 9 A.M.–4 P.M. For information contact Monmouth Battlefield State Park, 347 Freehold Road, Manalapan, NJ 07726. Tel. (908) 462-9616.

The Turning Point of the American Revolution. It may be doubted whether so small a number of men ever employed so short a space of time with greater and more lasting results upon the history of the world. . . . "May Liberty's Beacon Inspire Patriotism, Peace and Fellowship Amongst All Peoples."

Then and Now In the winter of 1776 Washington's army had suffered many military setbacks. Desertions and disease extracted a high toll. Supplies and morale were low. Backing among the colonists had dwindled. Many Americans supported the British; others simply no longer believed independence was possible—or desirable. The soldiers who stayed with the Revolutionary cause were desperately hungry and ill-clothed.

In early December Washington led his army into Pennsylvania for respite from the British pursuit. He ordered all boats seized up and down the river so that the enemy could not pursue. But the river iced over, making an assault possible anyway.

Washington's military options were to wait for a debilitating attack on his army or zap the enemy on a holiday, when they had been drinking. He determinedly chose the latter.

On Christmas afternoon, 2,400 Continentals assembled at the ferry of Samuel McKonkey. You can tour the stone McKonkeys Ferry Inn. It remains much the same as when Washington (according to lore) ate his Christmas dinner there in 1776. Drop in to the original Taylorsville Store, The Patriot, for a trip back in time to 1828. Here you can buy items like those sold in the old village and pick up a sandwich and cold drink. The history teachers/owners thrill kids with personal tours. Be sure to see the collection of paintings of George Washington in the visitor center.

On December 25, 1776, the watch stationed on Bowman's Hill reported to Washington that the coast was clear. It took the army 11 hours to cross the Delaware in the icy, quick current that night. The march toward the hard-fought victory at Trenton began about 3:30 A.M. in a driving winter storm. (The Hessians were surprised but not drunk.)

Today 20th-century bustle encroaches on the park, but the riverfront areas are protected. During a winter visit you can almost see what Washington faced that famous night.

Elsewhere in the Area The park is best toured as part of a visit to Trenton and the Old Barracks Museum. The Princeton Battle Monument is 12 miles northeast, Monmouth Battlefield is 30 miles east, and historic Camden is 37 miles south.

Ellis Island

Symbol of America's Immigrant Heritage

Location Off the tip of Manhattan in Upper New York Bay, near the shores of Jersey City, New Jersey. The site can be reached only by ferry.

Ellis Island National Monument is open daily, except December 25, 9:30 A.M.–5 P.M., with hours extended in summer. For information contact Superintendent, Statue of Liberty National Monument, Liberty Island, New York, NY 10004. Tel. (212) 363-7770. Call (212) 269-5755 for ferry ticket ($) and schedule information. Ferry tickets include a trip to the Statue of Liberty.

Frame of Reference Ellis Island was in use around the turn of the 20th century, 1892 through 1924, a period of heavy immigration to the United States by Europeans—the largest volunteer human migration in history. Ellis Island reopened to the public in 1990 after a $170 million renovation that ended a period of vandalism and decay since the island's abandonment in 1954.

Significance To these buildings in the shadow of the Statue of Liberty a huge wave of 12 million immigrants—mostly people fleeing poverty or political and religious persecution in European countries—entered the United States in search of work and their dreams. Here, a few hundred yards north of Lady Liberty, those apprehensive men, women, and children were "processed"—questioned and examined to ascertain if they met myriad health and social regulations—after their 3,000-mile journeys. Most then were sent on their way to mainland United States. About 3 percent were sent back home on medical grounds.

By 1910, 75 percent of the residents of New York City, Chicago, Detroit, Cleveland, and Boston were immigrants or children of immigrants. Today, 100 million Americans—about 40 percent of the nation's population—can trace their ancestry to this place. Ellis Island is the symbol of America's immigrant heritage.

About the Site The main building of the Ellis Island National Monument has been restored to its original appearance. This massive, three-story, brick-and-stone building is where immigrants first entered the Ellis Island complex. The second floor houses the huge registry room or Great Hall, once filled with wooden benches where sea-weary foreigners waited to hear their names called for initial questioning. The island was named after its late-18th-century owner, Samuel Ellis.

Today all three floors house the 200,000-square-foot Ellis Island Immigration Museum. The museum comprises four major exhibits designed to bring the immigrant experience to life; 30 galleries filled with original immigrant artifacts, oral histories, and ethnic music; several changing exhibits; and two theaters featuring the excellent, award-winning documentary *Island of Hope, Island of Tears*. The first floor has a snack bar and gift shop. The other buildings on the island (three connected islands, actually) stand unrestored, many of their windows broken or covered with plywood.

Hot Tips The Circle Line–Statue of Liberty Ferry travels at ½-hour intervals, 9 A.M.–5 P.M. daily, from Battery Park in lower Manhattan and Liberty State Park in Jersey City, New Jersey. Ferries make one round trip to both Ellis Island and the Statue of Liberty, so allow plenty of time for your visit, three to four hours. If you plan to visit both sites in one trip, allow up to one full day.

Upon entering the first floor, find the U.S. Park Service information booth. Here you can find out about ranger-guided tours, pick up maps, and get free tickets to *Island of Hope, Island of Tears*. You can rent audiocassettes available in several languages for self-guided tours. Television news anchor Tom Brokaw narrates a 28-minute audiocassette tour also available for rental. It is a park-enforced regulation that children must be chaperoned at all times, one adult for every 10 children.

It's wise to pack a snack for the visit, but food is available on both islands. Accommodations are available in nearby New Jersey cities and in New York.

The Best Stuff Orientation movies at historic sites often aren't worth your time, but *Island of Hope, Island of Tears* is a must-see. The 30-minute documentary tells the story of Ellis Island immigrants in their own words, featuring provocative footage of the Europe they left behind and the America that greeted them. The movie breathes life into the re-created turn-of-the-century Ellis Island. A 15-minute ranger talk precedes the film.

After the movie go sit on the original green wooden benches arranged at one end of Great Hall, as did the immigrants whose aged voices you just heard. Look out the massive, arched windows as did those anxious travelers, all of their possessions stashed in suitcases or cloth bags. (Some had nothing but the clothes on their backs.) The skyline of "the promised land," now more imposing, towered over choppy harbor waters.

The ferry ride to and from the island drives home the immigrant experience. Modern families huddle together on green benches of the crowded decks as the *Miss Freedom* glides by the Statue of Liberty. The boat slips into the dock at Great Hall; the American flag flies in the ocean winds. Maybe you can imagine the anxiety, possibly terror, mixed with the fatigue the farmers from small European villages felt as they stepped amid the huge buildings of Ellis Island. Said one immigrant woman in *Island of Tears* of this main building: "I couldn't take my eyes off that. It was like a whole city." You'll know what she meant.

Then and Now Most immigrants of 1892 to 1924 came to Ellis Island in the lower decks of great ships, in the third class called "steerage." The lucky few who traveled first or second class were examined upon the docked ships; the rest headed to the first floor baggage room of the main hall. Today you enter the baggage room as the immigrants did and walk up the restored staircase to the right where U.S. public health doctors began their examinations and watched to see which immigrants couldn't easily negotiate the long staircase.

Into the Great Hall the immigrants streamed, sometimes up to 5,000 a day. Then came the wait on the benches until their names were called. Most immigrants were processed in a day, beginning with a step up to the inspector's table. (One original table remains in the museum today.)

The questions, reflecting a succession of U.S. laws designed to keep out undesirables, began with "Do you have any money?" Paupers, idiots, lunatics, and immoral persons were not welcome. Those suspected of medical problems were detained for further examination. A complex of dormitories, dining halls, laundries, and hospitals grew around the main hall. Today you can visit an original dormitory on the second floor.

A walk-through exhibit explains the long medical examination the immigrants with suspected health problems faced. Doctors placed a chalk mark on their clothes to indicate the suspected problem. (A circle with an X over it indicated signs of mental illness.) Many, including pregnant women, were hospitalized. More than 350 babies were born in Ellis Island hospitals.

Today an exhibit, "The Peopling of America," behind the Baggage Room presents a three-dimensional statistical portrait of the United States' pageant of immigration. It carries the warning that population "facts" may not always be accurate, because they reflect changing attitudes about race, ethnicity, and national identification.

A plaque at the entrance to the exhibit puts our nation of immigrants in perspective. It reads "Since 1600, over 60 million people from throughout the world have come to the United States, creating a multiethnic nation unparalleled in history."

Elsewhere in the Area The Statue of Liberty and Castle Clinton, the first immigration station, are both at the harbor; Federal Hall, first capitol of the United States, is in Manhattan; Theodore Roosevelt's birthplace is at 28 East 20th Street; Ulysses Grant's Tomb is in Riverside Park; and the Alexander Hamilton Grange is at Convent Avenue and 141st Street.

Fort William Henry

Site of the Infamous Massacre of the French and Indian War

Location Eastern New York State on the southern shore of Lake George, one hour north of Albany. Take I-87 north to exit 21, east onto Highway 9N, north onto U.S. 9. The reconstructed fort is 3/4 mile on the right. From Montreal take the Northway (U.S. 87) south to exit 21. From Vermont take Route 149 west to Route 9 and turn north.

Fort William Henry ($), privately owned and operated, is open daily, from May through mid-June, 10 A.M.–5 P.M., from the end of June through Labor Day, 9 A.M.–10 P.M., and from September 2 through Columbus Day, 10 A.M.–5 P.M. For more information contact Fort William Henry, Canada Street, Lake George, NY 12845. Tel. (518) 668-5471.

Frame of Reference Fort William Henry was occupied during the French and Indian War (1754–63), which was part of the first true world war, known in Europe as the Seven Years' War. (The French and Indian War began two years before the Seven Years' War was officially declared.) French forces fired on the British at the fort for six days in August 1757 until the British surrender on August 9, 1757. The Native North American massacre of the surren-

Saratoga Battlefield: Irony 20 Years Later

It's ironic that a mere 30 miles southeast of Fort William Henry, where British and Americans fought side by side, stretches the Revolutionary War battlefield famous for a result that changed the course of American history—the decisive colonial victory over British forces at Saratoga convinced the French to join with American forces against Great Britain. The alliance tipped the scale toward colonial independence. It happened a mere 20 years after the French torched Fort William Henry.

In the fall of 1777 British forces under the command of General John "Gentleman Johnny" Burgoyne moved southward from Canada in a push toward Albany, New York. After a quick victory at Fort Ticonderoga, Burgoyne faced a series of military setbacks at the hands of patriot forces and pulled back to Saratoga.

There American Commander Horatio Gates and his 9,000 men waited on a hill over the road to Albany, now U.S. 4, between the hills and the Hudson River near Stillwater. Burgoyne's soldiers fought hard. Battles raged for nearly three weeks over several square miles. One American, General Benedict Arnold, later to become famous as a traitor, made a name for himself by leading a savage attack against German troops fighting for the British.

Burgoyne retreated to the heights of Saratoga where an American force that had now swollen to 20,000 surrounded him. He and his nearly 6,000 men were taken prisoner in what was to become one of the most decisive victories in history.

Today at Saratoga National Historical Park ($) you'll find a visitor center with a small museum, a network of hiking trails through the Adirondack

dered British troops as well as their Mohican, Mohawk, and colonial allies took place that night and early the next morning, on August 10, 1757.

Significance This is the reconstructed fort made famous by thousands of literary accounts of the 1757 massacre, including James Fenimore Cooper's classic *The Last of the Mohicans* and the string of movies that book has spawned. Eyewitness accounts vary widely but generally state that from this 50-foot-high promontory on Lake George, a badly outnumbered British force under Lieutenant Colonel George Monro held out for six days against a bloody bombardment by the French, who had about 3,000 Native North American allies from 30 to 40 tribal nations.

British forces at Fort William Henry surrendered to the French on August 9, 1757, after the French commander, Marquis de Montcalm, moved guns into point-blank firing range. Following the surrender frustrated Native North Americans allied with the French seized promised war plunder, and massacred the sick and wounded left behind in the fort. The French looked the other way.

Early the next morning the Native North Americans attacked and slaughtered most of the defeated British soldiers, colonial militiamen, Mohawks, Mohicans, and civilian wives and children on their way to British protection at nearby Fort Edward. (Estimates of the number slaughtered range from several hundred to several thousand.) The French then burned Fort William Henry to the ground. Although this simple fort endured a mere two years, its story still fascinates us two centuries later.

Mountains, and a nine-mile, self-guided auto tour road with 10 pullouts, markers, and monuments. Important battle sites (earthworks have been destroyed) are marked by posts.

- Eight miles north in Schuylerville (historic Saratoga) stands the 155-foot granite Saratoga Monument, erected in 1883. This was the site of Burgoyne's entrenched camp during the final days of the 1777 campaign. Ongoing renovations due to water damage keep the obelisk closed, but you can see four exterior niches that house life-size bronze statues of Saratoga war heroes: General Philip Schuyler, General Gates, and Colonel Daniel Morgan. The fourth niche is empty, the place where Benedict Arnold's statue should stand.
- The 1777 home of Philip Schuyler off Route 4 in Schuylerville is open for tours from Memorial Day through Labor Day, 9:30 A.M.–5 P.M.

The park is located 12 miles southeast of Saratoga Springs on U.S. 4 at NY 32, exit 12 off the Northway (U.S. 87). The visitor center is open daily, except Thanksgiving, December 25, and January 1, 9 A.M.–5 P.M. The park's nine-mile tour road is open daily, April 1 through November 30, 9 A.M.–5 P.M. For more information contact Superintendent, Saratoga National Historical Park, 648 Route 32, Stillwater, NY 12170-1604. Tel. (518) 664-9821.

▲

Historians generally credit Lieutenant Colonel Monro's stubborn resistance against Montcalm's power at Fort William Henry as the turning point in the French and Indian War. Monro broke the French momentum in this last of four colonial wars for European control of North America and its riches. By the end of the Seven Years' War, French power in North America had been eliminated, and the British had established a world empire on which the sun never set.

About the Site Fort William Henry occupies a few acres amid the amusement rides and refreshment stands of Lake George Village. From Canada Street (Route 9) it's easy to think the small log-and-mud structure with its four bastions further down the lake embankment is the site of a dressed-up bumper-car ride. The large sign in the parking lot reads "Fort William Henry, Ice Cream, Mini Golf."

On closer inspection, you'll see the entrance across the dry moat on the fort's north side. Inside you'll find the fort—authentically reconstructed on original foundations—a museum, the partially original dungeon, a large gift shop, a small theater for a brief orientation slide show, exhibits, and hourly living-history tours and demonstrations conducted by costumed guides.

Adjacent to the parking lot a log shelter protects the concrete-covered burial ground of men, women, and children who died during the 1757 siege. Their skeletal remains had been exhibited at the fort from the time they were exhumed during archaeological excavations in 1953 until they were given a final resting place in May 1993. Twenty-three large photographs on the walls show the preburial skeletons, some with screaming mouths and visible musket holes. A boulder on the asphalt sidewalk to the shelter marks the grave of an unknown soldier of the French and Indian War. In front of the shelter, there's a picnic table.

Hot Tips Plan to spend two hours. Be prepared to walk over gravel trails and negotiate steep stairs. For a better appreciation of what you'll see, read the 1826 Cooper classic before visiting, or check out one of the video versions. The latest *Last of the Mohicans* was released in 1992 (and is rated R). Food and accommodations are available in Lake George Village.

The Best Stuff The costumed guides from England's "144th Regiment Afoot" make the visit worthwhile. You'll witness a Royal British Grenadier—the original "shock troops," all over six feet (a "tall" order in colonial times)—toss a live grenade, fire a musket, and ignite a six-pounder cannon from the northwest bastion overlooking Lake George. This bastion is where Montcalm's forces first attacked. It was virtually destroyed in the ensuing bombardment. The guides give a lively account of what they're doing as the paddlewheel cruise ship *Minne Ha Ha* blasts her calliope from the lake. (Warning: The cannon detonation is very loud, although the demonstration uses only two ounces of gunpowder. Monro's men used two pounds of gunpowder. Frontier soldiers usually were deaf within two years of active duty—if they didn't die first.) Also check out these exhibits:

- **The Dungeon.** Kids will like this; it's spooky. In addition to solitary confinement cells and leg irons, you can see the dungeon's original 1755 fireplace.
- **The Fort Hospital.** Sanitation at the fort was abysmal, and many died here of filth and disease. This re-created hospital shows how primitive medical care was in the 18th-century military. Anesthesia was a swig of rum and a musket ball between the teeth. The drunken patient literally "bit the bullet" to deal with the pain of surgery. Among hundreds of artifacts found in archaeological digs at the site were musket balls with teeth marks on them. You'll find fort artifacts in the museum.

Then and Now Although British Major General William Johnson built Fort William Henry, named for the son of Britain's King George III, at this exact location, things have changed mightily in the last 240 years. In 1755 Johnson wrote, "I am building this fort at this lake where no house ever before was built, nor a rod of land cleared. . . ."

Johnson also changed the name of French-named Lake Sacrament to Lake George, for his English king. British spoils of war included a string of forts the French built along the colonial frontier, and they too were given English names.

Today there are still plenty of trees around Lake George, and if you stand on the north bastion overlooking the water and focus on the distant shoreline you can get the idea of what it looked like more than 200 years ago. But thousands of tourists sun on the beach across Beach Boulevard, the village teems with restaurants and motels, and the only screams are from thrill seekers on the Ferris wheel next door.

Elsewhere in the Area Fort Ticonderoga stands between Lake George and Lake Champlain, about 60 miles north just off I-87 at exit 28 on Route 74. This is another privately owned, reconstructed fort of the French and Indian War, originally built by the French in 1755 as Fort Carillon. The victorious British later renamed it. This fort also is famous as the site of the first American victory of the Revolution, in a surprise raid on May 10, 1775, by Ethan Allen with his Green Mountain Boys of Vermont and Benedict Arnold with Massachusetts volunteers. Here you can see military artillery, artifacts, and living-history demonstrations. Open from early May through late October, 9 A.M.–5 P.M. For information contact Fort Ticonderoga, P.O. Box 390B, Ticonderoga, NY 12883. Tel. (518) 585-2821.

◆Hidden Jewel◆

Seneca Falls

Site of First Women's Rights Convention

Location Central New York State, about 60 miles west of Syracuse. Take I-90 (New York State Thruway) to exit 41, then Route 414 south four miles to Route 5/20 east. The visitor center is located 15 minutes south of the Thruway and two miles east in downtown Seneca Falls on Route 5/20 east at 136 Fall Street.

Women's Rights National Historic Park is open daily, except Thanksgiving, December 25, and January 1, 9 A.M.–5 P.M., with extended hours in the summer. For more information contact Superintendent, Women's Rights National Historical Park, 136 Fall Street, Seneca Falls, NY 13148. Tel. (315) 568-2991. Other women's rights–related sites in the area are privately owned with varying days and hours of operation. For more information contact the Seneca County Chamber of Commerce, Routes 5 and 20, Seneca Falls, NY 13148. Tel. 1-800-732-1848.

Frame of Reference The mid-1800s was a time of social change and political turmoil centering on the antislavery movement. The First Women's Rights Convention was held July 19 and 20, 1848. The movement for women's right to vote continued through the early 1900s, until the 19th Amendment to the Constitution was ratified in 1920. The fight for gender equality continues today.

Significance In this sleepy town along the Seneca River, 300 reform-minded women, men, and children held an unprecedented convention to discuss women's social condition and need for full and equal rights with men. On July 20, 1848, 100 of the conventioneers—32 of them men, including ex-slave/abolitionist Frederick Douglass—boldly signed the Declaration of Sentiments, modeled on the U.S. Declaration of Independence signed 72 years earlier. "We hold these truths to be self evident: that all men and women are created equal, . . ." the new Declaration read. This convention spawned the revolution we now know as the Women's Rights Movement.

About the Site The park comprises Declaration Park, which features the remains of the brick Wesleyan Chapel where the convention convened, and a black, granite, 140-foot water wall engraved with the Declaration of Sentiments and a list of the signers. The wall runs the full length of the east side of the brick visitor center, a former firehouse, which houses a museum, bookstore, special exhibits, and a theater for a 25-minute orientation film. A life-size bronze sculpture of the organizers of the First Women's Rights Convention with key attendees dominates the visitor center lobby. Park rangers encourage visitors to touch the sculpture.

The park also includes the homes of convention planners Elizabeth Cady Stanton in Seneca Falls and of Mary Ann and Thomas M'Clintock in nearby Waterloo, where leaders drafted the Declaration of Sentiments. Access to these homes is by guided tours only. Sign up at the visitor center. Park rangers regularly offer tours of the chapel and interpretative talks centering on the 20-figure bronze statue.

The nature of Declaration Park is open and unfinished, signifying the continuing work toward women's equality. Wesleyan Chapel silhouettes the sky with stark metal beams and partial walls, all that remains of the original two-story structure.

Near the park the private National Women's Hall of Fame, opened in 1969, stands at 76 Falls Street. It is not part of the national park. One block east you'll find the Women's Rights National Resource and Educational Center at 116 Fall Street. Sign up for guided tours of the center's print shop at the visitor center. Park rangers also lead 45-minute walking tours of historic Seneca Falls from June through September.

Hot Tips Allow plenty of time for a leisurely visit—a couple of hours to half a day. You'll be absorbing not only the exhibits here but the entire drama of the fight for women's rights. It's a heady atmosphere. The town of Seneca Falls offers quaint shops and restaurants, nice sidewalks, little traffic, and delightful scenery to boot.

Numerous books tell the story of the fight for women's rights and its chief players, but young people may especially enjoy Norma Johnston's *Remember the Ladies*. The title comes from Abigail Adams's admonition to her husband, John, when he became the second president of the United States.

Parking is behind the visitor center or on the street. Food and accommodations are available in the Seneca Falls–Waterloo area.

The Best Stuff Be sure to watch the film *Dreams of Equality* early in your visit. The movie centers on a 19th-century Seneca Falls mother and her personal struggle with the controversial issues of women's rights that swirl about her at the time of the landmark convention. (She ends up attending the Women's Rights Convention but doesn't sign the Declaration of Sentiments.)

The film also explores the state of females in 19th-century America and today, showing the great strides women have made but subtly asking if things have changed enough. At one point a modern boy and girl engage in a lively discussion about how they feel about themselves. The girl laments how she often feels second-rate to braggart guys. Finally frustrated with her, the boy blurts out, "I just don't think it will ever be totally equal—unless we lose gender!" Exhibits throughout continue to offer points for discussion.

Questions—some answered with facts and some open to argument—fill the screen and spill over into the upstairs exhibits. Signs ask visitors "What were men afraid of?" "What did it mean to be a true woman?" "What do you want to be?" "Are there any toys here that you would not let your child play with?"

Debate continues as interactive video displays offer point/counterpoint discussions of today's issues such as pay equity, sexual harassment, child care, and job qualifications. Around the corner you're hit with displays of 1870 corsets and a selection of cosmetics reminding us that in 1989 surgeons liposuctioned 200,000 pounds of tissue from 130,000 American women. Eleven died.

Yep, a lot of questions are raised here; there is a lot to debate. Young people who might take current women's rights for granted should be intrigued.

Then and Now A famous 1773 tea party in Boston helped ignite the American Revolution two years thereafter. In 1848 a genteel tea party at the home of Jane Hunt in Waterloo sparked the women's revolution a mere six days later. At the 1848 birthday party, five women—Hunt, Lucretia Mott, Elizabeth Cady Stanton, Mott's sister Martha Wright, and Mary Ann M'Clintock—shared their anger and frustration about their own lives and the sorry lot of womanhood.

Stanton and Mott especially were indignant. Eight years earlier they had attended the World Anti-Slavery Convention in London with their husbands. The men were seated on the main floor and participated in debate. But Stanton and Mott were seated in the balcony with a handful of other attending women as silent spectators. Their resentments coalesced at that hot July tea party.

The very next week a procession of carriages ascended on the mill town of Seneca Falls after word quickly spread of Stanton and Mott's hastily organized convention. The 300 conventioneers, dressed in the cumbersome (often 20 pounds of petticoats and corsets) wool clothing of the day, discussed women's social condition in the Wesleyan Chapel, long used as a forum for controversial groups.

Quaker and abolitionist Lucretia Mott, very pregnant with her seventh child, shunned the convention of "confinement," which demanded that expectant women stay home, and rode miles in a carriage to attend. She spoke of "mother's rights."

Thus the Declaration of Sentiments was conceived and signed. Recriminations and controversy ensued. But the five organizers persisted, writing and lecturing and organizing. Another convention followed quickly in Rochester, New York, and women's rights conventions occurred annually until the outbreak of the Civil War in 1861.

Today casually dressed and educated women, with their daughters in tow, join the visitors here to absorb the story of the First Women's Rights Convention. Like the 12 miles of the Erie Canal that threads through Seneca Falls, the story of women's struggle for equality continues to wind its way through our history.

Statue of Liberty

Beloved Shrine of Political Freedom

Location On Bedloe's Island off the tip of Manhattan in Upper New York Bay. The monument can be reached only by ferry.

The Statue of Liberty National Monument is open daily, except December 25, 9:30 A.M.–5 P.M., with hours extended in summer. For information contact Superintendent, Statue of Liberty National Monument, Liberty Island, New York, NY 10004. Tel. (212) 363-7770. For ferry ticket ($) and schedule information telephone (212) 269-5755. Ferries take visitors to the statue and Ellis Island for one price.

Frame of Reference The Statue of Liberty was conceived in the wake of the French Revolution (1789–1801) and the Civil War in the United States (1861–65), when the ideals of liberty and stability burned bright in both countries. This gift from the people of France to the people of the United States was proposed in 1865 to commemorate the signing of the U.S. Declaration of Independence (1776) and the alliance of the two countries in the Revolutionary War. Lady Liberty was constructed in France in 1884, shipped to America in 1885, and reconstructed here in 1886.

Significance The giant copper statue of "Liberty Enlightening the World," known as the Statue of Liberty, stands at the gateway to the New World. It was one of the first images of America European immigrants saw as their boats approached the processing center of Ellis Island, a stone's throw away in the bay. The 151-foot-plus-1-inch statue has become one of the most enduring images of America and the freedom this country represents—a cherished monument with millions of visitors yearly.

About the Site The Statue of Liberty National Monument consists of the statue, the figure of a woman standing with her uplifted torch atop a 154-foot stone pedestal near the center of a 10.38-acre island, a visitor center, and a ferry dock. The star-shaped stone wall around the base of the pedestal, designed by American architect Richard M. Hunt, is the wall of an abandoned fort.

The Statue of Liberty, designed by French sculptor Auguste Bartholdi, is a study in numbers. She is built of more than 300 copper shells, each less than 1/10 inch thick, supported by an iron framework. Gustave Eiffel, builder of the famous Eiffel Tower in Paris, designed the massive inner framework. The statue's total height from pedestal bottom to torch top is 305 feet, 1 inch. She weighs 450,000 pounds. The pedestal rests on a 23,500-ton concrete foundation that goes 20 feet into bedrock. On the pedestal appears the famous chiseled sonnet by Emma Lazarus, "The New Colossus." It reads in part, "Give me your poor,/Your huddled masses yearning to breathe free."

Lady Liberty's torch-holding right arm extends 42 feet into the air. The torch, once glass and lit by mercury-vapor lamps, was refurbished as part of a bicentennial overhaul. Now it is covered in copper and painted gold. Lady Liberty holds the Tablet of Law bearing the date July 4, 1776, in Roman numerals. A broken shackle lies at her sandaled feet.

The visitor center houses a snack bar, a gift shop, and exhibits explaining how the idea of the statue was conceived, and how Lady Liberty was designed, constructed in France, shipped to this country, and reconstructed in Upper New York Bay.

Hot Tips The Circle Line–Statue of Liberty Ferry travels at ½-hour intervals, 9 A.M.–5 P.M. daily, from Battery Park in lower Manhattan and Liberty State Park in Jersey City, New Jersey. Ferries make one round trip to both Ellis Island and the Statue of Liberty, so allow plenty of time for your visit, about three to four hours. If you plan to visit both sites in one trip, allow four hours to one full day. It's wise to pack a snack for the visit, but food is available on both islands. Accommodations are available in nearby New Jersey cities and in New York. Do not attempt to climb to the crown of the statue if you suffer from claustrophobia, asthma, or acrophobia (fear of heights).

The Best Stuff Climbing a circular staircase up the hollow interior of the statue is guaranteed to get your heart pounding and make the visit unforgettable, especially for young people. But beware: this 22-story climb isn't for the faint of heart. The two staircases are narrow and have 354 steep steps. In warm months the interior of the copper statue can get mighty hot. Your hands get sweaty, and holding on to the stair rails becomes tricky. What's more, once you start your climb from the top of the pedestal, there's no turning back until you reach the crown. (This is definitely not recommended for younger children, but older kids may love it.)

It's a thrill to hike the steep steps past the folds of Lady Liberty's robe and see from the back side her three-foot mouth and giant eyes. And once you enter the seven-spiked crown, you've got spectacular views of the harbor and New York skyline from its windows and bragging rights to boot. You can also get great views at three different levels of the pedestal, accessible by elevator.

Note Sometimes when crowds are particularly large, park officials do not allow climbs to the crown. When the crown is open, waiting time for the climb can be from two to three hours. Take heart—the ferry ride past Ellis Island and around the front of the Bedloe's Island offers unique and memorable views of the statue.

Then and Now The idea for a monumental gift from France to America began with discussions in the Paris home of French scholar Edouard René Lefebvre de Laboulaye in 1865. The monument would express French republican ideals and cement friendship between France and America, a place where personal freedoms and economic stability apparently were thriving together. In the turbulent years after the French Revolution, such a monument may not have been possible in France, but at New York, America's immigrant gateway, the setting for the expression of ideals would be perfect. Bartholdi, inspired by colossal Egyptian monuments, designed the statue and picked the site for it.

The one condition of France's gift was that America had to finance and build a pedestal for the statue. The drive to finance Hunt's pedestal was difficult. Wealthy Americans objected to the statue on aesthetic grounds; the masses thought her frivolous. Only after Joseph Pulitzer, a Hungarian immigrant and publisher of the *New York World*, took on the job of soliciting donations were the funds raised. He blasted the wealthy and played on the emotions of the everyday man. Finally dedication of the pedestal and statue took place on October 28, 1886.

Today visitors crowd on board ferries with such names as *Miss Freedom* and gawk at the once-controversial statue. As the ferry rounds the island into the dock, visitors crowd to snap photographs of Lady Liberty, causing the boat to lean precipitously toward her side.

The Statue of Liberty is a World Heritage Site (1984), meaning that it makes a unique and important contribution to the world's cultural heritage.

Elsewhere in the Area Ellis Island and Castle Clinton, the first immigration station, are both at the harbor; Federal Hall, first capitol of the United States, is in Manhattan; Theodore Roosevelt's birthplace is at 28 East 20th Street; Ulysses Grant's Tomb is in Riverside Park; and the Alexander Hamilton Grange is at Convent Avenue and 141st Street.

Gettysburg

Bloodiest Battle, Turning Point of the Civil War

Location South central Pennsylvania, 39 miles south of Harrisburg, near the Maryland border. Take U.S. 15 to Route 134 west (Taneytown Road) three miles to the visitor center.

Gettysburg National Military Park Visitors Center is open daily, except Thanksgiving, December 25, and January 1, from mid-June through mid-August, 8 A.M.–6 P.M., and other months, 8 A.M.–5 P.M. The Cyclorama ($) is open 9 A.M.–5 P.M. For information on guided tours ($) and special programs contact Superintendent, Gettysburg National Military Park, 97 Taneytown Road, Gettysburg, PA 17325. Tel. (717) 334-1124. The town of Gettysburg is full of things to do and see including museums, theaters, camping, horseback riding, and theme railroads—all privately operated. For information contact the Gettysburg Travel Council, 35 Carlisle Street, Gettysburg, PA 17325. Tel. (717) 334-6274.

Frame of Reference The battle at Gettysburg was fought during the Civil War (1861–65), on three pivotal days, July 1 through 3, 1863.

Significance The battle at Gettysburg is considered the most important battle of the Civil War. Here, after three days of intense fighting, seven million bullets fired, and 51,000 casualties on both sides, the Confederacy reached the "high water mark" of its successes. From that point, the road for the South was to Appomattox and surrender. This also is the site of Major General George Pickett's famous charge and President Abraham Lincoln's celebrated Gettysburg Address.

About the Site The extensive park preserves most of the 42 square miles where the Civil War fighting took place in and around the farming village of Gettysburg. The town of Gettysburg is virtually a Civil War resort, offering privately operated museums, exhibits, recreation, food, and accommodations. The national park itself abounds with more than 1,300 monuments, markers, artifacts, and emotion. Bus tours ($) and guided auto tours ($) are offered, and park rangers provide guided walking tours. Auto tape tours ($) are sold in the visitor center.

The visitor center has an extensive museum, a large bookstore, and an electric map show ($) explaining the battle. Near the park, the 307-foot National Tower ($) affords a unique battleground view and a sound and light show. The Gettysburg Cyclorama ($) in the park displays a 360-degree version of Paul Philippoteaux's three-ton painting "Pickett's Charge" and offers a free film about the battle. At the visitor center you can catch a bus tour to President Dwight D. Eisenhower's home, a national historic site.

Hot Tips Plan to spend at least a day here. The park is so extensive that it's smart to pick a few sights for hands-on visits, especially if you are taking kids. You can order books and videos about the park in advance of your trip from the Gettysburg National Military Park Bookstore. For a brochure, contact Eastern National, 95 Taneytown Road, Gettysburg, PA 17325. Tel. (717) 334-4474.

An auto tour of the park takes about three hours. Park at the visitor center, and get a battlefield map. Separate walking tour maps of National Cemetery and the High Water Mark Trail are available. Take in the terrific museum, among the very best on the Civil War. The electric map's 30-minute review of the battle is a necessary introduction for your visit. Arrange guided tours from the visitor center. You can easily walk to the National Cemetery, Cyclorama, and the High Water Mark (site of Pickett's Charge) from the visitor center. Plan to drive to other historic stops.

Dress for the weather, and wear sturdy shoes. Closely supervise children—traffic can be heavy and terrain dangerous. Food and accommodations, including campgrounds, are available in Gettysburg. Picnic tables are at the site. Viewing the 1992 movie *Gettysburg* before your visit will make the experience especially meaningful.

The Best Stuff The main battlefield sites, especially if you can envision the drama depicted in the movie *Gettysburg* or in the many books written about the battle, pack an unforgettable emotional wallop. Make a beeline to these sites:

- **High Water Mark Trail.** Look over the site from Cemetery Ridge, where the battle climax took place. This is where General Pickett desperately led 12,000 Confederates into the roaring volcano discharge of 7,000 Union troops' artillery. Two in every three Confederates died in Pickett's Charge, more correctly called Lieutenant General James Longstreet's Assault, after the corps commander. Pickett led the main division at the front of the charge, but supporting brigades were under the charge of two other officers. The failure of Pickett's Charge ended the battle and meant that General Robert E. Lee's invasion of the North was over.
- **Devil's Den and Bloody Run.** The "awful, awful rocks," as one Alabama Rebel called them, remain the tangled maze of boulders where Confederate sharpshooters hunkered down to fire on Union soldiers occupying Big Round Top. Walk around (carefully) the exact place where wounded and dying men crawled into crevices to ride out the intense Union cannon fire from adjacent Big Round Top. Some died from the intense explosions of sound. A marker bearing a photograph taken at the site after the battle shows bodies everywhere among the rocks.

  Stand on a wooded bridge over Plum Run, where the wounded dragged themselves to the stream at Devil's Den. The water ran red with blood and became known as "Bloody Run."
- **Little Round Top.** This hill lay at the left flank of the fishhook battle line and was the most strategic terrain of the battle. Union soldiers took the high ground first and held it "at all hazards."

  Crouch behind the low stone breastworks the defending Maine soldiers hastily built on July 3, 1863, and envision the relentless assault by the doomed Confederates. The scene today remains almost as it was in 1863.

- **Gettysburg Museum of the Civil War at the visitor center.** Among an extensive display of weapons, uniforms, and artifacts, search out these items: musical instruments collected after the battle (young boys usually played the tunes for marching soldiers as well as carrying the litters of dead bodies); two bullets melded together in mid air; the floor beams of a nearby house with a series of large holes showing the track of a cannon shell—the cannonball itself remains lodged in a displayed house beam (look up at the ceiling to see this); and a surgeon's kit.
- **National Cemetery.** In the peacefulness of the 17-acre cemetery lie the remains of 3,500 Union soldiers killed at Gettysburg. (The Confederate dead were reinterred in Southern cemeteries.) The bodies were buried beginning four months after the battle. Until then, they had lain where they fell or in hastily dug graves. President Lincoln came here to make "a few appropriate remarks" at the request of Pennsylvania's governor following the ghastly battle. He delivered his now famous Gettysburg Address, the 212 words of which are inscribed on a marble wall of the Lincoln Memorial in Washington, D.C. A plaque marks the site where Lincoln stood.

  Take a hanky as you walk among the graves, arranged in a circle around the Soldier's National Monument near where Lincoln stood for his address. Some graves bear soldiers' names and ranks. Others, with inscriptions like "New York, 867 Bodies" and "Maine, 104 Bodies," signify common burial grounds. A series of metal plaques cast by the War Department commemorate the dead with an inscription from "The Bivouac of the Dead," written in 1847 by Theodore O'Hara after the Mexican War. One reads

  The muffled drum's sad roll has beat
  The soldier's last tattoo,
  No more on life's parade shall meet
  That brave and fallen few.

Then and Now Except for the many monuments and markers, much of the battlefield today looks as it did in 1863. The roads that crisscross the site are paved, and a few buildings to accommodate tourists dot the grounds, but pains have been taken to keep fields, rail fences, orchards, and surrounding forests as they were. An iron fence on Cemetery Ridge encloses the copse of trees that served as the beacon for Pickett's Charge. A simple monument marks the spot where Union fire mortally wounded General Lewis Armistead, the only Confederate brigade commander to pierce the Union line during the battle. (Armistead's 1850 sword, which he waved high with his hat on it as he led his men in the charge, now rests in the Museum of the Confederacy in Richmond. After the battle a Union soldier took it. At a reunion at Gettysburg in 1906 his family returned it to Armistead's family.) The North Carolina Monument, sculpted by Gutzon Borglum of Mt. Rushmore fame, memorializes the 26th N.C. Regiment, which suffered the highest losses at Gettysburg.

The Virginia State Memorial, a statue of Robert E. Lee astride his horse Traveller, marks the spot at the edge of the open field where the general watched Pickett's doomed charge, where he witnessed the Confederacy disintegrate and the Union preserved.

Elsewhere in the Area The Eisenhower National Historic Site is next to Gettysburg Park. Antietam Battlefield, Maryland, and Harpers Ferry, West Virginia, are about an hour's drive southwest of Gettysburg.

Independence Hall

Where the Declaration of Independence Was Born

Location Downtown Philadelphia, Pennsylvania, on Chestnut Street between 5th and 6th streets. To reach the park eastbound via I-76 and I-676, follow I-676 to right onto 6th Street to Chestnut Street. Westbound via U.S. 30 and Ben Franklin Bridge, as you cross the bridge, follow signs to 6th Street and Historic Area. Take 6th Street south to Chestnut, and turn left to the site. Southbound: via I-95, take exit 17 and go straight on 2nd Street to site area. Northbound: via I-95, take Historic Area exit and follow signs to 6th Street. Take Sixth to Chestnut, and turn right to site.

Independence National Historic Park comprises 24 historic sites, including Independence Hall, operated by government as well as private entities. The sites vary in days and hours of operation. The visitor center, located two blocks east of Independence Hall at Third and Chestnut streets, is open daily, 9 A.M.–5 P.M., in summer, 9 A.M.–6 P.M. There are no admission charges, but some sites, including Independence Hall, are by guided tour only.

For information contact Superintendent, Independence National Historical Park, 313 Walnut Street, Philadelphia, PA 19106. Tel. (215) 597-8974. For information on Carpenters' Hall contact Carpenters' Hall, 320 Chestnut Street, Philadelphia, PA 19106. Open daily, 10 A.M.–4 P.M., in January and February, closed Monday and Tuesday.

Frame of Reference This was a center of activity during the years of the nation's birth from 1775—when the Second Continental Congress met and ultimately adopted the Declaration of Independence (1776)—to the adoption of the Constitution of the United States in 1787. This "Birthplace of Liberty" housed events that took America from the colonial period (when England governed the country) through the Revolutionary and Confederation (under the Articles of Confederation) periods, and into the Federal (under the Constitution) period of history.

Significance In Independence Hall, formerly the State House of Pennsylvania and at that time the largest building in America, delegates from the 13 colonies to the Second Continental Congress unanimously adopted the Declaration of Independence on July 4, 1776. In front of Independence Hall stands a glass pavilion housing a famous symbol of freedom, the Liberty Bell, which was hung in the hall's tower in 1753. The famous bell rang out when the Declaration of Independence was first read publicly in the yard behind Independence Hall.

Independence Hall also is the site where George Washington accepted his appointment by Congress as the leader of the Continental army on June 16, 1775; 24 flags taken at the surrender of the British at Yorktown (the final battle of the Revolution) were lain at the feet of Congress and the Ambassador of France on November 3, 1781; where the Articles of Confederation were adopted and then ratified on March 1, 1781; and where, on September 17, 1787, the Constitution of the United States was adopted and then ratified the next year.

At the left of Independence Hall and its two wings is Philadelphia's Old City Hall, home of the first U.S. Supreme Court, 1791–1800. The building on the right of Independence Hall is Congress Hall, meeting place of the U.S. Congress from 1790 through 1800, the years Philadelphia served as the nation's capital.

About the Site The park encompasses about a dozen city blocks in downtown Philadelphia and offers a variety of important sites—24 in all—concerning our nation's colonial, Revolutionary, and Federal periods. Independence Hall and the Liberty Bell Pavilion dominate the park in William Penn's City of Brotherly Love, but crowds also gather in Independence Square (where the Declaration of Independence was first read publicly on July 8, 1776), Old City Hall, Congress Hall, Philosophical Hall (home of country's oldest learned society—begun by Benjamin Franklin in 1743), the First and Second Banks of the United States, Washington Square (Tomb of the Unknown Soldier of the Revolution), Carpenter's Hall (site of the First Continental Congress), Declaration House (where Thomas Jefferson drafted the Declaration of Independence), Franklin Court (site of Franklin's Home), City Tavern, Thomas Bond House, Bishop White House, St. Joseph's Church, Todd House, Christ Church, Christ Church Cemetery, Free Quaker Meeting House, and the other historic homes and shady gardens in the immediate area of Independence Mall.

Hot Tips Park in a parking garage if you're not taking public transportation. (Take the subway to Independence Mall.) On-street parking is tight and you can quickly violate the meter. There's a parking garage on 2nd Street between 3rd and Chestnut.

Plan your visit ahead of time; there's so much to see that you may be overwhelmed, especially if you're visiting with children. Allow half a day to see Independence Hall, the Liberty Bell, and a few other sites. Allow a full day if possible.

Start your visit at the visitor center. Pick up maps (available in 12 languages) and learn about various building hours and the myriad walking tours. Several programs, like "Fun with Franklin," are especially designed for children. The visitor center houses a theater, where a 28-minute orientation film, *Independence*, tells the park's story. There's also a gift shop as well as two floors of exhibits.

Kids Tip A cool souvenir is a reproduction of the original iron key to Independence Hall. The key really does fit into the keyhole of the original front door of the historic hall. (Other safeguards protect the entrance.) If park rangers aren't too busy, they've been known to let young visitors try their hand at unlocking the door.

Waiting time to tour Independence Hall can be an hour or more during the peak tourist season. Be prepared for a lot of walking along busy streets. Tours by trolley and horse-drawn carriages are available in the Independence Mall area. Food and accommodations are available in the immediate area.

The Best Stuff It's Independence Hall and the Liberty Bell that top the attractions list, although there are at least a dozen historic sites that are a close second. However long the lines, don't miss the guided tour of the two-story, Federal style (everything about the building is symmetrical) Independence Hall. You can enter the Assembly Room, where the Declaration of Independence and later the U.S. Constitution were signed, edging up to the stanchions ⅓ of the way into the green-walled room. Thirteen rectangular tables with floor-length green tablecloths are set in a semicircle around the elevated table where George Washington led the Constitutional Convention in 1787.

Park rangers re-create fascinating stories of the heated debates and the personalities that finally put together this document of freedom. This is the room where Franklin, at the Declaration signing, reportedly responded to John Hancock's assertion to his fellow signers that "we must hang together" by saying, "Yes, we must indeed all hang together, or most assuredly we shall all hang separately."

Until the spring of 1998 a utilities improvement project keeps the second floor of the building closed to the public. Most fascinating of the three upstairs rooms is the Long Gallery, which stretches 100 feet across the entire northern front of the building. During the nine months of 1777 when the British occupied Philadelphia, this former banquet hall served as a barracks for British soldiers and a hospital ward for captured American officers. You can gaze out the tall windows today and see approximately what those wounded men saw. The upstairs Governor's Council Chamber and the Committee of Assembly's Chamber are refurbished.

The glass Liberty Bell Pavilion in Independence Mall, across Chestnut Street from Independence Hall, allows viewing 24 hours a day. The interior of the pavilion and its exhibits are open from 9 A.M. to 8 P.M. Guided tours are available noon to 4 P.M. in the summer. The large bell was cast in a London foundry and inscribed with the Bible words, "Proclaim Liberty throughout all the Land Unto All the Inhabitants Thereof." It was hung in 1753 in the steeple of the new Pennsylvania State House, later to become Independence Hall. You can get up close to (but not touch) the famous, 2,000-pound bell and get a good look at the crack that unfortunately appeared the first time it rang. (The crack started out small but later became so large that the bell could not be used after 1846.)

The mostly copper bell rang out from Independence Hall steeple when the Declaration of Independence was read publicly on July 8, 1776, a tradition that continued on Independence Day until 1846. Abolitionists first used the bell as a symbol of freedom prior to the Civil War. The bell still hangs from its original wooden yoke of slippery elm.

It's also time well spent to visit the Declaration House at Market and 7th streets. The partially reconstructed house, owned by Jacob Graff on the outskirts of town in 1776, shows the rented rooms where a reluctant Jefferson toiled two weeks to create the draft of the Declaration of Independence. The scene has been painstakingly re-created.

Then and Now Today the peels of freedom regularly heard around Philadelphia come from the Bicentennial Bell, in a 130-foot brick tower at the visitor center. The bell was the British people's bicentennial gift to America in 1976. Tourists move among the throngs of locals going about their daily business, all enjoying the freedoms granted by the great documents created in the centuries-old buildings in this great city. In summer costumed interpreters and musicians roam the area. Most historic buildings are open for tour. The reconstructed City Tavern at Walnut and 2nd streets offers a lunch from yesteryear. Some homes require tickets (free at the visitor center). Philosophical Hall is not open to the public, and the First Bank of the U.S. is only an exterior restoration.

Elsewhere in the Area Visit Ben Franklin Memorial and Franklin Institute (housing a science museum and Omnitheater), Franklin's grave, Betsy Ross House, Philadelphia Museum of Art, Elfreth's Alley (oldest residential street in America), U.S. Mint (world's largest), City Hall (an architectural wonder), Afro-American Historical and Cultural Museum (first in America), Penn's Landing, the funky shops of South Street, and numerous theaters and museums.

You can see the silver pen set that Jefferson, Franklin, and Hancock used to sign the Declaration of Independence. *Richard Frear, National Park Service*

Valley Forge

Story of the Revolution's Darkest Winter

Location Southeast Pennsylvania, 18 miles northwest of Philadelphia on the banks of the Schuylkill River. From the Pennsylvania Turnpike (I-76) take Valley Forge exit 24 to U.S. 422 (Pottstown Expressway) north to Highway 23 west. The visitor center is located at the junction of North Gulph Road and Highway 23. Follow the signs.

Valley Forge National Historical Park ($) is open daily, except December 25, 9 A.M.–5 P.M. Costumed interpreters offer soldier-life demonstrations in warm months. For more information contact Superintendent, Valley Forge National Historical Park, P.O. Box 953, Valley Forge, PA 19482-0953. Tel. (610) 783-1077.

Where Washington Prayed

History depicts General George Washington as a brave and compassionate leader. Valley Forge legend supports this. Some 19th-century reports say the leader of the Contintental Army was spotted on his knees, praying in a wooded area near his Valley Forge headquarters. Modern historians generally regard this story as unsubstantiated and full of holes. Learning about the terrible winter in Pennsylvania, however, it's easy for a visitor to believe that a man of faith might have prayed somewhere on the grounds.

Frame of Reference The famous winter at Valley Forge took place during the Revolutionary War (1775–83), in the winter of 1777 to 1778.

Significance At this site, 12,000 ragtag colonial soldiers—enough to constitute a small town—camped for a long, miserable winter, marking the low point in the Revolutionary War. The soldiers, under the command of General George Washington, were preparing to fight British troops who had taken over Philadelphia, then the colonial capital. But that winter the young men fought only hunger, cold, disease, and boredom. Three thousand died.

This is a place where you can imagine what it was like to be a soldier in the Continental army during the darkest time of the American Revolution. Valley Forge gets its name from the iron forges along Valley Creek. Rampaging British troops razed the forges, built in the 1740s, and during the winter encampment of 1777 to 1778 only ruins of the forges remained.

Washington chose this encampment site because its two high hills, appropriately named Mount Joy and Mount Misery, provided lookout points and defensive advantages.

About the Site Valley Forge spreads over 4,000 rolling acres of grass and forest, a lovely emerald amid Philadelphia's bustling suburbs. Park highlights include impressive memorials, statues, replicas of soldiers' huts, George Washington's Headquarters ($), original defensive earthworks, historical homes used as officer headquarters, the Washington Memorial Chapel, and the Museum of the Valley Forge Historical Society.

The visitor center houses a museum, gift shop, and theater where you can view an 18-minute film, shown every half hour, depicting life during the war encampment. The museum displays an extensive collection of firearms, swords, and accessories from the Revolutionary era. The museum centerpiece is the white canvas sleeping marquee Washington used during the Revolution.

Your self-guided tour over 10 miles of road takes you past extensive remains and reconstruction of defensive earthworks. Pullouts dot the marked roadway winding past points of interest. A six-mile bike/foot trail and a ten-mile horse trail are open year-round. Scheduled bus tours are offered May to September.

Hot Tips You can tour Valley Forge by car, but it's a good idea to bring comfortable shoes for exploring the beautiful grounds and sites close up. There are three large picnic areas. Crowds of locals visit on sunny, warm weekends. Bring a kite and a picnic lunch. No fires, please. Food and accommodations are available in adjacent King of Prussia.

A good book for young people to read in advance is James E. Knight's *The Winter at Valley Forge: Survival and Victory*.

The Best Stuff Here are some Valley Forge sites you don't want to miss:

- **Soldiers' Huts.** What's most interesting about Valley Forge are the authentic replicas of the some of the 1,000 log huts the soldiers built for shelter. Step inside one of the 16-by-14-foot cabins and you practically can smell the green-wood smoke from the small fireplace at one end of the hut, like those where cold, hungry young men once huddled. Crude, wooden bunks line the walls. Notice how short they are—only about 5½ feet. Full-grown colonial men were smaller than men today. They fit perfectly well on the bunks. The plank beds are too unstable for you to lie on, but you can touch them to get an idea of what sleeping on them was like—not much comfort there.

  The cabins face each other along narrow "streets." The replicas are clustered in far-flung sections of the park in areas occupied by colonial troops in that winter of 1777 to 1778. Today monuments identify the sections where each state regiment camped. Soldiers from some states had more skills, built better huts, and suffered less. Likewise, some had better clothing and supplies because their home states had agreed to spend more money on the war effort.
- **Commemorative Arch.** Congress decided to build a huge arch, like ones you may see in Rome, Paris, or even New York City, to remember those who died at Valley Forge. The National Memorial Arch monument was dedicated in 1917 during World War I. In August 1997, the arch was rededicated on its 80th anniversary after $1.5 million in repairs. The inscription on the arch reads:

Naked and starving as they are
We cannot enough admire
The incomparable patience and fidelity
Of the soldiery.

These words are attributed to General Washington, February 18, 1775.

Many states have raised monuments to their long-ago heroes throughout the park. Check out the large display of statues and flags at the campsite of the Pennsylvania Regiment, by far the most extensive.

Washington's Headquarters. Washington later was headquartered in a stone country house that the army rented from a relative of the Potts family, ironworks owners for which the Pennsylvania town of Pottstown was named. This house stands just off of Highway 252 in the back of the park. After some restoration, it looks virtually the way it was that famous winter. Guides dressed in colonial garb answer your questions.

Then and Now The Valley Forge soldiers never had enough clothing or food. Men wrapped their legs and feet in strips of canvas torn from discarded tents. Many had no shoes at all. They stood on their hats when they stood at attention in the snow to protect their feet from the numbing cold. They often ate "fire cakes," made from flour and water. Some stole food from nearby farms. Now you can walk or hike up one of the high hills in Valley Forge and look southeast across Route 422 to see one of the largest shopping malls in America.

Fort Necessity: Washington's Only Surrender

Fort Necessity National Battlefield ($), 11 miles east of Uniontown in southwestern Pennsylvania, commemorates the events surrounding the start of the French and Indian War. At this tiny makeshift fort, now fully reconstructed, a French and Indian force surrounded a young George Washington on July 3, 1754, and forced his only military surrender. The confrontation at Fort Necessity was the opening episode of the French and Indian War.

Fort Necessity is open daily, except December 25, 8:30 A.M.–5 P.M. For information, contact Information Officer, 1 Washington Parkway, Farmington, PA 15437-9514. Tel. (412) 329-5512.

Disease killed most of the young men who died during the winter of 1777 to 1778. Typhus and smallpox, diseases now virtually gone because of vaccines and medicines, accounted for most of the deaths. Soldiers moved the sick to isolated hospitals in the countryside to contain the spread of illness. Because these places were so desperately miserable, many men suffered silently in their huts rather than risk hospitalization. Most, however, died in the makeshift military hospitals away from Valley Forge. There they are buried.

Elsewhere in the Area The John Audubon estate is in nearby Audubon, Pennsylvania.

3

SOUTH ATLANTIC

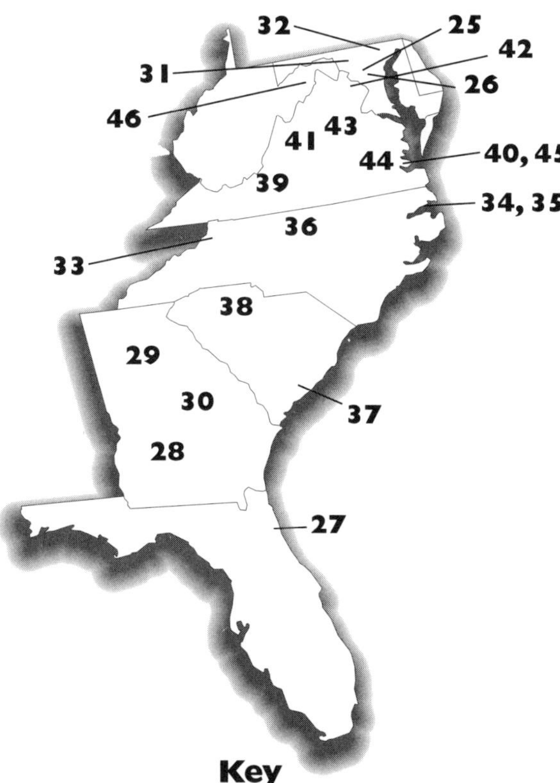

Key

Numbers correspond to site numbers on the map.

District of Columbia
25. Ford's Theatre
26. The White House

Florida
27. St. Augustine

Georgia
28. Andersonville
29. Martin Luther King Jr. National Historic Site
30. Ocmulgee

Maryland
31. Antietam
32. Fort McHenry

North Carolina
33. Cherokee Indian Reservation
34. Kitty Hawk
35. The Lost Colony
36. Greensboro

South Carolina
37. Fort Sumter
38. Kings Mountain

Virginia
39. Appomattox Court House
40. Jamestown
41. Monticello
42. Mount Vernon
43. Richmond
44. Williamsburg
45. Yorktown

West Virginia
46. Harpers Ferry

Ford's Theatre

Where Lincoln Was Assassinated

Location Washington, D.C., at 511 10th Street NW between E Street and F Street, five blocks east of the White House.

Ford's Theatre National Historic Site is open daily, except December 25, 9 A.M.–5 P.M. The theater is closed for rehearsals and matinees, usually Thursday, Saturday, and Sunday. For information contact Superintendent, Ford's Theatre National Historic Site, c/o National Capital Parks–Central, 900 Ohio Drive SW, Washington, D.C. 20242. Tel. (202) 426-6924.

Frame of Reference President Abraham Lincoln was assassinated—five days after Lee surrendered to Grant, ending the Civil War—on April 14, 1865.

Significance This is where John Wilkes Booth shot Lincoln, the 16th U.S. president. Lincoln died early the next morning in the back bedroom of a boardinghouse, the Petersen House, across the street from the theater.

About the Site Ford's Theatre National Historic Site comprises the theater, first used as a Baptist Church in 1833 and still in use for performances; the Lincoln Museum in the theater basement; and the Petersen House across the street, 516 10th Street, where Lincoln died. The home belonged to William Petersen, a tailor. The site is nestled among businesses and shops in a busy commercial area of the capital. At the time of Lincoln's death, this was the Tenth Street Neighborhood, one of the seediest in Washington.

Hot Tips There's limited pay parking in the area, so it's smart to take public transportation to the site. Or you can easily walk here while visiting other Washington attractions. Allow about 1½ hours for the free self-guided tour of the theater and visits to the museum and Petersen Home. Park rangers give lively informational talks at the site. Food and accommodations are available in the area.

The Best Stuff Just sitting in the wooden chairs of Ford's Theatre, where Washington society sat that fateful April night of 1865 during the assassination of President Lincoln, is moving. You can look up to the right of the stage—oversized in comparison to the theater capacity—and see the corner presidential box. Here Lincoln; his wife, Mary Todd; and two guests sat enjoying a production of *Our American Cousin* when John Wilkes Booth shot the president in the head, behind his left ear. Also look for these items:

- **Bloody Pillows.** The most interesting part of your visit may be a tour of the basement museum. There, encased in glass among an impressive array of artifacts connected with the assassination, are the long black coat Lincoln wore that night (one bloody sleeve was removed); several of the pillows, still stained with his blood, that doctors placed beneath Lincoln's head to comfort the dying man; the pistol Booth used to shoot the president; and the contents of Booth's pocket. (Booth, age 26, was a famous Shakespearean actor and was considered one of the most handsome men in America—a true matinee idol. Among his pocket contents are photographs of five women.) There's also a portion of the black mourning cloth that was draped on Lincoln's coffin as his body lay in state at the White House.

Death Room. At the Petersen House where Lincoln died, original contents in important rooms have been replaced by period furniture. The bed displayed in the back bedroom is similar to the one on which Lincoln succumbed to his head wound. The bed was not long enough to accommodate the lanky, six-foot, four-inch Lincoln. He had to lie diagonally across the bed.

Then and Now In the spring of 1865 Ford's Theatre, newly rebuilt after a fire in December 1862, was very popular. This was due mainly to owner John T. Ford's engaging productions with top-notch actors. The fact that the three-story, brick theater, with its mustard-yellow doors, was just north of two of Washington's poorest, most crime-ridden neighborhoods, didn't seem to matter.

Entertainment-hungry people traveled muddy 10th Street past sewage-polluted ditches for 495 performances from the theater's opening to its closing after Lincoln's assassination. Today's bustling paved street yields no clue to the rapidly growing city's problems of yesterday.

Reportedly, it was Mary Todd Lincoln's idea to attend the theater that night to celebrate the end of the Civil War. The Lincolns had asked Lieutenant General Ulysses Grant and Mrs. Grant to attend with them, but the Grants had other plans. So it was Clara Harris, daughter of New York Senator Ira Harris, and her fiancé, Major Henry Rathbone, who sat with the Lincolns in the enclosed section of the first balcony on April 14. The presidential box overlooked the stage from the right of the **U**-shaped balcony. The top balcony had the cheap seats purchased by the "lower class."

Now the presidential box and the theater, with its burgundy carpet and two large chandeliers, are restored to their 1865 appearance. Only the red damask sofa where Major Rathbone sat is original in the presidential box. Lincoln's rocking chair resides in a museum in Dearborn, Michigan.

When theater personnel received word of Lincoln's impending visit, they foraged the basement for something to make the box look presidential. They found red, white, and blue bunting and a framed picture of George Washington. They hung these items on the front of the box that fated night, and the items still hang there today.

Booth, a Southern sympathizer who blamed Lincoln for the South's problems, was part of a circle of conspirators who planned to kill the president and other key cabinet members. The night of April 14, Booth sneaked into the theater to launch the ghastly plan. He waited at the presidential box door. Plexiglas protects the box now, but visitors can walk right up to the narrow door that shielded Booth.

Booth was familiar with the play and knew when the audience would be riveted on a lone actor and laughing at his lines. At this moment, he shot Lincoln. When Rathbone intervened, Booth stabbed him, injuring him slightly. Booth then jumped from the box. He caught his foot on the decorative bunting and fell off-balance onto the stage. He broke a small bone in his left leg. Booth escaped through a back stage door and mounted a horse waiting there.

After a frantic 12-day flight to the South, authorities surrounded Booth and a co-conspirator in a Virginia barn, setting it ablaze. Historians debate whether Booth killed himself or whether one of his pursuers did so on April 26, 1865.

After the shooting Lincoln was moved to the Petersen House, where a dozen physicians attended him. They knew early on, however, that the president's wound was fatal. They could only comfort him. President Lincoln died on April 15, 1865, at 7:22 A.M.

Elsewhere in the Area Find the White House; Washington Monument; Mount Vernon; Smithsonian Institution; and 1806 Fort Washington, just south of D.C. exit 3 south from Capital Beltway (I-95).

You can view the bullet that killed President Lincoln and fragments of his skull at the National Museum of Health and Medicine on the campus of Walter Reed Army Medical Center at 6825 16th Street NW (weekend entrance on Georgia Avenue). Also on display is a section of John Wilkes Booth's spinal column revealing the path of the bullet that killed him.

The White House

The President's Home, Symbol of America

Location Downtown Washington, D.C., at 1600 Pennsylvania Avenue NW.

Self-guided White House tours are available to the public on a limited basis during peak tourist season. Tickets are free but available in a limited supply, year-round for public tours. Tours are offered Tuesday through Saturday, except Thanksgiving, December 25, and January 1, 10 A.M.–noon. Official functions may cause tours to be canceled or delayed. Call (202) 456-7041 for the latest tour information on a 24-hour recording.

Pick up tickets at the White House Visitors Center on 15th Street near the southeast corner at E Street. Hours are 7:30 A.M.–4 P.M. or until all tickets are distributed for that day's tours. The center is adjacent to the White House, just northeast of the Ellipse. Tickets are distributed on a first-come, first-served basis. (See Hot Tips in this section for more ticket information.)

For information on the White House contact White House, c/o National Park Service, 1100 Ohio Drive SW, Washington, D.C. 20242. Tel. (202) 208-1631.

Shortcut to Viewing Washington Monuments

So many wonderful sights fill the nation's capital that visitors easily can feel overwhelmed. Here's a memorable shortcut to viewing Washington's most important monuments. It's an enjoyable way to save time and walking. This tip is particularly useful if you have tired kids in tow.

Wait until evening, maybe a soft summer's night, and take public transportation to the Mall/West Potomac Park stop. Or you can drive and park in the area of the National Mall. Head for the Washington Monument. Climb the well-lit hill on which it stands at Constitution Avenue and 15th Street. The 555-foot stone-and-marble obelisk is open 8 A.M.–midnight in the spring and summer. Waiting lines for the elevator to the top of the monument are usually much shorter at night. (You also can climb the 897 steps to the top.)

From the small windows beneath the monument cap, you'll see Washington's famous buildings, monuments, and shrines winking at you with thousands of glowing lights. The clean lines of Pierre Charles L'Enfant's 1791 grand design for the city clearly stand out.

To the west, across the Reflecting Pool of Constitution Gardens, shines the Lincoln Memorial,

☛

Frame of Reference The White House has been the presidential residence from the earliest days of the American democracy (1800) to the present.

Significance This has been the home of every U.S. president except the first, George Washington, who chose the White House's precise location and approved its design. John

Adams, the second president, moved into the executive mansion on November 1, 1800. The White House, site of innumerable historic events, is Washington's oldest public building and is a symbol throughout the world of America and its president.

About the Site Officially dubbed the White House in 1901 by President Theodore Roosevelt, the 132-room executive mansion is the only residence of a head of state regularly open to the public, free of charge. The tradition began with the third president, Thomas Jefferson.

The stone mansion is painted white (thus its name) and faces Pennsylvania Avenue amid 18 acres of gardens and trees planted by presidents. The area is called President's Park. Regularly scheduled self-guided walking tours wind through five upstairs State Floor rooms and the entrance hall and offer views of three rooms on the ground floor.

The second and third floors are used only by the First Family and guests. The White House Visitors Center, which provides a video tour of the House, also includes a bookstore and informative exhibit.

Hot Tips Free tickets for a White House tour are high-demand items in Washington, a place always teeming with tourists. Arrive early at the White House Visitors Center to pick up tickets—required during peak tourist months—on the day of your tour. (Extremely limited guided tours can be arranged through your local congressional representative.)

An individual can obtain up to four tickets at the White House Visitors Center. Tickets are distributed on the morning of the tour. Tickets will note the time of your scheduled tour, and ticket holders queue at fenced-off bleachers near the White House 10 minutes ahead of time. Park rangers escort you to a White House side entrance—where you will walk through metal detectors and a phalanx of Secret Service agents—for your 20-minute tour.

where the colossal marble image of the 16th president watches over us. The Lincoln Memorial, along with the Vietnam Veterans Memorial (the Wall) adjacent to it, are the most-visited monuments in Washington.

To the south, overlooking the Tidal Basin, a 19-foot bronze Thomas Jefferson gazes from his classical-style memorial. A bit west on 15th Street the U.S. Holocaust Memorial Museum finds a home next to the Bureau of Engraving. To the north, across the Ellipse sits the White House. The domed U.S. Capitol dominates the view to the east, at the far end of the National Mall. The venerable buildings of the Smithsonian Institution surround the National Mall, and the Ulysses Grant Memorial overlooks the Reflecting Pool at its western end. The white U.S. Supreme Court building radiates from behind the Capitol building.

If the wait at the Washington Monument seems too long, a walk among the circle of American flags at its base will give you nearly the same heady effect. Or plop yourself down on the grassy hill and just breathe it all in.

Take a guide to the sites of Washington with you to ensure that you know what you're seeing. You can get a National Park Service brochure on the capital's major sites from National Capital Region Public Affairs and Tourism. Tel. (202) 619-7222. You also can pick up information at the Visitor Information Center, 1455 Pennsylvania Avenue NW, in downtown Washington. Tel. (202) 789-7000.

▲

Watching the continuously running ½-hour video *Within These Walls* at the visitor center helps you prepare for a White House tour. The White House Historical Association publishes many books about the White House. Many are available here. For information contact The White House Historical Association, 740 Jackson Place NW, Washington, D.C. 20560. Tel. (202) 737-8292.

Paid and free parking is available in the area. Check the visitor center.

Warning Stay within roped areas in the White House, and do not touch anything! Plain-clothes agents guard every room.

Kids Tip For a personal tour of the White House, kids can go on-line: http://www.whitehouse.gov/WH/kids/html/home.html

The Best Stuff Let's face it—most everything about the White House, the backdrop for many important events in this nation and the world, is interesting. And there's the added excitement provided by the possibility that you might catch a glimpse of the president, a member of the First Family, or a major political figure.

The five rooms open for public touring—the East Room, State Dining Room, and three salons named for their predominant colors, Green Room, Blue Room, and Red Room—are rich in detail, antique furnishings, important works of art, and history.

The gold East Room, the largest room in the mansion, is provocative and often photographed. This room, with its massive gilded mirrors and classical decor, houses the most important and oldest possession in the White House: a full-length portrait of George Washington by Gilbert Stuart. President James Madison's wife Dolley refused to leave the mansion during the British invasion of Washington, during the War of 1812, until the portrait was safely removed from the premises. The dramatic rescue took place shortly before the British burned down the White House on August 24, 1814.

Then and Now The White House has undergone near-constant change since its plans were on the drawing board of architect James Hoban in 1792. Hoban won a nationwide competition, suggested by Thomas Jefferson, to design the president's house.

On July 16, 1790, Congress passed the Residency Act, which established the capital on the banks of the Potomac River. The act empowered George Washington to choose the precise site for the city. French engineer Pierre L'Enfant created a city plan, with the president's house and the Capitol as focal points. Hoban supervised construction of the house, actually built ⅕ the size of the grandiose, original plans.

Today, after two total reconstructions, one following the 1814 burning, the second during the Truman administration (late 1940s–1952), change is the status quo at the White House.

Important meetings, bill signings, state dinners, and receptions continue day in and day out, as does the steady stream of regular people visiting the president's home.

Elsewhere in the Area See Ford's Theatre.

St. Augustine

Oldest Permanent European City in America

Location On the Atlantic Coast of northeastern Florida, 38 miles south of Jacksonville, 90 miles north of Orlando. From I-95 take U.S. 1 exit to site at State Road A1A.

Fort Castillo de San Marcos National Monument ($) is open daily, except December 25, 8:45 A.M.–4:45 P.M. For information contact Superintendent, Castillo de San Marcos National Monument, 1 Castillo Drive East, St. Augustine, FL 32084. Tel. (904) 829-6506. For information regarding privately operated sites contact St. Augustine Attractions Association, 166 San Marcos Avenue, St. Augustine, FL 32084, or the St. Johns County Visitors and Convention Bureau, 88 Riberia Street, Suite 250, St. Augustine, FL 32084. Visitor Information Center, Tel. (904) 825-1000.

Frame of Reference The Spanish established the colonial city of St. Augustine during Spain's northward expansion in the New World, beginning nearly 500 years ago. St. Augustine was settled in 1565, 42 years before the first English settlement in Jamestown. Historic sites here span the 16th to 19th centuries.

Significance St. Augustine is the oldest permanent city in America settled by Europeans. Here Spanish explorer Ponce de Leon, seeking the fabled Fountain of Youth, landed in 1513 on the coast he called *La Florida*, meaning "flowery." After driving out French colonizers, Don Pedro Menendez de Aviles later established this Spanish settlement in 1565. At St. Augustine in 1672 Spain began building the northernmost fortress of its western empire already established in South America and Mexico. The Castillo de San Marcos is the oldest masonry fort in America. The story of St. Augustine also tells the history of French, Spanish, and English struggles for "ownership" of the New World.

About the Site The many historic attractions of St. Augustine are spread over several square miles and represent developments over a period of several hundred years—the 16th century through the 19th. The oldest attractions of importance are the Fountain of Youth Archaeological Park ($), featuring the Landmark Spring, which Ponce de Leon supposedly hoped was the wondrous Fountain; the ancient Native North American town of Seloy; the towering Cross of Discovery, site of the first Christian burials in North America; excavations of the first 16th-century St. Augustine; and a planetarium.

Fort Castillo de San Marcos invites careful exploration and offers exhibits and living-history demonstrations. You also can stroll along the bustling streets of the authentically restored 18th-century Spanish Quarter ($), a living-history museum, and see the official state play, *Cross & Sword* ($), in an outdoor amphitheater.

Spanish St. Augustine, covering an area of several dozen square blocks, boasts the oldest European-built house in America—although an adobe house in Santa Fe makes the same claim, as well as America's oldest wooden schoolhouse ($). The area includes museums, dozens of colonial buildings, shopping outlets, and plenty of entertainment attractions.

Hot Tips There's something in St. Augustine to interest everyone in the family. You can park at one of eight parking lots and easily tour the colonial area on foot, or you can take a train tour ($$) or carriage tours ($$). For information on the narrated train tour contact the St. Augustine Sightseeing Trains at (904) 829-6545.

You can run up quite a tab if you try to see everything. Your best bet is to tour the fort, the Spanish Quarter, and, if there's time, the Native North American village Saloy and the site of the first St. Augustine. Food and accommodations are available in St. Augustine.

The Best Stuff Historic forts cover America, but the 300-year-old Castillo de San Marcos is among the most interesting. Not only is it the country's oldest masonry fort, but it is large, complex, and well preserved. The fort is built of coquina, a sedimentary rock of tiny seashells. It is a hollow square with four diamond-shaped bastions at each corner. The walls are 12 feet thick. Visitors enter through a single entrance shielded by the ravelin (a wedge-shaped outwork designed to protect the entrance). The vaulted underground powder magazine is the fort's oldest chamber; construction began in 1675. Also of interest are these items:

- **Shot Furnace.** The shot furnace is located on the cannon-laden seawall overlooking Matanzas Bay. This is where 19th-century soldiers heated cannonballs before launching them onto enemy wooden ships, setting them aflame.
- **Seminole Photos.** Exhibits in the lower part of the fort tell of the fort's many uses, but especially moving is the photo documentation of its years as a prison for Native North Americans captured during the Seminole war of 1835 to 1842 and during the later western military campaigns.
- **Spanish Quarter.** A stroll through the Spanish Quarter is fascinating and fun. Costumed guides and craftsmen re-create the 16th-century period when settlers and soldiers roamed among the old Spanish houses with iron grilles and overhanging balconies.

The town is the country's earliest example of European community planning. Narrow streets radiate from the broad Plaza de la Constitution with an interesting assortment of residences, shops (try a cool lemonade), and gardens. Kids may want to go inside the 200-year-old wooden schoolhouse at 14 St. George Street south of the historic city gates and get lessons from the "professor" and his wife. After a visit to the little schoolhouse, "pupils" receive a diploma.

Then and Now In the 16th century Spain had proven the most successful of the European superpowers in the New World. Already the Spanish had built vast and wealthy empires in the Caribbean, South America, and Mexico and had toeholds in the Mississippi Valley and California. Spanish "treasure fleets" regularly sailed from the New World along the Gulf Stream to Europe.

Spain was considered the most powerful nation in Renaissance Europe. Although Ponce de Leon had claimed Florida for Spain in 1513, France had tenuously settled at Fort Caroline (now a National Memorial) near Jacksonville. So Spanish King Philip II sent Menendez to drive out the French, which he did in very bloody fashion.

Menendez established St. Augustine as a base for operations. The fortified town remained under Spanish rule until 1763 when, in exchange for Cuba, Spain ceded it to the English, who had repeatedly attacked it, once occupied it, and even burned it down in 1665. (But the Spanish held the fort.) England returned Florida to Spain in 1783 when U.S. independence was recognized. In 1821 Spain sold Florida to the United States for $5 million and control of Texas.

Today remains of the colorful and war-torn past of St. Augustine, already a 210-year-old city by the time the Revolutionary War began in 1776, makes visiting here a historical treat.

Andersonville

Infamous Confederate Prison Site, POW Memorial

Location Central Georgia, just east of the town of Andersonville, 10 miles north of Americus and 40 miles southwest of Macon on Route 49 in Macon County. From the west and east take Route 26 east to Route 49 south. Follow signs to the visitor center and POW Museum. From the north and south take I-75 to Route 26 west to Route 49 south.

The Andersonville National Historic Site is open daily, 8 A.M.–5 P.M. A Memorial Day service is held on the Sunday prior to the legal holiday. For more information contact Superintendent, Andersonville National Historic Site, Route 1, Box 800, Andersonville, GA 31711. Tel. (912) 924-0343.

Frame of Reference Andersonville Prison, officially named Camp Sumter, was operated during the last 14 months of the Civil War (1861–65). The prison (opened to the public in February 1964) ceased to exist when the war ended in April and May 1865. Andersonville National Cemetery is part of the national cemetery system established by President Abraham Lincoln in 1862.

Significance Andersonville was the largest of the Confederate prisons during the Civil War, when more than 100 prison camps were in operation on both sides. On this 26½ barren acres surrounded by a 15-foot-high stockade, more than 45,000 Union soldiers were confined during the war, up to 32,000 at one time. Of these, 13,000 died from poor sanitation, malnutrition, disease, overcrowding, and exposure. This death rate was the highest among Civil War prisons.

When the POWs returned home at war's end, horror stories of the inhumane conditions at Andersonville ignited northern rage. Captain Henry A. Wirz, the prison commandant, was tried and hanged as a war criminal.

Andersonville today is a unique memorial. It not only honors the POWs of the Civil War, North and South, but it also memorializes all Americans taken prisoner in the 10 great wars in which Americans have fought, beginning with the Revolution.

About the Site The rural Georgia setting of the landscaped 475-acre park belies Andersonville's tragic story. The park includes the National Prisoner of War Museum, which offers a 27-minute video on Andersonville, a small POW museum, gift shop, and computer listing of Andersonville prisoners and guards. You can check to see if any family names are listed.

Visitors can walk the grassy prison site itself and see the carefully marked remains of water holes the prisoners dug, as well as larger holes that were entrances to escape tunnels. (Some prisoners did manage successful escapes while on work detail.)

A branch of Sweetwater Creek, which prisoners dubbed "the Stockade Branch," meanders between two hills that come together within the area once surrounded by the stockade. The disease-carrying Swamp served as the drinking water source, communal bathtub, and sewer system. In 1864 and 1865 thousands of "shebangs," crude prisoner-made shelters, dotted the barren slopes. A few replicas stand today.

Following photographs, drawings, and descriptions in prisoners' diaries, the prison has been partially reconstructed. The pine-log stockade, the double North Gate where prisoners entered, and some railings marking the deadline are partially reconstructed. The *deadline*, a four-foot-high railing of planks nailed to stakes, marked off four acres of "no-man's land," a band of ground 19-feet wide running parallel to the stockade. Confederates built it to keep prisoners away from the wall. Guards shot anyone crossing the deadline.

Several reconstructed "pigeon roosts," simple guard towers, stand at intervals along the stockade. Concrete posts mark the remainder of the outer stockade and inner deadline. Outside the stockade you can see the site of the Deadhouse, where the dead were stacked—up to 140 per day—until the bodies could be put in mule-drawn wagons and buried in the cemetery. Rings of defensive earthworks remain.

Twenty-three monuments dot the prison site and adjacent Andersonville National Cemetery, where white-marble headstones mark the graves of the 12,912 Union soldiers who died at Andersonville. About 400 simply read "Unknown U.S. Soldier." A stone canopy protects what prisoners then called "Providence Spring," a gurgle of fresh water that sprang up near the North Gate after a violent thunderstorm.

Ocmulgee

One of North America's Oldest "Public Buildings"

Beneath an ancient, man-made mound in central Georgia—a reconstructed circular earthlodge with its nearly 1,000-year-old clay floor still intact—is one of North America's earliest public buildings.

Native Americans of the Mississippian tradition (about A.D. 900–1540) probably built the circular, domed ceremonial chamber from clay, wood, and cane as a meeting place to discuss their social, political, and spiritual affairs. The earthlodge was one of several in this elite Mississippian outpost on the Macon plateau known as Ocmulgee. (*Ocmulgee* is a Native North American word meaning "bubbling springs.") The ancient town flourished here from about A.D. 900 to 1100, the same period of the mound cities of Cahokia and Moundville, although these mound cities were larger and more complex.

Today you can walk through a narrow, 20-foot passage into the interior of a grassy mound, where you can view the earthlodge, 42 feet in diameter, from behind a glass wall. An audio program explains the site.

Opposite the entrance is a raised clay platform shaped like a large bird, possibly an eagle. There are three "seats" sculpted into the clay platform and 47 additional seats sculpted into a semicircle around the lodge's periphery. The 50 or so people who met in this possible council house were probably the town's leaders.

The only artifact found at the site was a large pottery vessel, which most likely held the "black drink," a plant-based emetic, possibly used in religious ceremonies. A replica now sits in the lodge.

Most likely, the Ocmulgee inhabitants burned down the earthlodge when they abandoned the site around 900 years ago. The fire preserved key

☛

Hot Tips To make the most of your visit to this isolated place, you should learn about the Andersonville story before you go. Otherwise you could miss the prison's drama, which is only hinted at in the orientation video. Recommended reading includes *The Story of Andersonville Prison and American Prisoners of War,* written by staff members at the site for students, grade five through high school. Call the site for information. Also, the 1996 video *Andersonville* (rated R) gives the story a memorable, flesh-and-blood dimension.

Begin your visit at the National POW Museum, where you can park and pick up a map. You can walk or drive the narrow road that winds through the cemetery and around the prison periphery. Pullouts allow you to stop and walk around. Terrain is uneven, and the thick grass contains sandspurs. Watch for fire ants, snakes, and poison ivy, too. Wear closed shoes. Allow two to three hours for your visit. Food and accommodations are available in Americus.

The Best Stuff The most riveting aspect of the prison is, literally, holes in the ground. Twenty-seven holes, now capped and numbered, were small wells that prisoners dug for water. Larger ones nurtured a secret hope: escape.

Although one man tried to escape by having his friends carry him out as if dead, most prisoners tried to dig their way out. Their shebangs hid their work from the guards. Now you can see what's left of two escape tunnels, one which supposedly collapsed and killed two prisoners; the other, now encased in the roots of a giant oak, where one man crawled to safety. Both holes, about eight feet deep and five feet across, are enclosed by iron fences.

The POW Museum at the visitor center displays eerie souvenirs taken by departing Union soldiers: part of the gate, the gate key, and a prisoner's handmade shirt and trousers. Finding the graves in the cemetery of the Raiders, a marauding group of 200 or more murderers and thieves who preyed on fellow prisoners, brings home the greatest tragedy of Andersonville. The Regulators, a good-guy group of prisoners who banded together, finally stopped the Raiders. The Regulators rounded them up, tried them, and hung six of the leaders inside the prison.

evidence of original features, giving archaeologists a firm basis for this reconstruction. This earthlodge was the most spectacular find of 1930s archaeology.

The visitor center offers a 13-minute orientation film, gift shop, and museum with some hands-on exhibits that kids will like. Following a marked trail, you can also explore the remains of several flat-topped temple mounds, a burial mound, prehistoric trenches, and the sites of numerous thatched huts. The Great Temple Mound rises 45 feet above the rolling Georgia countryside. You can climb concrete and wooden stairs from its 300-by-270-foot base to the top for a splendid view of the area and historic Macon skyline. (Please do not climb any other mounds.)

Ocmulgee National Monument is located on the eastern edge of Macon, Georgia, on Walnut Creek, just off U.S. 80 east. Watch for signs. From I-75 exit take I-16 east, then take the first exit and follow U.S. 80 one mile east to the park. The park is open daily, except December 25 and January 1, 9 A.M.–5 P.M. For more information contact Superintendent, Ocmulgee National Monument, 1207 Emery Highway, Macon, GA 31201. Tel. (912) 752-8257.

▲

Then and Now The Confederacy chose Andersonville, a town that had 20 residents in 1864, as the prison site for several reasons: the location was far from the enemy line; it was in the heart of Georgia's breadbasket; and it had a water supply, slave labor, and a nearby railroad for transporting prisoners.

No matter. The plans for the prison were ill conceived, as neither side had prepared for a long war. Lack of food, sanitation, shelter, medical care, and space conspired to create one of the ugliest episodes of the Civil War. The 45,000 men imprisoned here from 26 states, including Southern states and the District of Columbia, suffered enormously.

Conditions in all Civil War prisons were horrendous. The Confederacy captured about 211,400 Union soldiers, of which 30,208 (14 percent) died in prison. Union forces captured about 462,000 Confederates, of which 25,976 (6 percent) died in prison.

Most of the graves of the Andersonville POWs are now marked with marble headstones bearing names, thanks to two people: a young prisoner from Connecticut, Dorence Atwater, who carefully kept records of deaths and smuggled the list out of the prison when he was released; and Clara Barton, founder of the American Red Cross.

With Atwater, Barton went to Andersonville after the war. They identified graves and marked them. The dead had been buried in rows, shoulder to shoulder, often naked and without coffins. A pink-granite monument here is dedicated to Barton.

Since becoming a national historic site in 1970, Andersonville has been a place for reflection, a place that honors America's POWs and commemorates their struggles. An exhibit hanging on a wall in the women's restroom (an appropriate place) hints at the Andersonville prisoners' trials. A sign tells how men with diarrhea or those incapacitated with other ills left human waste all over the stockade. This led to more illness and death.

The sign reminds us that Civil War soldiers had a better chance of living through combat than through prison confinement.

Elsewhere in the Area The Jimmy Carter National Historic Site, home of the 39th U.S. president, is in nearby Plains.

Martin Luther King Jr. National Historic Site

Memorializing the Civil Rights Leader, His Ideals

Location Atlanta, Georgia, east of the main downtown business district. From I-75/I-85 southbound take exit 95 at Piedmont/Butler/John Wesley Dobbs. At the second light turn left onto Auburn Avenue. Follow signs 3/5 mile to park. From I-85 north take exit 94 at Edgewood/Auburn Avenue and proceed to the second light. Turn right at light onto Auburn Avenue and follow signs 1/2 mile to park. The visitor center is located at 450 Auburn Avenue NE.

The visitor center at the Martin Luther King Jr. National Historic Site is open daily, except December 25 and January 1, 10 A.M.–5 P.M., with extended hours in season. Guided tours of the King birth home begin every half hour. There is a limit of 15 people per tour on a first-come, first served basis. Private organizations conduct tours of other important King sites in "Sweet Auburn," the neighborhood of King's youth. Days and times vary. Both the Park Service and private organizations schedule events.

For more information contact Superintendent, Martin Luther King Jr. National Historic Site, 450 Auburn Avenue NE, Atlanta, GA 30312. Tel. (404) 331-3920.

Frame of Reference Martin Luther King Jr. led the Civil Rights movement from 1955, when he emerged as the leader of the Montgomery, Alabama, bus boycott, to 1968, the acknowledged end of the Civil Rights movement. The movement for basic human rights peaked in 1963 with the March on Washington, where King delivered his famous "I Have a Dream" speech to 250,000 demonstrators. King was born in 1929 and was assassinated in 1968.

Significance King, who was awarded the Nobel Peace Prize in 1964, is the recognized leader of the Civil Rights movement. This turbulent period in the 1960s first was marked by nonviolent protests for racial equality—an activist approach King embraced—and later by race riots, which King disdained. The Baptist minister and author, who followed the teachings of the Bible and Indian pacifist leader Mohandas Gandhi, never veered from his passionate commitment to peaceful protests as the way to freedom.

History holds King the most eloquent spokesman for racial justice of the time. His teachings, dignified example, and leadership in the Montgomery boycott, the 1962 protest in Birmingham, Alabama (where he ended up in jail), and the 1965 Selma-to-Montgomery march inspired the Civil Rights movement.

This site, a combination of exhibits including King's grave, historically significant buildings, and the Martin Luther King Jr. Center for Nonviolent Change, memorializes the slain Civil Rights leader. It celebrates his ideals of justice, equality, and freedom.

About the Site The park comprises the Martin Luther King Jr. National Historic Site and the Preservation District that helps maintain the historic atmosphere of King's Sweet Auburn boyhood community. Sweet Auburn is still an active "town within a city" and straddles Auburn Avenue in east Atlanta.

The National Park Service owns 22 restored historical structures, some rented as private residences. The Historic Site includes King's birth home, an 1895 Queen Anne–style house at 501 Auburn Avenue; the 1922 brick Ebenezer Baptist Church, where King and his father were copastors from 1960 to 1968; the Freedom Hall Complex, which includes King's marble tomb and the Martin Luther King Jr. Center for Nonviolent Social Change, Inc. (referred to as "the King Center" and operated by the King Family); and several important Sweet Auburn buildings. The visitor center houses exhibits and a theater, where you can see a riveting 30-minute documentary on King and the Civil Rights movement.

The Preservation District includes about a dozen Sweet Auburn buildings, such as the Wheat Street Baptist Church, Royal Peacock Club, Sweet Auburn Curb Market, Butler Street YMCA, the *Atlanta Daily World,* and radio station WERD. The 100 businesses and public services along Auburn Avenue at the time of King's boyhood were all owned or operated by African Americans. Morehouse College, King's alma mater, is located outside the district but nearby.

Hot Tips Allow at least half a day for your visit. Better still, take a whole day and enjoy lunch in the neighborhood. Your first stop should be the visitor center. Here you can get maps and schedules of activities and sign up for guided tours of the boyhood home and neighborhood. Tours begin daily, except for December 25 and January 1, at 10 A.M. The last tours begin at 5 P.M. You also can pick up guide booklets for self-guided tours. Cassette and braille guides are available.

Park on the street or in a parking lot just north of the visitor center on John Wesley Dobbs Avenue. Allow one to two hours at the visitor center to see the movie and exhibits. Birth home tours take about 20 minutes. Allow one to two hours to visit the Center for Nonviolent Social Change, King's gravesite, and Ebenezer Church. The pavilion at the gravesite teems with activity, such as singing youth groups, so set aside time to enjoy.

The extensive gift shop at the King Center is full of wonderful books and theme items. Shirts bearing King quotes make great gifts. The center's Freedom Hall Auditorium offers a full list of performances ($).

Sidewalks and busy paved roads connect sites. Be prepared to walk. Take precautions against Atlanta's infamous heat and humidity in the summer. Food and beverages are available at the site. Accommodations are plentiful in Atlanta.

Two documentaries may help prepare you for your visit: *Eyes On the Prize* and *King: Montgomery to Memphis*.

This site could be the first stop on a Civil Rights journey that continues in Alabama.

The Best Stuff The movie, *A New Time, a New Voice*, shown in the visitor center theater is a top-drawer, three-hanky documentary on King and the Civil Rights movement. You won't forget Coretta Scott King talking about the first time she saw her future husband. "He's so short," she admits to thinking.

Footage of King exhorting the crowds and behind-the-scenes encounters bring tears to the eye. As 1960s race riots break out across the land, King, criticized for remaining nonviolent, passionately tells other leaders: "I'm sick and tired of violence! I'm not going to use violence!"

The walk-through exhibit hall weaves King's story into that of the Civil Rights movement through photographs, video and audio presentations, art (some life-size), and memorabilia. You can walk down a "highway" in Alabama amid statues of other civil rights marchers and their songs of freedom.

At the King Center museum, you'll find King's Nobel medal, his black robe with crimson sash, the suit he was wearing when he was stabbed by a mentally ill woman in New York in 1958, his personal Bible, handwritten speeches, and a "to do list."

The key attached to a green-plastic diamond with the words "Room 301, Lorraine Motel and Hotel, Memphis" dominates one display case. On April 4, 1968, as King stood on a balcony near room 301, which he had occupied on a mission to support striking sanitation workers, James Earl Ray assassinated him. King was 39 years old.

Then and Now Since 1986 America has celebrated King's birthday as a national holiday every January 15. Throughout the country, cities and towns have named streets and highways after him. In Atlanta the "peaceful warrior" rests as thousands flock to his gravesite yearly.

King's Georgia-marble crypt sits within a brick circular pod set in a bright blue reflecting pool. The inscription is a variation of a famous phrase from his "I Have a Dream" speech, delivered on the steps of the Lincoln Memorial: "Free at last! Free at last! Thank God Almighty, I'm free at last!"

Elsewhere in the Area At the Cyclorama in Grant Park visitors sit on a revolving platform and watch the Civil War Battle of Atlanta unfold. Stone Mountain, 16 miles east is the "Confederate Mount Rushmore," where huge images of Civil War leaders Robert E. Lee, Stonewall Jackson, and Jefferson Davis remain frozen in granite. Gutzon Borglum, who sculpted Mount Rushmore designed the monument.

The former Lorraine Motel on Mulberry Street in Memphis, Tennessee, is now the National Civil Rights Museum and is open to the public. Plexiglas encases King's motel room.

Antietam

The Bloodiest Single Day of the Civil War

Location North and east of Sharpsburg, Maryland, 70 miles west of Baltimore. From north, take Route 65 to the site; from east and west, take Route 34. Visitor center is on Route 65, one mile northwest of downtown Sharpsburg.

Antietam National Battlefield ($) is open daily, except Thanksgiving, December 25, and January 1, from September through May, 8:30 A.M.–5 P.M., and from June through August, 8:30 A.M.–6 P.M. The Annual Memorial Illumination takes place the first Saturday evening in December. Volunteers place 23,000 candles across the battlefield, each representing a battle casualty. For information contact Superintendent, Antietam National Battlefield, P.O. Box 158, Sharpsburg, MD 21782-0158. Tel. (301) 432-5124.

Frame of Reference The battle at Antietam took place a year into the Civil War (1861–65), on September 17, 1862, the single bloodiest day in America's history.

Significance This battlefield is significant for three reasons: First, it is the Civil War site where the most casualties were sustained in one day—more than 23,000. Second, although militarily the battle was a draw, General Robert E. Lee failed to effectively carry the war effort into the North—a death knell for the Confederacy. The Union, however, failed to end the war as President Abraham Lincoln had hoped. Third, Lincoln visited Antietam two days after the battle and subsequently made a decision that dramatically altered the course of the war: he issued the Emancipation Proclamation, ending slavery in rebellious states and rallying needed support for the Union cause.

About the Site Antietam National Battlefield covers 12 square miles along Highways 34 and 65 at Sharpsburg. It encompasses the cornfields where gunfire exploded cornstalks and human bodies alike; the Sunken Road—later dubbed "Bloody Lane"—where so many Confederate corpses piled up that Union soldiers ran across them to continue the battle; and the narrow Burnside Bridge, where a few hundred Georgia sharpshooters defended their position for hours against four Union divisions. (A division has 4,000 to 5,000 men.) Much of the battlefield is visible from the visitor center, located on a rise. The visitor center houses a small museum, gift shop, and theater, where you can see a great 26-minute orientation film, *Antietam Visit*.

Hot Tips Begin your tour at the visitor center, where you can pick up a map or rent an audiocassette to guide you through the battlefield. The best way to see the site is by car along a well-marked, eight-mile tour route. Stop at pullouts and walk areas of interest. Plan to spend two to three hours. If you have children from age 9 to 12, ask the park ranger for a copy of the *Antietam Battlefield Junior Ranger Program.* Kids can complete the activities and learn while touring the battlefield.

Sharpsburg is small and places to eat are limited. Accommodations and food are available in Hagerstown, Maryland, 10 miles north, or Frederick, Maryland, 20 miles east.

The Best Stuff The award-winning *Antietam Visit,* shown on the hour at the visitor center, is a fabulous must-see. It's a three-hanky experience that vividly re-creates the battle and President Lincoln's subsequent visit to the Union commander at Antietam, General George B. McClellan. Here are other highlights:

- **Battlefield View.** Go upstairs in the visitor center for a panoramic view of the battlefield through huge picture windows. You can compare what you see to a wall-size painting behind you by artist James Hope, a sidelined captain in the 2nd Vermont Infantry and eyewitness to the battle. His painting is based on sketches he made as the fighting raged.
- **Museum.** Check out the small but interesting museum downstairs. There's a surgeon's saw and a bandage from a battlefield hospital, as well as photographs and entries from soldiers' diaries.
- **Bloody Lane.** Take extra time for Sunken Road. There you can descend slate steps into the trench formed long ago by hooves and wagons on an old country lane. You can walk where the bodies of dead rebels lay piled up, their blood soaking into the soil.

  Look closely at the displayed reproduction of a photograph, taken by Alexander Gardner on September 19, 1862—two days after the fight—from that spot. You'll understand why battle survivors renamed Sunken Road "Bloody Lane." A stone walkup tower at the far end of the road offers a memorable bird's-eye view.
- **Burnside Bridge.** Just past Antietam National Cemetery, the stone Burnside Bridge arches over Antietam Creek. Here you can see the bluff where Georgia sharpshooters dug in and played a key role in McClellan's failure to gain a decisive win over Lee. Look for the towering "witness tree" on the right side of the bridge. This sycamore was standing on the day of the battle.

Then and Now Although Confederate forces were outnumbered two to one at Antietam and suffered losses of 10,700—¼ of the entire rebel army—Union General McClellan didn't gain a decisive victory that day. Federal losses were 12,410. President Lincoln was angry. He sent McClellan a one-sentence letter reading, "If you don't want to use the army, I should like to borrow it for a while." Later Lincoln removed McClellan from his command and sent him to New Jersey on recruiting duty. McClellan never held another command.

A visitor to Antietam National Battlefield today finds peaceful cornfields, a picturesque farm, and rolling meadows nestled against the scenic Blue Ridge Mountains. Park literature touts a Wildflower Tour. One hundred monuments dot the rural countryside, and strategically placed markers reveal details of the ghastly battle that took place 130 years ago. Locals say the silence and twinkling luminaries of the Memorial Illumination tell the Antietam story far better than anything else ever will.

Elsewhere in the Area Gettysburg Battlefield, Pennsylvania, is 65 miles north; Harpers Ferry, West Virginia, is 16 miles southwest. The home of Clara Barton, American Red Cross founder who tended the wounded at Antietam, is in Glen Echo, Maryland, just west of Washington, D.C.

Antietam National Battlefield covers twelve square miles. *B. J. Welborn*

Fort McHenry

Where "The Star-Spangled Banner" Was Born

Location Baltimore, Maryland. The fort stands at the tip of Locust Point, just south of the city's Inner Harbor. To get there from I-95 south take the Fort McHenry Tunnel. Bear right from the tunnel and take exit 55 to Key Highway, following signs to Fort Avenue, which deadends at the fort. From I-95 north take the Key Highway exit. Follow signs to Lawrence Street. Take a left on Lawrence to Fort Avenue and take another left to monument entrance.

Fort McHenry National Monument and Historic Shrine ($) is open daily, except December 25 and January 1, 8 A.M.–5 P.M., with extended summer hours. Special events and programs are regularly scheduled. Defenders' Day, celebrating the American victory in the Battle of Baltimore, is held the second Sunday in September. Group tours require three-day reservation notice. For information contact the National Park Service, Fort McHenry National Monument and Historic Shrine, Baltimore, MD 21230-5393. Tel. (410) 962-4299.

Frame of Reference The Battle of Baltimore took place during the War of 1812, called America's "Second War of Independence," on September 13 and 14, 1814.

Significance A young Washington lawyer, Francis Scott Key, penned the poem that later became our national anthem, "The Star Spangled Banner," while witnessing the fiery British bombardment of Fort McHenry, by Concreve rockets, during the Battle of Baltimore.

About the Site Fort McHenry today looks much the way it did in 1814, when Key wrote his famous words. The brick fort is star-shaped, with five bastions, following an old French design. It sits on a 53-acre site jutting into the Patapsco River below Baltimore's Northwest Harbor. There are exhibits in the fort, as well as in the visitor center, which houses a small gift shop and a theater, where you can view a 16-minute orientation film, *The Defense of Fort McHenry*.

Hot Tips Finding Fort McHenry can be difficult if approaching from the west. You'll be driving through the busy downtown area, and signs to the fort are nearly impossible to see. It's worth the extra time to bypass the city on I-695 until reaching I-95 and proceed to the site. A water taxi service operates daily around the Inner Harbor. Call (410) 563-3901 for water taxi information.

Park at the visitor center for a walking tour. Allow two hours. Don't touch the cannons, statues, or exhibits, and do not walk on the seawall. Watch children, especially near the water. Food and accommodations are available in Baltimore.

The Best Stuff The big attraction at Fort McHenry is an exact replica of the flag sewn by a Baltimore woman, Mary Pickersgill, at the request of fort Commander Major George Armistead. (You can visit Mary Pickersgill's "Flag House" and 1812 Museum at 844 East Pratt Street in Baltimore.) Major Armistead wanted to make sure that the invading British had no trouble seeing the 30-by-42-foot flag from a distance.

Bad weather, however, often prohibits the flying of the giant, 15-star flag (replica) above the fort. To see the original tattered flag, with 15 stars and stripes, visit the Smithsonian Institution's Museum of Natural History in Washington, D.C.

The original flag was preserved by Armistead's descendants, one of whom was nephew Lewis Armistead, who died leading a Confederate charge at Gettysburg. The rainy night in 1814 before Key wrote his poem Armistead flew a smaller flag. With the morning's calmer weather, he ordered his huge flag raised. That's the one Key saw "by the dawn's early light."

Smaller flag or not, after you watch the orientation film at the visitor center and the last strains of "The Star Spangled Banner" ring out, the curtain on a large picture window slowly draws back to reveal *the* flag waving over Fort McHenry. Almost everybody in the room gets tears in their eyes.

Also at the visitor center you can see the framed act signed by President Herbert Hoover declaring Key's poem our national anthem. A glass case protects a fragment from one of the "bombs bursting in air," too.

Then and Now The fort endured few alterations during its years of military use, as a key defense site in the War of 1812 through a final stint as an army hospital during World War I. You still can see remnants of the "dry moat" encircling the castlelike fort. U.S. Infantry troops were stationed in the moat in 1814. Another 1,000 military men gathered to defend Baltimore from a British naval onslaught.

The 15 United States had declared war against England on June 18, 1812, after the British had confiscated American merchant ships and cargo and forced U.S. seamen to serve with the English in the fight against Napoleon's France.

Fort McHenry was the key defense of Baltimore. British ships in the Patapsco River pummeled it with 1,500 to 1,800 shrieking, newly developed Concreve rockets for 25 hours. Key watched safely from the deck of a U.S. truce ship nearly two miles away in the Chesapeake Bay. The British had detained him while he was on a mission with the U.S. Commissioner of Prisoners to secure the release of an American prisoner, Dr. William Beanes. The mission succeeded, but the British kept Key and the commissioner overnight, fearing that the Americans had learned of their battle plans. The British let them go the next day.

British soldiers also advanced toward the fort by land. But the British ships withdrew after their land invasion failed to materialize, and they realized the exchange of fire from ship to fort was a standoff. Major Armistead ordered the smaller flag that had flown during the battle lowered and his giant cotton flag hoisted. The custom-made flag and the "rockets' red glare" inspired Key.

Today a walk through the sally port (entrance), ravelin (a wedge-shaped outwork designed to protect the entrance), and "bombproofs" (underground, arched chambers that protected men and artillery from shelling) takes the park's 600,000 yearly visitors back 180 years. Exhibits in the fort illustrate the site's various uses. Despite the intrusions of modern life everywhere at the watery edges of the park—ships, barges, cranes, and smokestacks, the most prominent with big blue letters reading Lehigh Cement—yesterday stubbornly endures.

Elsewhere in the Area Also in Baltimore are the Flag House and 1812 Museum, Maryland Historical Society Museum and Library (home of the original "Star Spangled Banner" manuscript), the U.S.S. *Constellation* (launched in 1797), Babe Ruth Birthplace and Baseball Center, and the Baltimore Maritime Museum. The Inner Harbor waterfront offers interesting shops, places to eat, and the National Aquarium.

Kitty Hawk

Where Man Achieved First Powered Flight

Location The Outer Banks of North Carolina, actually in Kill Devil Hills, about four miles south of Kitty Hawk and north of Nags Head on U.S. 158. From the north take U.S. 17 south to U.S. 158 east. From the south take U.S. 264 to U.S. 158 north. From the west take U.S. 64 to U.S. 158 north. The Wright Brothers Memorial Visitor Center is just off U.S. 158. Follow signs.

The Wright Brothers Memorial ($) is open daily, except December 25, 9 A.M.–5 P.M. For information contact Superintendent, Cape Hatteras Group, National Park Service, Route 1, P.O. Box 695, Manteo, NC 27954. Tel. (919) 441-7430.

Frame of Reference The dawning of the age of flight, less than a hundred years ago, was on December 17, 1903.

Significance Here brothers Orville and Wilbur Wright made the first powered air flight, flying their handcrafted airplane 120 feet and staying aloft 12 seconds. The brothers made four flights on that amazing first day in the history of flight. During the last flight of the day, the airplane flew 852 feet and stayed aloft 59 seconds. The brothers experimented with gliders for four years, making 1,000 glides to learn how to build and control an airplane before this date that ushered in the age of aviation.

About the Site Although the place where the Wright brothers flew is known as Kitty Hawk, the remote sandy beach is actually in the town of Kill Devil Hills, four miles south of Kitty Hawk. Earlier, however, the brothers had experimented hundreds of times with their glider on the high dunes of Kitty Hawk. These experiments paved the way for the first flight in their newest craft, one powered by a gasoline engine and propellers.

The site occupies a stretch of windswept sand and dunes on the narrow 300-mile stretch of land along North Carolina's coast called the Outer Banks. Kitty Hawk lies between the Atlantic Ocean and Albemarle Sound. Crowning the dominant Big Kill Devil Hill is a 60-foot granite monument honoring the Wright brothers. A large granite boulder marks the spot where the first powered flight left the ground. Numbered markers along the first path of flight indicate the distance of each of the Wright brothers' four flights.

The Wright brothers' 1903 camp buildings have been reconstructed of weathered wood. The larger building is the hangar where the brothers kept the airplane *Flyer*, used in the first flight. The second building is the workshop and living quarters that the brothers themselves constructed at the site.

A visitor center houses full-scale reproductions of the Wright brothers' 1902 glider and their 1903 *Flyer*. (The actual 40-foot winged biplane resides in the Air and Space Museum of the Smithsonian in Washington, D.C.) Exhibits at the visitor center tell the intriguing story of these scientists/mechanics, and park rangers' dramatic interpretative talks sometimes leave visitors misty-eyed. The gift shop offers books and items that kids will enjoy, such as a construction set for a model of the Wright brothers' airplane.

Hot Tips The Outer Banks can be reached by ferry at several points. For information about ferry schedules and reservations call 1-800-BY FERRY. U.S. 12 runs the length of the Outer Banks and merges with U.S. 158 near the memorial.

In summer months, sand at the site can be hot. Sand spurs abound. Wear closed shoes. Food and accommodations are available in surrounding resort communities. There are private camping sites nearby and at Cape Hatteras National Seashore.

The Best Stuff Exhibits, advance reading, and ranger stories of the Wright brothers and their historic flight make a visit to this isolated stretch of beach—the brothers' "outdoor laboratory"—memorable. Visiting only one part of this site doesn't reveal the brothers' careful planning, meticulous persistence, and undaunted faith in themselves that made their dream come true. But put everything together as you walk around this place, and you're hit with a deep sense of awe. Two regular, 30-something guys, who didn't even finish high school, solved the final riddles of flight that had befuddled their esteemed scientific predecessors. They put a manned, engine-powered, heavier-than-air flying machine into the air for the first time ever. These wiry brothers, owners of a bicycle shop in Dayton, Ohio, ushered in the entire planet's aviation age on this windswept, barren beach.

Why Did the Wright Brothers Choose North Carolina?

It was the big dunes surrounded by miles of flat beaches that lured the Wright brothers to Kitty Hawk. They felt it was the perfect place for their glider experiments. Nearly 100 years of scientific knowledge had proceeded these Ohio businessmen. They were determined to overcome the failures of previous experimenters and fly.

The brothers analyzed, tinkered, experimented, and tried and tried again. At one point, after realizing that data amassed by previous scientists for wing design were flawed, they almost came to the point of quitting. But instead the brothers, inseparable friends since childhood, built a wind tunnel and produced their own accurate data. (A replica of the simple wind tunnel resides in the museum at the Wright Brothers Memorial.) Using their air tunnel data, they also designed the first effective airplane propeller.

Ultimately the Wright brothers succeeded in flight through their wing design that could meet air flow and their ability to control their plane in banks and turns by the combined control of a rudder and "wing warping," a process of bending the wings. (The pilots achieved wing warping by swinging their hips in a cradle.) These inventions lay the foundation of modern aviation.

An on-the-spot photograph taken by one of the few witnesses captures the moment of man's first powered flight. The Wright brothers, dressed in coats and ties for the occasion, had set up the camera on a tripod near the launch rail. Though it took two tries and last-minute repairs, they released the plane at 10:35 A.M. Orville, lying flat in the center of the airplane, worked the controls.

☛

Visitors can walk the marked short distances of flight from the end of the reconstructed single rail from which the brothers launched their biplane. You can peer into the reconstructed hangar and one-room shack where the brothers ate (sometimes alongside their glider) and slept in burlap slings hung from the rafters. You realize that these young men planned to stay as long as it took to attain their dream of flight.

The museum at the visitor center tells the story of Wilbur and Orville's personal mission. Here you'll see the brothers' detailed drawings of their gliders and biplane, diaries, and documentary photographs. Correspondence with their father, a clergyman, speaks modestly of their triumphs and of their all-too-frequent failures. The telegram the brothers sent home announcing to their father that they had achieved powered flight is a matter-of-fact report of times and distances.

The plane rose; the photographer snapped. The plane flew at an airspeed of 38 mph for 120 feet in 12 seconds before hitting the sand. That was it. Man had escaped the confines of the earth forever.

The words inscribed around the base of the Monument to Flight on Big Kill Devil Hill beautifully tell the story of that day: "In commemoration of the conquest of the air by the brothers Wilbur and Orville Wright, conceived by genius, achieved by dauntless resolution and unconquerable faith."

Note The Aviation Trail in Dayton, Ohio, preserves other important Wright brothers sites.

▲

Then and Now Except for the visitor center, monuments, and stabilizing grasses on the dunes, the wide expanse of white sand here looks much the same as it did during the Wright brothers' sojourns. You can see the prime oceanfront properties surrounding the site from Big Kill Devil Hill. There are always visitors and an ocean breeze.

Elsewhere in the Area Fort Raleigh is in Manteo, and Cape Hatteras National Seashore is nearby.

The dawning of the age of flight, less than a hundred years ago, was on December 17, 1903.

Photo courtesy Wright Brothers Memorial Visitors Center

The Lost Colony

England's Ill-Fated New World Settlement

Location On Roanoke Island near Manteo on North Carolina's Outer Banks. The site is 92 miles south of Norfolk, Virginia, and 67 miles southeast of Elizabeth City, North Carolina. From the north take U.S. 158 to U.S. 64/264 west to the site. From the south and west take U.S. 64/264.

Fort Raleigh National Historic Site is open daily, except December 25, 9 A.M.–5 P.M., in summer, 9 A.M.–8 P.M. For more information contact Superintendent, Cape Hatteras National Seashore, Route 1, P.O. Box 675, Manteo, NC 27954. Tel. (919) 473-5772.

America's oldest outdoor drama (opened in 1937), *The Lost Colony* ($), runs nightly throughout the summer (except Sunday) at 8:30 P.M. in the site's Waterside Theatre. For information write The Lost Colony, P.O. Box 40, Manteo, NC 27954. Tel. 1-800-488-5012.

Frame of Reference More than 400 years ago, as the English struggled to settle the New World, colonists first landed at Roanoke Island in 1585. That colony failed. A later colony of people, "the Lost Colony," landed in 1587 and built Fort Raleigh. By 1590 it had mysteriously disappeared.

Greensboro

Woolworth: Where the Civil Rights Mass Movement Began

The Civil Rights movement began with the Montgomery bus boycott in 1955. After an incident at a North Carolina Woolworth lunch counter in 1960, it became a genuine mass movement.

On February 1 of that year, four African American students at North Carolina Agricultural and Technical State University sat down at a "whites only" lunch counter at a Woolworth store in downtown Greensboro. When asked to leave, the men remained seated.

Within a week the "sit-in" movement had spread to towns throughout North Carolina; within a month it had moved to a half-dozen Southern states. Nonviolent "sit-ins," "kneel-ins," and "wade-ins" at white-only restaurants, public schools, and other public buildings captured media attention. Following the militant nonviolent precepts of Martin Luther King Jr. and other leaders, protesters refused to retaliate, even when struck or dragged off to jail. Black and white college students throughout America became involved in the 1960s Civil Rights movement.

Today a section of the lunch counter from the F. W. Woolworth in Greensboro, complete with four stools, stands in the Smithsonian Institution's National Museum of American History in Washington, D.C. An authentic sign above the counter reads "Super Jumbo Banana Split 39¢."

Currently the empty Woolworth store on South Elm Street in Greensboro is boarded up, awaiting full funding for its transformation into the International Civil Rights Center and Museum.

Significance This verdant island is the place where the English explorers managed a tenuous foothold on the new continent in the late 16th century. They called their new colony "Virginia," after the virgin Queen Elizabeth I. The most famous of the English endeavors here, however, was the expedition put together by Sir Walter Raleigh, a favorite of Queen Elizabeth, in 1587. This ill-fated settlement became known as the Lost Colony. Raleigh's first expedition in 1584 was exploratory. Some of the colonists of the settlement returned to England in 1585 after conflicts with Native North Americans.

The 116 colonists of this ill-fated settlement of the "Cittie of Ralegh" disappeared during a three-year absence (1587–90) of their artist/governor John White. He had returned to England for badly needed supplies. When White returned, the settlement's houses had been taken down, personal effects were scattered, and no one could be found. White's baby granddaughter, Virginia Dare, the first English child born in the New World, was among the missing.

White found only the letters *CRO* carved on a tree. Also the word *Croatan*, the Native North American name of nearby Hatteras Island, was carved on a post. There was no carved Maltese cross, the agreed upon signal of trouble. Searches for the colonists proved fruitless. What happened to the beleaguered band of men, women and children has remained a mystery for more than four centuries.

About the Site The 150-acre wooded site includes a reconstruction of the colony's earthen Fort Raleigh, sites of the settlers' homes, the privately

Cherokee Indian Reservation

Chapter in the Trail of Tears

In the western tip of North Carolina, 52 miles west of Asheville, North Carolina, and 33 miles south of Gatlinburg, Tennessee, the Qualla Boundary, known as the Cherokee Indian Reservation, spans 56,000 acres in five counties. This is home for the descendants of the Cherokee who escaped the 1838 U.S. government's removal to permanent Indian territory in the West. The Cherokee called this forced journey (to what is now Oklahoma) *Nunahi-Duna-Tlo-Hilu-I*, or "Trail Where They Cried." It has become known as the Trail of Tears.

About 1,000 Cherokee escaped the government roundup by hiding in the mountains of North Carolina and Tennessee. Some had special agreements to stay. In 1868 they established their tribal government in the town of Cherokee and are known as the Eastern Band of Cherokee Indians. The Cherokee, the second largest Native North American tribe, call themselves *Ani'Yun'wiya*, or the Principal People.

The reservation land was purchased by a white man, Will Thomas, who presented the land to the Cherokee people in the late 1800s. About 10,000 Cherokee are enrolled members of the Eastern Band. The ancestral homeland of the Cherokee is the southern Appalachian Mountain region in the states of North Carolina, Tennessee, Georgia, Kentucky, and Alabama.

Cherokee survivors of the Trail of Tears established their capital in Tahlequah, Oklahoma, in 1841.

The Cherokee Indian Reservation in North Carolina offers visitors the opportunity to learn of Cherokee history and the Trail of Tears. Pick up maps

operated Elizabethan Gardens ($), nature trails, and the Waterside Theater. The outdoor drama *The Lost Colony* was written by Pulitzer Prize–winning playwright Paul Green.

The visitor center houses a museum displaying artifacts excavated at the site, exhibits, and John White's watercolors; a theater where you can view a 17-minute orientation film; and a gift shop featuring handmade crafts. Park interpreters tell the story of the fort, the settlers' hardships, and the well-to-do English who supported the New World expeditions.

You'll find the *Elizabeth II*, a replica of a 16th-century ship similar to the one that brought the 1585 settlers to Roanoke, docked at Roanoke Island near Manteo. The ship has a museum.

Hot Tips To make your visit more enjoyable, be sure to catch Green's semifictional outdoor drama. With nearly 150 actors, authentic costumes, fireworks, special effects, and plenty of beating Native North American drums, the play gets your pulse going and catapults you back into the perilous times for European settlers here long ago. The outdoor production, though slow-moving in spots and featuring language unfamiliar to American ears, offers something for the whole family. Allow three hours for the evening play.

Allow an hour to see Fort Raleigh and the museum, more time if you want to visit the formal Elizabethan Gardens. The Garden Club of North Carolina created the gardens as a memorial to the first colonists and as an example of the garden estates of the colony's rich backers.

and information at the visitor center. Sites on the reservation include these:

- **Oconaluftee Indian Village** ($), U.S. 441 north. This re-creation of a 1750 Cherokee Indian village gives hands-on insight into rituals, arts, and everyday life. Cherokee guides escort visitors.
- **Oconaluftee Pioneer Farmstead** ($), two miles north of Cherokee on U.S. 441. This reconstructed farmstead portrays pioneer mountain life.
- ***Unto These Hills* outdoor drama** ($) in the Mountainside Theater, U.S. 441 north. The summertime, nightly drama is the nation's most-viewed outdoor drama. It tells of the Cherokees' dances, legends, rituals, and the Trail of Tears.
- **Cherokee Cyclorama,** Highway 19N. Life-size figures help tell the Cherokee story.
- **Museum of the Cherokee** ($), Highway 441 north. This excellent museum tells Cherokee history through displays, hands-on activities, and videos (one on the Trail of Tears). Visitors can enter a full-size Cherokee home—a conical, wooden hut. The museum also has a bookstore.
- **Qualla Arts and Crafts Mutual,** across from the museum. This is a sales outlet for Cherokee crafts and art.

There are also gardens, hiking trails, recreational activities, and picnic grounds. Campgrounds are available in the area and at the adjacent Great Smoky Mountains National Park. Fishing is by permit only. Shops and restaurants crowd the area. Tourism is the Cherokee economic lifeblood.

For more information contact Cherokee Tribal Travel and Promotion, P.O. Box 460, Cherokee, NC 28719. Tel. 1-800-438-1601 or (704) 497-9195.

▲

Food and accommodations are available in Manteo and surrounding resort communities. Private campgrounds are nearby and at Cape Hatteras National Seashore.

The Best Stuff It's fascinating to explore the exact place where the earliest English settlers endured untold hardships—and failed to establish a permanent colony. After intensive archaeological studies, Fort Raleigh has been built within the confines of its original moat. This first British fort in Virginia has earthen outer walls enclosing about 50 square feet. It is essentially square, with two pointed bastions facing each other and a larger octagonal bastion. Raleigh's explorers built it as protection from Native North Americans and other European forays.

Then and Now It's ironic that the scene of the settlers' hardships and disappearance 400 years ago sits today amid a vacationer's paradise. Hunger, disease, and Native North Americans hostile to the settlers are long gone, replaced by restaurants, hotels, and tourists relaxing and fishing on the beaches. North Carolina continues to have a large population of English ancestry.

After Queen Elizabeth's death, the new King James I, suspecting plots against him, stripped Sir Walter Raleigh of his numerous offices and privileges. Raleigh was arrested, tried, and condemned to die. Instead he spent 13 years in the Tower of London. King James briefly released him in 1616 to lead another expedition. Again Raleigh's actions incurred the King's wrath, and Raleigh was beheaded under his old death sentence.

Although Raleigh's settlements in the New World were temporary, Great Britain later established a permanent colony called Jamestown, in Virginia, in 1610 and went on to dominate America's early development.

When North Carolina established its capital in 1792, it was named Raleigh, after the man who sparked England's impulse to conquer the New World. The town of Manteo is named after the friendly Native North American chief who helped the settlers of Raleigh's colony.

Elsewhere in the Area See Kitty Hawk.

Fort Sumter

Where the Civil War Began

Location Charleston Harbor, Charleston, South Carolina. Fort Sumter is accessible only by boat from harbor points in Charleston and Mount Pleasant, South Carolina.

Fort Sumter National Monument is open daily, except December 25, from April 1 through Labor Day, 10 A.M.–5:30 P.M.; hours vary at other times of the year. For information contact Superintendent, Fort Sumter National Monument, 1214 Middle Street, Sullivan's Island, SC 29482. Tel. (803) 883-3123.

Tour boats ($) leave from City Marina on Lockwood Drive, just south of U.S. 17 on the Ashley River waterfront in Charleston, and from Patriots Point in Mount Pleasant, across the Cooper River east of Charleston. For boat tour information contact Fort Sumter Tours, Inc., 205 King Street, Suite 204, Charleston, SC 29401. Tel. (803) 722-1691.

For information on Charleston historic sites contact the Charleston Trident Convention and Visitors Bureau, P.O. Box 975, Charleston, SC 29403 Tel. (803) 853-8000.

Frame of Reference The Civil War began on April 12, 1861, when Confederate forces fired on Federally held Fort Sumter. After Union surrender, Federal bombardment of the Confederate-held fort continued until evacuation on February 17, 1865.

Significance Here is where the Civil War began. Confederate forces fired on the fort, named for Revolutionary War hero Thomas Sumter of South Carolina, after a small Federal garrison refused to leave. A fierce exchange of cannon fire ensued until Federal forces surrendered on April 14, 1861. Fort Sumter was one of many coastal forts built after the War of 1812. Construction began in 1829 and was still unfinished in 1860.

South Carolina had become the first state to secede from the Union in December 1860. In February 1860 delegates from seven states met in Montgomery, Alabama, and adopted a constitution for the Confederate States of America. Jefferson Davis was elected president. As Confederates began seizing Federal forts, the small Federal force stationed at Fort Moultrie on Charleston Harbor secretly moved to Fort Sumter, just completed at the mouth of Charleston Harbor. South Carolina authorities demanded withdrawal.

President Abraham Lincoln decided to send provisions to the 96 Union men stationed there. South Carolina volunteers occupied Fort Moultrie and three other forts circling Charleston Harbor. On April 11, Brigadier General P. G. T. Beauregard, who had taken command of Confederate troops at Charleston, demanded that the Union commander, Major Robert Anderson, surrender the fort. Anderson refused.

At 4:30 A.M. on April 12, 1861, Confederate forces began shelling Fort Sumter. The Civil War had erupted. Two days and 3,000 shells later, Anderson surrendered to

Beauregard, his former West Point student, and his men marched out of the fort and boarded a ship for New York.

Although Union forces heavily bombarded the Confederate-held fort during the war, it was never retaken. Fort Sumter became a symbol of Confederate defiance and Union resolve. Today its crumbled remains symbolize the Civil War itself.

About the Site Fort Sumter sits on a three-acre, man-made island, a speck in the vast Charleston Harbor, where locals claim the Ashley and Cooper rivers merge to form the Atlantic Ocean. You might expect Fort Sumter to look something like the Pentagon, considering its fame. But today's fort is a specter of devastation—a beaten-down, haunting reminder of war.

What you see are three battered walls, rising merely feet above sea level in places. Inside the once-five-sided structure are the partial ruins of the officers' quarters, sally port (entryway), enlisted men's barracks, parade ground, first-tier casemates (gun rooms), and 11 of the actual 100-pound Parrott guns fired from Fort Wagner on nearby Morris Island against Fort Sumter.

In the remaining gun room ruins, you can see several projectiles fired from Morris Island protruding from the wall. Half of the fort (right flank wall and gorge wall), which was virtually destroyed, is now buried and not accessible. You can, however, walk atop the buried area to view the harbor, guarded by several field artillery pieces like those used by the Confederates, and replicas of the five flags that have flown over the fort.

A granite monument in memory of the Union defenders who died during the opening bombardment of the Civil War stands at the edge of the parade grounds.

Besides destruction from Union bombardments, the fort suffered a later ignominy that rendered it almost unrecognizable. In 1899, during the Spanish-American War, a huge concrete battery known as Battery Isaac Huger was built across the center of the fort. The parade grounds were filled in with sand. After the U.S. government declared the site a memorial in 1932, half of the grounds were excavated in the 1950s. That half today is the portion opened to the public. The Battery Huger has been renovated. Its rooms now house a museum and small gift shop. In 1948, following World War II, the fort became a national monument.

Hot Tips You should purchase your tour boat tickets at the docks in Charleston or Mount Pleasant at least 15 minutes before boarding times. Free parking is available. Boats have snack bars. It takes 45 minutes to reach the fort, but the trip from Charleston allows you to see the historic, rainbow-colored houses (Rainbow Row) along the harborside battery. Allow three hours. Dress for the weather. Watch children closely. Do not go beyond rails or chain barriers in the fort. The fort has uneven surfaces and steps. Food and accommodations are available in Charleston and Mount Pleasant.

For a fascinating look at the battle of Fort Wagner, a Union move to overtake Fort Sumter, check out the 1989 movie *Glory*.

The Best Stuff The boat ride through Charleston Harbor and the approach to Fort Sumter offer some of the most exciting moments of your visit. Much around the fort remains the same as it was 130-plus years ago (only five generations) when the low-country South Carolina skies were alive with artillery shells. It's easy to imagine how genteel Charlestonians excitedly took to their roofs with picnic baskets to see early-morning artillery fire on April 12, 1861.

Rebel Soil. Want to get an idea of what it was like to be a rebel under a constant barrage of Yankee fire during the war? You can wander through the remains of what once were 5-foot-thick, 50-foot-high walls and feel their resolve. You can come close to shattered bulwarks, view cannons, and walk the soil where stubborn Confederate soldiers literally dug in to resist Federal gunfire, flames, and hunger.

Original Flags. Nothing brings home the drama of Fort Sumter more than the flags displayed in the museum at the fort. You can see the actual tattered Stars and Stripes that flew over the fort during the 34-hour Confederate bombardment of April 12 and 13, 1861. Also displayed is the South Carolina Palmetto flag. This flag flew over Sumter after Anderson's Union forces surrendered the fort to the Confederates.

Then and Now Although Federal guns hurled nearly seven million pounds of metal at Fort Sumter from surrounding forts, Confederate losses totaled only 52 dead and 267 wounded. All the while, laborers and slaves inside the fort worked around the clock, fortifying shattered walls with sand, masonry fragments, and bales of cotton.

The South never left Fort Sumter until the advance of General William T. Sherman's Union troops from Savannah. Then they evacuated.

Fort Sumter was a source of great irritation for the North. The Port of Charleston had become the only loophole in the naval blockade of the Atlantic Coast. Badly needed war supplies for the Confederacy came into Charleston; out went cotton and other goods as payment.

To close the port of Charleston and capture the city, Federal forces needed to capture Fort Sumter, which, of course, they never did. Federal troops did, however, capture Fort Wagner, one of a trio of other forts surrounding the harbor. From Fort Wagner on Morris Island Union troops fired powerful cannons on Sumter, almost reducing it to rubble.

Visitors aboard the tour boats can glimpse portions of the ruins of Fort Wagner, as well as Fort Johnson and Castle Pinckney around the harbor. On Sullivan's Island visitors can walk through Fort Moultrie, which saw heavy action in the Revolutionary War and was occupied by both Union and Confederate troops in the Civil War.

Elsewhere in the Area The 1771 Old Exchange and Provost Dungeon, 122 East Bay Street, Charleston, houses a portion of Charles Towne's wall of 1680 to 1718. Here in 1773 citizens met to protest the Tea Act. In the dungeon, South Carolina signers of the Declaration of Independence were imprisoned.

Also visit Charles Towne Landing, off Route 171, three miles northwest of downtown Charleston, site of the first permanent English settlement in South Carolina and the original 1670 fort; Powder Magazine, 79 Cumberland Street, Charleston, the oldest public building in the city (c. 1713); Dock Street Theater, 135 Church Street, one of oldest theaters in America; Boone Hall Plantation, America's most photographed plantation, just north of Charleston on Highway 17; and Middleton Place, Ashley River Road (Highway 61). Civil War walking tours depart daily in-season from the Mills House Hotel Courtyard, 115 Meeting Street.

Kings Mountain

Where Overmountain Men Turned the Tide of Revolution

Location North central South Carolina, 15 miles southwest of Gastonia, North Carolina, and 10 miles east of Gaffney, South Carolina. From the north, south, and west take I-85 to Highway 216 six miles east to the park. From the east take U.S. 321 to York, then east via Route 161 north. Follow signs.

Kings Mountain National Military Park is open daily, except Thanksgiving, December 25, and January 1. There are living-history encampments the first weekend in May and the weekend nearest October 7. For information on hours contact Superintendent, Kings Mountain National Military Park, P.O. Box 40, Kings Mountain, NC 28086. Tel. (864) 936-7921. An Overmountain Victory National Historic Trail reenactment, beginning September 23 in Abingdon, Virginia, precedes annual commemorative ceremonies at Kings Mountain on October 7. For information contact the Overmountain Victory Trail Association, Inc., Sycamore Shoals State Park, Elizabethton, TN 37643. Tel. (615) 543-5808.

Frame of Reference The Battle of Kings Mountain was fought on October 7, 1780, five years into the Revolutionary War (1776–81), when British military strategy centered on exploiting loyalist and patriot divisions in the South.

Significance On this rocky spur of the Blue Ridge, Americans fought Americans in a savage battle that thwarted the Crown's strategy to end the colonial rebels' bid for independence. England planned to exploit hot divisions of loyalty in the South, thus conquering the region and ending hope of Revolutionary victory.

But that dream came to a screeching halt at Kings Mountain—named for an early settler—as a swarm of "Overmountain Men," angered by British threats to "lay waste (their) country by fire and sword," sought revenge. The Overmountain Men wanted to settle old scores as well as punish these fellow countrymen for their loyalties to the Crown.

The Overmountain Men led patriots to victory at Kings Mountain with a secret weapon they used in their everyday life: the frontier rifle. The dead-eye accuracy of the Overmountain Men's slender rifles, plus their deadly aim, honed by years of hunting small game, spelled crushing victory over the loyalists and their scatter-shot muskets.

This unexpected victory shattered the Crown's southern strategy and was a major turning point in the Revolutionary War. The British never regained their military momentum. Surrender at Yorktown followed one year later.

About the Site Except for a parking lot and the visitor center, Kings Mountain (not to be confused with the North Carolina town nearby) probably looks much as it did 220 years ago. A 1½-mile, self-guided foot trail through a forest leads to the still timberless top of the rocky mountain, which stands 60 feet high, 600 yards long, and 60 to 120 feet wide. Plaques along the battlefield trail explain developments in the battle and mark significant places of action.

At the grassy mountain top, a granite obelisk commemorates the battle, citing the heroism and patriotism of those who participated where the tide of battle turned in favor of the American colonies. Descendants of the Americans killed here erected the monument.

Along the paved forest path you will find the grave of Major Patrick Ferguson, the Loyalist commander and the only British-born participant in the battle. A plaque marks where he fell mortally wounded from his horse. Nearby a boulder and plaque show visitors where President Herbert Hoover addressed 75,000 people at a celebration of the battle's centennial.

The visitor center houses a gift shop and a small museum with exhibits explaining the battle and frontier life. An excellent 18-minute film, *Kings Mountain: Turning Point in the South*, runs every half hour in the theater. In summer months a costumed park ranger gives a demonstration on the Brown Bess musket, used by the loyalists, and the long rifle, the weapon of the Overmountain Men. The park has a horse trail and hiking trails.

The Battle of Kings Mountain

Cruel Ironies and Vengeance

Major Patrick Ferguson, the only professional British soldier from the British Isles at the Battle of Kings Mountain, led American-born soldiers serving in the British military and loyal colonists (Tories) against patriot volunteers and colonial militiamen (Whigs) from several southern states. Ferguson had hoped to continue a string of British victories in South Carolina. The British then planned to take the rest of the South.

What Ferguson hadn't counted on was the angry swarm of southern Overmountain Men among the patriot forces, out for bloody vengeance after Ferguson's public threat to the "set of mongrels" to "lay waste (their) country with fire and sword."

The Overmountain Men began their trek to Kings Mountain from the remotest western corners of Virginia and North Carolina, the region people called the "overmountain country." Walking along a 220-mile route through the Appalachians, today's Overmountain Victory Trail, their ranks swelled from 1,500 to 1,800 as militiamen and volunteers from three southern states joined them. This frontier force tracked Ferguson and his men to Kings Mountain. Here, with his troops ensconced on high ground, Ferguson planned to annihilate the enemy.

But the Overmountain Men carried a weapon that would prove the greatest menace Ferguson's 1,100 loyalists had ever faced—the slender rifles of the frontier. The rifles, combined with the buckskin-clad "backwater man's" deadly aim—honed by a lifetime of hunting small, swift game, and fighting Native North Americans—wreaked cruel havoc on Ferguson's men. Crouching behind trees and rocks,

Hot Tips You can experience Kings Mountain in about two hours. If you plan to hike, wear sturdy shoes. Trails become steep in places. Bring your own beverages. A contour map and

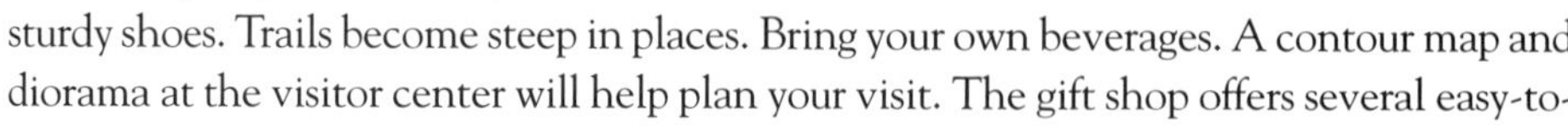

diorama at the visitor center will help plan your visit. The gift shop offers several easy-to-read books on the battle. To better understand and savor what you see, read Wilma Dykeman's slender book *With Fire and Sword: The Battle of Kings Mountain 1780*.

Food and accommodations are available in surrounding small towns as well as York and Gaffney, South Carolina, and Gastonia, North Carolina. Campsites are available at nearby Kings Mountain State Park. No picnicking is allowed at the battlefield.

The Best Stuff The story of the Overmountain Victory Trail and the Battle of Kings Mountain is just plain good. You're not going to leave this site without a renewed sense of the best and the worst of the Revolutionary War, and possibly America.

As the story of the decisive battle unfolds in the visitor center's theater and in trail markers, you'll learn of the fierce independence, courage, and steely determination that the Overmountain Men brought here. You'll also see their other side: vindictiveness and cruelty.

Picturesque plaques along the ridge bear quotes from patriot officers, like Colonel John Sevier, future six-time governor of Tennessee. His Overmountain regiment attacked from the west side. "In God and our rifles we trust!" he shouted. The battle cry of patriot hero Colonel William Campbell reveals the mindset that decisive day: "Shout like hell and fight like demons!"

Then and Now From the air, Kings Mountain looks like a giant human footprint. From today's vantage of more than 200 years, the frontiersmen's brief hour of battle here leaves an indelible portrait of what we like to think of as the true American character.

the Overmountain Men picked off the loyalists one by one as they defended the mountain. Ferguson and 225 of his men died, 163 were wounded, and 716 were taken prisoner. The patriots lost only 28 men; 62 were wounded.

Ferguson's detachment, in a last-ditch try for victory, relied on an ill-fated bayonet charge down the mountain. The Overmountain Men polished off a victory with their trusted rifles. It's a cruel twist of history that years before, Major Ferguson himself had invented the breechloading rifle. British Commander Lord Cornwallis had forbade its use.

The patriot victory gave America's Continental army both a moral boost and precious time to reorganize. The British learned to not underestimate the rebel character or to rely on loyalist recruits. In the South the tide had turned. The British never regained earlier military momentum. Their Yorktown surrender occurred one year later.

The story of Kings Mountain actually began years before the battle. It's a story of civil unrest, both in Britain, where pressure to end the war was mounting, and in North Carolina, where hatred between the east and west as well as between loyalists and patriots had reached a boiling point. British military leadership thought it would be an easy task to recruit volunteers in this state where political, religious, social, and economic resentments abounded. Their southern strategy was to take South Carolina, then North Carolina, then Virginia, home of the colonial capital. The war would be over.

But this story is full of twists and turns. Fear of independence and a keen sense that British rule was best for the colonies motivated the loyalists. Fear of the Crown and a keen sense of self-determination motivated the Overmountain Men. They formed a

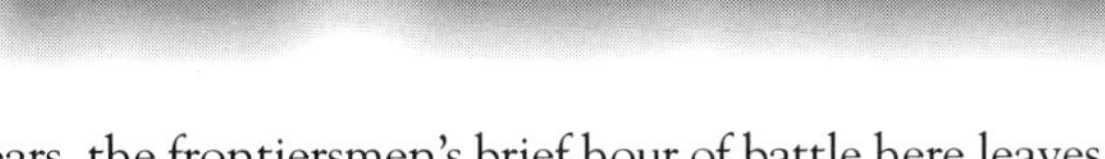

The arched, stone monument that marks the grave of Major Ferguson, respected at the time by both British and Americans, was erected in 1930 as a memorial. Its carved message reflects today's international sentiments: "From the citizens of the United States of America in token of their appreciation of the bonds of friendship and peace between them and the citizens of the British Empire."

In the Kings Mountain forest visitors will find two witnesses to yesterday's battle—a towering, 12-foot round poplar tree that was but a sprig that day and the gurgling spring where the dying washed their wounds.

volunteer citizen army on their own, not compelled by Congress or any state power. They followed leaders they democratically chose; they fought as they had taught themselves. And they destroyed Cornwallis's left flank and his grand plan by simply refusing to give in.

The story of Kings Mountain heroism, however, turns ugly in its final chapters. Three times the Overmountain Men charged up the hill. Three times they were driven back down. Finally the Overmountain Men realized that Ferguson's volleys were zinging right over their heads and that the Overmountain Men's rifles were hitting their marks. Then they yelled the frontier war whoop learned from the Native North Americans and charged.

Once the real fighting started, the Overmountain Men refused to end it. Even as the slain Ferguson's men brandished white handkerchiefs, pleading "quarter" (mercy), the Overmountain Men remembered past British atrocities and continued their slaughter. (Some say the backwoodsmen didn't know what a white flag meant.) Wounded loyalists were left unattended. The victors and greedy local citizens plundered the bodies. Marauding hogs and wolves later feasted on the dead.

A final bloody epilogue occurred when the Overmountain Men beat and hacked prisoners of war on the march to a POW camp. The Overmountain Men also tried a few POWs for breaking open houses, killing the men, turning the women and children out of doors, and burning the houses. Some were hung; some captives escaped. In the end, only 130 fellow Americans were delivered to prison.

▲

Appomattox Court House

Where Robert E. Lee Surrendered

Location South central Virginia, 18 miles east of Lynchburg and 3 miles northeast of the town of Appomattox. From U.S. 460 or U.S. 460 Bypass take Route 24 north 11 miles to the park entrance.

Appomattox Court House National Historical Park ($) is open daily, except Thanksgiving, December 25, January 1, Martin Luther King Jr. Day, and Presidents Day, 8:30 A.M.–5 P.M. Special programs take place in warm months. For information contact Superintendent, Appomattox Court House National Historical Park, P.O. Box 218, Appomattox, VA 24522. Tel. (804) 352-8987.

Frame of Reference The Civil War ended here on April 9, 1865.

Significance This out-of-the-way village, the seat of the then-new county of Appomattox, is where General Robert E. Lee, commanding general of the Army of Northern Virginia, surrendered his men to Lieutenant General Ulysses S. Grant, chief of U.S. forces, signifying the end of the Civil War (1861–65). The village was called "Appomattox Court House," an 19th-century means of signifying where the county courthouse was located, not the actual building. In fact, Lee's surrender to Grant took place in a private home in the village, not the public courthouse, which was closed that Palm Sunday 130 years ago.

About the Site A visit to Appomattox Court House is a trip back through time to a place of special meaning in American history. The tiny, out-of-the-way village of 1,700 acres has been restored essentially to its April 1865 appearance, with 13 original buildings and 9 other structures—including the McLean house, where the Lee-Grant surrender took place—reconstructed on their original sites.

The handful of historic country roads in the village are open only to pedestrian traffic for self-guided tours. In warm months costumed interpreters answer your questions as if it were the summer of 1865. You can go inside most buildings, including the McLean house, the brick courthouse (now home to the visitor center), Clover Hill Tavern, and the county jail. There's a small but interesting museum in the courthouse. Markers and exhibits dot the park. The town of Appomattox offers restored and reconstructed buildings.

Walk the muddy Old Richmond–Lynchburg Stage Road circling the courthouse, where in 1865 nearly 30,000 Confederate soldiers marched before Union soldiers to lay down their arms three days after the formal surrender. Outside the village you can visit the sites of Lee's and Grant's headquarters, as well as a cemetery, where soldiers who were killed on the day of surrender are buried. An impressive monument erected by North Carolina marks the furthest advance of its troops that April 9.

Hot Tips Pick up a map for your walk through the village at the visitor center in the two-story brick courthouse. Allow two hours plus time to see the surrender-related sites outside the village. The once-dirt country roads are now gravel, but a visitor can still mire in red mud. Park in the lot off Route 24 for the village tour. Other marked lots along Route 24 allow parking at the cemetery, headquarters sites, and North Carolina Monument.

Two short slide shows at the visitor center are shown every other half-hour. "Appomattox" recounts the surrender and the events leading up to it. The other is a compilation of excerpts from diaries of soldiers participating in the surrender. Take a snack or eat before your visit; food is not available in the park. Accommodations and food are available in the town of Appomattox or in Lynchburg. Camping is possible at nearby Holiday Lake State Park and at private campgrounds.

The Best Stuff The soul of the village is the reconstructed brick house of Wilmer McLean, where Lee and Grant met face-to-face in the Victorian parlor and quickly hammered out the surrender terms that Palm Sunday. The original three-story 1848 house was purchased in 1863 by McLean, a merchant, in an ironic attempt to escape the ravages war had brought to his former home in Manassas, Virginia. It was by far the finest building in the village and, because the courthouse was closed on Sunday, Lee's emissary chose the home as the appropriate site for the surrender. Be sure to see these items:

- **Surrender Room.** The 18-by-21-foot room is furnished exactly as it was on April 9, 1865, according to eyewitness accounts of the surrender. (Unfortunately, there were no photographers present at the hastily arranged moment.)

It's also unfortunate that witnesses, without McLean's permission, took much of the contents in the white-walled room as souvenirs after the signing. Reproductions, however, are precise, including the specially loomed, red-and-green-patterned carpet. Only a sofa and two vases on the black marble mantel are original to the room. The museum displays the table on which Lee and Grant signed the final surrender terms.

In another tale of fortune-seeking, investors in 1893 dismantled the entire McLean house itself. They had big plans to display it in Chicago and later in Washington, D.C. The house was laid out on the front lawn brick by brick and stick by stick, but the investors soon ran out of money. The house remained there uncovered and vulnerable to thieves and souvenir-seekers until 1941.

Only 5,000 of the 60,000 original bricks remained when the village became a park, and the house was rebuilt only after extensive research. Today the original bricks form part of the house front between the front two windows.

- **Parole Pass Press.** In the final surrender terms Grant allowed Confederates who laid down their arms to return home, never to be held as prisoners of war. To ensure that the men would not be arrested or disturbed, he had paroled prisoners' passes printed and filled out during the days between his meeting with Lee and the surrender parade—also a condition of surrender—on April 12.

In a front room of the brick 1819 Clover Hill Tavern sits an authentic handcranked portable Civil War printing press. It's like one that cranked out paroled prisoners' passes for Confederates after the surrender. (Few of these portable war presses, often found in generals' quarters, survive. Others are in the Smithsonian.)

The portable presses ran night and day in the two-story tavern, cranking out about 28,000 8-by-3-inch passes. Though small, this piece of paper meant a big guarantee—safety on the grueling walk home for the defeated Army of Northern Virginia.

Surviving Artifacts. Despite souvenir hunters, the museum in the visitor center houses a few important surrender items. Here you can see the white towel used as the Confederate truce flag, the broken wooden pencil Lee used to correct Grant's original draft of the surrender terms, working drafts of the terms, and the signing table. (The Museum of the Confederacy in Richmond, Virginia, displays the pen Lee used to sign the final terms as well as the uniform he wore that day.)

Then and Now The village of Appomattox Court House, a settlement called Clover Hill until the county of Appomattox was established in 1845, never had a population of more than 120, about 30 families. And the stage line and railroad never brought real prosperity.

When the courthouse burned down in 1892 the county seat was moved to the town of Appomattox. The tidy tree-lined village on a windy ridge is a page from the everyday life of a rural stagecoach stop. And with a little imagination—and strategically placed historical plaques—you can almost see Lee's army in its final dreary moments of dissolution.

The surrender parade that Grant insisted upon lasted from 6 A.M. until 1 P.M. on April 12, 1865, four years to the day that Southern rebels fired on Fort Sumter. The Confederates' last month of existence had been filled with hunger, exhaustion, and casualty-heavy battle as Union forces relentlessly pursued.

Grant's successful siege of Petersburg, Virginia, had forced Lee to retreat westward. Lee's dispirited army was down to about 20,000 ragtag men facing a Union army of more than 60,000. After the loss at Petersburg, the Confederate evacuation of Richmond, and a failed attempt to break surrounding Union lines at Appomattox, Lee made the agonizing decision to surrender rather than face more suffering and losses.

Today the surrender road, actually the Old Richmond–Lynchburg Stage Road, peters out from a graveled walkway to a grassy stretch at the village edge. Walk past the fields of wildflowers and mountain vistas as the thousands of Confederates did that day, their feet turning the road, from the Appomattox River to the courthouse, into a sea of red mud. Quiet and dignity prevailed as 6,000 Federal troops lined the road and looked on, "honor answering honor," as one diarist wrote.

Stand on the small porch of the wooden Kelly house overlooking Surrender Triangle, where the widow Kelly watched the Confederate troops unfurl their tattered flags and pile their weapons, some crying and kissing their muskets good-bye. For all practical purposes, the Civil War was over.

Elsewhere in the Area Red Hill, Patrick Henry's re-created last home and burial site, is located in Brookneal, 27 miles south of Appomattox in Charlotte County.

Jamestown

First Permanent English Colony

Location Southeastern Virginia, about 60 miles east of Richmond on the James River. From the north and south take I-95 to I-64. From the east and west take I-64. Follow signs from I-64 to Colonial Parkway and entrances to historic sites.

Jamestown Settlement ($), operated by the Commonwealth of Virginia's Jamestown-Yorktown Foundation, is open daily, except December 25 and January 1, 9 A.M.–5 P.M. The National Park Service operates James Island ($), in concert with the Virginia Society of Antiquities ($), and it is open daily, except December 25, 8:30 A.M.–4:30 P.M., with extended hours April through October. For information on special events and programs at both sites contact Superintendent, Colonial National Historical Park, P.O. Box 210, Yorktown, VA 23690. Tel. (757) 898-3400.

Frame of Reference Jamestown was settled during the early colonial period (1607–99).

Significance Jamestown, named for King James I, was the first permanent English settlement in America, 13 years before the Pilgrims landed at Plymouth Rock and 42 years after the Spanish settled St. Augustine, Florida.

Jamestown was the capital of Virginia for 92 years before the last of a series of disastrous fires sent the capital upriver to Williamsburg. The original settlement of 104 men and boys was located on James Island. The Virginia Company of London sponsored the settlement in search of fortune. This was the first center of religious, social, economic, and political life in England's New World.

About the Site The site consists of two parts: the 1,500-acre Jamestown Island, the archaeological site where the 1607 colony began; and Jamestown Settlement, the 20-acre re-creation of that colony adjacent to the island. Jamestown is part of the Colonial National Historical Park, which includes Yorktown, eight miles northeast along the Colonial Parkway.

The foundations of many homes and buildings on Jamestown Island have been excavated. Whitened bricks cover these foundations to protect them and allow easy viewing. Information stations with audio programs guide visitors. (Do not touch ruins.)

The Jamestown Settlement encompasses an authentic replica of the original James Fort, Powhatan's Village, a museum, and reconstructions of the three ships that brought the first settlers here from England. Near the park entrance a reconstructed glass house, where costumed interpreters create handblown glass, gives visitors insight into one of the foremost enterprises of the island.

Two driving tour loops, one three miles and one five miles long, offer a good way to explore Jamestown Island. Here the towering remains of the 1617 Jamestown Church walls are the only above-ground structure of the colony. It is one of the oldest English-built edifices in America and symbolizes the founding of a nation.

Hot Tips Set aside half a day for both sites. Jamestown Settlement is a hands-on exhibition. You should allow at least two hours at the site so that children can try on costumes, hear about the settlers' difficult life from interpreters, go inside the lodges at Powhatan's Village, explore the fort, and board the replicas of the three ships that brought the first adventurers across the Atlantic.

Begin your walking tour at the entrance lobby. Don't miss the excellent museum that tells Jamestown's story. A 20-minute orientation film adds to the experience. Pick up a *Junior Ranger Program* (which also can be used at Yorktown) to give the kids projects during their visit.

Be prepared for a lot of walking (wear rugged shoes), some on dirt paths. Summer weather can be buggy and muggy. Food and accommodations are abundant in Williamsburg and in Yorktown. A café and extensive gift shop are adjacent to the museum. You can rent audiotapes for an auto tour of James Island in the bookstore. Allow one to two hours. Commercial bus tours ($$) are available, too.

The Best Stuff Exploring the narrow confines of the three wooden ships that brought the English settlers here—the *Discovery*, the *Godspeed*, and the *Susan Constant*—is a blast. How did 105 people manage to live on these vessels during that long, problem-plagued journey and keep their sanity? Plenty of good photo opportunities exist here. Also look for these items:

- **Powhatan's Mantle.** The museum's Powhatan Native American Gallery displays a replica of Chief Powhatan's mantle. The 7½-by-5½-foot mantle, or "match-coat," the name given it by the Algonquian Native North Americans who inhabited the area in 1607, is made of four white-tail-deer hides sewn together. Thousands of shell beads sewn on the mantle form a pattern depicting a human figure. Animals and 34 circular designs flank the figure.

  This mantle belonged to the ruling chief of the 30-plus tribes of the area. Native North Americans called him Wahunsunacock. The English called him Emperor Powhatan or the King of Virginia. There's no definitive information on the use or origin of the mantle. The original resides in a museum at Oxford University in England.
- **Stories of Pocahontas.** Powhatan's daughter was Pocahontas, who married colonist John Rolfe in 1614, possibly inside a wooden church at James Fort. She met Captain John Smith when she was 11. This famous girl helped smooth relations between settlers and the Native North Americans. Look for her statue in the park.
- **Glass House.** Costumed artisans blow glass objects in the reconstructed glass house near the remains of the original 1608 one. Settlers built the house to produce glass for British trade. (Tobacco, however, became the better deal.) Watch as the finisher reheats pieces of glass in the "glory hole" of the clay furnaces. You can purchase beautiful handblown pieces here.

Fort James. Exploring the wattle-and-daub, thatched-roof houses inside the re-created stockade fort is great fun. Kids can put on re-creations of the heavy chain armor and metal infantry helmets the fort guardians wore as they anxiously watched for Native North American and Spanish attacks. Until recently historians thought the site of the original fort was under water. But remains of a palisade on land have been tentatively identified as part of the triangular wall built around the fort almost 400 years ago.

Then and Now Half of the first 105 island settlers died, and of the 550 settlers of "James Towne," 440 died in the "starving time" of 1609 to 1610. Burley leader Captain John Smith kept the colony together with the aid of Pocahontas and friendly Powhatan. It may have helped that he told the English gentlemen who were "above" manual labor that those who did not work would not eat.

More men and women came later, and African slaves arrived in 1620. The inhabitants cultivated tobacco, expanded the settlement, and, despite more setbacks, willed Jamestown to survive.

Today a network of granite monuments tells of the events and people of the colony that nearly met extinction.

Elsewhere in the Area Colonial Williamsburg is 8 miles north at the end of Colonial Parkway. Yorktown is 16 miles northeast. Nearby, descendants of Pocahontas still live on reservations.

The Pamunkey Reservation is located 15 miles north of Williamsburg, 10 miles south of Route 30 near West Point. Here you'll find Chief Powhatan's grave and a museum reviewing the history of the people. Pocahontas is buried in England. She died there of smallpox on a trip that won over the hearts of British royalty.

At the nearby Mattaponi Reservation Museum you can see Pocahontas's necklace and other Native North American artifacts.

Monticello

Thomas Jefferson's Home

Location Central Virginia, three miles southeast of Charlottesville. From I-64 traveling east take exit 121A; from I-64 traveling west take exit 121. Take Route 20 south. Turn left onto State Highway 53, and follow signs to the parking area.

Monticello ($) is open daily, except December 25, from November through February, 9 A.M.–4:30 P.M. and from March through October, 8 A.M.–5 P.M. Visits are by guided tour only. There's a brief shuttlebus ride from a parking lot to the mountaintop home. The Thomas Jefferson Memorial Foundation, Inc., owns and operates Monticello. For information contact the Development and Public Affairs Department, Monticello, P.O. Box 217, Charlottesville, VA 22902. Tel. (804) 984-9800. The Monticello Visitor Center is open daily in warm months, 8 A.M.–5:30 P.M., and in winter months, 8 A.M.–5 P.M.

Frame of Reference Monticello was a residence during the life of Thomas Jefferson (1743–1826), author of the Declaration of Independence and the third president of the United States. Jefferson also served as governor of Virginia, Minister to the Court of Louis XVI of France, Secretary of State, and vice president of the United States.

Significance This was Jefferson's mountaintop home from 1768, when he began construction, to his death here on July 4, 1826. Monticello was the center of Jefferson's private life and is an autobiographical monument to his varied interests and ingenuity. He designed the house himself and filled it with items that uniquely describe his life and many accomplishments. Jefferson, his family, and his descendants are buried here. Monticello is considered one of America's architectural masterpieces.

About the Site Jefferson described Monticello, which means "little mountain," as his "essay in architecture." He built, remodeled, and rebuilt the brick three-story, 21-room home over 40 years, reflecting the father of American architecture's pleasure in "putting up and pulling down."

The thrill of visiting the mansion, once the center of a 5,000-acre plantation, is savoring Jefferson's ingenious adaptation of inventions; examining the delightful twists and turns of the Roman neoclassic architecture and decor of his custom-built home; and beholding the gardens, orchards, and mountain beauty surrounding it. The house is 100 percent original. Visiting Monticello is almost like visiting the man who contributed so much to America.

Guided tours include only the first floor of the home, although guides are available for scheduled tours of the gardens.

Near the site entrance at the intersection of I-64 and Route 20 the Monticello Visitor Center offers fascinating exhibits that chronicle the life of this extraordinary man. More than 400 personal possessions and artifacts from Monticello are on display. The visitor center houses a gift shop and theater where you can see a 30-minute film, *Thomas Jefferson: the Pursuit of Liberty*. The film runs daily at 11 A.M. and 2 P.M.

Hot Tips At the visitor center you can purchase resource packets, designed for the classroom, that you may use during visits with kids. For information on this and school programs contact the Monticello Education Department, P.O. Box 316, Charlottesville, VA 22902. Tel. (804) 984-9853. Allow two hours to visit Monticello. In season, long lines for guided tours may require additional time. Add another 1½ hours for the museum and movie at the visitor center.

Snacks are available at the Monticello ticket booth on the grounds. Picnic facilities and a greenhouse offering Monticello plants stand nearby. Food and accommodations are available in Charlottesville. For a trip into history, catch the luncheon buffet at 1784 Michie Tavern near Monticello on Route 53.

The ticket booth gives $2 bills as change. The bill features Jefferson's portrait and an engraving of the signing of the Declaration of Independence and is the perfect Monticello souvenir.

The Best Stuff The moment you step into the entrance hall at Monticello you experience Jefferson's thoughtful, ingenious personality. The airy, two-story room functioned as a greeting hall for guests and as Jefferson's private museum. The room houses paintings, sculptures, 350 maps and globes, and Native North American artifacts. Here Jefferson hung moose, deer, and elk antlers from the western expeditions of Lewis and Clark (directed by him when he was president) according to size, so that guests could make comparisons.

A glass exhibit case protects bones of a woolly mammoth, extinct for 10,000 years, brought from Kentucky by William Clark. The Jefferson-designed seven-day clock towers next to the arched front door. A network of weights and cables shows the day of the week on this unique timepiece. You have to go into the basement to see the bottom of the clock (Friday and Saturday). Jefferson designed the clock for his Philadelphia home during his days at the Continental Congress. It didn't quite fit Monticello's wall, so Jefferson solved the problem with a hole in the foyer floor.

The best stuff also includes these:

- **Jefferson's Cabinet or personal study.** Between the library of 10,000 volumes and the master bedroom, this many-sided room was where Jefferson read (in seven languages), wrote letters (nearly 20,000 in his lifetime), and conducted scientific experiments. A five-sided revolving bookstand Jefferson designed allowed him to read five books at once. Here Jefferson received word the Louisiana Purchase was completed.
- **Jefferson's Bedroom.** The bed rests in an alcove between the bedroom and cabinet so that Jefferson could retire from either room. The bedroom features a skylight (Monticello boasted 13 of these, which were rare at the time), a walk-up closet over the bed, and a wooden medicine chest. Jefferson served as his own physician, studying and experiment-

ing with herbs. The polished chests have 150 glass bottles filled with homegrown herbs. The library has 150 medical books. The six-foot, three-inch bed is where Jefferson died on July 4, 1826—the 50th anniversary of the Declaration of Independence.

Mulberry Row. Here is where you can learn about the complex African American community at Monticello. This 1,000-foot-long dirt road was the center of activity to support Monticello for the 60 years of Jefferson's residency. Seventeen structures stood among the mulberry trees that lined this road. These included slave cabins, a stable, wood- and iron-working shops, and a smokehouse. Only three partial stone buildings survive today. An orchard and a two-acre vegetable garden, re-created from Jefferson's extensive records, spread over land next to Mulberry Row.

Exhibits. Don't pass up the extensive exhibit of Jefferson's possessions and Monticello artifacts at the visitor center. Note especially the display of the contents of Jefferson's pockets, including a red-leather pocketbook, the knife he used to scrape mud from his boots, and his "ivory notebook," small strips of ivory that spread out like a fan. Jefferson carried these notebooks for his copious notes, making observations on everything from the law to the weather. He was one of the first systematic observers of American climate and made daily notations of temperature. Jefferson also attached an odometer to the carriage he designed to record its mileage.

Kids will be interested in copies of letters Jefferson wrote to his daughter, instructing her on the use of her time. He suggested she read French from 3 to 4 P.M. and "exercise yourself in music" from 4 to 5 P.M. Jefferson himself was an accomplished violinist.

Then and Now Monticello and its grounds continually undergo study and restoration. The search for additional original Monticello items never ceases. Today false fronts have replaced Jefferson's vast book collection; the originals became the nucleus for the modern Library of Congress. Full restoration of the "dependencies"—rooms concealed under wings of the house and connected by an all-weather passageway—continues, although the roped-off rooms are opened.

You can peer into the refurbished kitchen and bottling room, where slaves Ursula and Jupiter transferred cider from 126-gallon kegs to bottles. Dusty bottles line the shelves in the wine cellar today.

In Monticello itself modern machines measure heat and humidity. Today, instead of important guests (many uninvited and staying up to three weeks) and a houseful of extended family and 12 grandchildren, tourists from around the world roam the estate.

A short walk takes you to the family cemetery, where Jefferson and many of his 2,000 descendants are buried. Some graves are as recent as 1995. The inscription on the marble obelisk marking Jefferson's grave is as he instructed:

> ***Here was buried Thomas Jefferson, Author of the Declaration of American Independence, Of the Statute of Virginia for Religious Freedom, and the Father of the University of Virginia.***

Jefferson made no mention of his political positions, which he called "his duty."

Mount Vernon

The Home of George Washington

Location Eastern Virginia, 16 miles south of Washington, D.C. From Alexandria or Arlington take the George Washington Parkway to the site. From Richmond or Fredericksburg take U.S. 1.

Mount Vernon ($) is open daily, from November 1 through March, 9 A.M.–4 P.M., from April through August, 8 A.M.–4 P.M., and from September through October, 9 A.M.–5 P.M. For more information contact Mount Vernon Ladies' Association, Mount Vernon, VA 22121. Tel. (703) 780-2000.

Frame of Reference George Washington (1732–99), first president of the United States, made Mount Vernon his home from 1754 to 1799.

Significance Washington lived at this 500-acre estate on the Potomac River, inherited from his half-brother Lawrence, until his death here at age 67. This was his home during the 6½ years he lead the Continental army during the American Revolution and the years he served as first president of the United States (1789–97), although he spent little time at his beloved Mount Vernon during those years.

At Mount Vernon Washington, America's pioneer farmer, laid the foundation for modern agriculture and made innovative advancements in the breeding of farm animals. Washington and his wife, Martha, are buried here.

Mount Vernon, America's most-visited home, preserves the personality, intelligence, and interest of the nation's first president and humanizes the famous man represented in the familiar pictures and statues.

About the Site Washington's three-story white mansion with its bright red roof sits amid 30 acres of woods and grounds, gardens, courtyard, a complex of restored outbuildings that housed services for the family, a slave burial ground, and the Washington family tomb. The mansion seems reversed, with a wide, columned porch overlooking the Potomac River. Fourteen rooms on two floors are open for guided public tours. Restoration of the estate continues. A museum next to the mansion exhibits Washington's personal and household possessions. Summer hands-on educational exhibits include a Revolutionary War tent with life-size fiberglass mule and an up-close and personal look at the first president in the film *George Washington: Pioneer Farmer.*

You can see an exact reconstruction of the innovative 16-sided wheat-threshing barn Washington designed. Dedicated in September 1996, the 52-foot-diameter, wood-and-brick, two-story barn was where horses walked over harvested crops on the top floor to "tread out" grain, which dropped through small gaps in the floor to the lower level.

Hot Tips Allow three hours for your visit. You can reach the site by bus ($), or rail ($) from downtown Washington, D.C., or you can drive there. Parking is free. Mount Vernon also is part of several tour packages you can purchase in the capital. For transportation information contact Metro Bus and Rail, (202) 637-7000; Fairfax Connector, (703) 339-7200; Tourmobile Sightseeing Tours, (202) 554-7950; Told Line, (202) 289-1995; or All About Town, (202) 393-3696.

The *Potomac Spirit* offers boat cruises to the site from mid-March to October. Tel. (202) 554-8000. Food and accommodations are available in Washington. You can eat lunch or dinner at the Mount Vernon Inn on the grounds. The site also has a snack bar and two gift shops.

The Best Stuff The guides at Mount Vernon reveal the human side of the man who once lived life to the fullest here. They intertwine details of the estate with details of the first U.S. president's life, leaving you with the impression that you have visited Washington's personal world. The things you see (and that Washington touched) as you walk through the house evoke the elegant, thoughtful, intelligent nature of the man who led the United States in its early years. Keep an eye out for these revealing treasures:

Farmer George

George Washington was one of the first American agriculturists. He experimented with plants, trees, and shrubs imported from all over the world to the botanical garden at Mount Vernon. During the Revolutionary War, General Washington wrote home regularly with meticulous instructions on the care of his Mt. Vernon plantation. The subject of farming appears in his writings more than any other subject. Now you can stroll through this area of restored plants and crops and buy Mount Vernon plants and seeds from a shop at the site.

Sheep roam the estate's paddock, reminding visitors that Washington improved his breed of sheep so that they yielded more than twice the average amount of wool. He also may have been the first American farmer to raise mules. Today three mules—Jake, Blue, and Kate—call the estate home.

Washington's last months at Mount Vernon are reported to have been both busy and happy. He attended to his thriving farms, performed civic duties, and entertained guests. Today Mount Vernon is the destination of a million visitors annually from around the world, making it America's most-visited home as well as one of the country's oldest ongoing preservation projects.

The home stands as a monument to Washington, who was described by Henry Lee (a Revolutionary War general, member of the Continental Congress, and governor of Virginia) as "first in war, first in peace, first in the hearts of his countrymen."

- **Bastille Key.** The iron key to the notorious Paris prison where kings and ministers had imprisoned men and women at will, the Bastille, is inconspicuously mounted on the wall beside the main staircase. The key was a gift to Washington from Marquis de Lafayette. Lafayette, a young French nobleman, played an important role not only in the American Revolution, but in the 1789 French Revolution that began with the storming of the Bastille. Washington was Lafayette's friend, father figure, and admired fellow defender of liberty.

- **Where Washington Slept and Died.** You can look into an intimate upstairs room and see where Washington *really* slept for much of his life. This bedroom, called "Mrs. Washington's Room" (she bathed and dressed here; he used his downstairs study), is also the room where he died. Washington was an unusually tall man measuring 6 feet, 2½ inches (average height at the time was 5 feet, 9 inches), and his 6½-foot, mahogany, sycamore, and tulip-poplar bed was built especially for him in 1795 at the direction of Martha.

  Washington died on December 14, 1799, after catching a chill while riding his horse for five hours around his farm in cold rain and hail. His attending doctors, as they often did in that day, performed frequent bloodlettings in an effort to cure him. He steadily weakened, then died. Martha was sitting at the foot of this bed at the moment of his death.
- **The Mount Vernon Museum.** On the north lane of the estate, the museum displays personal possessions of George and Martha Washington. Included are the general's military equipment and swords, his silver-handled toothbrush, and a lock of his white hair. You can see Martha's satin wedding slippers and a bust of Washington, widely considered the best likeness of him, modeled at Mount Vernon by French sculptor Jean Antoine Houdon.

Then and Now Thanks to the group of persistent women who organized the Mount Vernon Ladies' Association (1853)—the oldest national preservation organization in America—Mount Vernon has been preserved and looks much as it did in Washington's day. Then it was the centerpiece of an 8,000-acre estate of five farms. The outer walls, made of stucco striated to look like stone, are kept bright white. The rooms have been restored as records indicate they were then, including the vibrant blue of the west parlor walls and the vivid greens of the small and main dining rooms—colors that Washington believed aided digestion. In the large dining room, on April 14, 1789, Washington learned he had been elected president. Areas of the house are roped off to protect the original furnishings.

Elsewhere in the Area George Washington's birthplace is re-created about 30 miles southeast of Mount Vernon. The George Washington Birthplace National Monument is 38 miles east of Fredericksburg in northeastern Virginia. Washington's first home no longer stands, but a similar memorial house has been constructed on the plantation on a tributary of the Potomac River.

Here you can tour a working colonial farm and imagine the boy George playing wildly in the orchard where he chopped down the cherry tree. For more information contact Superintendent, George Washington Birthplace National Monument, National Park Service, R.R. 1, P.O. Box 717, Washington's Birthplace, VA 22443. Tel. (804) 224-1732.

Richmond

Capital of the Confederacy, Union Prize

Location Richmond is located in Central Virginia. From the north and south take I-95; take U.S. 64 from the east or west.

Richmond National Battlefield Park is open daily, except Thanksgiving, December 25, and January 1, 9 A.M.–5 P.M. For information contact Superintendent, Richmond National Battlefield Park, 3215 East Broad Street, Richmond, VA 23223. Tel. (804) 226-1981. The Museum of the Confederacy ($) stands downtown at the corner of Clay and 12th streets, next to the Medical College of Virginia. Museum hours are Monday through Saturday, 10 A.M.–5 P.M., and Sunday, noon–5 P.M.

The White House of the Confederacy ($), next to the museum, is open for guided tours only during regular museum hours, except for Tuesday and Thursday, when tours begin at 11:30 A.M. For information on the Museum of the Confederacy and the White House of the Confederacy, contact the Museum of the Confederacy, 1201 East Clay Street, Richmond, VA 23219. Tel. (804) 649-1861. The city's Civil War monuments can be viewed any time. For information on Virginia's Civil War Trails, call 1-888-CIVIL WAR.

Frame of Reference Richmond was the capital of the Confederacy during most of the Civil War (1861–1865). Confederates evacuated the city on April 3, 1865, the day after the fall of Petersburg.

Significance The southern city was not only the capital of the Confederacy, but a principal manufacturing and medical center as well as a main military supply point. Richmond was the primary physical and psychological objective of the Northern army from the beginning to the end of the four-year Civil War. Virginia was the "buffer state" between North and South and site of an estimated 60 percent of the fighting and ¼ of the major battles.

"On to Richmond" was a familiar rallying cry for Union troops. The city withstood seven major "On to Richmond" military campaigns during the war, two of which—the Seven Days' Battles of 1862 and Lieutenant General U.S. Grant's successful 10-month siege of Petersburg of 1864 to 1865—brought Union forces so close to the heavily entrenched city that Union soldiers set their watches by Richmond church bells.

But it was not until Petersburg fell that General Robert E. Lee and his army were forced to flee westward on April 2, 1865. Virtually unprotected, the Confederates evacuated Richmond the next day, leaving their city in flames and ruin. Lee's surrender at Appomattox quickly followed (six days later), marking the end of the Confederacy and the reuniting of a nation.

About the Site This thriving capital city lies in the heart of Virginia, which from 1861 to 1865 was the heart of the Confederacy. A visit to Virginia's Civil War past must include Richmond, the center of four bitter, violent years in American history.

In and around Richmond, you'll find six major Civil War battlefields; the refurbished Confederate Executive Mansion, which served as the Southern White House from 1861 to 1865; the Museum of the Confederacy, one of the most riveting Civil War museums in the country; and "Monument Avenue," featuring statues of famous Confederates, including Lee and Stonewall Jackson.

In the Hollywood Cemetery at Cherry and Albemarle streets lie the graves of some 18,000 Confederate soldiers and celebrities, including General George Pickett, J. E. B. Stuart, and Confederate President Jefferson Davis. The Richmond Battlefield Park Visitor Center introduces you to a network of Civil War battlefields surrounding the city. Cold Harbor and Fort Harrison have smaller orientation centers, staffed seasonally. Markers help explain the park's 11 historic sites and battlefields.

The Virginia Historical Society ($), 428 N. Boulevard (at the corner of Kensington Avenue), exhibits important Confederate artifacts, including J. E. B. Stuart's coat and blood-stained sash.

In addition, you can visit St. John's Church, at 2401 East Broad Street downtown. This is where Patrick Henry spoke his famous words on March 23, 1775, "Give me liberty . . . or give me death!" fanning the flames of the American Revolution.

Hot Tips To sample Civil War Richmond, plan to spend half a day. If you want to visit the 11 units of the Battlefield Park, allow accordingly for the 80-mile auto tour. Start your tour at the Battlefield Visitors Center, 3215 Broad Street, where you can pick up park maps and audiocassettes, catch a brief orientation slide show, and view exhibits. Allow two hours for a combined visit to the Confederate White House and the Museum of the Confederacy.

Historic Richmond Tours offers ½-day van tours ($$) of the Seven Days' Battles and the city. Call (804) 780-0107 for information.

If you wish to follow the path of Lee's retreat from Petersburg south of Richmond to Appomattox, you can buy a packet with two books, a map of the 20-stop auto route, and a cassette telling about the sites. Pick up the packet at either the Appomattox or Petersburg parks. For more information call 1-800-6 RETREAT. Allow a day for this self-guided auto tour.

The Best Stuff The richly ornate Victorian interior of the Confederate White House tells fascinating stories of what occurred here during the Civil War. Two-thirds of the furnishings are original. This was the site where the Confederate Cabinet met with Jefferson Davis around the massive mahogany dining table, where "starvation balls" featuring "Jeff Davis fruit punch" instead of imported wine were held in the central parlor, and where President Lincoln paced in the red velvet–wallpapered library after the fall of Richmond. Kids might be interested in seeing the east portico balcony from which Davis's five-year-old son (one of six children) fell while walking on the railing. He died of his head injury.

The treasures of the Museum of the Confederacy rank at the top of Civil War collections. Among the artifacts on three floors you'll find these:

- **Lee's Uniform.** The gray wool, brass-buttoned uniform Robert E. Lee wore at his surrender at Appomattox and the decorated sword he carried are here. The sword, a gift from admirers, is inscribed "General Robert E. Lee from Maryland, 1865." You'll also find a tent filled with Lee's personal effects, including his boots, hat, gloves, cot, saddle, revolver, chest, and sash.
- **J. E. B. Stuart's Gear.** You can see military gear of the flamboyant cavalryman J. E. B. Stuart, including his plumed hat, wool uniform, and saddle.
- **Stonewall Jackson's Death Mask.** The plaster death mask of Lee's most-trusted general, Stonewall Jackson, is on display. Jackson died after sustaining a shoulder wound at the Battle of Chancellorsville. (His left arm was amputated and ceremoniously buried. He subsequently died of pneumonia.) Lee reportedly later said that if General Jackson had been at his side in Gettysburg, he would have won.
- **Armistead's Sword.** See the 1850 sword that General Lewis Armistead brandished as he lead the Southern brigade that spearheaded the ill-fated Pickett's Charge at Gettysburg.
- **Davis Suit.** This is the gray wool suit Jefferson Davis was wearing when U.S. troops captured him in Georgia soon after Lee's surrender.
- **Custer Table.** A small, oval table from the parlor at the McLean House where Lee surrendered is here. The name Custer is roughly inscribed on its underside.

Then and Now As Richmond's 203,000 residents go about their daily business, Civil War reminders keep their city in the vortex of Civil War history. The Richmond Battlefield Visitors Center occupies a modest building on a grassy hill where the largest of the five war hospitals of the city (Chimborazo) stood. Supposedly a Richmonder who had visited South America named it after a volcano in Ecuador. More than 76,000 Confederate sick and wounded were treated in the 40-acre hospital complex. The entire area is now a park in a quiet residential neighborhood.

The business of running the 12th most populated state fills the grand, downtown capitol building, once home to the Confederate Congress. Physical signs of the roaring flames that consumed the waterfront along the James River and the pandemonium that accompanied the city's frantic evacuation are long gone. You can still see remains of the complex lines of fortifications that encircled the city and earthworks on the battlefields, but tranquility prevails as Richmond church bells ring out the hour.

Today musicians play "Taps" around the country at ceremonial occasions. This song was composed near here 130 years ago by two Union soldiers in memory of their fallen comrades.

Elsewhere in the Area Maggie L. Walker (prominent African American and first woman to found a bank) National Historic Site is at 3215 East Broad Street. Petersburg National Battlefield ($) is 20 miles south of Richmond. For information contact Superintendent, Petersburg National Battlefield, P.O. Box 549, Petersburg, VA 23804. Tel. (808) 732-3531.

Williamsburg

Influential Capital of Colonial Virginia

Location Southeastern Virginia, about 50 miles east of Richmond, between the James and York rivers. From the north and south take I-95 to U.S. 64 east. Follow signs to the visitor center just off Route 132. From the east and west take U.S. 64.

Colonial Williamsburg is open daily. Purchase tickets at the visitor center. Ticket prices are $26 for adults, $15 for children 6 to 12, and free for children under 6. Multiday ticket packages are offered; visitor center hours vary seasonally. Ticket price includes use of all buses. Buses run 8:50 A.M.–10 P.M. Buildings are open 9:30 A.M.–5:30 P.M. Special programs and tours take place year-round. For information contact the Colonial Williamsburg Foundation, P.O. Box 1776, Williamsburg, VA 23187-1776. Tel. (757) 220-7645 or 1-800-HISTORY.

Frame of Reference Williamsburg's peak of influence occurred from 1699 to 1779, when Williamsburg served as Virginia's capital. The colony's government was moved from Jamestown, the first permanent English settlement in America, upriver to this more desirable location in 1699. Richmond became the state capital in 1780.

Significance This beautiful "modern" city was the commercial, social, and cultural center of pre-Revolutionary America's largest and most influential colony. It is the site of pivotal events, involving colonial celebrities such as George Washington, Patrick Henry, Thomas Jefferson, and George Mason, that led to the Declaration of Independence in 1776 and later to the Bill of Rights and the U.S. Constitution. Today Colonial Williamsburg is the world's largest living-history museum.

About the Site Colonial Williamsburg, one mile long and half a mile wide, has been authentically restored to its grand, 18th-century appearance. It comprises more than 500 buildings, including 88 original colonial structures. Museums, exhibitions, 90 acres of gardens and greens, and day and evening interpretative programs abound. Exact restorations include the Governor's Palace, which served as the residence for seven royal British governors and the first two governors of the Commonwealth of Virginia (Patrick Henry and Thomas Jefferson). The most important restored building in the city is the Capitol building, where the Fifth Virginia Convention unanimously called for American independence on May 15, 1776. Work here led directly to the nation's Bill of Rights and the U.S. Constitution.

Hot Tips Visiting Colonial Williamsburg is a wonderfully entertaining and educational experience for the entire family, except very young children. There are a ton of things to do and see in this re-created world of colonial Virginians, so allow plenty of time for your visit—at least five to six hours, preferably a day or two. The historic area is open only to pedestrian traffic, and to enter most historic buildings and the museums you must have a ticket. The area is like a historic Disney World. Lines into the buildings by guided tours can be long but are worth it.

Begin your visit at the visitor center, where you can watch the 8-minute orientation video or a 37-minute movie, *Williamsburg: The Story of a Patriot,* in the spacious theater. Then take a shuttlebus to the site. There are places to eat and gift shops in and around the historic area. Lodging is plentiful in Williamsburg. The area is a vacation wonderland, with countless stores, malls, attractions, restaurants, and motels in the area.

Walking areas in the park are brick and gravel. Be prepared for a lot of walking. Many objects and furnishings in exhibition buildings are rare and fragile: do not touch!

The Best Stuff Do not miss the movie *Williamsburg: The Story of a Patriot* before your visit. Filmed in and around Williamsburg's colonial buildings, the movie takes you up close and personal with Washington, Jefferson, Patrick Henry, and some regular people who nurtured our country's independence and freedom. Visits to the colonial Capitol, Raleigh Tavern, and Bruton Parish Church have more meaning after this well-done introduction. And you'll leave with new insight into colonial America and the powerful events leading to the Revolution. Among the best stuff are these sites:

Governor's Palace. The two most important buildings in town are the Governor's Palace and the Capitol. Engaging costumed interpreters guide small groups through both, pointing out details and regaling visitors with anecdotes. The lavish three-story palace is reconstructed of handmade brick on its original foundations. Colonial social life revolved around the palace, considered one of the most beautiful buildings in the 18th-century British Empire. A highlight is the entrance hall, where 774 muskets, swords, pistols, and bayonets in artistic arrangements on the walls and ceiling greet you. This was a public-relations ploy to remind visiting colonists of British power.

The governor's guests danced the minuet in the two-story gilded turquoise ballroom at the rear of the palace. The stately opening dance lasted up to three hours beneath huge portraits of Queen Charlotte and King George III. Then the fatigued and hungry guests retired to the elegant gold Supper Room and feasted beneath the enormous crystal chandelier. Visiting these rooms today, you can almost hear the tinkle of a gilded pianoforte like the one nestled in a corner of the ballroom.

The Capitol. This three-story building stands at the east end of Duke of Gloucester Street, the main street in the restored city. Restored trade sites, homes, and exhibits line the mile-long avenue.

An open portico connects two oval wings of the Capitol, reflecting Britain's bicameral (based on two legislative branches) form of government. The left wing housed the Governor's Council, 12 wealthy landowners loyal to England, appointed for life by the governor. The council met around an oval table upstairs. Downstairs is the General Court, where colonists charged with serious crimes were tried. The governor presided over the proceedings.

The right wing was home to the elected Virginia legislature, called the "House of Burgesses." Representatives elected from the Virginia colony, which stretched from the

Atlantic to the Great Lakes to Mexico and covered an eight-state region, sat on facing tiers of long benches and governed the colony.

Here a 29-year-old Patrick Henry, later called the "orator of the Revolution," launched a series of fiery speeches (amid shouts of "Treason!") against the Stamp Act of 1765. A bronze plaque beneath a sprawling oak beside the Capitol concisely tells the story of this place:

> ***Here Patrick Henry kindled the flames of Revolution by his resolutions and speech against the Stamp Act, May 29–30, 1765. The first step taken toward the Union of the States. May 15, 1776, Here declared the colonies free and independent States. June 12, 1776, the work of George Mason laid the foundation for the Bill of Rights and on June 29, 1776, for the Constitution.***

- **Original Jail.** Check out the Public Gaol (jail), an original building, with dark cells and straw-covered floors where insufferable heat or frostbite was the prisoners' enemy.
- **Colonial Post Office.** Mail a postcard here and your mail gets a handstamped, 18th-century cancellation.

Then and Now John D. Rockefeller Jr. began restoration of Colonial Williamsburg in 1926, banning all remnants of the tawdry Model-T era that had intruded upon the decaying former capital. Today's three million annual visitors get hands-on history lessons on the tumultuous time when old loyalties to England ran head-on against the new stirrings of freedom eloquently voiced by Patrick Henry.

When the Virginia Convention voted in 1776 for independence, it gave its clear instructions to the Virginia representative to the Second Continental Congress meeting at that time in Philadelphia, Richard Henry Lee. Lee, who was personally against calls for independence and the inevitable war that would result, nevertheless introduced the resolution for Independence. Congress passed Lee's resolution on July 2, and on July 4, 1776, it adopted the Declaration of Independence.

Elsewhere in the Area Colonial Williamsburg is only a few miles from Colonial National Historical Park, which includes Jamestown, Yorktown, and the scenic Colonial Parkway. The oldest academic building in America is part of the nearby College of William and Mary.

Yorktown

Where the British Surrender Ended the American Revolution

Location Southeastern Virginia, 80 miles east of Richmond along the York River. From the north and south take I-95 to U.S. 64 east. From the west and east take U.S. 64. Yorktown lies at the eastern end of the scenic Colonial National Parkway connecting it to Williamsburg and Jamestown.

Yorktown Battlefield is part of the Colonial National Historical Park and is open daily, 8:30 A.M.–5 P.M., with extended hours from April to October. Special celebrations take place every October 19. For more information contact Superintendent, Colonial National Historic Park, P.O. Box 210, Yorktown, VA 23690. Tel. (757) 898-3400. The Yorktown Victory Center ($) museum is open daily, except December 25 and January 1, 9 A.M.–5 P.M. For information contact the Jamestown-Yorktown Foundation of the Commonwealth of Virginia at (757) 253-4838. The village of Yorktown offers privately operated colonial and Revolutionary sites with varying days and times of operation.

Weird War Cries, Germ Warfare, and Night Fighting

Cornwallis chose coastal Yorktown as the station for his troops and naval support because of its strategic mid-Atlantic location. He surrounded Yorktown with redoubts and earthworks. Washington, after a string of demoralizing Continental army defeats in the summer, was looking for the chance to deliver a fatal blow to the British forces. His plans to take New York City from the British didn't pan out, so he decided to seize the opportunity presented by Cornwallis's encampment of nearly ⅓ of the British forces in the United States at Yorktown.

With empty tents set up in New Jersey and fake troop movements, Washington temporarily fooled the British in New York into thinking he still planned to attack there. Leaving some troops behind to guard the city, he relentlessly hurried his Continental army with 5,000 French troops under General Rochambeau 400 miles south beneath a scorching August sun.

Meanwhile, a French-British naval skirmish at Yorktown left French ships blocking Cornwallis's sea escape route. A delighted Washington encamped upriver at Williamsburg. His full army gathered, plus

☛

Frame of Reference Yorktown was the site of the end of the Revolutionary War (1775–83), October 6 to 19, 1781.

Significance Here, General George Washington's army, aided by French troops, bombarded the British under the command of General Charles Earl Cornwallis with 15,000 bombs and cannonballs over nine days. This was the last major battle of the Revolutionary

War. Cornwallis's defeat was a blow from which the British could not recover, and his surrender on October 19, 1781, essentially ended the military fight for independence. Great Britain, however, would stall for two more years before granting independence.

About the Site A Yorktown visit should include a tour of the well-maintained and partially reconstructed Revolutionary battlefield, a walk through the 1691 village of that name with its colonial dwellings, and a stop at the Yorktown Victory Center, a living-history museum of the American Revolution. All are in close proximity.

The seven-mile auto Battlefield Tour includes original British earthworks and reconstructed colonial earthworks, two reconstructed fortified redoubts, cannon and mortar used in the battle, a terrific museum, Surrender Field, and the home where surrender terms were negotiated. Rangers offer battlefield tours in warm months. The battlefield visitor center houses a museum, which features a special children's exhibit, the walk-through half-replica of a British frigate. You'll also find part of the tent (in a climate-controlled, sealed exhibit) that Washington used at Yorktown. The rest of the tent is displayed at the Smithsonian Museum of American History in Washington, D.C. A 16-minute orientation movie at the visitor center theater puts the climactic battle into perspective, depicting the drama of the frustrations Washington faced.

the French troops. Trapped between French ships and Continental troops, Cornwallis seemed doomed. Smallpox also had taken a terrible toll on the British troops.

Desperately, Cornwallis, in a germ-warfare action, ordered the disease-contaminated clothing and equipment of dead soldiers strewn along the road from Williamsburg to Yorktown. He hoped the deprived Continental army troops would take the coveted items and thus spread the deadly pox into their camps. American spies heard of the plan, however, and Washington ordered his men to ignore all British goods along the road when the troops pulled out of Williamsburg on September 28.

With the arrival of Washington's forces, Cornwallis pulled his men into the inner trenches. Washington ordered his troops immediately into the abandoned outer works. Then on the night of October 6, 1,000 volunteers crept forward under cannon fire and stealthily dug a second siege line within 800 yards of the British inner works. Cornwallis hadn't heard or seen the Americans furiously working in the dark!

Now the Americans were within cannon-firing range. They dragged in the heavy artillery, and on October 9 the bombardment began. On October 11 Washington again ordered a second siege line dug. By morning, the trench was within 400 yards of the enemy.

☛

Museums, historic sites, and colonial homes line the narrow streets of historic Yorktown, a smaller village today than it was in colonial times. Visit the cave that supposedly served as Cornwallis's headquarters, the home of Virginia Governor Thomas Nelson Jr. (damaged by Washington's cannon fire), and a reproduction of the largest-known pottery factory in colonial America. For more information call (757) 890-3300.

The Yorktown Victory Center features more than 500 period artifacts, living-history exhibits, a 1780s farm site, and a Continental army encampment. Kids will love it.

Hot Tips You can tour the village and battlefield by car, but to get the most out of the visit plan to walk a good deal. The battlefield walking tour is mostly over grass on uneven terrain. Yorktown village has no sidewalks. Pick up maps of the town and battlefield at the Yorktown Visitor Center or battlefield visitor center.

Even if pressed for time, take the 30-minute, 300-yard walking tour of the siege lines, guided by a park ranger. You can see the actual sites where the armies of Washington and Cornwallis entrenched and faced each other (within 400 yards!) and hear a stirring recount of the battle.

Camping and picnic areas are nearby. Food and accommodations are available in Yorktown.

The Best Stuff The museum at the visitor center is well done and interesting, offering kids memorable hands-on experiences. But the best stuff lies unassumingly on the battlefield. Although you can't walk on the now-grassy earthworks (trenches with mounds of dirt facing the enemy side), you can stand exactly where the British dug 1½ miles of earthworks, trying to ride out Washington's relentless cannon bombardment.

During the Civil War, the original mounds were enhanced by Confederate troops to their present eight-foot height. Artillery actually used in the bombardment stand around the battlefield, placed approximately where they were in 1781. Across 400 yards of open field, you can see reconstruction of the earthworks of Washington's second siege line—dug in one night, 3½ feet deep, 7 feet wide, and 750 yards long.

Reconstruction of Redoubts (forts) 9 and 10, 120-foot mounds ringed with sharpened logs and 12-foot trenches, loom in the distance. You can climb the pentagon-shaped Redoubt 9, hunker in the hollowed center, and stand atop the mounds edging the parapets where Cornwallis's men frantically fired their muskets.

Only Redoubts 9 and 10 kept Washington's inner siege line from stretching to the York River and cutting off all hope of Cornwallis's escape. On October 14 Washington ordered night attacks to capture the two hills. Fighting was fierce and hand-to-hand. Colonial and French troops had unloaded their muskets to keep them from discharging and warning the British. They relied on their courage and bayonets. To ensure that they were not mistaken for the British in the dark, the Frenchmen screamed "Rochambeau! Rochambeau!" as they surged forward. Not quite able to mouth the French name, the continentals allegedly shouted, "Rush 'Em Boys! Rush 'Em Boys!" The redoubts fell quickly.

From these strategic heights, Washington built his largest artillery batteries, able to fire into any part of Yorktown. Today the sharpened "logs" ringing the redoubts are concrete, and the reconstructed mounds are overgrown with grass and wildflowers.

At dawn on October 17, 100 cannons opened fire on the British at close range. About 9 A.M., a young boy in a red coat climbed upon the British defense works and beat his drum, signaling Cornwallis's desire for a conference to arrange surrender. Surrender came on October 19. This defeat was a blow Great Britain could not overcome. America had secured independence.

Washington's army, allied with French troops, took the redoubts in intense and bloody hand-to-hand combat. Cornwallis's troops had built them to ensure that Washington and his allies could not reach the York River and surround them. Continental army troops took Redoubt 9, and the French swiftly followed suit at Redoubt 10.

Then and Now Walking the battlefield today is a thrilling experience if you're at all familiar with the dramatic story of the battle. (Wonderful books for youth are available.) Today's battlefield is cleared of trees but not quite to the extent that Cornwallis cleared them before battle. He wanted no interferences with his artillery fire. The field is dotted with flags and informational plaques. There also are bronze reminders of the 1862 Civil War standoff between Union and Confederate troops preceding the Union offensive into Richmond.

From a key position in the break between the original British inner earthworks and the outer works that Cornwallis abandoned early on, you can see reconstructed Redoubts 9 and 10 and the reconstructed second siege line that Washington's men frantically dug under British fire and cover of darkness. You can imagine how it was during the battle, when Washington's French-American army of 16,000 to 17,000 men bombarded the 7,000 to 8,000 British and German troops for nine days (October 9–17) from those trenches and others.

Harpers Ferry

Where John Brown Raided the Federal Arsenal

Location West Virginia, 65 miles northwest of Washington, D.C., where the Shenandoah River joins the Potomac and where West Virginia, Maryland, and Virginia meet. From West Virginia and Virginia take U.S. 340 to the visitor center, located just south of the highway. A traffic light on U.S. 340 marks the turnoff to the visitor center. Follow the signs.

Harpers Ferry National Historical Park ($; $5 per vehicle; $2 per bus passenger; $3 per walk-in visitor) is open daily, except December 25, 8 A.M.–5 P.M., and in summer months, 8 A.M.–6 P.M. Park rangers conduct tours, and living-history programs are available in warm months. For information contact Superintendent, Harpers Ferry National Historical Park, P.O. Box 65, Harpers Ferry, WV 25425. Tel. (304) 535-6223.

Frame of Reference The raid at Harpers Ferry took place during the tumultuous period leading up to the Civil War (1861–65), on October 16, 1859.

Significance This town is where the famous abolitionist John Brown staged his raid on the federal arsenal in an ill-fated plot to steal the 100,000 weapons stored here, then march South and arm slaves. Brown planned that the freed slaves would join in his guerrilla anti-slavery uprising. Brown's raid in Harpers Ferry (named for town founder Robert Harper, a Philadelphia millwright who once managed a ferry service here) threw gasoline on the flames of North-South division. The Civil War erupted 18 months later.

The rich, multilayered history of this partially restored river village also boasts many significant events in the areas of industry, transportation, environment, the Civil War, and African American history.

Many historic luminaries visited this crossroad, including George Washington (who worked with Congress to establish the federal armory and arsenal here), Thomas Jefferson, Meriwether Lewis (who loaded supplies here before his famous journey West), Robert E. Lee, Stonewall Jackson (who led the capture of 12,500 Union troops here, the largest surrender of U.S. soldiers in the Civil War), George Armstrong Custer (who met his wife here), Abraham Lincoln (who visited on his way to Antietam battlefield), Frederick Douglass, and W. E. B. DuBois (founder of the NAACP) who hosted the second Niagara Movement here in 1906.

The former Storer College cements the town's significance in African American history. The college opened in 1865 in an abandoned armory building and dedicated itself to educating former slaves. Frederick Douglass was a trustee. With desegregation, the college closed in 1955.

About the Site From the visitor center, you'll take a shuttlebus to the ½-square-mile Lower Town, where 16 restored buildings and exhibits, media presentations, and costumed interpreters take you back to pre-Civil War days. The restored John Brown's Fort, in which Brown and his followers barricaded themselves during the final moments of his raid, stands near The Point of the town, along the Shenandoah River, at Arsenal Square.

You can walk the stone streets and brick sidewalks among ruins of 19th-century buildings. You'll find museums, shops, restaurants, and the National Park Bookshop, all housed in brick, stone, and white-clapboard historical structures. Some businesses are privately operated. You'll also see plenty of rolling water and lovely mountain vistas from a network of hiking trails. The Appalachian Trail intersects the park.

Adjacent to the town, the ruins of Virginius Island, a 19th-century industrial town once surrounded by the Shenandoah River and the Chesapeake & Ohio Canal, welcome exploration. Short walks take you to Civil War fort ruins on Camp Hill. (The village's easy transportation and strategic location between Union and Confederate lines made it a hot Civil War property. The site changed hands between the North and the South eight times during the war.) On Camp Hill, where Civil War soldiers pitched tents and drilled, the original Storer College building stands. It now houses National Park Service offices.

John Brown: Famous, Fiery Antislavery Activist

Among the loudest antislavery voices in the mid-1850s was that of John Brown (1800–59). Born to an New England abolitionist family, Brown, with some of his 20 children (most had died), played a violent role in the "Bleeding Kansas" hostilities over slavery in the new territory. Brown went into hiding after a gory massacre of proslavery settlers in Kansas for which he claimed responsibility. He later emerged with New England backers who believed in his plan to wage war with freed slaves as allies against the South.

Brown, ever the activist, raided the Harpers Ferry arsenal in 1859 with his "Army of Liberation," which included three of his sons and some free African Americans. The group overtook the town, seizing several strategic points and hostages. Cornered by local militia, the band held up in the fire engine house, but later U.S. Marines under the command of Robert E. Lee stormed the building and captured Brown. Ten men were killed, including two of Brown's sons. Seven men, including Brown, were taken prisoner. Five escaped.

Brown was brought to trial in nearby Charles Town, found guilty of treason against the Commonwealth of Virginia, and hanged on December 2, 1859. Northern glorification of Brown and Southern disdain of Brown's violent (some said insane) actions and abolitionist beatification, drove a wedge dividing the country even deeper.

Hot Tips Plan to spend at least half a day at the site. A full day is more realistic. Your first stop should be the visitor center, where you can pick up information and maps. After reaching the Lower Town by shuttlebus, first visit the information center on High Street, where there's a small museum.

Dress for the weather, and wear comfortable shoes. Some streets are steep; the brick-and-stone walkways and steps can be slippery. Traffic may be heavy, and the rivers have dangerous currents, so keep a close watch on children. Picnic only in designated areas. No fires are allowed. Restaurants dot High Street, Hog Alley, and Potomac Street, but they are crowded in tourist season. Food and accommodations also are available in nearby Charles Town, West Virginia.

Before visiting Harpers Ferry, read about John Brown. The poet Robert Penn Warren wrote a stirring tribute. Brown's role in bringing on the Civil War is symbolized in a mural in the Kansas State House. Other famous paintings show the fiery abolitionist as a martyr. After his death Union soldiers memorialized Brown by singing this ditty as they went into battle: "John Brown's body lied a-moldering in the grave, But his soul goes marching on. . . ."

The Best Stuff The riveting story of John Brown's 1859 raid on the arsenal places his "fort" at the top of the must-see list.

"John Brown's Fort" stands as the only survivor of the old Harpers Ferry Armory, a cluster of structures that included two arsenal buildings. The small rectangular building has three arched doors and the remains of a cupola atop its slate roof. The building, actually the armory's 1848 Fire Engine House, is where a desperate Brown and 21 of his followers held hostages during a 36-hour siege.

Storer College alumni placed a plaque on the fort's outer wall in 1918. It reads:

> ***That this nation might have a new birth of freedom, That slavery should be removed forever from American soil, JOHN BROWN and his 21 men gave their lives. To commemorate their heroism, this tablet is placed on this building, which has been known as John Brown's Fort.***

Today visitors go inside the fort to sit on wooden benches and hear ranger talks about John Brown's raid.

Then and Now On the eve of the Civil War, Harpers Ferry was a vibrant industrial town. The rivers produced power for the town's mills and factories. Shops, churches, and taverns dotted the landscape, strategically located between the North and South, and at a juncture of the Baltimore & Ohio Railroad, the Winchester & Potomac Railroad, and the Chesapeake & Ohio Canal. Robert Harpers's ferry service, which flourished in the mid-1700s, had become obsolete as bridges spanned the rivers.

Repeated floods, many in recent years, have taken a toll. Little remains of the original town today. Robert Harper's house, the oldest building here, still survives. Wetlands fill the abandoned canals, and only ruins remain of the mills, tannery, iron foundry, pulp company, and federal arsenal where workers produced 600,000 weapons. Interchangeable parts were first introduced at the arsenal. The Upper Town of Harpers Ferry remains a residential area.

Elsewhere in the Area Antietam National Battleground is located 16 miles north.

4

EAST NORTH CENTRAL

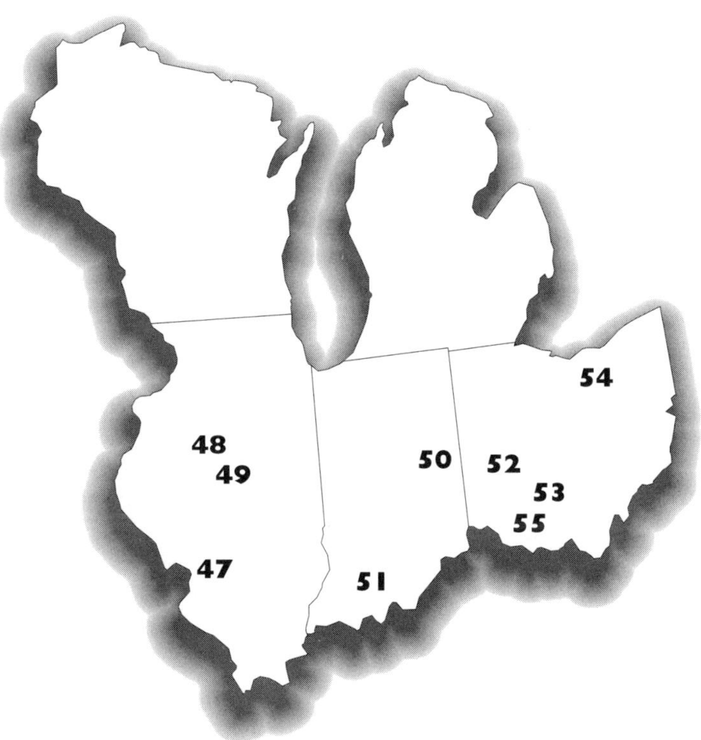

Key

Numbers correspond to site numbers on the map.

Illinois

47. Cahokia
48. New Salem
49. Springfield

Indiana

50. Levi Coffin House
51. Lincoln Boyhood Home

Ohio

52. Dayton Aviation Trail
53. Hopewell Mound City
54. Oberlin
55. Serpent Mound

Note: The **Lincoln Heritage Trail** *(not marked above) runs through Illinois, Indiana, and Kentucky.*

Cahokia

Prehistoric America's Largest Mound City

Location Southwest Illinois, eight miles across the Mississippi River east of St. Louis, three miles west of Collinsville, Illinois. From the east and west take U.S. 55/70 to exit 6. From U.S. 255 north and south take exit 24 to Collinsville Road, then go south onto Ramey Street. Follow signs to Interpretive Center.

The Interpretive Center at Cahokia Mounds State Historic and World Heritage Site is open daily, except Thanksgiving, December 25, January 1, Martin Luther King Jr. Day, Presidents Day, and Veterans Day, 9 A.M.–5 P.M. Ranger-guided tours are offered seasonally and special programs are offered year-round. Kids' Day is held in May. Heritage America celebration is held the last weekend in September. For information contact Cahokia Mounds State Historic Site, 30 Ramey Street, Collinsville, IL 62234. Tel. (618) 346-5160.

Frame of Reference The Cahokia mounds date back to about 1,000 years ago, during the latter part of the prehistoric Mississippian culture (A.D. 800–1000) of Native North Americans. The mound-building society that lived at Cahokia thrived here for about 500 years, reaching its zenith between 800 and 900 years ago (A.D. 1100–1200). The site was first inhabited about 1,300 years ago (A.D. 700). After a period of decline, Cahokia was abandoned by A.D. 1400 for unknown reasons.

Significance Cahokia was the largest prehistoric mound city in North America, reigning as the most influential cultural center of the Mississippian society. The planned city was the largest and most sophisticated prehistoric Native North American city north of Mexico. Cahokia's most massive mound, the 100-foot-high, 14-acre Monks Mound, is the largest prehistoric earthwork in the world. At its height Cahokia had about 20,000 residents.

The site, which French explorers named in the 1600s for a subtribe of the Illini Indians, the Cahokia, was the regional center for numerous outlying hamlets and villages. Major satellite towns existed throughout the area, including large mound cities in St. Louis and East St. Louis. Mounds from these cities no longer exist.

Among the other major Mississippian regional centers of prehistoric southeastern America, only the second-largest mound city, located in today's Moundville, Alabama, rivaled the influence of Cahokia. The people of Cahokia believed their Great Chief, who lived atop Monks Mound, was brother of the sun. Many artifacts excavated here display sun symbolism; rituals may have involved sun worship. Translated, *Cahokia* means "the city of the sun."

About the Site The 2,200-acre site preserves the heart of what once was a six-square-mile city with possibly 120 man-made, earthen mounds and hundreds of pole-and-thatch homes arranged in rows. Today 68 mounds survive. Archaeologists have found many home sites. The most common mounds are rectangular-shaped platform mounds, which probably had buildings on top and were used for ceremonies. Other mounds are conical, containing burials; six are ridges. Ridge mounds may have marked special boundaries, but their function is unclear.

A portion of a high, wooden stockade has been reconstructed. Cahokian workers rebuilt the two-mile stockade three times. The wooden, bullet-shaped stockade had bastions (guardhouses) at equal intervals. It surrounded Monks Mound, a huge open plaza, several important mounds, and homes of the elite. Each stockade took about 20,000 trees to build. Homes of people of lesser social standing stood outside the stockade. Farming fields lay at the edge of the diamond-shaped city boundary.

Monks Mound, named for the French Trappist monks who lived nearby in the early 1800s, was home of the Great Chief. On this enormous mound of four terraces, the Great Chief, head of a complex social order, conducted ceremonies and governed the city. A massive building stood on the summit of the mound, which contained an estimated 22 million cubic feet of earth. Ancient workers mounded the earth basketful by basketful.

The mounds were built in successive stages over long periods of time. Work on Monks Mound may have spanned 300 years. Some think the mound may once have covered 23 acres, more area than the Great Pyramid of Egypt covered. Visitors today can climb 154 wooden steps to the top terrace of Monk's Mound.

The site has a reconstruction of a sun calendar, known today as "Woodhenge." A central observation post stands at the center of the 410-foot circle of 48 large, red-cedar posts. The entire calendar aligns with solstices and equinoxes. Excavations show that Woodhenge, named for the famous, prehistoric stone assemblage in England, Stonehenge, was rebuilt at least five times at this exact location. You can also find these at the site:

- **Museum.** Cahokia's expansive Interpretive Center houses a top-drawer museum and an impressive theater. Here visitors can view a prize-winning, 25-minute orientation slide show, *City of the Sun*, on the hour. The museum's many exhibits, artifacts, hands-on activities, and murals of America's prehistoric civilization are unrivaled. Its centerpiece is a full-size re-creation of a Cahokian neighborhood. Visitors can wander through the village and absorb an average day in the community of 1,000 years ago.

  The Interpretive Center also houses a museum gift shop and café.

- **Tour Trails.** Three self-guided, marked walking trails allow close-up visits to the huge Twin Mounds, Monks Mound, and Woodhenge. It's smart to drive from the Interpretive Center to Monks Mound and Woodhenge. Both now are located across busy Collinsville Road, which intersects the site. Parking lots are at the Woodhenge and Monks Mound sites. The Twin Mounds trail begins at the Interpretive Center.

  A short trail from the Twin Mounds trail leads to Mound 72. Excavations at this small, ridge mound have found 300 ceremonial and sacrificial burials, including four men with heads and hands missing. The main burial seems to be that of a male ruler, about 45 years old, laid on a blanket of 20,000 seashells.

Only about 1 percent of the ancient sites at Cahokia have been excavated and scientifically studied. Excavations have revealed more than 80 buildings—mostly single-family dwellings—thousands of artifacts, and hundreds of human burials.

Hot Tips Plan to spend a full day here. Allow 45 minutes for each of the three walking trails. Dress for the weather, and wear sturdy shoes. Terrain is uneven and can be muddy. Trails are made of wood chips. Monks Mound steps are steep and can be slick. Self-guided tour tapes and gear are available for loan at the information desk in the Interpretive Center. Tour booklets are sold in the gift shop for one dollar. A six-mile nature/cultural trail is open year-round. In summer the public can watch outdoor excavations in progress.

Visitors who plan to take notes in the museum must obtain a permit from the Information Desk. (The museum staff worries that writers will prop notebooks on the display cases and scratch them.)

Do not climb any of the mounds except Monks Mound, where you must use the steps. Do not leave children unsupervised.

The Cahokia Mounds Museum Society book, *Cahokia: City of the Sun*, gives an excellent overview of the site and its history. Order it in advance of your visit.

There's a picnic area on Collinsville Road across from Monks Mound. Food is available at the site. Food and accommodations are found in Collinsville.

The Best Stuff This magnificent park runneth over with gee-whiz sites. But these top the list:

- **Monks Mound.** It's a strenuous climb, but what a view you'll have! Imagine how the Great Chief looked down upon his mighty city 1,000 years ago. Today you'll see a green park at your feet, a crisscross of busy highways, and the St. Louis skyline with its famous Gateway Arch etched against the sky to the west.
- **The Interpretive Center Complex.** This is among the best museums in America. The State of Illinois built the 33,000-square-foot, $8.2-million complex, which opened in 1989. It's an architectural and historic showplace. Outstanding exhibits include an explanation of urban stress in Cahokia, where the population density was 4,000 people per square mile; a basic, prehistoric tattoo kit; and a re-creation of a chieftain burial. Five sunken wells inside the gallery show excavation areas. The award-winning orientation show, using 13 slide projectors, is a must-see.

Then and Now The residents of Cahokia and other Mississippian mound-building communities were successors of the Hopewell civilization centered about 1,000 years prior in Ohio. The Cahokian urbanites took their civilization to more sophisticated levels. We do not know why residents slowly abandoned this mound city, but overpopulation, drought, and decline in resources probably led to economic and political instability.

An 1819 map shows that 26 mounds much like those at Cahokia stood inside the boundaries of St. Louis, an area that was a Cahokian suburb in ancient times. None of the mounds survive in St. Louis, once nicknamed "Mound City."

Each year Cahokia is visited by half a million people. Cahokia is a World Heritage Site, meaning that it makes a unique and valuable contribution to the world's cultural legacy.

Elsewhere in the Area The Jefferson National Expansion Memorial is in St. Louis, 20 miles west; Brooks Catsup Bottle, a 170-foot-high water tank shaped and decorated as a big catsup bottle is on Highway 159 in Collinsville.

Monk's Mound is the largest prehistoric earthwork in the world. *Illinois Historic Preservation Agency*

Springfield and New Salem

Heart of the Land of Lincoln

Location Springfield, the capital of Illinois, is located in the central part of the state. New Salem is 20 miles northwest of Springfield. The Lincoln Home Visitor Center is located in downtown Springfield at 426 South 7th Street. From the north and south take U.S. 55 to downtown exits. Follow brown signs to "Lincoln Home Area," several blocks east of the State Capitol. From east and west, take U.S. 36 to downtown exits. Park ($) at the visitor center on 7th Street, a one-way street.

To reach New Salem, leave Springfield via Jefferson Street, which becomes Route 97. Follow Route 97 to the New Salem park entrance, seven miles northwest of Salisbury and two miles southeast of Petersburg.

The Lincoln Home National Historic Site is open daily, except Thanksgiving, December 25, and January 1, 8:30 A.M.–6 P.M., with extended hours in summer. For more information contact Superintendent, Lincoln Home National Historic Site, 413 South 8th Street, Springfield, IL 62703. Tel. (217) 492-4150.

In addition, 10 Lincoln-related sites in Springfield welcome the public. They are owned and operated by federal, state, and local governments, as well as by private

TOP 10 SITE

Lincoln Heritage Trail

The most interesting way to learn about Abraham Lincoln is to follow the Lincoln Heritage Trail. This self-guided auto tour begins at Lincoln's birthplace near Hodgenville, Kentucky. It winds hundreds of miles through rural areas and cities in Kentucky, Indiana, and Illinois, where Lincoln is buried in Springfield. Among the two dozen sites along the trail are these:

- Abraham Lincoln Birthplace National Historic Site, three miles south of Hodgenville, on U.S. 31E. Here spreads the 348-acre Sinking Spring Farm that Abraham Lincoln's father, Thomas, bought in 1807 for $200. A 19th-century log cabin, symbolizing the tiny, dirt-floored home where Lincoln was born, stands enshrined in a granite, neoclassical temple. Fifty-six granite steps, one for each year the 16th U.S. president lived, take you up to the grandiose structure. The original "Sinking Spring," where the Lincolns drew water, still bubbles next to the six-columned temple. Hiking trails and picnic tables are located at the site.

  The visitor center houses a museum and theater, where you can see an 18-minute orientation film, *Lincoln: The Kentucky Years.* In the lobby, the museum displays the preserved cross section of the huge Boundary Oak that marked a corner of the Lincoln farm. (The oak died in 1976.)

  The site is open daily, except Thanksgiving and December 25, at 8 A.M. Closing times vary. For information contact Superintendent, Abraham Lincoln Birthplace National Historic Site, 2995 Lincoln Farm Road, Hodgenville, KY 42748. Tel. (502) 358-3137. The Lincoln Museum is located nearby in the Hodgenville town square.

entities. Days and hours of operation vary. For more information contact Springfield, Illinois, Convention and Visitors Bureau, 109 North 7th Street, Springfield, IL 62701. Tel. 1-800-545-7300 or (217) 789-2360.

Lincoln's New Salem is open daily, from March through October, 9 A.M.–5 P.M., and from November through February, 8 A.M.–4 P.M. It is closed during most state holidays. For information contact Lincoln's New Salem, R.R. 1, P.O. Box 244A, Petersburg, IL 62675. Tel. (217) 632-4000.

Springfield and Lincoln's New Salem are important sites along the Lincoln Heritage Trail.

Frame of Reference Abraham Lincoln (1809–65) lived in New Salem and Springfield during his adult life. He lived in New Salem for six years, from 1831 to 1837, when he was elected to the Illinois State Legislature at age 28. He lived in Springfield for 24 years, from 1837 to 1861, when he left for Washington, D.C., as president-elect at age 52.

Significance Here in the heart of today's Land of Lincoln, the future 16th president of the United States matured from a somewhat aimless young man into a purposeful lawyer and politician. Lincoln spent 30 years in Illinois, almost his entire adult life. Visits to Lincoln's New Salem Village and the Springfield he loved open a treasure chest of history. Here you will find tangible reminders and uncommon insights into the man who played one of the most important roles in the history of the United States. You can literally walk in the footsteps of Abraham Lincoln.

About the Sites Springfield and Lincoln's New Salem can be visited separately or together as a full-day adventure.

LINCOLN'S NEW SALEM

Lincoln's New Salem is where a 20-something Lincoln spent six years working odd jobs and studying law under the oaks. Here the future president earned the nickname "Honest Abe," for repaying a loan he and a friend had taken out to buy a general store that failed.

New Salem is an authentic log-cabin village, reconstructed

- The Knob Creek Farm, Kentucky, six miles east of Hodgenville on U.S. 31E. An 1800s log cabin re-creates the Lincoln family farm where they lived from 1811 through 1816. The cabin is open April 1 through November 1. For information contact Lincoln Boyhood Home–Knob Creek, Hodgenville, KY 42728. Tel. (502) 549-3741.
- Lincoln Boyhood National Memorial, Lincoln City, Indiana.
- Lincoln's New Salem State Historic Site, Illinois, 20 miles north of Springfield.
- Lincoln Home National Historic Site, 413 South 8th Street, Springfield, Illinois.

For more information on the Lincoln Heritage Trail, contact the Indiana Tourism Development Division (Tel. 1-800-289-6646), the Kentucky Department of Travel Development (Tel. 1-800-225-TRIP), the Illinois Bureau of Tourism (Tel. 1-800-223-0121), or the individual sites. Also contact the Lincoln Museum, 200 East Berry Street, P.O. Box 7838, Fort Wayne, IN 46802-7838. Tel. (219) 455-3864.

Other Lincoln sites around the country include Mount Rushmore in South Dakota; Ford's Theatre and the Lincoln Monument, both in Washington, D.C.; and the memorial where Lincoln delivered the Gettysburg Address at Gettysburg Battlefield in Pennsylvania.

▲

on the actual site of the 160-year-old settlement where Lincoln lived. The village, within a 700-acre park, includes 23 reconstructed buildings. Visitors walk dirt roads among homes, stores, a blacksmith shop, the Rutledge Tavern, a grist mill, a schoolhouse, barns, woodsheds, and even outhouses. The cooper shop is original. Period furnishings adorn each log structure.

Visitors can go inside some of the small buildings, including the schoolhouse, and experience what life was like for Lincoln and his frontier neighbors. Chatty costumed interpreters pepper their tales of New Salem life with stories of Honest Abe.

A grand visitor center houses an intriguing museum, gift shop, and theater where you can see an excellent 18-minute orientation film, *The Turning Point*. A souvenir shop and bookstore are located next door. The site has a seasonal campground, picnic area, and amphitheater that offers a variety of productions in summer months.

Also in summer, visitors can learn about steamboat travel on the Sangamon River via hourly boat trips aboard the *Talisman*.

SPRINGFIELD

The centerpiece of the city Lincoln loved is the two-story house where the Lincolns lived for 17 years. The green clapboard house is the only home they ever owned. The site includes four blocks of Lincoln's neighborhood, most of which has been restored. Interpretive signs along the wooded boardwalks mark 13 houses of Lincoln's neighbors. The lovely neighborhood of graveled streets and once-high prestige is only a short walk from the law offices and the Old State Capitol where Lincoln worked.

The Lincoln Home Visitor Center houses a bookstore and two theaters, where you can see a movie on Springfield and a filmed tour of the Lincoln home. Scheduled visits to the home are by ranger-guided tour only. Tour-group size is limited. Pick up tickets for this free tour at the information desk.

These are other Lincoln-related sites in Springfield:

- **Lincoln-Herndon Law Offices ($).** Corner of Adams and 6th streets across the mall from Old State Capitol. See this by guided tour only. This is the only surviving building in the immediate area where Lincoln practiced law for 23 years. The offices are furnished much as they were when the future president and his third law partner, William H. Herndon, rented space on the brick building's third floor.
- **Lincoln Family Pew.** First Presbyterian Church at 7th Street and Capitol Avenue.
- **Lincoln Ledger.** Lincoln's original account at Marine Bank is on display at the Bank One lobby across 6th Street from Old State Capitol.
- **The Old State Capitol.** This stately, columned building was reconstructed in the mid-1960s with its original exterior sandstone blocks. First built in 1839, the capitol has been restored inside and out to its 1850s appearance. Here the future president's political career took shape. Lincoln gave his famous "House Divided" speech in the semicircular House of Representative chamber in 1858.

  Costumed actors offer a program, *Mr. Lincoln's World at the Old Capitol*, on Friday and Saturday, except in May.
- **The Lincoln Tomb.** Oak Ridge Cemetery, north of downtown. Enter at 1500 Monument Avenue or North Walnut Street. The graves of Lincoln and his family lie within the white granite monument with an obelisk towering 117 feet above the ground. A statue of Lincoln, the U.S. coat of arms, and four military groupings grace the exterior. A bronze Lincoln Head

at the entrance is a replica of the carving by Gutzon Borglum, which resides in the U.S. Capitol. Visitors enter the tomb by a bronze front door into a stately rotunda, then pass through a circular walkway to the red-marble monument marking Lincoln's burial site. Statuary along the walkway depict Lincoln's career. His wife and three sons are buried nearby in the tomb.

Young people especially will enjoy the solemn ceremonies held every Tuesday at 7 P.M., June through August. Soldiers in Civil War costumes lower the American flag, somberly fold it, and present it to someone in the crowd.

Most of Springfield's Lincoln-related sites can be reached by a self-guided walking tour from the Lincoln Home Visitor Center. Plan to drive to Lincoln's tomb north of the downtown area. Trolley($) and carriage tours($) are available downtown.

Hot Tips Set aside a full day to visit all the sites. Pick up maps at the visitor center. A detailed guide of Mr. Lincoln's neighborhood sells for 50¢. Walking is on boardwalks, bricks, and city sidewalks. Surfaces near the Lincoln Home are uneven. Watch for heavy traffic. Food and accommodations are available in the immediate area.

At Lincoln's New Salem limited fast food is available seasonally. A restaurant is located at the park entrance (limited winter hours). Food is available in Petersburg. Dress for the weather. Village "streets" can be dusty or muddy.

The Best Stuff Innocuous scenes in Springfield present surprising epiphanies: the Lincoln Home Victorian parlor, where Lincoln learned of his nomination for the presidency; the front bedroom; the black horsehair sofa in the law office, where Lincoln read the morning newspaper out loud, driving his law partner crazy; and the somber Lincoln Tomb evoke feelings of patriotism and reverence.

Kids will love New Salem and the steamboat ride, a visit to the tavern and a walk to the outhouse. The village offers an exciting, hands-on way to study, as the orientation movie puts it, "this place that changed the man and changed the course of history."

Then and Now Lincoln arrived in New Salem village on the riverboat on which he worked soon after leaving his father's Illinois home. The museum records his neighbors' recollections.

The restored houses in Mr. Lincoln's Springfield neighborhood function as offices today. Trendy restaurants surround Lincoln's law office and the Old State Capitol. But tour guides and interpretive programs at the sites succeed in turning back the clock to Lincoln's time.

Before he left Springfield on February 11, 1861, Lincoln told his law partner to keep their firm's signboard up. When he left Washington, he said, he would return to practice law in Springfield. Herndon later wrote that the president-elect clasped his hand warmly, "and with a fervent 'good-bye,' he disappeared down the street, and never came back to the office again."

Elsewhere in the Area The Illinois State Capitol offers guided tours Monday through Friday, 9 A.M.–3:30 P.M.; the Capitol Complex Visitors Center, 425 South College Street, houses historic exhibits; the Governor's Mansion, the nation's third oldest, offers guided tours Tuesday and Thursday mornings; Oliver P. Parks Telephone Museum is at 529 7th Street; and the 1850s Clayville Stagecoach Stop is 12½ miles west of Springfield on Route 125.

Lincoln Boyhood Home

The Frontier Farm That Shaped a President

Location Southern Indiana in Lincoln City, 30 miles northeast of Evansville, on Highway 162, 8 miles south of I-64. From I-64 take Highway 231 south (exit 57) to Highway 162. Follow signs to the park entrance on Highway 162.

Lincoln Boyhood Home National Memorial ($) is open daily, except Thanksgiving, December 25, and January 1, 8 A.M.–5 P.M. Lincoln Living Historical Farm buildings are open only mid-April through September and briefly in October. Living-history demonstrations and ranger talks take place in summer. For information contact Lincoln Boyhood National Memorial, P.O. Box 1816, Lincoln City, IN 47552. Tel. (812) 937-4541.

Frame of Reference This was Abraham Lincoln's home during his boyhood years from December 1816 to mid-1829.

Significance On this site, in what was called the "Little Pigeon Creek Settlement," stood a small farm hewn from rugged wilderness where the lanky boy who would become the 16th president of the United States grew to manhood. The hardscrabble farm life on Pigeon Creek helped shape Abe during his formative years from age 7 to age 21. Activities in Lincoln's life here included splitting rails, plowing, planting, playing, reading by the fireplace, grieving for his mother, Nancy Hanks Lincoln—who died here when he was 9—and attending school "by the littles." This farm has become part of American folklore. Here is where you can learn about the basic childhood values that sustained the man who led the country through America's darkest period—the years of the Civil War.

About the Site The stone, semicircular Memorial Visitor Center—with sculptured stone panels depicting Lincoln's life, and two connecting Memorial Halls—dominates the site. The state of Indiana built the memorial as a tribute to Lincoln and his family. In addition to Lincoln Hall and Nancy Hanks Lincoln Hall, the visitor center houses a museum, gift shop, and theater. Here you can see a 24-minute orientation film on the young Lincoln, *Here I Grew Up*, narrated by the late U.S. Senator Everett Dirksen.

The Lincoln Living Historical Farm is a re-creation of a self-sufficient Indiana frontier farm just like the 100-acre farm Lincoln's father, Thomas, claimed here in the early 1800s. Although no buildings survive from the original Lincoln farm, the site is authentic. A Lincoln Cabin Site Memorial features the bronze-cast hearth and sill logs of a tiny pioneer cabin, thought to be the remains of the true Lincoln home. A stone wall surrounds the hearth site.

The spring from which young Abe and sister Sarah drew water gurgles here, and you can walk the shady hill where Nancy Hanks Lincoln and other pioneers are buried. An iron fence encloses the small cemetery and the white, arched memorial stone erected on Nancy Hanks Lincoln's grave in 1879.

The 1800s log cabin that represents Lincoln's boyhood home is a tiny, one-room cabin chinked with mud. It has one front window, a front and back door, a small hearth with a log chimney, and a loft.

Three trails crisscross the site. The short Lincoln Boyhood Trail connects the visitor center, cemetery, Cabin Site Memorial, and the farm. The Trail of Twelve Stones begins at the farm and loops back to the cemetery. This unique path offers a hands-on way to teach kids about Lincoln's life. Stones from important sites, such as Gettysburg, Mary Todd Lincoln's home, and the U.S. Capitol, tell the story. The one-mile Lincoln Boyhood Nature Trail takes you through a forest like the one where Abe played as a boy.

A 120-foot flagpole across from the visitor center is the setting for flag-lowering ceremonies on holidays and special occasions, including Lincoln family birthdays. The "garrison" flag used in the ceremonies measures 20 by 28 feet and weighs 45 pounds.

Hot Tips Allow two hours for your visit. Pick up a map and trail guides at the visitor center. Trails consist of gravel and dirt; one includes many steps. Watch for poison ivy, insects, and snakes. Bring beverages. Picnic tables are at the site. Food and accommodations can be found in the nearby towns of Santa Claus and Dale. Camping facilities are available in Lincoln State Park adjoining the memorial. You can mail a postcard from a post office in the visitor center. The postmark will read "Lincoln City."

Levi Coffin House

"Grand Central Station" of Underground Railroad

One of the antislavery movement's most famous leaders was Levi Coffin, a North Carolina Quaker who moved to Newport, Indiana (later called Fountain City), in 1826. During the 20 years Coffin and his wife Catherine lived in Newport, their eastern Indiana home was a refuge for more than 2,000 fugitive slaves, all of whom reached freedom.

When pursued fugitives finally made their way to this rural section of eastern Indiana, all trace of them seemed to disappear. Legend has it that frustrated slave hunters often said, "There must be an Underground Railroad and Levi Coffin must be the president and his house the Grand Central Station."

Coffin's friends convinced him to write *Reminiscences* in order to leave a record of the antislavery movement. Coffin mentioned few names, but his book is a rare record of the 19th-century covert operation.

Today you can visit the Coffins' original eight-room Federal-style brick house where slaves found sanctuary. Among the slaves Coffin helped may have been "Eliza," whose story is told in Harriet Beecher Stowe's 1852 fictional *Uncle Tom's Cabin*. The home, a National Historic Landmark, is located in downtown Fountain City.

To reach the Levi Coffin State Historic Site ($), take U.S. 70 to U.S. 27 north about seven miles. The site is open from June 1 through August 31, Tuesday through Saturday, 1–4 P.M., and from September 1 through October 31, Saturday only, 1–4 P.M. It is closed July 4.

For information, contact Levi Coffin State Historic Site, P.O. Box 77, Fountain City, IN 47341. Tel. (765) 847-2432.

Younger children will enjoy *The Abraham Lincoln Childhood Home Coloring Book* by G. W. Sanders.

The Best Stuff This site breathes life into cherished images of the young Lincoln splitting rails amid a winter frost, or the lanky youth reading *The Life of Washington* before a log-cabin hearth. The historical farm and museum capture the humble beginnings of the man who became an eloquent spokesperson for democracy and a celebrated hero. Here is the best stuff:

- **The Cabin.** Staff dressed in period clothing cook, spin, feed hogs, plow fields, and make lye soap in the yards. Visitors can climb thick wood pegs stuck in the wall beside the cabin hearth. (The six pegs took up less room than a staircase in the one-room cabin.) Take a look in the loft and see what Abe's "bedroom" may have looked like. The plank floor of the 18-by-16-foot cabin was an improvement made in a "prenuptial agreement" between Thomas Lincoln and his second wife, a widow named Sarah Bush Johnston (whom Abe called "my best friend"). She wouldn't live on a dirt floor. She also asked that the walls be whitewashed, which they were.
- **Snakeroot and homework.** The museum exhibits focus on the Lincolns as "Indian territory" pioneers. Look for the display about Nancy Hanks Lincoln's death from "milk sickness," a disease caused by drinking the tainted milk of cows that have ingested a toxic plant called snakeroot. Lincoln later said of his mother, "All that I am or ever hope to be, I owe to my loving angel mother." Study the mounted snakeroot plant and look for it on the farmstead.

  In the museum, you can see copies of four surviving pages of Abe's arithmetic copy book. A re-creation of a typical cabin interior uses hearthstones excavated from the original Lincoln cabin site.

Then and Now This Indiana farm was but one stop along a series of homesites for Thomas Lincoln's family—from Boston to Pennsylvania, Virginia, Kentucky (where Abe was born), and finally to Illinois (where the adult Abraham practiced law).

After 14 years at the Little Pigeon Creek Settlement, Thomas reportedly sold 80 acres of his farm for $125 and traded the fertile 20 acres used for crops for a horse. The Lincolns piled all their worldly goods, including the sturdy, portable front door, into three wagons. The Lincoln Trail Memorial and the Lincoln Memorial Bridge now mark the spot where they crossed the Wabash River from Indiana to Illinois in 1830.

Elsewhere in the Area *The Young Abe Lincoln*, a musical outdoor drama, is performed nightly except Monday, mid-June through August, in the amphitheater at Lincoln State Park next to the Lincoln Boyhood Home. Tel. (812) 937-4710.

Dayton Aviation Trail

Chronicling the Story of Flight

Location Southwestern Ohio, in and around the city of Dayton, called the "Birthplace of Aviation." The visitor center for the Dayton Aviation Heritage National Historical Park is located at 22 South Williams Street downtown. Take West Third Street to Williams, or take U.S. 35 to the Germantown Avenue exit north to Williams Street.

Aviation Trail sites have varying days and hours of operation. The visitor center/Wright Cycle Company Shop for the Dayton Aviation Heritage National Historic Park is open from Memorial Day through Labor Day, weekdays, 8 A.M.–5 P.M., Saturday, 10 A.M.–4 P.M., and Sunday, noon–4 P.M.; the rest of the year, open weekends only, except by appointment. As of Memorial Day 1998, plans call for the visitor center to be open daily except for Thanksgiving, December 25, and January 1, from 9 A.M.–4:30 P.M. For more information contact Dayton Aviation Heritage National Historic Park, P.O. Box 9280, Wright Brothers Station, Dayton, OH 45409. Tel. (937) 225-7705.

For information on other related sites contact Aviation Trail, Inc., Wright Brothers Branch, P.O. Box 633, Dayton, OH 45409. Tel. (937) 443-0793.

Frame of Reference The Trail chronicles the story of flight from ancient times, through the Wright brothers initial work here in 1896, into modern times. The Trail also offers glimpses of the future.

Significance This is where you can experience the unique aviation heritage of Dayton, the Wright brothers' hometown, expanded and polished into the everything-you-may-ever-want-to-know story of flight. Beginning with one of Orville and Wilbur Wright's bicycle shops, you can move on to the prairie field where they perfected their airplane. Next comes an intriguing lineup of monuments, museums, and parks. You can cap the hands-on experience with an amazing up-close-and-personal display of hundreds of aircraft at the Wright-Patterson Air Force Base.

About the Site Dayton's story of flight development is told through a self-guided auto tour of the Dayton Aviation Trail, which includes 45 separate sites, both private and public, some spectacular and some obscure. About a dozen demand time for visiting; others need only drive-by attention.

The federal Dayton Aviation Heritage National Historic Park encompasses four sites, all centering on the Wright brothers. (The park also includes the home of African American writer Paul Laurence Dunbar, a boyhood friend of the brothers.) Other sites range from the United States Air Force Museum—where you'll see an eye-popping display of more than 250 aircraft and missiles, many parked wing-over-wing inside three enormous hangars—to the Wright family graves. The park, authorized in 1992, is under development.

You'll find the national park visitor center in the restored, two-story brick Wright Cycle Company Shop. Here you walk on the wooden floors where Orville and Wilbur trod as they ran their bicycle repair business and printing shop and contemplated flight. The shop houses several original Wright artifacts, including their heavy wooden repair table. The Trail's other sites include:

- **Wright Flyer III.** Carillon Historical Park, 2001 South Patterson Boulevard. Orville himself supervised the restoration of this biwinged flying machine that the brothers used to perfect the art of flying. The *Flyer III* rests in Wright Hall, which Orville helped design. Next door stands a replica of the bicycle shop where the Wrights designed the world's first airplane. (The original building, once located on West 3rd Street downtown, is on display at Greenfield Village in Dearborn, Michigan. You'll find the first airplane the Wrights flew at Kitty Hawk, North Carolina, in the Smithsonian's Air and Space Museum in Washington, D.C.)
- **Huffman Prairie Flying Field,** Wright-Patterson Air Force Base, east of Dayton. In this last remnant of Ohio prairie, the Wrights flew their airplane in 1904 and 1905, mastering the principles of controlled flight. Here, too, they opened the world's first permanent flying school, the Wright Company School of Aviation, where more than 100 of the world's first aviators learned to fly. The Wright's reconstructed hangar stands in the field. From I-675, take Wright-Patterson AFB Areas A&C exit (exit 17) and enter Gate 12A. Stop at the visitor center for a pass and map.

The Wrights operated a print shop in the brick building called the "Hoover Block" in downtown Dayton adjacent to the Wright Cycle Shop. Park plans call for the restoration of this three-story building. The third floor will display the Dave Gold Memorial Parachute Museum. (Dayton is also the birthplace of the modern parachute.)

- **The United States Air Force Museum,** Wright-Patterson Air Force Base on Springfield Street (Route 444) at Gate 28B. Watch for signs.
- **Wright Brothers Memorial,** Route 444 at Kaufman Road, also on the base. The towering, pink-granite shaft overlooks Huffman Prairie Field.
- **Hawthorn Hill,** the Wright home, 901 Harmon Avenue. Although now housing a business, the grand home is worth driving by.
- **Woodland Cemetery,** Wright family burial site, 118 Woodland Avenue.
- **Kettering-Moraine Museum,** 35 Moraine Circle South, houses an exhibit of Wright family memorabilia.
- **Old Court House Museum** of the Montgomery County Historical Society, 7 North Main Street, offers an exhibit on the Wright family.
- **International Women's Air and Space Museum,** 26 North Main Street, Centerville, Ohio, just south of Dayton on Route 48. Highlights achievements of women in aviation and the role of the Wright brothers' sister Katherine in their achievements.
- **Wright B Flyer, Inc.,** Dayton General Airport South, 10550 Springboro Pike, Miamisburg, about ten miles southwest of Dayton. The *Flyer B* is a workable replica of the Wright's first mass-produced airplane (1910–11). Enthusiasts exhibit and fly it.

Hot Tips Don't think you're going to pop into Dayton for a couple of hours and get the whole story. Plan to spend at least a day or two. Get maps in advance. Getting around the trail is confusing. Your first stop should be the Air Force Museum to begin your tour with a bang. There's a tourist information center, open daily, 9 A.M.–5 P.M., with a parking lot. Get your maps and information about sites here.

The only complete listing of all 45 aviation-related sites comes in a 134-page soft cover book, *A Field Guide to Flight: On the Aviation Trail in Dayton, Ohio*, by Mary Ann Johnson. It's available at the national park visitor center, Dayton bookstores, or by mail. Send $14.95 (plus 85¢ sales tax, if you are an Ohio resident) to the Aviation Trail, Inc., Wright Brothers Branch, P.O. Box 633, Dayton, OH 45409. (Make your check payable to the Aviation Trail, Inc.)

You can picnic at the Wright Brothers Memorial on shady Wright Hill as modern jets from Wright Field rumble overhead. Take snacks for your visit to the Air Force Museum, where picnic tables are available but no food can be purchased. Food and accommodations are available throughout the Dayton area. City buses stop at the museum. You can rent audiocassette tour guides of the museum in the gift shop. A short bus ride takes you to a museum annex displaying 50 more aircraft.

A great way to end your Dayton tour is with a visit to Carillon Historical Park ($). The kids will love climbing aboard the lovingly restored 1903 Barney and Smith train car and the City Railway trolley. Plan to spend several hours here among the historic buildings and exhibits. The park is open May 1 through October 31; hours vary. Tel. (937) 293-3638. Snacks are available.

The Best Stuff The Air Force Museum is fabulous; it's probably one of the most interesting museums you'll ever visit. You can walk right up to its 250 aircraft and missiles, weaponry, exhibits, and audiovisual programs to learn the history of flight from man's earliest dreams into the space age. Stare down the needle-nose of the world's first operational Stealth aircraft, first flown in 1983. The price tag for the V-shaped, black war plane that can fly at 684 mph was $43 million. Walk drop-jawed under the white underbelly of an immense, 157-foot-long, 185-foot-wingspan "Stratofortress" used in Vietnam. Sit inside a giant flying "Globemaster" next to a World War II Jeep. Plans call for the first presidential jet, Air Force 26000, to be displayed in the museum. Presidents Kennedy, Johnson, and Nixon used this jet.

Note Oils from hands damage the aircraft. Do not touch!

The IMAX Theater ($) schedules four movies about flight, and the extensive gift shop is an odyssey itself. The museum is open daily, except Thanksgiving, December 25, and January 1, 9 A.M.–5 P.M.

Then and Now Dayton fairly shouts about its aviation heritage. Trolley cars named "Wright Flyer" tool around town. Aircraft from Wright Field (named for the famous brothers) rumble overhead during U.S. Army Air Corps testing. On Wright Hill a bronze plaque with wings reads "In commemoration of the courage and perseverance and the achievements of Wilbur and Orville Wright. . . . They brought aviation to the world."

Elsewhere in the Area The Neil Armstrong Air and Space Museum in the astronaut's hometown of Wapakoneta, Ohio, is about sixty miles north of Dayton off I-75.

Hopewell Mound City

Two-Thousand-Year-Old Ceremonial Graves of "Golden" Culture

Location South central Ohio, three miles north of Chillicothe on Highway 104 in the Scioto River Valley. Take U.S. 35 to Highway 104. Park entrance is two miles north.

Mound City ($), the only complete unit of the Hopewell Cultural National Historic Park currently accessible to the public, is open daily, except Thanksgiving, December 25, and January 1, from Labor Day through mid-June, 8:30 A.M.–5 P.M.; with extended hours in summer. Special events are regularly scheduled, including Archaeology Day and bird walks. In addition to Mound City, the federal park includes Hopeton Earthworks, High Bank Works, Hopewell Mound Group, and a portion of the Seip Earthworks. The state-owned Seip Mound, inside the earthworks 17 miles west of Chillicothe, is open to the public.

For more information contact Superintendent, Hopewell Cultural National Historic Park, 16062 State Route 104, Chillicothe, OH 45601. Tel. (614) 774-1125.

Frame of Reference The Mound City flourished during the first two centuries A.D. during the height of the Hopewell culture of prehistoric Native North Americans from about 100 B.C. to A.D. 500. The Hopewell culture falls into the Woodland tradition of prehistoric Native North Americans (1000 B.C.–A.D. 1000).

Significance This prehistoric ceremonial cemetery survives as one of the most interesting, extensive, and well-preserved clusters of mounds in the Midwestern area where the Hopewell culture flourished. Here the elite and illustrious from the upper tier of the society were buried, along with their fabulous possessions ceremoniously scattered about them. The Hopewell people established a complex, hierarchical society—a complete break from the autonomous communities that had preceded it in ancient America. The society, simply called Hopewell, can be thought of as prehistoric America's golden age.

The Hopewell society of Woodland Native North American Indians is distinguished by the construction of large, geometric earthworks (earthen walls) and a wide-ranging trade network. The trade network encompassed the entire eastern half of what is now America. The Hopewell culture was named after Hopewell Mound City here, which is one of the culture's major constructions. This burial site itself was named for the Hopewell family, which owned the site in the 1890s when excavations began. Two local amateur archaeologists, Ephraim G. Squier and Edwin H. Davis, first documented the mounds here in 1848.

When prehistoric people first arrived on the North American continent from 40,000 to 10,000 years ago, many migrated to the fertile Ohio River Valley just below the receding glaciers. Archaeologists have distinguished two distinctive types of ancient mound-building cultures that eventually developed and were centered in the Ohio Valley. These are the Adena culture (beginning about 3,000 years ago) and the Hopewell culture (about 2,000 years ago). The later, prehistoric Mississippian culture was centered further south and west.

The Hopewell built larger and much more elaborate earthworks than their predecessors. Their sphere of economic, social, and possibly religious influence was unprecedented on this continent. The Hopewell also was the first North American society to raise art to the level of symbolism. It was the first society on the continent to have a class of professional artists, possibly supported by the elite.

The Hopewell Mound City and other sites of important ancient earthworks in the Hopewell Culture National Historic Park lie in the Scioto Valley north and south of Chillicothe. This valley has the largest number and greatest diversity of ancient earthworks in North America.

Mound City represents only the burial aspect of a complex and influential society that prospered for almost 600 years. Other mound sites within the Midwestern center of Hopewell society were ceremonial, possibly used for great festivals and celebrations. One such site stands across the river from Mound City and is an inaccessible

Finding Ohio's Mounds

The Ohio River Valley was a center for America's prehistoric people for thousands of years. The first of the complex, organized societies here was the Adena culture of 3,000 years ago (800 B.C.–A.D. 100), followed by the Hopewell culture (200 B.C.–A.D. 100). (The cultures overlapped.) These societies built thousands of mounds in the area. Across southeastern America, up to 200,000 mounds may have existed.

Prehistoric mounds survive today in 17 states, spanning from the upper Midwest over to North Carolina and down to Florida.

Ancient people built three basic types of mounds: burial, ceremonial (usually flat-topped to support buildings), and effigy, which may be burial or ceremonial. The use of some mounds is unknown. Outstanding examples of effigy mounds are Ohio's Serpent Mound in Adams County and the Effigy Mounds in eastern Iowa. Ohio also has the largest conical burial mound, in Miamisburg. The largest platform mound reigns in Cahokia, just east of St. Louis near Collinsville, Illinois.

Of the thousands of mounds and earthworks that once dotted Ohio, urban expansion and agriculture have destroyed most of them. Mounds in other states have also met the same fate. Only 15 to 20 percent remain nationwide.

Nevertheless, in addition to Hopewell Mound City, these important earthworks survive in Ohio and are open to the public:

- **Serpent Mound.**
- **Miamisburg Mound,** Miamisburg, Ohio, is the largest conical burial mound in Ohio and possibly the United States. The mound, almost 3,000 years old, measures 877 feet in circumference and was originally more than 70 feet high. Visitors can climb 116 steps to the mound summit.

☛

part of the federal park. The Hopewell people lived in small, autonomous villages scattered around the ceremonial mounds.

Hopewell Mound City is one of three major sites of Hopewell society in the Scioto Valley. One, in the western part of the state near Cincinnati, is almost destroyed. The other is the Newark Earthworks, which once enclosed four square miles, northeast of Mound City.

About the Site Mound City comprises 23 remaining burial mounds of different shapes and sizes on 13 grassy acres within an earthwork. The largest mound is elliptical and 65 feet long and 14 feet high. The wall, nearly square in shape with rounded sides, has two opposite, unobstructed entrances, one facing the Scioto River.

All of the mounds in the "City of Graves" have been excavated through the years and restored to their original appearance. The many artifacts and human remains—some skeletal and some ashes—found within the mounds are in storage or on display in prestigious museums throughout the world. You can see a few of these artifacts in the small museum at the site's visitor center.

The visitor center also houses a bookstore and theater where you can view an excellent 17-minute orientation movie, *Legacy of the Mound Builders*. The movie is especially good at fitting the age of North American Mound Builders into world history: while the Greeks were building temples, the Hopewell were building mounds, the narrator tells us.

You can walk among the grass-covered mounds as well as observe the site of several mounds that have been removed to reveal the

- **Fort Ancient,** Miamisburg, Ohio, is a system of 3½ miles of unusual earthworks built 2,000 years ago by the Hopewell Native North Americans on a bluff. Centuries later the Fort Ancient Native Americans built a settlement at the foot of the bluff.
- **Seip Mound,** Paint Creek Valley, off U.S. 50 southwest of Chillicothe. Visitors can climb this 20-foot burial mound once surrounded by two miles of earthworks. Partial earthworks remain.
- **Flint Ridge State Memorial,** in Glenford at 7091 Brownsville Road SE. This was a mother lode of flint used by prehistoric people.
- **Fort Hill State Memorial,** southwestern Ohio south of U.S. 50. Hopewell hilltop enclosure, near Serpent Mound.
- **Moundbuilder State Memorial,** Newark. This circular enclosure was part of Hopewell earthwork complex.
- **Story Mound,** Chillicothe at junction of Delano Road and Cherokee Street. This burial mound is nearly 20 feet high. Get directions at the Hopewell Visitor Center.
- **Leo Petroglyphs State Memorial,** five miles northwest of Jackson, off U.S. 35. This sandstone cliff has 37 incised, prehistoric drawings.

The Ohio Historical Society owns and operates many of the ancient earthworks in Ohio. For more information contact the Ohio Historical Society, 1982 Velma Avenue, Columbus, OH 45601. Tel. (614) 297-2300.

A reconstructed village of a 12th-century ancient culture, SunWatch, is located south of downtown Dayton, just off I-75. For information contact SunWatch, 2301 West River Road, Dayton, OH 45418. Tel. (937) 268-8199.

You can get information on prehistoric mounds in individual states from the U.S. Park Service and state tourism offices.

outline of the wooden charnel houses once inside the mounds. Bodies were cremated in special clay basins of these charnel houses and the bodily remains lavished with worldly possessions. The Hopewell then destroyed the charnel houses and built mounds over them, basketful by basketful. They usually built the mounds in phases to accommodate later burials.

A ¾-mile nature trail encircles the site and skirts the Scioto. Several push-button audio programs help explain Mound City. Rangers lead group tours with prior arrangement.

Hot Tips Allow three to four hours at the site. The area inside the earthen wall is grassy, and the hiking trail is gravel. Stay off the mounds! Ask a ranger for a copy of the park's *Junior Ranger Program*. Kids can earn a neat badge for completing the activities. The Park Service also offers an inexpensive coloring book, titled *The Hopewell Indians*, that nicely explains the Hopewell culture.

Watch the orientation movie first. Without a basic knowledge of prehistoric Native North American cultures, a visit here could be dull; with it, it's very exciting. Check out local libraries and bookstores before visiting. A booklet by Bradley T. Lepper of the Ohio Historical Society, *People of the Mounds: Ohio's Hopewell Culture*, is absorbing and helpful. A reprint by John B. Carlson from the magazine *Early Man 1979* is wonderful. You can find both at the visitor center. The center also sells wonderful replicas by Ohio artists of the ancient pottery pipes and bowls excavated here.

What Does *Prehistoric* Mean?

The word *prehistoric* means "before history," the time before people recorded events in writing. Since early Native North Americans had no written language, the term *prehistoric* refers to the time in North America before the arrival of European explorers, who wrote about their adventures.

Historic times in the New World western hemisphere obviously came after historic times in the Old World eastern hemisphere, where some scholars speculate written language may have developed nearly 5,000 years ago.

America's historic times generally begin in the 16th century.

The Best Stuff To enjoy these earthworks, do some work ahead. With advance reading, you'll spend an unforgettable few hours here imagining life 2,000 years ago. Walking the woodland trail around an ancient cemetery, you can sense what people long ago may have felt while approaching this sacred ground. The serene trail takes you down steps to an overlook at the river. Was this the place where villagers dragged boats ashore and brought their elite dead up the bluff to the mounds?

Across the river lie the remains of the Hopeton Earthworks. There immense earthworks enclose a circle and a square, each larger than the Mound City enclosure. The prevailing thought is that Hopeton served as a great ceremonial center. It's amazing to think of how this now-overgrown area of river valley, still teeming with varied wildlife, once must have moved to the rhythm of a lost society.

Then and Now The land where Hopewell National Park stands today was a choice piece of real estate in prehistoric times. The Scioto connected to other great rivers, including the Ohio 60 miles south, allowing ancient "interstate" travel. The Hopewell could move far and wide in a sophisticated trade network, and people from a great portion of North America could have come here bearing treasures. A welcoming microclimate allowed a wide variety of plant and animal life unusual in similar locales.

What we truly know of Hopewell, however, comes only from the treasures taken from the mounds. The Hopewell had great artists. Their symbolic and beautiful creations in clay and copper were buried along with pearls, mica, and pipes. We don't know, however, why the Hopewell built the mounds. What motivated them to undertake projects involving such intense labor and time? They left no written records.

Until the summer of 1996, one mound here, called Mica Mound for the many sheets of mica covering the four cremated bodies, was cutaway for viewing. Through the glass wall, the sliced-open mound revealed a square clay basin, made by ancient hands, where the cremated bodies had lain. The ashes were on display, but the Park Service has removed these, citing an increased sensitivity to displaying human remains. Now the mound has been restored.

During World War I, a sprawling military training post, Camp Sherman, crossed the mounds, and many were flattened. A barracks was built into the Elliptical Mound. Fortunately the mound floors were spared, and mound restoration began in the 1920s by the Ohio Historical Society. Mound City became a federal site in 1923. Controlled excavations continued into the 1960s.

We don't know how or why the Hopewell society ended. By the time European explorers arrived, the mounds were overgrown and Native North Americans did not know their story.

The Hopewell earthworks was not a political center like the later Mississippian culture chiefdoms found at Moundville, Alabama, and Cahokia, Illinois. Some archaeologists, however, do speculate that Hopewell primarily was a religious center, a sort of Mecca. Others say it was predominately a trade center.

Elsewhere in the Area The outdoor historical drama *Tecumseh!*, about the struggles of the Shawnee Indian leader, plays evenings at the Sugarloaf Mountain Amphitheater in Chillicothe during summer months. For information and tickets contact *Tecumseh!*, P.O. Box 73, Chillicothe, OH 45601-0073. Tel. (740) 775-0700.

The Ohio Historical Center is located in Columbus.

Oberlin

Beacon of the Underground Railroad

Location Northeast Ohio, 30 miles southwest of Cleveland. Take Ohio Turnpike (U.S. 80/90) to Highway 10/U.S. 20 to the exit at Highway 511. Drive north into downtown Oberlin.

Individual sites vary in days and hours of operation, but public parks and the Westwood Cemetery are accessible during the day. For more information about Oberlin contact the Oberlin Chamber of Commerce, 20 East College Street, Oberlin, OH 44074-1613. Tel (440) 774-6262. For information on other Ohio Underground Railroad sites contact the Lorain County Visitor's Bureau, 611 Broadway, Lorain, OH 44052-1803. Tel. (440) 245-5282 or 1-800-334-1673.

Frame of Reference The underground railroad operated during several decades before and during the Civil War (1861–65).

Significance This quiet town exhibited a unique unity and zeal as possibly the most important station along the Underground Railroad, the legendary slave escape network to freedom. Townspeople gained international attention as a "hotbed of abolitionists" in 1858 when a daring mob rescued a fugitive slave who had hidden in Oberlin from slave catchers and a U.S. marshal. If runaway slaves could make it to Oberlin, freedom—often in Canada—was virtually guaranteed.

In 1859 three former slaves who gained their freedom with the help of the Oberlin Underground Railroad joined John Brown during his raid on the federal arsenal at Harpers Ferry, West Virginia. One of them died in the raid; two were later hanged for their participation. In all nine Oberlin families, some black and some white, have been documented as participants in the Oberlin Underground Railroad.

Oberlin College, which dominates the town, was the first U.S. institution of higher learning to enroll African Americans and women. In 1862 Mary Jane Patterson was the first black woman to receive a college degree in America, from Oberlin College.

This college town celebrates its heritage, maintaining a palpable sense of dedication and purpose to people of all races. Oberlin is a living monument to freedom and a necessary stop for people interested in the Underground Railroad.

About the Site Historic sites connected with the Underground Railroad in Oberlin include these:

- **The 1842 First Church in Oberlin** (corner of Main and Lorain streets) where the Oberlin Anti-Slavery Society met. This also was the site for a memorial service for the two men hanged after John Brown's raid, as well as the funeral site for an orphaned, four-year-old fugitive slave child.

- **Martin Luther King Jr. Park** (corner of Vine and Pleasant streets behind post office) memorializes the Civil Rights leader and the "Harpers Ferry Three."
- **Oberlin Westwood Cemetery** (entrance on Morgan Street) is the final resting place for former slaves and leading abolitionists.
- **Underground Railroad Sculpture** (outside Talcott Hall on Oberlin campus at corner of Professor and West College streets).
- **Allen Memorial Art Museum** (corner of East Lorain and Main streets) houses important African and African American art. The museum is open Tuesday through Saturday, 10 A.M.–5 P.M., and Sunday, 1 P.M.–5 P.M. It is closed on Monday.
- **A network of Civil War–era houses** that served as stops on the Underground Railroad, including the Shurtleff/Monroe House ($). Guided tours are offered only on Tuesday, Thursday, and the first Sunday of the month, at 1, 2, and 3 P.M. Giles W. Shurtleff commanded Ohio's first black regiment in the Civil War. James Monroe was Oberlin's leading abolitionist who became a U.S. congressman.

You can also enjoy various community artwork, including the Underground Railroad Quilt at Oberlin Community Center, 80 South Main Street, and an outdoor mural on an office building on Highway 511.

Hot Tips This is not a site for young children. There are no bells and whistles here; the site is cerebral, the sum of its parts. Older children who have studied the Underground Railroad in school should enjoy it.

Get a map for your self-guided Oberlin walking tour from the Oberlin Area Chamber of Commerce, located downtown beside the Oberlin Inn on Main Street. Most sites are an easy sidewalk stroll from the chamber, but you may want to drive to Westwood Cemetery. Allow a leisurely ½-day.

Food and accommodations are available in Oberlin and nearby towns.

To help ensure that older children appreciate the town's heritage, visit your local library or bookstore and get books for younger readers on celebrated abolitionists they probably have learned about in school, such as Harriet Tubman, Sojourner Truth, and Frederick Douglass.

The Best Stuff Don't miss the Underground Railroad sculpture, with its eight true-size railroad ties rising 15 degrees into the air.

At the first fork in the lane through Westwood Cemetery, you'll find a six-foot monument to the runaway slaves who took refuge in Oberlin and died there. The town had these words carved into the monument's black marble:

> ***In memory of the fugitive slaves whose journey to freedom brought them to Oberlin. Shielded by an Almighty arm, Thy griefs and sufferings now are o'er, Beyond the reach of tyrant's harm, Freed spirit, rest forever more!***

Near the monument, a marker shows the grave of Lee Howard Dobbins, the four-year-old fugitive slave orphan who died in 1853.

At Martin Luther King Jr. Park, look for the monuments to those who died with John Brown and one commemorating the "Oberlin Wellington Rescue," when citizens rescued the captured fugitive slave John Price in 1859. Price was waiting in the nearby town of Wellington for return by train to the South. Beneath a preserved photo of the 20 Oberlinians jailed in the incident, all dressed in their Sunday best, the citizens of Oberlin have left visitors with this thought: "With their comrades in the abolition cause . . . they kindled hopes of freedom for us all."

Then and Now When the college and town were founded in 1833 the strongly religious citizens of this small community were devoted to Christian principles of justice, equality, and peace. They felt slavery was an affront to these principles. Oberlin College and the intricately bound town united to guarantee freedom to any slave who made it to this refuge just south of Lake Erie and Canada.

The first recorded Underground Railroad activity took place in spring of 1837, when a former college student transported slaves by wagon toward Canada. Stories abound about Oberlin slave rescues, hidings, and escapes to freedom.

Serpent Mound

Ohio's Quarter-Mile-Long Effigy of Mystery

Location South central Ohio, 34 miles east of Cincinnati, about 30 miles southwest of Chillicothe. From the east and west take Highway 32 or U.S. 50 to Highway 73 north and south. The site in Adams County is about 17 miles south of Hillsboro and 5 miles north of Locust Grove on Highway 73.

Serpent Mound State Memorial Visitor Center ($; $4 per vehicle) is open daily, from Memorial Day weekend through Labor Day, weekdays, 9:30 A.M.–5 P.M., Saturday and Sunday, 10 A.M.–5 P.M., and from after Labor Day through October and April through mid-May, Saturday and Sunday, 10 A.M.–5 P.M. For information contact Serpent Mound State Memorial, 3850 State Route 73, Peebles, OH 45660. Tel. (937) 587-2796. The Ohio Historical Society operates the site. Contact the organization at 1982 Velma Avenue, Columbus, OH 43211-2497.

Frame of Reference Serpent Mound was built about 900 years ago, A.D. 1070 plus or minus 70 years.

Significance Prehistoric Native North Americans built this enigmatic mound of stone and earth in the shape of a giant, uncoiling snake for unknown reasons. Serpent Mound reigns as the most famous and most visited of the ancient mounds, but it may also be the least understood. The ¼-mile-long snake is the largest effigy mound in North America. This site may be the first archaeological memorial in the United States. The Ohio legislature passed laws to protect it in 1888.

About the Site The great serpent uncoils in seven deep curves atop an isolated ridge 90 feet above Ohio's Brush Creek. An asphalt walking path with benches encompasses the effigy, generally following its curved, 1,348-foot form undulating over the hilly terrain. The effigy, restored in 1889 after early archaeological exploration, averages 20 feet wide. Height varies from 2 to 6 feet.

You can view the snake from above on a 25-foot, steel walk-up tower built in 1908. Four stone steps allow you to walk over the coiled tail on the cliff overlooking Brush Creek. A small museum houses exhibits on the mound and on archaeologist Frederick Ward Putnam of Harvard University's Peabody Museum. Putnam conducted the first systematic archaeological study of the serpent and three burial mounds also in the park.

The burial mounds were built by people of the Adena culture (beginning about 3,000 years ago) who lived here long before Serpent Mound's construction by the later Fort Ancient people.

Hot Tips Allow 1½ hours to take in Serpent Mound, the museum, and the burial mounds.

The park has picnic tables. Food and accommodations are available in nearby towns and Hillsboro. However, a gift counter in the museum does offer light snacks.

The primitive restrooms have no running water. Bring disposable wipes for washing hands.

A hiking trail winds around the base of the ridge. Use extreme caution on this trail, which has loose stones and steep drops. Watch out for young children when climbing the observation deck and walking near the creek.

The Best Stuff This is a fun place to see on your way to somewhere else, possibly the Hopewell sites of Chillocothe. Walk around Serpent Mound and contemplate the theories of its existence. Was it an ancient plea for rain? A prehistoric calendar? A symbol of religious fervor? A charm to ward off evil? No human bones or artifacts have been unearthed here to give clues to why prehistoric people built Serpent Mound or why they chose this sacred place. (The lack of human remains, however, has ruled it out as a burial mound.) Some investigators have noticed that a portion of the cliff's face, protruding beneath the serpent's head, resembles a snake, hence the name. Check it out for yourself.

Then and Now Early Ohio settlers knew of Serpent Mound, but it was formally introduced to the scientific community in 1848 by Ohio archaeologists Ephraim G. Squier and Edwin H. Davis in their *Ancient Monuments of the Mississippi Valley*. They also mapped the Hopewell Mounds and others. Drawings through the years vary. Sometimes the large oval looks like a striking snake's head; other drawings show it as an eye on the snake's head. At times the oval appears to be a toad or an egg that the snake is swallowing.

A stone "wall" may have once traversed the oval. Small horns may have been below the head, and a "tongue" may have extended from the head. Today, after centuries of erosion and reconstruction, it looks like a mere oval with openings on each side. A scraggly cottonwood clings to life in the oval's center.

Since 1887 Serpent Mound has served as a public park attracting gawkers and picnickers alike. Renewed archaeological studies in 1991 spawned new theories about Serpent Mound, including one that embraces the astronomical alignments of the snake's curves. This theory boosts the argument that the effigy was a calendar marking planting and harvesting seasons or the time of religious and ceremonial activities. The snake has been an important symbol from prehistoric times. Native North Americans still regard the mound as a sacred place.

Elsewhere in the Area See Finding Ohio's Mounds.

5

WEST NORTH CENTRAL

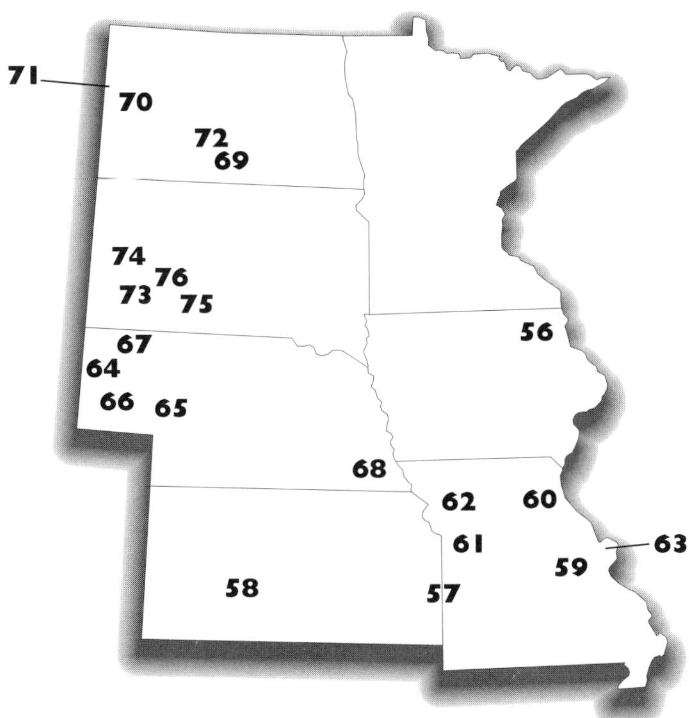

Key

Numbers correspond to site numbers on the map.

Iowa
56. Effigy Mounds

Kansas
57. Fort Scott
58. Fort Dodge

Missouri
59. Daniel Boone's Home
60. Hannibal
61. Independence
62. Pony Express Stables
Pony Express Trail
(see National Trail System Map on page xv)
63. St. Louis

Nebraska
64. Agate Fossil Beds
65. Chimney Rock
66. Scotts Bluff
67. Fort Robinson
68. The First Homestead

North Dakota
69. Fort Abraham Lincoln
70. Fort Buford
71. Fort Union Trading Post
72. Knife River Indian Villages

South Dakota
73. Crazy Horse Memorial
74. Deadwood
75. Wounded Knee
76. Mount Rushmore

Effigy Mounds

Prehistoric Burial Sites in the Shape of Animals

Location Northeastern Iowa, on the western bank of the Mississippi River, across from Prairie du Chien, Wisconsin, and three miles north of Marquette, Iowa, on Highway 76.

Effigy Mounds National Monument Visitor Center ($) is open daily, except Thanksgiving, December 25, and January 1, from Memorial Day through Labor Day, 8 A.M.–6:15 P.M., and the rest of the year, 8 A.M.–4:30 P.M. Reservations are required for school groups. For more information contact Superintendent, Effigy Mounds National Monument, R.R. 1, P.O. Box 25A, Harpers Ferry, IA 52146-7519. Tel. (319) 873-3491.

Frame of Reference The oldest effigy mounds here are more than 2,000 years old; the newest are about 700 years old. (Some conical mounds are 2,500 years old; their construction began in the Hopewell period.) The Effigy people built the mounds from around A.D. 350 to A.D. 1400, in the late Woodland period of prehistoric America (1000 B.C.–A.D. 1000).

Significance Effigy mounds built in the shape of animals are unique to the upper Mississippi Valley. This park preserves a spectacular group of these ancient ceremonial mounds of effigies—cameo representations of living creatures such as eagles, falcons, bison, deer, turtles, lizards, and, in particular, bears. Prehistoric mounds are found in much of America, but animal effigy mounds such as these exist only in areas of southern Wisconsin, southeast Minnesota, and northeast Iowa. Why the Effigy people built these low-relief shapes remains a fascinating mystery.

About the Site Within the park's 1,481 acres rise about 200 mounds, 29 of which take the form of effigies. The rest are conical, compound, or linear. A typical effigy is 3 to 4 feet high and 75 feet long. Bird wingspans may reach 100 feet. The largest effigy, the Great Bear Mound, is 137 feet long and 70 feet wide at the shoulder.

The Yellowstone River divides the park into north and south units. Eleven miles of hiking trails connect the mounds. Park at the visitor center to reach the north unit, where you can view the Great Bear Mound, Little Bear Mound, and others. This unit boasts spectacular scenic views from bluffs of the Mississippi Valley. The unit has six miles of gravel trails. The shortest is a two-mile loop.

Trailside exhibits and markers tell the story of the mounds.

To reach the south unit, park at the Iowa Department of Natural Resources (DNR) day-use area on Highway 76, ½ mile south of the visitor center. This unit has five miles of hiking trails over old logging and military roads. The trail to the Marching Bear Group is a four-mile loop.

The visitor center features a model of the monument, a museum showing artifacts and a natural-history display, and a theater where you can see a 14-minute audiovisual program, "Earthshapers."

Hot Tips Allow a day for your visit. Don't come here if you don't like hiking. If you do and if you have an interest in prehistoric America, this is a great outdoor experience. Visit with older kids only. Your first stop should be the visitor center. Come prepared for the weather, and bring insect repellent in warm months; there are a lot of mosquitoes. Watch for ticks and poison ivy on the trail. Stay clear of the cliffs. Do not disturb the mounds or anything else in the park.

Although the visitor center has drinking fountains, bring water or beverages. Picnicking is not allowed at the site, but tables can be found at the Iowa DNR day-use area and at Pikes Peak State Park on Highway 340, two miles south of McGregor, Iowa. Food and accommodations are available in Prairie du Chien.

The Best Stuff Walking this sacred prehistoric area is a feast for the eyes and spirit. Some of the cliffs overlooking the Mississippi are 300 feet high and afford remarkable views. From the Third Scenic View, you can see the islands that make up the Upper Mississippi River National Wildlife and Fish Refuge. The plant and animal life thrive in abundance; watch for the white-tailed deer and red fox.

Then and Now When white settlers moved into this region in the early 1800s, their farming and logging began a process of destruction of the mounds. Local groups began a movement to preserve those mounds remaining, and the site was declared a national monument in 1949.

Although we don't know why the effigy mounds were built, we do know how. Archaeological studies have revealed that Effigy people first outlined their shapes with shells, then mounded dirt, basketful by basketful, within the outline. Ceremonial fires burned at the head, flank, or heart of the animal.

We also don't know what happened to the Effigy Mound builders, if they left the region or stayed in place and changed their culture. We do not know who their descendants are. We have only their works to enjoy.

Elsewhere in the Area Historic Prairie du Chien has many interesting sites including Villa Louis Historic Site, Fort Crawford Medical Museum, and Mississippi paddleboat cruises. For information contact Prairie du Chien Area Chamber of Commerce, P.O. Box 326, Prairie du Chien, WI 53821. Tel. 1-800-PDC-1673.

Fort Scott

Legendary Frontier Fort of Nine Lives

Location Eastern Kansas, near the Missouri border, 90 miles south of Kansas City and 60 miles northwest of Joplin, Missouri. From the north and south take U.S. 69 to the town of Fort Scott. From the east take U.S. 64; from the west, U.S. 54. The park is located downtown near the intersection of U.S. 69 and U.S. 54. Watch for signs.

Fort Scott National Historic Site ($) is open daily, except Thanksgiving, December 25, and January 1, 9 A.M.–5 P.M., with extended summer hours. Year-round activities include a Mexican War encampment the first weekend after Labor Day and American Indian Heritage Weekend the second weekend in October. For information contact Superintendent, Old Fort Boulevard, Fort Scott, KS 66701. Tel. (316) 223-0310.

For information on the historic town of Fort Scott contact Visitor Information Center, 231 East Wall Street, Fort Scott, KS 66701. Tel. 1-800-245-FORT.

Frame of Reference Fort Scott was occupied periodically during the mid- to late-19th century, during American westward expansion and the establishment of a permanent Indian frontier. The U.S. Army built the fort in 1842 and abandoned it in 1853 as the frontier moved further west. But the fort's military life revived periodically during 1862 to 1873. Civil War troops occupied fort buildings in 1862, selling them to private citizens in 1865. The town of Fort Scott and the fort buildings then went on to host significant historic events and military reoccupation through 1873.

Significance Like the proverbial cat, this small but strategic frontier fort lived nine lives during its legendary three decades of history. The fort reflects the story of the chaotic American frontier and the dark Civil War era. It is America's only restored military post of the 1842 to 1853 frontier period.

Fort Scott, named for Winfield Scott who was appointed General-in-Chief of the Army in 1841, stood along the "Military Road," a string of forts running along the frontier from Minnesota to Louisiana. At the time the string of frontier forts divided white settlements from the permanent Indian territory.

The 155-year-old fort's nine historical lives are as follows: protector of the American frontier, participant in the Great Sioux War, safeguard for Santa Fe Trail travelers, participant in the Mexican War, peacekeeper in the "Bleeding Kansas" period, Civil War supply center and hospital, gathering point for the nation's first recruited black soldiers, guardian of California gold-seeking trails, and protector of the railroad builders.

Fort Scott's history is laced with exploits of elite frontier troops known as the Dragoons. Dashingly outfitted in blue uniforms with red sashes, gold epaulets, and high hats with large tassels, these highly trained men could fight on foot or horseback. They were proficient with a variety of weaponry. These frontier warriors, stationed not only at Fort Scott but other contemporary forts, impressed friend and foe alike.

About the Site Fort Scott has been restored to its 1848 appearance, with 20 structures and 33 historically furnished rooms open to visitors. Four of the green, wooden buildings are original, including the 1843 hospital, 1845 officer housing, quartermaster storehouse, and post bakery. Reconstructions include the infantry barracks, Dragoon stables, Dragoon barracks, post headquarters, guardhouse (jail), and magazine. The buildings surround an open parade field with reconstructed magazine and well canopy. Visitors also can view the remains of privies and a restored tall-grass prairie.

A visitor center, housed on the first floor of the hospital, has a small bookstore. The two original hospital wards upstairs are authentically furnished. The infantry barracks next door house a small museum and video nook, where an orientation video tells the Fort Scott story. Tours are self-guided, but rangers offer guided tours and interpretative programs seasonally. Pick up a map at the visitor center.

The town of Fort Scott, the second-oldest white settlement in Kansas, offers a picture-book walk through history with its rows of restored Victorian shops, brick streets, historic homes, and parks. The 1862 Fort Scott National Cemetery, one of 12 original national cemeteries, is nearby.

The Forts of Kansas

Here is a list of historic forts in Kansas. An asterisk (*) indicates best bets for a family visit. These sites are easily accessible, can be toured fairly quickly, and offer attention-grabbers that might appeal to kids.

- **Fort Leavenworth,** 7th Street and U.S. 73, Leavenworth. This is the oldest U.S. Army fort in continuous use west of the Mississippi. Built in 1827, the fort is home of the U.S. Army Command and General Staff College. The Frontier Army Museum, 100 Reynolds Avenue, is open Monday through Saturday, 10 A.M.–4 A.M., Sunday, noon–4 P.M., and closed Easter, Thanksgiving, Christmas, and New Year's Day. Tel. (913) 684-5604.
- **Fort Riley,** exit 301 off I-70 in Junction City. This fort was built in 1853 and still is active. Here Lieutenant Colonel George Custer formed his 7th Cavalry Regiment in 1866. The fort's schools served as the center for the evolution of cavalry tactics and training. Today it is a major army training center. The U.S. Cavalry Museum is open daily, except holidays, Monday through Saturday, 9 A.M.–4 P.M., and Sunday, noon–4:30 P.M. Tel. (913) 239-2737.
- ***Fort Larned,** 6 miles west of Larned on Highway 156. The fort is one of the best surviving examples of Indian wars–era frontier forts. The fort has nine original buildings, a reconstructed blockhouse, 40 furnished rooms, restored parade grounds, visitor center, orientation film, museum, and bookstore. It offers guided tours and living-history programs. It is open daily, except Thanksgiving, December 25, and January 1, 8 A.M.–5 P.M., 6 P.M. summer. Tel. (316) 285-6911.
- **Fort Hays,** U.S. 183 Alternate in Hays. This fort includes four original buildings and living-history demonstrations on summer weekends. It is open daily except holidays, Tuesday through Saturday,

Hot Tips Allow three hours to see the fort and town. Be prepared to walk over rough and sometimes muddy terrain and to negotiate steep stairs. Dress for the weather. The town offers hourly trolley tours April 1 through the first weekend in December. Food and accommodations are available in Fort Scott. Picnicking is available at Gunn Park. Campgrounds are nearby.

The Best Stuff With a little information and imagination, two stories of the fort come to life here: the Dragoons and the fiery events during the Bleeding Kansas period from 1855 to 1861.

The life of Dragoons stationed at Fort Scott was usually uneventful. But in 1845 they were part of a famous excursion known as the Kearney Expedition. Led by Colonel Stephen W. Kearney, the Dragoons joined a 2,000-mile-long military trip across the West in 99 days. The expedition was to protect travelers on the Oregon and Santa Fe trails. The flashy Dragoons also helped to impress the Native Americans and the British with American power, which was the mission's true goal.

Today, Fort Scott visitors can get a flavor of the Dragoons' dashing life in the 210-foot-long Dragoon stables, where 30 horse stalls are fully reconstructed.

Two Fort Scott buildings remind us of the town's position in the vortex of the Bleeding Kansas struggles preceding Kansas's admission to the Union. After the Kansas Territory had been created in 1854, Kansas settlers had the right to decide if the territory would enter the Union as a free state or a slave state. Landowners

9 A.M.–5 P.M., and Sunday and Monday, 1 P.M.–5 P.M. Tel. (913) 625-6812.

***Fort Dodge,** five miles east of Dodge City on Highway 154. Several buildings are open to the public for self-guided tours. This site currently serves as Kansas Soldier's Home. Tel. (316) 227-2121.

Fort Dodge can be part of a tour of legendary **Dodge City.** Here visitors can walk or take auto tours of the most notorious of the Western cowtowns. You'll get a real sense of the late 19th-century Wild West and the era of the American cowboy.

Sites here include the Boot Hill Museum, Santa Fe Trail ruts tract, Fort Dodge Jail, a one-room schoolhouse, the historic homes and reconstructed businesses of the original Front Street, 16 miles of brick streets, Gunfighters Wax Museum, statues, and the re-created Long Branch Saloon. (Parents may remember this structure made famous on the TV series "Gunsmoke" that ran from 1955 to 1975.) In addition, Boot Hill Cemetery gives mute testimony to the cowtown's violent past.

For information on Dodge City, contact Dodge City Convention and Visitors Bureau, P.O. Box 1474, Dodge City, KS 67801. Tel. (316) 225-8186.

Fort Harker, located on private property on the west side of Kanopolis on Highway 140. This is open to the public only during Fort Harker Days, the second weekend in July. Tel. (913) 472-4071.

Fort Wallace, just east of Wallace on U.S. 40. All that remains of the original fort is the old post cemetery, enclosed by stone walls within the Wallace Township cemetery. The rest of the original site is on private property. Call for access. Tel. (913) 891-3538.

For information on historic forts in Kansas, contact the Department of Commerce and Housing, Travel and Tourism Development Division, 700 Southwest Harrison, Suite 1300, Topeka, KS 66603. Tel. 1-800-2-KANSAS, ext. 30. Ask for the brochure on Kansas frontier forts or one titled *Guarding the Plains.*

▲

clashed—sometimes violently—over the issue. Adding fuel to the flames was the fact that Kansas and Missouri were on opposite sides of the issue. Missouri "border ruffians" crossed the border into Kansas on election day to vote for proslavery candidates. Border squabbles were common and often violent.

The former Fort Scott, located right on the Missouri-Kansas border, found itself in a unique situation. The fort's old officer quarters had become the Fort Scott Hotel, known locally as "the free-state hotel." Here agitators who opposed slavery and wanted Kansas to enter the Union as a free state gathered.

Directly across the former parade ground, in the former army barracks, stood the Western Hotel. This was known as the proslavery hotel, where folks on the opposite side of the issue gathered. Fighting between the two camps often erupted. The army again was brought back to Fort Scott in February 1858 to restore peace.

Today the antagonistic "hotels" still face each other but are restored and furnished as they were in the frontier days of the fort.

Then and Now Ironically, a military presence at Fort Scott wasn't really needed until after the army abandoned the fort in 1853. The frontier was relatively quiet. No fighting ever occurred at the fort itself. A soldier's life consisted of tedious drills and boring work at the fort spiced with rare military excursions into Indian territory and in the Mexican War. Alcohol abuse, illness, desertions, and harsh punishment for small infractions were part of life.

By the early 1850s a small village surrounded the fort. In the decade after the frontier had passed, the village and fort played key roles in the Bleeding Kansas squabbles, the Civil War, and the Santa Fe Trail.

By 1869 plans to extend the railroad, specifically the Missouri River, Fort Scott and Gulf Railroad, ignited violent land disputes. Again, the army returned to Fort Scott, this time to protect railroad workers. With the coming of the railroad in 1872, the town of Fort Scott boomed and put down deep roots. The army abandoned the fort again in 1873. This time was truly the last time.

Elsewhere in the Area Marais des Cygnes Massacre Site, where Missouri border ruffians gunned down 11 Kansas men in 1858 over land squabbles is 30 miles north of Fort Scott. The state site is located just northeast of Trading Post, Kansas. Exit U.S. 69 at a country road one mile north of Highway 52. Follow signs east. For information contact Marais des Cygnes Massacre State Historic Site, R.R. 2, P.O. Box 157, Pleasanton, KS 66075-9487. Tel. (913) 352-6174.

Hannibal

Home of Tom, Huck, Becky, and Mark Twain

Location Northeastern Missouri at the Illinois border, 85 miles west of Springfield, Illinois. To reach the Hannibal Historic Area, take U.S. 36 (Mark Twain Avenue) into the downtown area at Mississippi Riverfront. The Mark Twain House and most related sites are located in or near a pedestrian mall between Main and 3rd streets at Hill Street, one block south of U.S. 36. Follow the signs.

Historic Hannibal sites are privately operated. Days and hours of operation vary. The Mark Twain Boyhood Home and Museum ($) is open daily, except Thanksgiving, December 25, and January 1, in summer months, 8 A.M.–6 P.M., in spring and fall, 8 A.M.–5 P.M., from November through December, 10 A.M.–4 P.M., from January through February, 10 A.M.–4 P.M., Sundays, December through February, noon–4 P.M., and in March, 9 A.M.–4 P.M. For information contact Mark Twain Boyhood Home and Museum, 208 Hill Street, Hannibal, MO 63401. Tel. (573) 221-9010. Guided tours ($) of the home and nearby related sites begin at the adjacent Museum Annex.

Mark Twain's House

You can visit the Hartford, Connecticut, house Twain had built in 1874 and lived in with his family until 1891. At this lavish mansion, Twain wrote seven major works, including *Tom Sawyer* and *The Adventures of Huckleberry Finn*. The historic Mark Twain House ($) is open daily, except Thanksgiving Day, December 24 and 25, January 1, and Easter. Hours vary by season. Visits are by guided tour only.

For information contact Visitor Center, The Mark Twain House, 351 Farmington Avenue, Hartford, CT 06105. Tel. (860) 493-6411.

The Mark Twain Cave ($) is open daily in summer, 8 A.M.–8 P.M., from April through early October, 9 A.M.–6 P.M.; and from November through early March, 9 A.M.–4 P.M. For more information contact the Mark Twain Cave, P.O. Box 913, Hannibal, MO 63401. Tel. (573) 221-1656.

For information on other historic sites in Hannibal, contact the Hannibal Visitors and Convention Bureau, 505 North 3rd Street, Hannibal, MO 63401. Tel. (573) 221-2477.

Frame of Reference Hannibal was the boyhood home of Samuel Langhorne Clemens (1835–1910), better known as Mark Twain (his pen name), during the era when steamboats dominated the Mississippi and slavery inflamed the nation. The Clemens family moved to Hannibal in 1839 when Twain was four. Twain left Hannibal as a young man at the outbreak of the Civil War.

Significance This town on the Mississippi River, 100 miles north of St. Louis, is famous as Mark Twain's boyhood home. Twain was the first great American writer born and raised west of the Appalachian Mountains and the first to write in an American vernacular. His works raised the level of humor to high art; his books and lectures made him a world celebrity. Twain's works have been translated into more than 60 languages.

Hannibal, a frontier village of 2,000 people in Twain's youth, is the setting of his greatest books, including *The Adventures of Tom Sawyer* (1876) and *The Adventures of Huckleberry Finn* (1884), considered his masterpiece. Twain's characters and much of what he wrote about were taken directly from his youth here.

A historic area at the town's waterfront, where the Mississippi yawns half a mile wide, protects the writer's boyhood home. The small area also includes a handful of the other homes and buildings that played important roles in Twain's formative years and later in his books. So securely are Twain's boyhood adventures etched into American's memory that 179-year-old Hannibal dares bill itself as America's hometown.

What's In a Name?

When Samuel Langhorne Clemens became a writer, he used a term familiar to his boyhood on the shores of the Mississippi River as his pseudonym. When the riverboats huffed into Hannibal, a leadsman in the bows would constantly heave a line into the river waters and call out the depths. When he saw that the river's depth was two fathoms deep, the leadsman would cry out "By the mark, twain!" This meant the boat was safe, with 12 feet of water beneath it. The exclamation "mark, twain" was a welcome sound in Hannibal.

About the Site Several blocks of the riverfront are dedicated to Twain's boyhood. The town has transformed a brick section of Hill Street between Main and 3rd streets into a pedestrian mall. Twain sites here include Twain's quaint, two-story, clapboard boyhood home, fully restored in 1990; the Mark Twain Museum next door in a historic stone building; the Mark Twain Museum Annex behind the Twain home; the J. M. Clemens law Office, where Mark's father presided as Justice of the Peace in 1841; the 1830s Pilaster House/Grant's Drug Store, where the Clemenses once lived upstairs and the drug store operated downstairs; and a whitewashed replica of "Tom Sawyer's fence."

The museum houses Twain memorabilia, first editions of Twain's works, one of the writer's famous white suits, and a series of Norman Rockwell paintings used for editions of *Tom Sawyer* and *Huck Finn*. The Annex offers an orientation slide show.

Also in the pedestrian mall area are Becky Thatcher's House ($), the 1840s home of Twain's childhood sweetheart Laura Hawkins, immortalized as Tom Sawyer's love, Becky Thatcher; the Haunted House on Hill Street Wax Museum ($); the bronze Tom and Huck statue by Frederick Hibbard at the foot of Cardiff Hill; the sites of Muff Potter's jail and Huck's house; and the Mark Twain Memorial Lighthouse atop Cardiff Hill. The white, wooden lighthouse was first dedicated in 1935 in celebration of the 100th anniversary of Twain's birth.

The entire historic area teems with restored Victorian buildings, now housing candy stores, ice cream parlors, antique shops, souvenir stores, theme restaurants, and exhibits.

Private companies offer tours ($) by trolley, train, and riverboat.

The Mark Twain Cave ($) (Cameron Cave), one mile south of Hannibal on Highway 79, offers guided tours, restaurants, a large gift shop, and camping. Here Tom, Becky, and Huck explored the far reaches of the cave, as did the young Clemens. Hannibal offers a variety of entertainment venues with Mark Twain themes.

Hot Tips The entire family should enjoy this site. Allow half a day. Plan to spend more time if you're interested in the tours and related attractions. Begin at the Twain Boyhood Home and Museum near the U.S. 36 bridge over the river. Guided tours of related attractions begin in the Museum Annex. Park on the street or in small, nearby parking lots. Pick up information and maps at the visitor center at the site. Dress for the weather, which can be extreme. Walking is mainly on sidewalks. Wear a light wrap in the cave, where the year-round temperature is 52 degrees.

Snacks and food are available in the historic district. Food and accommodations are in the immediate area. Campgrounds are nearby and at the Mark Twain State Park in Florida, Missouri, 40 miles southwest.

The Best Stuff Shuffling around this picturesque town and eating ice cream and gawking at the Twain sites is delightful. Older kids who've read about Tom and Huck in school will enjoy this trip back in time, as will their parents. The quaint shops, the brick street, the mighty Mississippi riverfront, the riverboat—together, they evoke bygone days of paddleboats, pirates, childhood, and dreams.

The trip's top attention-grabber is the Mark Twain Cave. Walk inside the cave's mouth, shaped like the letter A and find the excitement Tom and his buddies found. The 55-minute tour loop reveals fantastic limestone formations like Alligator Rock, Injun Joe's Canoe, and Hanging Shoe.

Then and Now Twain's sleepy 1840s village that awoke only when the riverboats arrived now has 18,000 residents. The riverboats still roam the river blowing their whistles, but only for show. Tour guides point out Jackson Island and Lovers' Leap.

Floods have wiped out much of the riverfront. Today a low flood wall built in 1993 protects the historic district from Mississippi flood waters. Hannibal tapped into the tourist industry during the 1960s. Now 250,000 visitors flock here each year.

The peripatetic Twain moved into a Hartford, Connecticut, mansion in 1870 after marrying Olivia L. Langdon, then he moved to New York in 1900. He died in 1910. During a late-life interview in India, Twain was quoted as saying, "All that goes to make the me in me is a small Missouri village on the other side of the globe."

Elsewhere in the Area Mark Twain's modest birthplace welcomes visitors at the Mark Twain State Park in Florida, Missouri. The Molly Brown Dinner Theater, 200 North Main, stages theme musicals; the 1878 Old Jail Museum is at 201 South 4th Street; the Mark Twain Outdoor Theater is at Clemens Landing, U.S. 61 south; and the Mississippi Riverboat Mark Twain riverboat tours begin from the foot of Center Street.

Independence

Where the Oregon, California, and Santa Fe Trails Began

Location Western Missouri, 20 miles east of Kansas City. To reach Independence's Historic Area, take Highway 24 into town. Exit at Liberty or Delaware streets. Follow the blue signs. The National Frontier Trails Center is located at 318 West Pacific.

The National Frontier Trails Center ($) is open daily from April through October, Monday through Saturday, 9 A.M.–4:30 P.M., and Sunday, 12:30–4:30 P.M., from November through March, Monday through Friday, 10 A.M.–4:30 P.M., and weekends, 12:30 P.M.–4:30 P.M. For more information contact National Frontier Trails Center, 318 West Pacific, Independence, MO 64050. Tel. (816) 325-7575.

For information on Independence contact City of Independence, Tourism Department, 111 East Maple, Independence, MO 64050. Tel. 1-800-748-7323 or (816) 325-7111.

Frame of Reference Independence was founded in 1827, during America's 19th-century period of westward expansion. Its heyday of immigrant activity was in the 1840s and 1850s.

Significance All three of the great routes that took settlers West during America's westward expansion—the Santa Fe, Oregon, and California trails—began in or near Independence. The town, auspiciously located on the Missouri River at the westernmost edge of the frontier, competed ferociously—and very successfully—with other towns along the river to equip the pioneers, tradesmen, soldiers, and adventurers who thronged here in the 1800s.

The town reigned supreme as the principal jumping-off point to the West until the violent upheavals prior to and during the Civil War brought the wheels of westward migration to a grinding halt. After the war, politics and economic advantages made Kansas City the place where emigrants' new lives began.

But in its heyday, Independence's public square hummed every spring with strangers of all types: pioneer families, trappers, traders, missionaries, soldiers, gold-hungry speculators, and adventurers. Entrepreneurs and businesses of all types vied for their business: blacksmiths, wagon makers, hotels, saddle and harness shops, stables, and saloons. At one point Independence boasted 40 blacksmith shops. Business was lucrative. Immigrants paid $145 for one iron wagon axle. A bill of sale displayed at the National Trails Center proves it.

The land surrounding Independence became a virtual tent city as emigrants prepared for their journeys and waited for just the right moment to depart. Most arrived by paddleboat from St. Louis, the Gateway of the West. For those headed to Oregon, the grass at the square needed to be about four inches high when they left. The timing meant that they would cross the Rockies just before the snows began.

Today the Queen City of Trails preserves its story of exploration, acquisition, and settlement of the West.

About the Site Independence trails sites include these:

- **The National Frontier Trails Center.** Located in a historic mill, the Trails Center presents the story of overland trade and migration to the West. The center houses a museum full of artifacts, chronological exhibits, and passages from trail diaries; a spacious theater with an excellent, 18-minute introductory film; and a museum gift shop. The center's Merrill J. Mattes Research Library contains many rare books. Make an appointment for research. The museum presents fascinating stories like that of Hiram Young, an ex-slave whose durable, handmade wagons became legendary.
- **Historic Independence Square,** downtown between Liberty, Maple, Main, and Lexington streets. The courthouse where future U.S. President Truman began his political career as a judge still dominates the public square. Granite monuments on the north and south sides of the courthouse commemorate the beginning of the Oregon and Santa Fe trails.
- **Auto Routes.** The Trails Center is located on the Santa Fe Trail Route. The Oregon and California trails begin at the public square at Liberty and Maple streets. Follow signs to begin trail tours.

Hot Tips This is a site for older family members with an interest in America's great Western trails. Get information and maps in advance. Finding your way around town is tricky. Allow two to three hours for your visit. You can buy a walking guide to Independence Square at the Trails Center for one dollar. Outside walking is on sidewalks. Food and accommodations are available in Independence.

The Best Stuff Following the great Western trails is rising in popularity and may become the next great American vacation excursion. If you're among those who plan to cruise the continent, the museum and movie here send you off with a better understanding and deeper appreciation of what earlier trail travelers faced. You won't find what's offered here anywhere else.

Then and Now By the time fortune-seekers began heading to Santa Fe in 1821, Independence was a village of a few hundred people. In the busiest Oregon Trail years of the 1840s and 1850s, a common sight was a pioneer father yelling commands to a newly acquired yoke of oxen near the Square. Oxen were the beast of choice to pull the prairie schooners loaded with about 2,000 pounds of essentials across the continent to Oregon.

Paved streets and sidewalks now surround the once-grassy Independence Square where the first chapters of the trails were written. Shops, banks, restaurants, and businesses fill the low buildings that face the square now as then. Although the city's population is about 120,000, Independence Square's ambiance is still that of a small town.

Elsewhere in the Area Other Independence sites include the Harry Truman Home, Library, and Museum; 1859 Jail, Marshal's Home and Museum; 1827 Jackson County Log Courthouse; Mormon Visitors Center and Mormon Temple; 1881 Vaile Mansion; 1855 Bingham-Waggoner Estate; and other historic homes.

Pony Express Stables

Where the Legendary Mail Rides Began

Location St. Joseph, in western Missouri at the Kansas border. From the north and south take U.S. 29; from the east and west take U.S. 36. From U.S. 36 take the 10th Street exit. Stay left onto Penn Street. The Pony Express Memorial is located at 914 Penn Street. Follow the blue signs.

The Pony Express National Memorial ($) is open daily, except Thanksgiving, December 24, 25, and 31, and January 1, from June through September, Monday through Saturday, 9 A.M.–6 P.M., and Sunday, 1 P.M.–6 P.M., and from October through May, Monday through Saturday, 9 A.M.–5 P.M., and Sunday, 1 P.M.–5 P.M. For information contact the Pony Express National Memorial, 914 Penn Street, P.O. Box 244, St. Joseph, MO 64502-0244. Tel. (816) 279-5059 or 1-800-530-5930.

Frame of Reference The Pony Express began operation on April 3, 1860, the decade after California's population explosion following the 1849 discovery of gold and statehood in 1850. It officially discontinued mail service to California on October 27, 1861.

Significance From these original Missouri stables, a skinny, teenage rider on a bay mare galloped off on a 2,000-mile, 10-days-or-less mail route to Sacramento, California, launching the Pony Express. The 100 young Pony Express riders' daring races against time, terrain, and tempests made the mail-delivery enterprise legendary, if not profitable. Pony Express entrepreneurs selected St. Joseph, a frontier metropolis of 9,000 in 1860, as the mail route launch site because it was the first town on the Missouri River reached by both the telegraph and railroad. Messages sent here from the East would be immediately expressed West in a fraction of the time they could reach California by boat or stagecoach. The Pony Express rider motto was "faster and still faster."

The completion of the transcontinental telegraph ended the need for a speedier mail service. Although the Missouri-to-California Pony Express failed financially and lasted a mere 18 months, it provided a critical information link at an important time in history. As the Civil War erupted, the Pony Express allowed faster communication between East and West, forging a vital link that helped keep the new state of California in the Union.

The spirited image of the lone mail carrier on horseback overcoming tremendous odds to reach a goal evoke deep-seated American ideals 140 years later. The Pony Express represents the conquering of the West. It symbolizes the American Dream. This humble brick building in St. Joseph commemorates the legendary Pony Express.

About the Site Much of the exterior of the Pony Express Stables, once named Pikes Peak Stables, is original. The building now houses a museum with artifacts excavated at the site, 21 exhibits—including a walk-in Pony Express relay station—a gift shop, and a video-viewing area. Here visitors can see a fact-filled, 15-minute video, *The Pony Express*. The museum protects the original well that supplied water for the Pony Express horses. You can pump the well yourself.

Inside the restored stable doors, a life-size exhibit re-creates the first ride of the Pony Express. An audio program allows visitors to join the cheering crowd on Penn Street as "Johnny Fry," wearing the official red shirt and blue pants of the Pony Express, streaks into history.

The memorial was created in 1959 after a succession of local companies had occupied the one-story, one-gable building. Before that period, the structure had functioned as horse stables for 43 years. Archaeological digs at the sites from 1989 to 1993 resulted in full restoration. A deep, square hole inside the museum, purposely left from excavations, shows the stable's 1855 and 1888 stone foundations.

A bronze, life-size Pony Express memorial statue at the Civic Center downtown commemorates the courageous, adolescent mail carriers who became American heroes.

Hot Tips Allow two hours for your visit. Parking is on the street or at small lots in the area. A small park across Penn Street has picnic tables. Food and accommodations are available in St. Joseph.

Books about the Pony Express are plentiful. The museum's best-seller is Raymond and Mary Lund Settle's *Saddle & Spurs*. A good bet for young readers is Jacqueline Geis's *The First Ride*. The shop sells a video titled *Pony Express Riders*.

The Best Stuff The best things are the hands-on exhibits that illuminate the ever-fascinating Pony Express story, including these facts:

- **The Pony Express founders,** William Russell, Alexander Majors, and William Waddell,

Restoring the Pony Express Trail

Most of the original Pony Express Trail has been obliterated by time or human activity. Segments of the trail are purely conjecture. Double track dirt roads on both private ranches and federal land cover much of the trail now. Clear traces of the original trail are visible only in Utah (133 miles on public lands) and California.

The National Park Service is developing a Comprehensive Management and Use Plan for the Pony Express National Historic Trail. When completed, the plan will describe the official auto tour route, mark the trail, and list historic sites.

Plans are underway to open to the public approximately 120 historic sites along the Pony Express Trail, which traverses eight states. These will include 50 stations, most of which are ruins now.

For more information on plans for the Pony Express Trail contact National Park Service, Long Distance Trails Office, 324 South State Street, Suite 250, P.O. Box 45155, Salt Lake City, UT 84145-0155. Tel. (801) 539-4093.

The only original Pony Express Home Station survives in Marysville, Kansas, 100 miles west of St. Joseph. For information contact Marysville Pony Express Barn, 106 South 8th, Marysville, KS 66508. Tel. (913) 562-3825.

started the service to get government mail contracts worth $1 million. In the end, they lost $200,000.

Riders had to be young, weigh less than 120 pounds, and be of good moral standing. The 1860 help wanted poster reads

> ***PONY EXPRESS***
> ***St. Joseph, Missouri to California***
> ***in 10 days or less.***
> ***WANTED***
> ***Young, Skinny, Wiry Fellows***
> ***not over eighteen. Must be expert***
> ***riders, willing to risk death daily.***
> ***Orphans preferred.***
> ***Wages $25 per week.***
> ***Apply, PONY EXPRESS STABLES***
> ***St. Joseph, Missouri***

Young riders galloped for 80 to 100 miles a day over prairies, plains, and mountains at an average speed of 10 mph. Riders changed mounts every 8 to 15 miles, each riding 60 to 120 miles, with 160 way stations along the way. Gear included the leather *mochilla,* a four-pouch saddlebag for letters, a rifle, and a Colt revolver. Some stations were called home stations, where fresh riders took over and weary ones slept. They were 75 to 100 miles apart. Four hundred men were hired to operate the crude stations around the clock.

The original Pony Express mail charge was five dollars for one ounce plus five cents for each additional ounce. Charges were later reduced to one dollar per ounce.

Buffalo Bill Cody was probably the most famous rider, and, at 15, the youngest rider. He rode 322 miles in less than 22 hours using 21 horses. The museum provides a list of other Express riders.

One Pony Express rider died in action, but 150 horses were killed. None of the 35,000 letters was lost.

Then and Now Like some of its less-illustrious Eastern forerunners, the Pony Express was a private business venture. Before 1860 minor express mail routes ran from Boston to New York and later to St. Louis along a first Pony Express route. The Southern Overland Mail in the West took mail from St. Louis to San Francisco by stagecoach in 24 days. Boats transported mail through the Gulf of Mexico, by mule through Panama, and up the Pacific coast in six weeks.

The Pony Express did deliver on its pledge of speedier mail service. President Lincoln's inaugural message was whisked to California in 7½ days. The Express's bust as a business pales in the glow of the horsemen who streaked off into American legend.

Elsewhere in the Area Also in St. Joseph find the Patee House Museum, an 1858 elegant pioneer hotel that served as early Pony Express headquarters. The site includes the reconstructed offices of Russell, Majors, and Waddell. Also see the St. Joseph Museum, 1100 Charles Street; Glore Psychiatric Museum, St. Joseph State Hospital, second floor; Jesse James Home, 12th and Penn streets, where the famous outlaw was killed; Society of Memories Doll Museum, 12th and Penn streets; National Military Heritage Museum, 701 Messanie Street; and Knea-Von Black Archive, 1901 Messanie Street.

St. Louis

Gateway to the West, Salute to Jefferson

Location East central Missouri on the Mississippi River. The Jefferson National Expansion Memorial is located at downtown St. Louis's riverfront. From the intersection of U.S. 70, U.S. 64, U.S. 55/70, and U.S. 55, take the Memorial Drive exit. Follow signs to the memorial and parking area ($).

The Jefferson National Expansion Memorial ($), which includes the Museum of Westward Expansion and the Gateway Arch, is open daily, in summer months, 8 A.M.–10 P.M., and the rest of the year, 9 A.M.–6 P.M. The Old Courthouse is open daily, 8 A.M.–4:30 P.M. For more information contact Superintendent, Jefferson National Expansion Memorial, 11 North 4th Street, St. Louis, MO 63102. Tel. (314) 425-4465. Fee packages include the tram ride to the top of the arch and choice of wide-screen theater movies.

For information on St. Louis contact the St. Louis Convention and Visitors Commission, 1 Metropolitan Square, Suite 1100, St. Louis, MO 63102. Tel. 1-800-916-0095 or (314) 421-1023.

Frame of Reference St. Louis was founded in 1764 and was important as a gateway city during most of the 19th century, the period of America's westward expansion. This era begins with President Thomas Jefferson's Louisiana Purchase in 1803 and closes with the declared end of the American frontier in 1890.

Significance Established as a French fur-trading post near the point where the Missouri River empties into the mighty Mississippi, St. Louis served as America's conduit to western trade, exploration, and settlement for most of the 19th century. The history of St. Louis, named by its French founder, Pierre Leclede, after France's King Louis IX, preserves the story of America's expansion from the Atlantic to the Pacific. The memorial commemorates this historical era.

St. Louis's role as gateway to the West began with the return of Lewis and Clark here in 1806. They had just completed their groundbreaking "Voyage of Discovery" to the Pacific, initiated by President Jefferson. With maps and information of the western lands now available, explorers and fur traders soon clogged St. Louis's waterfront, stocking up for forays into the wilderness. Trappers returned with furs. St. Louis firms bought the pelts, processed them, then shipped them back East and on to ports around the globe. St. Louis became the world's fur-trading center.

When beaver hats fell out of fashion around 1840, the city was well into a second boom. This boom was in westward-bound settlers, brought to St. Louis by the steamboats that glutted its waterfront. Sometimes, 100 steamboats moored simultaneously where the arch stands today. Pioneers to Oregon and California outfitted here for their journeys west. St.

Louis was the jumping-off point where white settlement ended and the West began. For a while the great trails to the West originated here.

The completion of the Eads Bridge over the Mississippi River in 1874 enabled the railroad to come to town. The steamboat era came to a screeching halt.

About the Site Visitors enter the Gateway Arch and Museum of Westward Expansion beneath the arch. In the spacious lobby of the underground museum complex, you'll find an information desk, kiosks with accessibility information, a tram ticket window along the east wall, an extensive gift shop, and video nooks showing previews of movies currently shown in the two theaters. One theater always features the film *Monument to the Dream*, which tells how the 630-foot, stainless steel arch—America's tallest man-made monument—was constructed. Movies in the second theater change periodically.

Visitors can take a heart-stopping, four-minute tram ride to the top of the Gateway Arch, where there's a 65-foot-long observation room lined with small windows. On a clear day, you can see up to 30 miles.

The west wing of the museum complex houses the Museum of Westward Expansion. The museum spreads in a semicircle around a bronze statue of Jefferson. Visitors walk among life-size exhibits, wall-size photographs, and representative artifacts as the story of the settling of the West chronologically unfolds. Rangers offer regularly scheduled tours of the museum and special programs.

A lush, 91-acre riverfront park with benches and reflecting pools surrounds the memorial. Just north of the Gateway Arch, a renovated nine-block, upscale commercial area, Laclede's Landing, preserves the remaining warehouses from the city's steamboat days.

The memorial also includes the Old Courthouse, built between 1839 and 1862, two blocks west. The arch frames the courthouse, crowned with America's first iron dome. The shiny dome served as a beacon for 19th-century steamboat captains when docking in St. Louis's crowded waterfront. Between the courthouse and the arch, the landscaped Luther Ely Smith Square protects the site where warehouses once bustled with fur traders.

The courthouse, a dramatic example of 19th-century public architecture, was the site of the famous and controversial Dred Scott slavery case in 1847. The subsequent Supreme Court decision in the case further split North and South, contributing to the Civil War.

The stately building houses four museum galleries, special exhibits, dioramas depicting St. Louis history, two restored 1800s courtrooms, a gift shop, and a theater. On the quarter hour, the excellent 30-minute movie *Gateway to the West* traces the history of St. Louis. Courthouse tours are self-guided. You can rent audio tour cassettes and headgear in the gift shop.

Hot Tips Allow half a day to a full day for your St. Louis visit. Set aside two hours to tour the Expansion Museum and for the arch tram ride. In the summer, however, waits of up to an hour for the tram ride are common. Visits to the Old Courthouse take about 1½ hours. Watch for uneven surfaces and heavy traffic. Use stair rails in the Old Courthouse. The sloping walkway into the arch becomes slippery when wet or icy.

Large groups should make tram reservations. For information contact Bi-State Development Agency, Arch Reservations, 707 North 1st Street, St. Louis, MO 63102. Tel. (314) 982-1410.

The Museum of Westward Expansion is cerebral and not meant for young children. Do not touch anything in the museum. Students in grades four and up, however, will enjoy the park ranger's interpretative talks in the museum.

Food and accommodations are available in the immediate area.

The Gateway Arch World Wide Web address is http://www.st-louis.mo.us/

The Best Stuff Cool attention-grabbers at this site ensure a memorable visit for all ages, except for very young children. These include the following:

Gateway Arch. Park literature terms the tram ride up the hollow legs of the arch "a sensory experience." Try *white-knuckle experience*. It's fun, but this ride is not for persons afraid of heights, closed spaces, or loud noises. Two trams, each with eight barrel-shaped passenger capsules, descend tracks inside the arch legs. Engines periodically (and noisily) upright the capsule as it moves through the curved legs. Visitors can look through windows into the open space of the legs.

The Gateway Arch, designed by famed architect Eero Saarinen, designer of Washington's Dulles International Airport, is built to sway as much as 18 inches. And sway it does. You won't forget this experience.

The Old Courthouse. The galleries and movie here harbor rare nuggets of history. Top billing goes to the remains of "the Rock House" of 19th-century fur trader Manual Lisa. The house sat on the bluff where the settlement of St. Louis began.

Daniel Boone's Home

In Defiance, Missouri, 35 miles west of St. Louis, stands the stone four-story home that famed frontiersman Daniel Boone built between 1799 and 1812. Here Boone and his family lived on the Missouri frontier. Boone died here in 1820.

The Georgian-style home has walls 21/2-feet thick with portholes. Visitors can tour the Daniel Boone Home ($), which is furnished with many belongings that the Boones actually owned and used. The home boasts seven walnut mantels, intricately carved by the great woodsman himself.

Boone, considered one of the greatest figures of the American frontier, is known for his explorations of Kentucky and the West of the 18th century. He led the group that blazed the Wilderness Road, America's first Oregon Trail, through the Appalachian Mountains and Cumberland Gap in 1775.

The Daniel Boone Home is open for guided tours daily, except Thanksgiving, December 25, and January 1, from March 1 through October 31, 9 A.M.–6 P.M., and from November 1 through the last Sunday in November, 11 A.M.–4 P.M.; winter weekend hours vary. Boonesfield Village, a 19th-century living-history village, is under development at the site.

For more information contact Historic Daniel Boone Home and Boonesfield Village, Inc., 1868 Highway F, Defiance, MO 63341. Tel. (314) 987-2251.

American Indian Peace Medal Exhibit. This unique collection of gold and silver medals amazingly—although inadvertently—recounts the U.S. government's relationship with Native North Americans. The collection, the largest of its kind on display in the world, begins with an engraved silver medal of the George Washington administration and ends in 1869 with the Grant administration.

Then and Now The Gateway Arch is among America's most popular historic stops, with 4 million visitors annually. The innovative Eads Bridge still spans the Mississippi, attracting architects from around the world. St. Louis's historic waterfront, where once dreamers "jumped off" to a better life, remains a hive of activity in this great commercial center.

Elsewhere in the Area You can see Ulysses S. Grant National Historic Site, Grant's home at 7400 Grant Road; Grant's Farm; tours of the ancestral Busch family estate; St. Louis Zoo, one of the best in America; historic Lafayette Square; Museum of Transportation, 3025 Barrett Station Road; and Missouri History Museum at the Jefferson Memorial in Forest Park, featuring an exhibit on the 1904 St. Louis World's Fair. The fair commemorated the Louisiana Purchase. Also nearby are Cahokia Mounds, 8 miles east near Collinsville, Illinois; and Mastodon State Historic Site, 20 miles south of St. Louis on I-55.

Agate Fossil Beds

Mother Lode of Mammal Fossils and Red Cloud Artifacts

Location Northwest Nebraska, 23 miles south of U.S. 20 at Harrison, Nebraska. From Harrison, take Highway 29 south to the monument entrance. Site is 34 miles north of U.S. 26 via Highway 29. Visitor center is 3 miles east of Highway 29 on River Road.

The Agate Fossil Beds National Monument Visitor Center is open daily, 8 A.M.–5 P.M.; summer hours are extended. Trails are open from dawn to dusk. For more information contact Agate Fossil Beds National Monument, c/o Superintendent, Scotts Bluff National Monument, P.O. Box 427, Gering, NE 69341. Tel. (308) 668-2211.

Frame of Reference The site encompasses two distinct eras. The first was 13 to 25 million years ago, when now-extinct mammals walked a Miocene savanna here. The second was less than 100 years ago, from the late 1800s, when the last of the Sioux and Cheyenne were confined to reservations, to the early 1900s, when the legendary Sioux chief Red Cloud and his followers gave gifts and tribal treasures to rancher James Cook. Cook's pioneer ranch here contained the rich quarry of fossilized mammal remains.

Significance This dry, isolated site curiously preserves two lost and disparate epochs: a chapter of evolution called the Age of Mammals of the Miocene Epoch and the remains of a Native North American civilization that began on this continent from 11,000 to 40,000 years ago. The fossils in beds of sedimentary rock formed about 19 million years ago. The beds are one of the richest concentrations of fossilized mammal remains ever discovered. The fossils come from a relatively recent era of evolution. (The earliest fossil traces of life on earth date from 3½ billion years ago. The period of the first dinosaurs began around 225 million years ago.)

The museum at the visitor center not only documents the site's rich fossil finds but also preserves valuable artifacts of the Sioux and Cheyenne tribes, whom James Cook befriended.

Cook, a man of unusual abilities and vision, and famous Sioux chief Red Cloud were friends. After the U.S. Army finally confined Red Cloud and the rest of his hold-out tribe to reservations, the Sioux and Cheyenne regularly visited Cook's Agate Springs Ranch from the Standing Rock Reservation in South Dakota. They brought gifts and entrusted Cook with tribal treasures. Crowded storage vaults and a museum at the site contain several hundred prized Native North American artifacts—ceremonial garb, war clubs, ghost shields, moccasins, and a letter from Red Cloud. These gifts and treasures document the story of a lost civilization, as Red Cloud hoped they would.

About the Site The site's rich deposits of agate—a fine-grained, variegated quartz—give Agate Fossil Beds its name. The park encompasses 2,700 acres and protects the exceptionally rich fossil beds, the prairie, and a wide range of plants and wildlife. The visitor center's new and expanded museum houses rare fossil exhibits—many hands-on—and the Cook Collection of Native American artifacts. Included in the collection are Red Cloud's war shirt and pipe bag; a handpainted cowhide depicting scenes from the Battle of Little Big Horn; the ceremonial gown of Red Cloud's wife, Good Road; and the leather sheath legendary Sioux chief Crazy Horse wore when he died.

The horizontal fossil beds are two to three feet thick. They lie near the surface of two hills, Carnegie and University hills. The beds are made of sedimentary rock, formed about 19 million years ago by the compression of mud, clay, and debris left by wind and water. You can walk a two-mile loop from the visitor center through the prairie, across the Niobrara River, and up and around the hills where the fossils lie.

The hills are capped with hard agate, which resists erosion and protects the softer layers below. The fossil deposits, first excavated in 1904, once were part of the flat landscape at the Niobrara, which has changed courses through the millennia. The river now meanders through the prairie almost half a mile away. You can see sun-whitened fossilized bones of now-extinct mammals—skulls, long leg bones, curbed rib cages—embedded in the dry, grayish hillsides. Clear coverings protect most exposed bones. An estimated 75 percent of the fossil-bearing areas of the hills remain unquarried.

The visitor center houses a small bookstore and a theater, where an orientation film runs regularly. Nature lovers will enjoy the identification cards for the flora and fauna along the self-guided prairie tour located near the visitor center door.

Hot Tips Allow two to three hours at the site. It takes about an hour to hike the trail. Dress for seasonal weather extremes. The visitor center has a cold-beverage machine, but bring water for warm-weather hiking. Sheltered picnic tables are on the site. The trail to the fossil hills is narrow but paved. It becomes very steep in places, which can be difficult for some; the altitude here is 4,000 feet above sea level.

Watch for rattlesnakes and falling rocks. Beware of roaming bison. Don't hike the area alone. Food is available in nearby towns. Food and accommodations are available in Harrison, Scottsbluff, and Chadron, about 50 miles northeast.

To learn about the Agate Springs Ranch, the Cook Collection, and Red Cloud, read a wonderful book by James Cook's granddaughter, Dorothy Cook Meade, *Heart Bags & Hand Shakes* (1994). James Cook's own books, *Fifty Years on the Old Frontier* (1923) and *Longhorn Cowboy*, published shortly after his death in 1942, give trenchant, firsthand looks at the frontier days here.

The Best Stuff Seeing fossilized mammal bones in big-city museums is interesting. But walking into wilderness prairie and seeing fossils where they have lain for millions of years is a lot better. At Agate Fossil Beds, you'll find fossilized bones of the Menoceras, a before-unknown rhinoceros with two horns; the Moropus, a large mammal about 7 feet at the shoulders; and the Dinohyus, the "terrible pig." This monstrous beast was about 10 feet long and 7 feet high at the shoulder and had a huge head with large tusks. Back at the museum you can pick up sample fossils to examine.

You'll also see the fossilized skeleton of a now-extinct beaver. This strange, ancient beaver dug large, corkscrew tunnels into the prairie. These fossilized tunnels, called *daemonelix,* lie exposed in eroded bluffs of the park. Allow 45 additional minutes to hike the trail to the daemonelix site.

Then and Now A *savanna* is a grassland scattered with clumps of trees. The savanna at Agate today remains much as it was millions of years ago. The Niobrara River is deeper and swifter than in earlier days, when it was wide and shallow. Modern additions include a ranch and the remains of the "Bone Cabin," which housed excavation parties in the early 1900s. The animals roaming here today include pack rats, bull snakes, and deer. Those of 20 million years ago more closely resembled what you find now in Africa.

Projectile points found here show that Native Americans roamed the area 11,000 years ago; the latest were the Sioux and Cheyenne. White settlers arrived 150 years ago.

James Cook was the first white man to discover fossils on the land he inherited from his father-in-law in 1878. He brought in scientists from universities and museums to study his find, housing them at his ranch. The fossils they unearthed now reside in museums throughout the country.

Spend a Night at a Genuine Frontier Fort

You can stay overnight at Fort Robinson, the military post where, on September 5, 1877, guards killed famous Oglala Sioux chief Crazy Horse as he attempted to escape imprisonment. Now a Nebraska state park, this site offers lodging in the enlisted men's barracks or officers' quarters as well as at modern camping sites. Overnight stays are available from the second weekend of April through the third weekend of November. Primitive camping is allowed year-round. Lodging units vary from one room in the barracks to the entire Comanche Hall, the 1909 Bachelor Officers' Quarters. The hall accommodates 60 people. Rates are moderate.

The sprawling base of restored adobe, brick, and wood buildings stands on 22,000 acres in the heart of the rugged Pine Ridge region of northwest Nebraska, just west of Crawford on U.S. 20. The Crazy Horse Memorial rises 80 miles north in South Dakota.

The park offers a full agenda of family activities ($), including jeep rides, mountain biking, horseback riding, and hayrides through wild countryside where buffalo really do roam. There are also stagecoach rides, chuckwagon cookouts (buffalo stew anyone?), theater productions, and building tours, as well as visits to a fort museum and the Trailside Museum. The University of Nebraska operates the Trailside Museum. Exhibits include fossils and a complete Ice Age mammoth skeleton.

For reservations and more information contact Fort Robinson State Park, 3200 Highway 20, P.O. Box 392, Crawford, NE 69339-0392. Tel. (308) 665-2900.

Elsewhere in the Area The unique geological makeup of this area of Nebraska and South Dakota makes for an exciting array of fossils. Nearby fossil sites include Toadstool Area, five miles north of Crawford; Trailside Museum (Ice Age mammoth skeleton), at Fort Robinson; Black Hills Petrified Forest, near Piedmont, South Dakota; and the Museum of Geology in Rapid City, North Dakota.

Chimney Rock

Most Famous Oregon Trail Landmark

Location Western Nebraska, about 20 miles east of Scottsbluff and 3½ miles south of Bayard on the south side of the North Platte River. Take U.S. 27 from Bayard to the intersection of Highway 92 and turn right. Watch for a sign at a gravel road on the left, which takes you to the visitor center.

Chimney Rock National Historic Site facilities ($), operated by the Nebraska State Historical Society, are open daily, in winter, 9 A.M.–5 P.M., and in summer, Monday through Saturday, 9 A.M.–6 P.M., and Sunday, 10 A.M.–6 P.M. For information contact Director, Chimney Rock National Historic Site, P.O. Box F, Bayard, NE 69334-0680. Tel. (308) 586-2581.

Frame of Reference Chimney Rock was a major Oregon Trail marker during the Oregon Trail years, beginning about 1841. It ceased this role about the time the transcontinental railroad was completed in 1869.

Significance This solitary clay, ash, and sandstone spire near the North Platte River served as a beacon to the Oregon Trail emigrants.

The powerful natural feature is the most-written-about land formation in the diaries of Oregon Trail emigrants. Seeing this then-chimney-shaped landmark signaled that the journey to the far West was ⅓ over. Chimney Rock was not only a guide but a source of intrigue and inspiration. The severely eroded rock stands today as one of the most important symbols of the American West.

Scotts Bluff

You can walk an eight-foot-wide section of the Oregon Trail carved by thousands of pioneer wagons at Scotts Bluff National Monument ($). The site is located five miles southwest of the town of Scottsbluff on U.S. 29, and two miles west of Gering via Highway 92. This enormous bluff rises 800 feet above the prairie at Mitchell Pass. It was a famous milepost for Oregon Trail emigrants. The eroded wagon ruts here are especially deep.

The monument is open daily, in summer, 8 A.M.–6 P.M. and from Labor Day through Memorial Day, 8 A.M.–5 P.M. Summit Road is open daily, in summer, 8 A.M.–5:30 P.M., and from Labor Day through Memorial Day, 8 A.M.–4:30 P.M. For information contact Superintendent, Scotts Bluff National Memorial, P.O. Box 27, Gering NE 69341-0027. Tel. (308) 436-4340.

About the Site Visitors can view Chimney Rock ¼ mile away from a patio at the visitor center or through wall-size windows. A fence encloses the area. (You can see the rock from miles away, and easily from U.S. 92/26, which is the approximate route of the Oregon Trail.) Hiking to the base of the rock is allowed only by a crude trail south of the visitor center. Park at the trail head. The visitor center houses a museum, small gift shop, and theater where you can watch an excellent orientation film, *Chimney Rock and the American West.* The museum features a fascinating exhibit on Chimney Rock, as well as exhibits—some hands-on—on the Oregon Trail and the Western frontier.

Hot Tips It's worth getting off the highway and stopping to contemplate this rock that held so much meaning for the emigrants. If you plan to hike to the base, boots and hiking clothes are essential. Take water. Terrain is difficult. Watch for bison, rattlesnakes, and yucca plants. Food is available in nearby Bayard; food and accommodations are available in Scottsbluff.

The Best Stuff Gazing upon Chimney Rock is what you came for, and that's the best thing going. Don't miss the film and exhibits, however. You'll learn how this symbol of the West conjured up entirely different images for travelers depending on their backgrounds. To Native North Americans it was "Elk's Penis." More staid emigrants wrote of the rock as a funnel, column, Beacon Hill, potato hill, and lightning rod. Some compared the rock to the then-already-famous Bunker Hill and Washington monuments. You'll also find out how erosion has changed the rock's shape through the years.

Then and Now It's likely that the rock's present shape of twin points, one higher than the other, will endure several centuries more. Forty-niners passing here during the California gold rush recorded the height at 360 feet from base to top, based on shadow measurements. Today the 35-million-year-old rock reaches 325 feet. It stands 4,225 feet above sea level near the base of a towering bluff.

Elsewhere in the Area Other well-known Oregon Trail sites include Courthouse Rock and Jail Rock, on Highway 88 south of U.S. 26 near Bridgeport, and Scotts Bluff.

The First Homestead

Commemorating the Sodbusting Pioneers

Location Southeastern Nebraska, 40 miles southwest of Lincoln and 4½ miles northwest of Beatrice. From the north and south take U.S. 77 to U.S. 136 west to Highway 4 west at Beatrice to visitor center. From the east and west take U.S. 136 to Highway 4.

Homestead National Monument of America is open daily, except December 25, in summer, 8 A.M.–6 P.M., and in other seasons, 8:30 A.M.–5 P.M. Special tours and living-history demonstrations are given in summer. For information contact Superintendent, R.F.D. 3, P.O. Box 47, Beatrice, NE 68310. Tel. (402) 223-3514.

Frame of Reference In the second half of the 19th century during the settlement of the last great expanse of the West—the arid grasslands between the Missouri River and the Rocky Mountains—Congress passed the Homestead Act in 1862. It went into effect on January 1, 1863. Most of the homesteads were staked by the 1890s, but Congress didn't repeal the Homestead Act until 1934.

Significance This is the site of possibly America's first homestead, that of Daniel Freeman, a Union scout in the Civil War. Freeman, from Iowa, signed up for his land shortly after midnight on the day the Homestead Act took effect. The Homestead Act opened up the plains and prairies of the West by giving 160 acres (¼ mile square) to anyone who lived on the land for five years and improved it.

Under the Homestead Act, 1.6 million homestead applications were filed and 274 million acres were claimed. Most homesteaders came from the Ohio and Mississippi valleys. Many settlers, especially European emigrants, bought grant land—about 200 million acres—from the railroad companies.

Freeman's cabin is gone, but the land where it stood from 1865 to 1890 today represents the spirit of the pioneers who settled this region under the Homestead Act. Although no sod homes, or soddies, were built at this site, the monument honors the sodbusters who tamed the great American desert with ingenuity, hard work, and sheer willpower, transforming the area into productive farms.

About the Site The park comprises 163 acres, 100 acres of which are restored tall-grass prairie. Tall-grass prairie, which spans the moister, far-eastern area of the Plains, is so called because the component grasses can grow eight to nine feet high.

Here visitors will find the approximate site of the cabin occupied by a "squatter" before Freeman staked his claim. Squatters could buy land at $1.25 an acre after six months. The area also marks the sites of Freeman's log cabin and the brick house the Freeman family occupied from 1876 to 1916. Another log cabin built in 1867 on a nearby homestead and moved here as an exhibit allows visitors to see what pioneer life was like here in the 1880s. The Palmer-Epard cabin is made of mixed hardwoods and homemade bricks set in lime mortar.

A 2½-mile, self-guided walking tour also takes you around the restored prairie past the Freeman graves. A quarter mile west of the visitor center, the restored, one-room Freeman School is open for seasonal tours and living-history demonstrations. Before closing in 1967, this brick building was the oldest operating one-room schoolhouse in Nebraska.

The visitor center offers exhibits, a diorama of a homestead with surrounding fields, a mural with a sod house, a farm implement display—including a sodbusting "grasshopper" used on homesteads—and an 18-minute orientation slide program, *The Free Land*.

Hot Tips Pick up the award-winning trail guidebook *The Changing Prairie* at the visitor center. Allow two hours for your visit. Prepare for the weather, and wear sturdy shoes. The walking trail drops off steeply in places. Check for ticks. Do not disturb the grasslands. You can walk to the Freeman School, but rangers recommend driving there. Park in a small lot at the site.

There's a small picnic area at the site. Food and accommodations as well as campgrounds are available in Beatrice (pronounced Be-AT-ris).

The Best Stuff What's great about this site is the story it evokes. Most of the legends of the West—those of the Oregon Trail emigrants, the Pony Express riders, the U.S. Cavalry, the great Native North American chiefs, the cowboys—seem quite romantic. But the story of the sodbusters who tackled the difficult conditions of America's heartland is unromantic indeed.

After Congress passed the Homestead Act, thousands and thousands of dreamers found the price was right to settle millions of acres of open land. It was free. So they packed their belongings into wagons, headed west, and staked their claims. Then came the reality check. Life here was hard. The land held very little water. Lack of water in the westernmost reaches near the Rockies meant virtually no trees, and no trees meant no wood to build homes. (In the easternmost areas, where Homestead National Monument is located, more rainfall allowed trees to grow, so pioneers could build log cabins.)

Arid conditions also meant that native vegetation had adapted by growing a dense and sturdy root system. Pioneer farmers who attempted to plow their land had to literally bust through the matted root systems of grasses entrenched in the sod, hence the moniker *sodbusters*. Farmers used the mats of broken sod left in the fields to build their sturdy, weather-resistant homes. The soddies have come to symbolize this homesteading era in the American West.

The thick tangle of roots in the sod ensured that the slabs of "Nebraska marble" and "Kansas brick" kept their shape. Soddies often were built into hills. Grass grew on the soddie roofs, and buffalo chips burned in the iron stoves. Meals were served on family china set nicely on a packing crate that served as a table. As railroads pushed into the sod-house frontier, trains loaded with wood portended the rise of the familiar frame house.

In the 1860s a new invention called the "grasshopper" plow sliced the sod vertically, then turned it aside to reveal a furrow for planting. Other inventions, such as windmill water pumps and threshing machines, eventually lightened the farmers' workload and boosted production, even if they brought the burden of debt.

The innovation that may have most dramatically changed the face of the homesteading frontier was the 1873 invention of barbed wire. Now homesteaders without wood could cheaply and effectively enclose their property. Barbed wire ended the open range that, until that point, Western ranchers had enjoyed. Of course nasty battles over land rights ensued.

The Great Desert's environmental hazards, some of biblical proportions, also plagued settlers: prairie fires, tornadoes, hail storms, and swarms of crop-eating locusts. But, as the Plains Native Americans had known for centuries, middle America was actually a mosaic of climates and geological conditions. Survival—even prosperity—was possible.

Wide bands of differing climatic conditions determined not only housing types but types of plants and animals and eventually the region's cash crops: corn and wheat.

Then and Now The U.S. government declared the end of the frontier in 1890. The conquest of the Native North Americans, government land giveaways, and the transcontinental railroad meant that all areas of America, including the Great American Desert, had been settled.

Today enormous ranches and agribusinesses splay across the landscape of the homesteading past. Some of America's least-populated states dominate this region, however. This last frontier's sturdy individualism remains an ideal for Americans everywhere.

Elsewhere in the Area Nebraska has more than 100 surviving sod houses. Some are open to the public. Gothenburg, in south central Nebraska, has a Sod House Museum at the I-80/Highway 47 intersection, open May through September. For information call (308) 537-3505.

Toadstool Park near Fort Robinson in northwest Nebraska also has a soddy. The Dowse Sod House stands on Highway 183 between Sargent and Ansley in central Nebraska's Custer County, known as the Sod House Capital of the World. Tel. (308) 628-4231. For information on Custer County, contact the Custer County Historical Commission, 255 South 10th Street, Broken Bow, NE 68822. Tel. (308) 872-2203.

Forty miles south in Marysville, Kansas, the Marysville City Park off U.S. 77 exhibits a sod-house replica. Marysville also has the only original Pony Express Home Station remaining. A Pony Express Museum is nearby. An original Pony Express Way Station stands in Gothenburg.

Fort Union Trading Post

The American Fur Company's Colorful Success Story

Location The North Dakota/Montana border, 24 miles southwest of Williston, North Dakota, and 21 miles north of Sidney, Montana. From Williston take U.S. 2 west to Highway 1804 south to the park entrance. From Sidney, take Route 200/58 to 58 north to the entrance on Highway 1804.

The Fort Union Trading Post National Historic Site is open daily, except Thanksgiving, December 25, and January 1, from Memorial Day through Labor Day, 8 A.M.–8 P.M. and the rest of the year, 9 A.M.– 5:30 P.M. A four-day fur-trade rendezvous takes place over the third weekend in June. For information on tours, living-history programs, encampments, and special events, contact Superintendent, Fort Union Trading Post National Historic Site, R.R. 3, Box 71, Williston, ND 58801. Tel. (701) 572-9083.

Frame of Reference The post operated in the mid-19th century, during the decades of intense fur trading in the wilderness of the West. Fort Union was established in 1828. In 1867, investors sold the fort to the U.S. Army, which soon dismantled it.

Significance Here, near the junction of the Missouri and Yellowstone rivers—frontier interstates—John Jacob Astor's American Fur Company dominated the ruthlessly competitive fur trade on the Northern Plains for a record 39 years. This behemoth of free enterprise operated from 1828 to 1867 and provided the early wealth of Astor, who at his death in 1848 was the richest man in America. Fort Union, called a fort because of its defensive palisade and guard towers, was the largest and finest of a string of fur-trading posts along the Northern Plains rivers.

The fort was a frontier melting pot, serving as host to eight Native North American tribes; an eclectic mix of trappers, explorers, scientists, and employees; and distinguished residents and guests. Among the rich and famous who visited the post were John James Audubon, German Prince Maximilian, and renowned artists George Catlin and Karl Bodmer, who left valuable historic records.

Fort Union Trading Post preserves the rich legacy of the American Fur Company as well as the brief and colorful period of fur trading on the American frontier.

About the Site The post is partially reconstructed on its original foundation to appear as it did at its lucrative height around 1851. The post includes the wooden palisade walls enclosing a 220-by-240-foot quadrangle, two stone bastions, a towering flagstaff, the grand Bourgeois House (headquarters for the post superintendent), Indian Trade House, and the foundations of the support buildings such as ice house and dwelling range. Up to 100 employees toiled here in the fur-trading era. The towering white main gate overlooks the Missouri River. Everything is whitewashed and gleams in the sun, just as it did 160 years ago.

The visitor center occupies the Bourgeois House and houses a gift shop and a museum, which displays some of the two million artifacts excavated at the site. The plains surrounding the fort provide an authentic—and isolated—mid-19th-century setting, thanks to strict land controls. Visitors can follow a hiking trail through a grassy flood plain to the riverfront where frontier boats once landed. Costumed interpreters offer lively talks about life here during the fur-trading years.

Hot Tips Allow two hours for your visit. Dress for seasonal weather extremes. The visitor center has a beverage machine; picnic tables are located near the river. The Trade House sells handcrafted items like those traded for furs here in the 19th century. Food and accommodations are available in Williston and Sidney.

The Best Stuff You'll remember the story of Fort Union's aggressive public relations/advertising campaign long after you leave. The imaginative campaign began with the post's founder and first bourgeois, Kenneth McKenzie, and was probably the reason the post came to dominate the Western fur trade. To get customer attention, McKenzie had the entire post whitewashed; an eye-catching, iron channel catfish placed atop the flagpole; and the red-roofed Bourgeois House made ever grander. And although it was against the law to supply liquor to Native North Americans, Fort Union saw it as a necessary item of trade.

Fort Buford

Where Sitting Bull Surrendered

Fort Buford, five miles east of Fort Union, was established in 1866 as the Guardian of the Great Confluence. The partially original fort guarded the junction of the Missouri and Yellowstone rivers.

Here military supplies arrived to support the U.S. Army during the Plains Indian Wars. Later infantry and cavalry stationed here policed the international boundary and guarded construction of the Northern Pacific Railroad.

But Fort Buford may be best known as the place where the famous renegade Sioux leader Sitting Bull surrendered to the U.S. Army. The fort, subject to many Native North American attacks, also imprisoned other famous Native North American leaders: Chief Joseph of the Nez Perce, Gall of the Sioux, and Crow King of the Sioux.

The fort was expanded many times during its 29-year use, from a few adobe buildings to a complex of wooden structures. Today only two original structures and a cemetery remain in a corner of a wide prairie. Other building sites are marked.

The aged warrior, venerated leader, and holy man Sitting Bull has come to symbolize the Plains Indians' stubborn refusal to allow white civilization to end a culture and way of life. Sitting Bull shunned treaties and the reservations. He became supreme chief of the Lakota (called Sioux by whites) and Cheyenne, and as such was the spiritual leader of the Indians at the Battle of Little Bighorn in 1876.

Sitting Bull believed that he and his fellow warriors had the right and duty to challenge traditional Native North American rivals as well as white men who dared defy them. The U.S. Army regarded Sitting Bull and his war parties as its toughest opponents on the Plains.

The heart of the enterprise's competitive edge was the Trade House. Here the Bourgeois guaranteed customer satisfaction and, hence, product loyalty. Step up into the reception room immediately to the left of the Main Gate and see more of these marketing tools. Here post employees received tribal chiefs with toasts, exchanges of gifts, pipe smoking, elaborate meals, and friendly conversation before uttering even a word about business.

Then and Now The American fur trade, which had a heyday of only 20 years, declined around the time of the Civil War (1861–65). Many factors ended the trade, resulting in the demise of Fort Union, including smallpox among the Native North Americans brought by white settlers, the preference of members of high society for silk hats over beaver ones, and attacks by hostile Sioux that brought the full force of the military out West.

In 1864 the army took over the post until a new fort could be built. Nearby Fort Buford opened in 1866, and the Northern Fur Company, which had tried to continue the fur trade at Fort Union, gave up hope of profit and sold the post to the army in 1867. Troops dismantled the fort and used the materials to complete Fort Buford.

Today nothing disturbs the dry prairie surrounding Fort Union but Highway 1804, telephone wires, a distant ranch, and the Great Northern Railroad tracks. Fort employees complained in their diaries of boredom and isolation. Time passes slowly here, as it always has.

Following the cavalry defeat at Little Bighorn, the government stepped up its campaign to quell Native American resistance with renewed warfare and threats to cut off rations at reservations. Most chiefs signed new treaties. Sitting Bull refused. Instead, he and his followers fled to Canada. Authorities there ultimately forced him back over the border. The great chief, with 87 surviving followers, surrendered to the army at Fort Buford in 1881.

Sitting Bull became a prisoner of the U.S. government for two years. Later he toured the country as part of Buffalo Bill Cody's Wild West Show. In 1890 at the Standing Rock Reservation, now on the border of the Dakotas, a Native North American soldier, believing the chief was trying to escape, shot and killed Sitting Bull, who was then in his mid-50s.

Today the Sitting Bull Surrender Room is part of Fort Buford's former officer quarters built in 1872. The whitewashed, clapboard house has its original dark wood floor and white stucco walls. The Surrender Room stands to the right of the entrance hall. The building houses a small museum that tells Fort Buford's story. Here visitors can view a six-minute orientation video and enjoy terrific living-history presentations about the dreary life faced by a young soldier wearing a recycled Civil War uniform.

Fort Buford State Historic Site is open daily, from May 16 through September 15, 8 A.M.–5 P.M. Off-season tours are available by appointment. For more information contact State Historical Society of North Dakota, North Dakota Heritage Center, Bismarck, ND 58505. Tel. (701) 328-2666.

▲

Elsewhere in the Area Five miles east stands Fort Buford, where famed Sioux chief Sitting Bull surrendered to the U.S. Army after fleeing Canada.

Hot Tips Kids will enjoy reading about Sitting Bull's exceptional life and the last years of the Plains Indians' way of life depicted in several books written for young people. Among them is Jane Fleischer's *Sitting Bull, Warrior of the Sioux*. Picnicking facilities are available in a lovely state park at the confluence of the Missouri and Yellowstone rivers. Sitting Bull's grave is on the Standing Rock Reservation, 30 miles south of Bismarck.

Knife River Indian Villages

Commemorating a Lost Way of Life on the Plains

Location Central North Dakota, 60 miles north of Bismarck and ½ mile north of Stanton. From the south take U.S. 83 to Highway 200A north through Stanton to Route 31 and the park entrance. From the north take U.S. 83 to Highway 200 to Route 37 and the park entrance.

The Knife River Indian Villages National Historic Site is open daily, from Memorial Day through Labor Day weekend, 8 A.M.–6 P.M., and the rest of the year, 8 A.M.–4:30 P.M. For more information contact Superintendent, Knife River Indian Villages National Historic Site, R.R. 1, P.O. Box 168, Stanton, ND 58571. Tel. (701) 745-3309.

Frame of Reference The final stage of the Plains Village Period of Native North Americans was A.D. 1000 to 1885. About 1525 the first of the five villages at Knife River, North Dakota, was settled. The remains of three now exist. (Some historians suggest that the first settlement actually occurred 700 years ago, as early as 1300.) The last village was permanently abandoned in 1845. The villages were occupied at different intervals, some

Fort Abraham Lincoln

Custer's Last Home

The whole family will enjoy this reconstructed, hands-on fort, six miles south of Mandan, North Dakota, near Bismarck off Highway 1806. Built in 1873 the fort once housed the famous Seventh Cavalry and its leader, Lieutenant Colonel George Armstrong Custer. It was from Fort Abraham Lincoln that Custer and his men departed under the command of Brigadeer General Alfred Terry to meet their destiny at the Battle of Little Bighorn. This was Custer's last post and home.

The fort, built around Cavalry Square, includes the custom-built Victorian home of Custer and his wife, Libbie; cavalry barracks; infantry post; commissary; granary; and On-a-Slant Indian Village, a re-created small Mandan community that existed here from 1650 to 1750.

While Fort Abraham Lincoln is not the site of a major historic event, the park is one of the most interesting and fun stops in America's outback. Costumed interpreters welcome you as if the year were 1875, just before Custer departed to meet his destiny. "Are you here to attend Mrs. Custer's ball tonight?" they might ask.

You can tour the authentically furnished "Custerized" house replica and go inside several Mandan earthlodges reconstructed on the exact sites where once 75 earthlodges stood. The tribe's village was built on sloping ground, hence the name, "On-a-Slant." By the time Lewis and Clark explored the region, the village was in ruins. The Mandan were living along the Knife River, some 60 miles north of here.

Allow two hours at the fort. Food and accommodations are available in Mandan and Bismarck. For information contact Bismarck Convention and Visitors Bureau, Tuscany Square, 107 West Main Avenue, Bismarck, ND 58501. Tel. 1-800-767-3555.

overlapping, in a 300- to 500-year period. Explorers Lewis and Clark stopped here on their Voyage of Discovery (1804–1806). Excavated projectile points indicate the site was first inhabited 11,000 years ago.

Significance This strategic site at the confluence of the Knife and Missouri rivers allowed the Native Americans who settled here a lifestyle of permanency unique in the Northern Plains. The grassy plateau and the crossroads of rivers—the Missouri flowing north-south and the Knife flowing east-west—provided rich soil, protection, and transportation lines for agriculture and a far-ranging trade network that permitted two tribes, the Mandan and the Hidatsa, to thrive here. The Hidatsa was the tribe of Sakakawea (Sacajawea), the young woman who served as interpreter on the Lewis and Clark expedition.

Waves of smallpox brought by white traders virtually wiped out the Knife River villages, once home to 8,000 to 10,000 people. Modern farming has all but eradicated remains of the villages. Little of the prairie grasslands or rare Missouri River floodplain forest that once surrounded the villages now survive, but conservation efforts are underway.

The 1,075-acre park preserves the remnants of the culture and agricultural ways of the Northern Plains Indians. Knife River Indian Villages is the only park the federal government has set aside to commemorate the Native North American.

Sakakawea

The true story of Sakakawea may not be the one you learned in school. One thing is for sure—the popular legend of this Shoshone girl has generated a good deal of controversy among historians.

Sakakawea truly did live at the Knife River in the Awatixa Hidatsa village of Metaharta, after being captured by the Hidatsa in Montana when she was 12 years old. The state of North Dakota adopted the spelling of her name as *Sakakawea,* Hidatsa for "Bird Woman." Wyoming and several Western states have adopted the Shoshone word *Sacajawea,* meaning "Boat Launcher." (How to pronounce the name is a touchy topic in this part of the West.)

The Hidatsa sold Sakakawea to a French fur trader, Toussaint Charbonneau, who later married her. Sakakawea and Charbonneau had an infant son, Jean Baptiste, when Lewis and Clark hired Charbonneau as an interpreter for the famous Voyage of Discovery. Sakakawea, who probably was only 14 or 15 at the time of the voyage, helped Lewis and Clark identify landmarks, obtain horses, and interpret the language of her native people. The Voyage captains wrote in their journals that the presence of a young, female Native North American and her infant helped gain the trust of all Native North Americans they encountered.

Historians disagree about Sakakawea's life and death after her trip to the Pacific with Lewis and Clark. Some say she lived a long and good life among the Native North Americans. Others claim she died young and unhappy, longing for her people. Some say her role in the Voyage of Discovery was minor; others call her a true heroine of the West.

You can see a bronze statue of Sakakawea and her infant son on the Capitol grounds in Bismarck.

About the Site You may find that holes in the ground never have had such meaning. What remain today of three villages along the west bank of the Knife River are circular depressions, 6 to 30 feet in diameter, where hundreds of round earthlodges stood. At least five inches of soil insulated the earthlodges, arranged close together at this site 200 to 300 hundred years ago.

You can take self-guided or in-season ranger-guided walks from the visitor center to two village sites, the Awatixa and the Awatixa Xi'e (Lower Hidatsa) on a 1½-mile gravel walking trail. The Big Hidatsa Village, two miles north, can be reached on foot or by car on a paved road.

Look carefully and you can see *travois trails*. These parallel lines were created in the soil by *travois*, load-carrying platforms tied with rawhide onto long poles. Animals dragged the travois among villages, creating deep ruts that served as roads.

The visitor center houses a museum, much of it hands-on and geared toward kids; a small gift shop, featuring crafts handmade by Mandan and Hidatsa descendants; and a theater. A moving, 15-minute orientation movie tells of the villages through the eyes of Buffalo Bird Woman, who grew up here. She was interviewed extensively before her death in 1930.

An authentic earthlodge replica just outside the visitor center highlights a park tour. The earthlodge, melding into landscape, is accessible only by guided tour as staff levels permit. Additional park trails vary in length from ⅗ to 7 miles, taking hikers through the prairie and woodland ecosystems. In winter, some trails are open for cross-country skiing.

Hot Tips Be prepared for temperature extremes and dress accordingly. December to February lows average 5 degrees to below 0 degrees Fahrenheit; June to August temperatures average 80 to 90 degrees Fahrenheit. Winter brings blowing snow, and in summer there are hoards of insects. Plan to spend about three hours in this time capsule of the American West. Food is available in Stanton and nearby communities. Accommodations can be found in Hazen, 15 miles west, and in Bismarck.

The story of the Knife River Villages comes alive in the lovely text, photographs, and illustrations in the booklet *M-'e E'cci Aashi Awadi* by Noelle Sullivan and Nicholas Peterson Vrooman. Look for it in the gift shop. For a special treat, read the descriptions of this Missouri River region in *The Journals of Lewis and Clark*, edited by Frank Bergon.

The Best Stuff Visitors may find a stroll through the blowing sweetgrasses of this restored prairie the most fascinating part of the trip. Add to that a tour of the earthlodge by park ranger Lauren Yellowbird, whose ancestors lived here; the drawings of the village made by frontier visitors shown in park literature; the provocative story of a lost way of life as told by Buffalo Bird Woman; and the now-grassy symmetry of the close-knit village remains, and you can visualize the teeming villages of a fallen civilization.

Then and Now The villages that existed here live in the pages of books, museum displays, and thousands of excavated artifacts. Most of these artifacts, tools, and pottery shards are housed here in a climate-controlled vault at the site. The abandoned village earthlodges were destroyed by raiding Sioux, the meanderings of the Missouri River, and flooding caused by dams.

Now the eroded shores of the Missouri where Mandan children once played are fenced off and marked with signs warning visitors to stay off or face fines and/or imprisonment. As you walk the mowed grasses around the earthlodge depressions, locusts scatter beneath your feet.

The earthlodge you visit now was authentically constructed in 1992 for more than $100,000. It's outfitted with a $30,000 security system. Step inside the buffalo-hide door with its hollow buffalo hoof "doorbell" and discover a culture that included horses corralled inside, a sacred "shrine" area, indoor sweatlodges, and homes constructed and owned by the women.

Women also tended the fields in this agriculture-based society. As Buffalo Bird Woman says in the orientation film: "We cared for our corn in those days just as we would a child." Men spent their time hunting, seeking spiritual knowledge, or horse raiding.

Natural objects such as seashells found at the site tell of the villages' extensive trade network. But the villages also had their own trade good: Knife River flint. The river here is so named because the Hidatsa and Mandan people made knives and projectile points from this malleable flint, mined in nearby quarries. (Check out a sample of Knife River flint at the visitor center.)

The Hidatsa who survived the smallpox epidemics held on at Knife River until 1845. Then they and the last of the Mandan moved two days up the Missouri River and established Like-a-Fishhook Village. The Arikara tribe from further south joined them in 1862. The federal government relocated the people to reservations in 1885. Today they are known as the Three Affiliated Tribes.

Elsewhere in the Area Fort Mandan, a replica of the fort Lewis and Clark built in 1800 to 1805, is three miles west of Washburn, North Dakota; Fort Clark site, where the American Fur Company operated a major fur-trading post, is also near Washburn; Three Affiliated Tribes Museum is just south of New Town; Roosevelt National Park is in the Badlands along U.S. 85; and Fort Abraham Lincoln is just west of Bismarck.

Crazy Horse Memorial

The Second Colossus of the West—in Progress

Location The Black Hills of southwestern South Dakota, about 40 miles southwest of Rapid City, South Dakota. The Crazy Horse Memorial entrance is 16 miles southwest of Mount Rushmore on U.S. 16/385, and 11 miles north of the town of Custer, South Dakota.

The Crazy Horse Memorial ($) is a not-for-profit educational and cultural project financed totally by fees and contributions. The mountain sculpture is a work in progress. The memorial is open daily, in summer, 6:30 A.M.–dark, and the rest of the year, 8 A.M.–dark. Laughing Water Restaurant at the site is open May through mid-October. The Volksmarch takes place yearly in the first weekend in June. Then the public has direct access to the carving, walking up to the face. For information contact Crazy Horse Memorial, Crazy Horse, South Dakota 57730-9506. Tel. (605) 673-4681.

Frame of Reference The work of "sculpting" the great Sioux leader Crazy Horse from the Black Hills mountain began in 1947 and continues today. The memorial's progress depends on funding, and no completion date has been set.

Significance The Crazy Horse Memorial began as a dream of an aging Lakota (Sioux) chief, Henry Standing Bear, who approached Korczak Ziolkowski with his idea to show whites that Native North Americans also had heroes. Ziolkowski, a self-taught sculptor of note who had worked on Mount Rushmore, agreed. Lakota chiefs decided the mountain should be carved into the image of the Oglala (a branch of the Sioux) chief Crazy Horse, whose courageous short life and tragic death carried great symbolism.

The sculptor, who looked like a bearded mountain man, saw an opportunity to "right a little bit of wrongs" done to Native North Americans. He made the humanitarian project a lifelong work. Ziolkowski planned Crazy Horse as a three-dimensional monument, created from a whole mountain. When finished, the memorial will reign as the world's largest sculpture.

The sculpture depicts Crazy Horse answering a question posed to him by a white fur trader, "Where are your lands?" The chief sits astride his horse, his arm extended, his finger pointing to the East from which the white man came. Crazy Horse's reply: "My lands are where my dead lie buried."

Though not as well known as neighboring Mount Rushmore, the Crazy Horse Memorial attracts throngs of enthusiastic visitors year-round. They witness the sculpture in the making. The 70-room Crazy Horse complex is a thriving center of Native North American culture, also a work in progress.

About the Site The Crazy Horse Memorial comprises the 600-foot mountain that one day will be a completed image of the Sioux chief; the sculptor's Crazy Horse model—1/34 the size of the mountain version; and a half-dozen buildings centered on a wooden veranda. Here you can observe the work in progress. (The sculpture is 1½ miles from the observation deck. For 25¢ you can peer through mounted telescopes and see sculptors at work with jackhammers as mountain goats look on.)

The complex includes the log Ziolkowski home and studio, a three-wing Indian Museum housing one of the region's foremost Native American collections, the Native North American Educational and Cultural Center, an extensive gift shop, and the Laughing Water Restaurant. Two rustic theaters offer orientation films on the memorial. Visitors can take a scheduled bus trip ($) to the base of the monument.

Since Ziolkowski's death in 1992, his large family has carried on the project of carving the monument in pegmatite granite. Ziolkowski lies buried in a vault in the mountainside here, its steel doors bearing the epitaph he wrote for himself: "KORCZAK, Storyteller In Stone, May His Remains Be Left Unknown."

Sleep in a Tepee, See Wounded Knee

You can camp in a tepee at the Minnekahta Tepee Village, ½ mile south of Hot Springs, South Dakota, on Highway 385, just south of Custer State Park. You can sleep in a Sioux tepee lodge or pitch your own tent along the Minnekahta River, the river of warm water. Activities include a journey to Wounded Knee, site of the 1890 Lakota massacre, the final chapter of the Plains Indian Wars. (A monument stands over the mass grave of many of the victims of the Seventh Cavalry.) The journey also takes you to the site of the historic Ghost Dances and Red Cloud's burial site on the Pine Ridge Reservation.

For more information, telephone (605) 745-1890.

Hot Tips There's no hiking here, but you will be walking around at a high altitude. Some may experience physical discomfort. Allow 1½ hours for your visit, more if you take the 25-minute bus trip. Be sure to visit the restaurant, where free coffee is a tradition.

Kids may enjoy mailing a postcard postmarked "Crazy Horse" to friends from the 22-year-old post office.

Souvenir Tip You also can pick up a free souvenir rock blasted from the mountain. The rocks are in bins near the entrance.

A visit here will have more meaning if you learn about Crazy Horse beforehand. The book *Crazy Horse: The Strange Man of the Oglalas* by Mari Sandoz is very popular.

The Best Stuff First of all, there's the sheer size of this emerging monument, called the "fifth face of the Black Hills" that will be 641 feet long and 563 feet high when finished. Crazy Horse's single, handcarved chief's feather will tower 44 feet into the air. The space under his pointing arm can hold a 10-story building. The heads of all four Mount Rushmore presidents can fit into Crazy Horse's long-haired head; a five-room house can fit into one of his nostrils.

Participating in the annual Volksmarch onto the monument is memorable to say the least. And two nights per year the mountain crew at Crazy Horse sets off a spectacular "night blast" of fireballs on the unfinished sculpture. The event takes place on June 26, the birthday of Ziolkowski's wife Ruth, and on September 6, the dual anniversaries of Crazy Horse's death and the 1908 birth of the sculptor.

Then and Now No documented photo of Crazy Horse exists. In drawings, he's the one out front at the Battle of Little Big Horn with his trademark lightning bolt painted across his face, an eagle on the right side of his head, and hail marks over his body. Crazy Horse's "colors" were blue and yellow. Sculptor Ziolkowski, a Bostonian orphan of Polish descent, made a composite of the warrior from "word pictures" given to him by old Native North Americans who had known the chief during his brief 34-year life.

After Ziolkowski and Chief Standing Bear chose the site for the memorial and purchased land from the federal government, the sculptor used 179 gallons of white paint to outline the future sculpture. You can still see the six-foot-wide line where blasting has not yet occurred.

By today 8½ million tons of rock have been dynamited away. Work continues according to Ziolkowski's specifications. He

Deadwood: Witness Wild Bill Hickok's Demise

The town of Deadwood, South Dakota, has its roots in Lieutenant Colonel George Armstrong Custer's discovery of gold in "them thar hills," the Black Hills, that is. Gold seekers threw up the original wooden buildings in this mining town in 1875. Successive fires and floods wiped them out, but townsfolk soon rebuilt them with native stone.

Corporate mining downsizing almost killed the town in the 1980s. But in 1989 South Dakota approved limited-stakes gambling for the city of Deadwood. Much of the gambling take was earmarked for preservation and restoration of Deadwood's many special buildings.

The reborn town, a national historic landmark, is best known as the place where James Butler Hickok (better known as Wild Bill Hickok), let down his guard during a poker game on August 2, 1876, and took a .45 bullet in the back. (This was only weeks after Custer was slain in the Battle of Little Big Horn.) A drifter named Jack McCall, who claimed the "prince of pistoleers" had killed his brother, shot the infamous, gun-slinging ex-sheriff.

Like a passel of others at the time, Hickock had come to Deadwood seeking his fortune. What he actually got is now part of Western legend.

During summer months, you can witness the four-times-daily reenactment of Hickok's killing and the aftermath at Saloon #10 on Deadwood's historic Main Street. The reconstructed saloon also displays Wild Bill's death chair and 1,043 items, historical and otherwise. Saloon #10 bills itself as the only museum in the world with a working bar.

Visitors can walk among 100-year-old Victorian buildings along the historic Deadwood downtown. You'll also find museums, the Broken Boot Gold Mine, and Mount Moriah Cemetery, where Wild Bill and his pal Calamity Jane are buried. You can walk genuine brick streets and ride the Deadwood Trolleys. Look for Crazy Horse sculptor Korczak Ziolkowski's granite tribute to Wild Bill.

Hot Tips History books provide the facts on Wild Bill, but to sample the legend, watch the 1996 movie *Wild Bill* before your visit.

For more information on Deadwood and other South Dakota historic sites, contact South Dakota Tourism, Room 602, 711 East Wells Avenue, Pierre, SD 57501-3369. Tel. 1-800-S DAKOTA.

and his wife, Ruth, prepared three books of detailed plans for the project before his death at age 74.

Twice Ziolkowski turned down $10 million in federal funding for the project. He wanted money from regular people to pay for his vision. In the orientation film Ziolkowski explains his life mission, his voice cracking with emotion. He says, "When the legends die, the dreams end, and when the dreams end, there is no more greatness."

Crazy Horse's nine-story-high face looms above hikers on the Crazy Horse Volksmarch. The 10K hike, which draws more than 10,000 visitors, is the nation's largest Volksmarch. Held the first weekend in June, it is the only time the public has access to the mountain carving in progress. *Robb DeWall*

Mount Rushmore

Patriotic Colossus of the West

Location The Black Hills of southwestern South Dakota, 25 miles southwest of Rapid City, South Dakota. Mount Rushmore rises 2 miles southwest of Keystone, South Dakota, on Highway 244. From Rapid City, take U.S. 16 south to U.S. 16A south to Highway 244 west. Watch for directional signs.

Mount Rushmore National Memorial is open daily, year-round. The Orientation Center is open daily, except December 25, from Memorial Day through Labor day, 8 A.M.–10 P.M., and the rest of the year, 8 A.M.–5 P.M. The Sculptor's Studio is open daily, in summer, 9 A.M.–5 P.M. For information on the many ranger talks, tours, special events, and the Sculpture Lighting Ceremony, contact Superintendent, Mount Rushmore National Memorial, P.O. Box 268, Keystone, SD 57751. Tel. (605) 574-2523.

Frame of Reference Work on carving the faces of the four U.S. presidents in granite began at Mount Rushmore in 1927 and ended in 1941.

Significance Mount Rushmore began in 1923 as a dream of a state historian of South Dakota to attract tourists. His original idea for the sculptures was to represent Western pioneer history. But noted sculptor Gutzon Borglum, who agreed to carve the mountain face, had a different idea.

Borglum was inspired to carve the heads of U.S. presidents, first George Washington, Abraham Lincoln, and Thomas Jefferson, then later Theodore Roosevelt. Borglum, also the sculptor behind Georgia's monument to the Confederacy, Stone Mountain, believed these men best represented America's first 150 years. The men stood for the nation's founding (Washington), preservation (Lincoln), growth (Jefferson), and development (Roosevelt).

Today Mount Rushmore is considered America's shrine of democracy. Borglum's colossus has become a great symbol of America around the world. The site attracts 2.8 million visitors a year, up to 30,000 per day in the summer. Rangers here call it the fast food of U.S. parks.

About the Site Mount Rushmore National Memorial encompasses 1,270 acres, including the carved mountain, towering about 400 feet above the park's columned grand entrance. The faces are about ¼ mile from the entrance. You can visit Borglum's second studio, where his Mount Rushmore model stands at a 1/12 scale of the mountain, and see the sites of the original studio. Nightly at 9 P.M. in summer, visitors gather in the large amphitheater at the foot of the memorial for a 20-minute talk about the four presidents, a film called *Four Faces on a Mountain*, and the ceremonial lighting of the memorial. Park rangers schedule 30-minute nature walks and 45-minute children's talks about Mount Rushmore's history. For a closer view of the monument, visitors can hike the one-mile Presidential Trail (as of this writing only partially finished) to the mountain base. At press time, the Presidential Trail was partially finished. The full trail is scheduled to open in summer 1998.You can walk under the presidents' heads and look up the eight nostrils on four, 21-foot granite noses. A new 5,200 square-foot visitor center museum with exhibits, a large Grand View Terrace, and two theaters featuring a 13-minute orientation film, also are scheduled to open in summer 1998.

An orientation center and bookstore show a continuous four-minute film telling the history of the memorial. There is also an expansive gift shop and restaurant on the premises.

The town of Keystone is chock full of shops, restaurants, attractions, and museums, including the Rushmore-Borglum Story museum ($) and gift shop.

Hot Tips Park in one of five parking lots outside the grand entrance. During peak tourist season, you may have to circle around for a parking space; but be patient—turnover is quick at the fast-food park. The park may be difficult for some to experience. It's 33 steps up to the grand portico, and, remember, you're already way up there, 5,245 feet above sea level. Warning to those with heart or respiratory problems: the altitude and steep terrain can conspire to make hiking dangerous. Stay on the trail and boardwalk. There is no climbing allowed on the monument.

Plan to spend at least two hours here, more if you want to enjoy the ranger talks. Eating at the restaurant and poking around the big gift shop are great fun, too.

Kids Tip Pick up the *Mount Rushmore Junior Ranger Program* booklet at the orientation center. Also, an educational activity book, *Discover Mount Rushmore*, is a great follow-up for the trip home.

You can find food, accommodations, and plenty of things to do in Keystone. The area abounds with campgrounds, including those at Custer State Park and Black Hills National Forest. You can see Mount Rushmore and other area sites from an aerial tramway ($) in Keystone, and while touring by helicopter [individual ($$) or group ($$$)] from a site just outside the Crazy Horse Memorial entrance on U.S. 16/385.

The Best Stuff The faces at Mount Rushmore are huge: 60 feet tall with 18-foot-wide mouths. Besides the thrill of seeing this big, big monument, the best thing is the evening program. It brings home the rich experience of just being here. Visiting Mount Rushmore is truly an adventure in patriotism.

Plan to have your pulse race and eyes water at the evening Sculpture Lighting Ceremony. The 30-minute program ends with the singing of the National Anthem as lights illuminate the famous presidential faces. The ranger talks are quite good.

Then and Now While the days of blasting, drilling, and polishing the granite faces are long gone, preservation work continues. National Park Service crews inspect the monument yearly and patch small cracks with a silicone-based mixture that Borglum himself devised. So far, there's been no major damage.

Borglum chose this mountain, named earlier for New York lawyer Charles Rushmore—who ensured that his moniker remained by donating $5,000 toward the sculpture—because of the weather-resistant nature of the mountain's Harney Peak granite. Native North Americans viewed the Black Hills as a holy place; locals referred to the mountain as "Slaughterhouse Hill."

Borglum liked the way the sun shown on the mountain, which was large enough to accommodate his grand vision. The gray granite appears gleaming white in bright sunshine. It erodes one inch every 1,500 years. So we can enjoy Mount Rushmore for the next 100,000 years!

The U.S. government paid for 85 percent of the sculpture's $1 million price tag; the rest was raised by schoolchildren nationwide. Borglum died before the monument's completion, but his son Lincoln directed the final phase of carving. Today rubble from the blasting still covers the mountainside beneath the faces.

Mount Rushmore's formal dedication ceremony took place in 1991, the monument's 50th anniversary.

Elsewhere in the Area Rushmore-Borglum Story museum is in Keystone; Crazy Horse Memorial is 16 miles southwest; Custer State Park is 9 miles south; and Wind Cave National Park is just south of Custer State Park.

6

EAST SOUTH CENTRAL

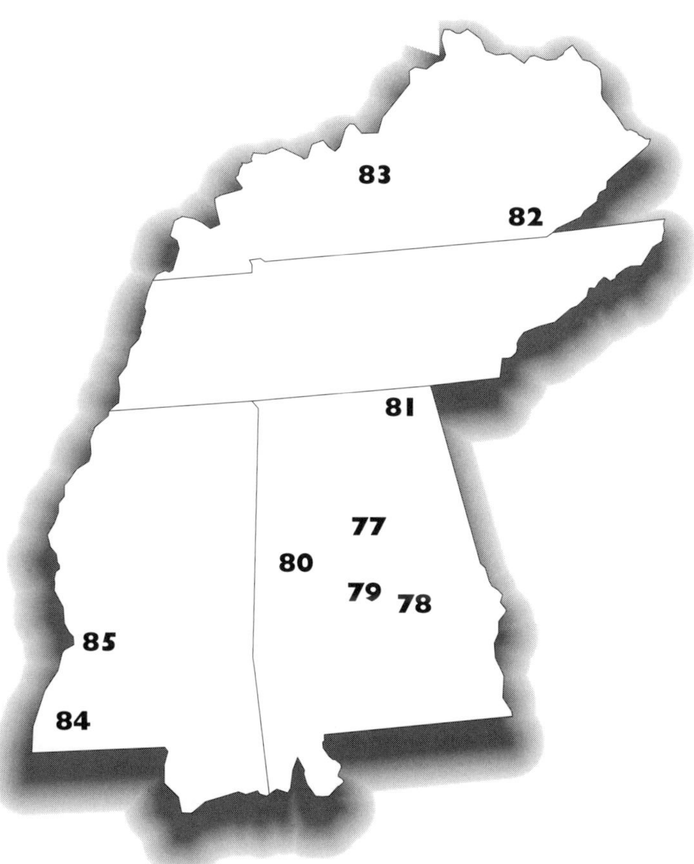

Key

Numbers correspond to site numbers on the map.

Alabama

77. Civil Rights Journey: Birmingham
78. Civil Rights Journey: Montgomery
79. Civil Rights Journey: Selma
80. Moundville
81. Russell Cave

Kentucky

82. Cumberland Gap
83. Lincoln's Birthplace

Mississippi

84. Natchez
85. Vicksburg

The Natchez Trace (see National Trail System Map on page xv)

Civil Rights Journey

Montgomery, Birmingham, and Selma

Location The three cities form a triangle in the heart of Alabama. Montgomery, the state capital, is located in the state's southeastern quadrant. Birmingham is 94 miles north of Montgomery; Selma is 49 miles west of Montgomery.

For more information on Alabama's Civil Rights Journey contact the Alabama Bureau of Tourism and Travel, P.O. Box 4309, Montgomery, AL 36103-4309. Tel. 1-800-ALABAMA. Ask for a booklet titled *Alabama's Black Heritage*. Government and private entities operate individual sites. Days and times of operation vary.

You may wish to preface your Alabama Civil Rights Journey with a visit to the Martin Luther King Jr. National Historic Site in Atlanta, 154 miles east of Birmingham.

Frame of Reference The Civil Rights movement flourished from the mid-1950s through the 1960s. Seeds of the movement were sown in 1955, when Rosa Parks refused to yield her seat on a bus to a white man, sparking the Montgomery bus boycott of 1955 to 1956. Protests for racial equality and human rights took place in Birmingham in 1962, and the famous Selma-to-Montgomery march occurred in 1965. The Civil Rights movement suffered a devastating blow with Martin Luther King Jr.'s assassination in 1968.

Significance Events in these Alabama cities, and the involvement of acknowledged Civil Rights movement leader Martin Luther King Jr. in them, epitomize the 1960s fight for racial justice and equal rights.

MONTGOMERY

It was in Montgomery, birthplace of the Confederacy, on December 1, 1955, that a weary African American seamstress named Rosa Parks refused to give up her seat on a bus to a white man, defying local Jim Crow laws. Her arrest ignited latent resentments in the city's African American community.

Under King's leadership, Parks's action resulted in the yearlong Montgomery bus boycott. The U.S. Supreme Court later ruled Montgomery's segregation law unconstitutional. Montgomery's state capitol came to symbolize legalized racial inequality. Civil Rights marchers in the Selma-to-Montgomery voting rights march of 1965 congregated on the capitol steps to voice their demands for freedom. The march riveted the nation.

BIRMINGHAM

In 1963 King and the group he and other African American leaders had formed in 1957 to fight for black Civil Rights, the Southern Christian Leadership Conference (SCLC), took on Birmingham. King considered Alabama's largest city the most segregated city in

America. The SCLC organized the African American community. In 1963 King led a series of nonviolent demonstrations in the city. The police commissioner, Eugene Bull Connor, proved to be an unwitting friend to the movement. He used attack dogs, tear gas, electric cattle prods, and fire hoses on the demonstrators as millions of outraged Americans watched on television.

The police actions mobilized national support for the movement. But King was arrested. From his jail cell, King wrote his famous *Letter from Birmingham City Jail*. On September 15, 1963, a bomb at Birmingham's 16th Street Baptist Church killed four African American girls attending Sunday school. The atrocity was a turning point in the Civil Rights protest. President John F. Kennedy became a high-profile advocate of new Civil Rights legislation.

SELMA

Selma solidified the Civil Rights movement. In 1965 the long struggle for African American voting rights culminated in a 50-mile march from Selma to Montgomery. Led by King, hundreds of Civil Rights marchers planned to take their protest to the steps of the Alabama capitol. But at the Edmund Pettus Bridge over the Alabama River, law enforcement officers attacked the marchers. That day, March 7, became known as "Bloody Sunday."

Two days later, again with King in the lead, the marchers peacefully turned around at the point of confrontation. On a third try on March 21 a swelled crowd of 4,000 marched over the bridge down Highway 80. U.S. national guardsmen, sent by President Lyndon B. Johnson, protected them. With heavy media coverage, the crowd continued to grow. Five days later 25,000 marchers reached Montgomery. President Johnson signed the Voting Rights Act on August 6, 1965.

About the Sites The Birmingham-Selma-Montgomery triangle features many historic landmarks associated with the Civil Rights movement. The cities have erected memorials, monuments, museums, and markers that commemorate the people and events of the nonviolent struggle for racial justice and equality four decades ago. Here are the most significant sites:

- **Birmingham.** The newly created Civil Rights District, including the Birmingham Civil Rights Institute (560 16th Street North), tells the story of the Civil Rights movement, then and now. Kelly Ingram Park (5th Avenue North at 16th Street) was the site of mass meetings in the 1960s. The park's Freedom Walk features sculptures commemorating events of 1963. The 16th Street Baptist Church is across 16th Street from the Institute and catty-corner to the park); the Greyhound Bus Station (North 19th Street), was the site of a violent attack on the Freedom Riders of 1961.
- **Selma.** The National Voting Rights Museum and Institute (1012 Water Avenue, near the Pettus Bridge) displays a record of events and people who made Civil Rights history; the Martin Luther King Jr. Street Historic Walking Tour (which begins at the corner of Jeff Davis Avenue and Martin Luther King Jr. Street) is a self-guided tour of the area where the voting rights activities organized (including the Brown Chapel AME Church, which served as protest headquarters); the Edmund Pettus Bridge (downtown over Alabama

River) is where law enforcement officers confronted marchers; and the Selma-Dallas Courthouse (Alabama Avenue and Lauderdale Street) was the destination of most of the voting rights protest marches.

Montgomery. The city's Civil Rights Memorial stands at the corner of Washington and Hull streets, on the grounds of the Southern Poverty Law Center. Maya Lin, architect of the Vietnam Memorial wall in Washington, D.C., designed the black-granite sculpture. The impressive work uses flowing water to evoke the Civil Rights movement and honor the 40 people killed during the struggle.

Other Montgomery sites include the Dexter Avenue King Memorial Baptist Church (454 Dexter Avenue), where Martin Luther King Jr. was minister when he led the bus boycott; the Rosa Parks arrest site (corner of Moulton and Montgomery streets), where the seamstress refused to give up her bus seat; the gleaming, 140-year-old Alabama State Capitol, where Selma marchers gathered on the wide front steps; the Greyhound Bus Station (Court Street), site of riots when angry mobs met Freedom Riders in 1961; and a long list of buildings, exhibits, statues, plaques, and museums associated with or commemorating the Civil Rights movement.

Hot Tips To visit all three cities, allow two to three days. If you begin in Atlanta, add another day. Plan to spend three hours in each city. It's important to give kids background information about the Civil Rights movement before your visit. The King site in Atlanta does this beautifully, as does the Civil Rights Institute in Birmingham. Many books are available on King and the movement, several written especially for kids. Check out the PBS documentary *Eyes on the Prize* at your local video store. Many parents have personal memories of the 1960s. This trip affords a great opportunity to share them with the family.

The Best Stuff Everything along the Alabama Civil Rights Journey tells an absorbing story. Regardless of time constraints, don't miss these:

Birmingham Civil Rights District. A sign reading "A Place of Revolution and Reconciliation" greets you on the brick Freedom Walk at Kelly Ingram Park. You walk past life-size sculptures depicting riveting scenes from the 1963 Civil Rights movement. Art includes "Police Dog Attack," "Children's March," "Ministers Kneeling in Prayer," and "Freedom Wall," in which a man and woman huddle against the building as fire hoses spray them. Crossing the street, you learn more in the domed Civil Rights Institute's circular series of galleries. Round and round you go, up a slightly inclined walkway, past rooms full of photographs, memorabilia, and video shows. The sites house the original door of King's Birmingham cell and a burned-out Greyhound bus.

Selma's Pettus Bridge and Voting Rights Institute. Now-adult children of the 1960s may recall the television footage of the confrontations at this steel, arched span leading out of downtown Selma. A plaque at its foot now tells of the Selma movement, while an overhead sign bearing a Confederate flag on the bridge itself reads "Selma Welcomes You." Among the walls of photographs in the small Voting Rights Institute, opened in 1993, stretches the "I Was There" wall. Here you'll find handwritten comments from Selma marchers. Look for Rosa Parks's. If you don't have time to walk the several blocks of Martin Luther King Jr. Street, you can drive most of it and read the plaques of the 12 stops from the car. Pick up a map of historic Selma at the Chamber of Commerce, 513 Lauderdale Street.

The Civil Rights Memorial. This centerpiece of the journey glistens in water-cooled black granite amid the gleaming white-marble government buildings that fill Montgomery's wide, hot streets. A circular table, the top of an off-angle, inverted cone, records the names of the 40 men, women, and children who died in the Civil Rights struggle. It chronicles the history of the movement. Water bubbles from the table's center and flows evenly across the top. As at the Vietnam Memorial wall in Washington, visitors can brush their fingers across the carved names and dates that radiate from the center like hands on a clock. The first entry begins with Rosa Parks's arrest, then goes to June 20, 1964, when Freedom Summer brought 1,000 young Civil Rights volunteers to Mississippi; to March 25, 1965, when Viola Gregg Liuzzo, a housewife and mother from Detroit, was shot and killed by a Klansman in Selma. The story ends with King's assassination in 1968.

On a curved wall behind the table, water flows over King's often-quoted words taken from the Bible. He said he would not be satisfied, "until justice rolls down like waters, and righteousness like a mighty stream."

King's 1885 brick church, Court Square, and the capitol are within easy walking distance. So is the First White House of the Confederacy at 644 Washington Avenue. The capitol's senate chamber, where delegates from seceding states organized the Confederate government in 1861, has been restored to its Civil War appearance.

Then and Now Most sites along the Civil Rights Journey look today as they did during the Civil Rights movement. Some change has been inevitable: Birmingham's still-active 16th Street Baptist Church has been restored, and even sleepy Selma has grown. Alabama today reminds visitors of the way things were, how much America has changed, and how far we have to go.

Martin Luther King Jr. National Historic Site in Atlanta. King's house is the second from the left.
National Park Service

◆Hidden Jewel◆

Moundville

Remains of the 1,000-Year-Old Ceremonial Center

Location West central Alabama, on the banks of the Black Warrior River in Moundville, 15 miles south of Tuscaloosa. Take Highway 69 from Tuscaloosa and head south. Watch for directional signs in the town of Moundville to the entrance.

Moundville Archaeological Park ($) is open daily, 8 A.M.–8 P.M. The museum is open daily, except for major holidays, 9 A.M.–5 P.M. For more information contact Moundville Archaeological Park, P.O. Box 66, Moundville, AL 35474. Tel. (205) 371-2572. The park has been part of the University of Alabama since 1928.

Frame of Reference Moundville was occupied about 1,000 years ago, during the last of three overlapping prehistoric cultures that flourished then vanished in North America. The Moundville society was part of the Mississippian culture (A.D. 1000–1540), a lost civilization of Mound Builders. The city was mysteriously abandoned before DeSoto's exploration of the Southeast in the 1540s.

Significance Moundville was an ancient fortifed chiefdom, a sophisticated city of about 3,000 people organized around a supreme chief. This chiefdom served as the ceremonial center for a network of satellite settlements housing 10,000 people. It was one of three major hubs of Mississippian civilization. The ruins of one is in Oklahoma; the other is in Georgia. Neither is as elaborate as Moundville.

What distinguishes Moundville today is the large number of mounds that survive in this sparsely populated farming area. Ancient people built flat-topped ceremonial mounds to support temples, council buildings, and homes of the elite here. Moundville's 60-foot Temple Mound is the second largest prehistoric mound in the country. The largest is in Cahokia, Illinois, eight miles east of St. Louis. The reconstructed, 700-year-old temple atop Temple Mound is open to the public and offers a unique experience.

Although thousands of prehistoric Native North American mounds dot southeastern America, Moundville's cluster of survivors is among the most significant. The ancient city's voluminous archaeological finds have been especially revealing.

About the Site The 317-acre park comprises 20 ceremonial mounds of various sizes, still rising majestically in the river mists after centuries of decay. The mounds occupy a plateau some 60 feet above the Black Warrior River. The mounds average 12 to 15 feet high. They generally surround an open space that served as a large central plaza in Moundville's heyday 800 years ago.

Open areas around the mounds were sites of hundreds of wood-and-mud homes. Open fertile lands along the river served as ancient cornfields for this intensely agricultural society.

Moundville has four lakes, formed when ancient hands mined the soil to construct the mounds. The lakes probably were stocked with fish. An unknown number of mounds at the site are not visible or have been destroyed by modern agriculture.

At the far end of the park a museum houses artifacts unearthed at the site, exhibits, a gift shop, and a theater where visitors can select from a menu of 21 informational videos. Viewing is by request. Near the river you can visit replicas of ancient Mississippian village homes outfitted with life-size dioramas. A boardwalk nature trail winds through the forest along the river. A conference center overlooks the river and is available for rental. There is an adjacent campground.

Hot Tips Don't be deterred by the site's remoteness. Follow the signs through the farmlands; you're on the right trail. Allow three to four hours at the site, longer if you hike the trails. Wear sturdy walking shoes. Use insect spray in warm months. No walking is allowed on the mounds, except on the steps provided at Mound B, the Temple Mound. Take water or beverages. Picnic tables are located at the site overlooking the river.

The videos provide excellent lessons in America's native prehistory. Without watching at least one, your visit to Moundville might be confusing. Highly recommended for all ages: the 15-minute version of *Moundville, Journey Through Time*. Food is available in the town of Moundville. Accommodations are available in surrounding towns and Tuscaloosa.

The Best Stuff Nothing "tops" the thrill of hiking the 82 wooden steps—located where the original earthen ones were—up the sloped side of Mound B. The restored rectangular temple (about 25 by 20 feet) has been reconstructed where it actually stood. Walk inside the waddle-and-daub structure (made of woven rods and twigs and mud) with a thatched roof of palm leaves. Life-sized models behind a shield of glass depict a religious rite.

Because the Mississippians left no written records, we don't know exactly what the rites were for or how they were performed. But evidence suggests that the sacred fire seen here was common. The fire, possibly representing the sun deity, has four logs pointing in the four cardinal directions: north, south, east, and west. Tattooed Native North Americans dance around the flames. Skulls without bodies unearthed here indicate that human sacrifice may have been part of the Moundville culture.

Then and Now We have but the barest outline of the Moundville story, told only by things left behind. Found in official excavations: 3,000 burials and associated cultural material, 75 home sites, 100 clay fire basins, weapons, pottery fragments, and jewelry. Looters took many objects before controlled excavations began in the early 1900s.

Some think the religious symbolism here may have been inspired by Mexican concepts, stories of which were brought here by tradesmen of the more advanced Aztec society. We don't know what inspired the ritual mound building. Experts theorize Moundville dwellers may have voluntarily built the mounds in a religious fervor. It's also possible the mounds were a product of forced labor, built to glorify chieftains.

We do know the ancient people built the ceremonial complex over many years, basketful by basketful. We also know that 85 percent of Moundville people had deliberately deformed skulls caused by a cradleboard fitted on infants' heads. Experts suspect that the

15 percent with normal skulls occupied the lowest social status. Kinship to the chieftain apparently determined social status; closest relatives had the highest status.

The story of Moundville and the other major centers of Mississippian culture in southeastern America ends in a cloak of mystery. The frenzied and labor-intensive mound building was relatively brief, ending for unknown economic, social, or political reasons. Chiefdoms may have disintegrated into smaller units after prolonged crop failures. Populations could have became so large that kinship to chieftains became meaningless. No proven direct link exisits between modern Native North American tribes and the Mississippian Mound Builders. Moundville's majestic remains leave only a provocative silence.

Elsewhere in the Area The Alabama Museum of Natural History is located at the University of Alabama on 6th Avenue in Tuscaloosa. You can view Moundville artifacts at the Paul W. Bryant Museum at 300 Paul W. Bryant Drive, Tuscaloosa.

For information on the two other major Mississippian mound centers, contact Spiro Mounds Archaeological State Park, Route 2, P.O. Box 339AA, Spiro, OK 74959. Tel. (918) 962-2062. And contact Etowah Indian Mounds State Historic Site, 813 Indian Mound Road SW, Cartersville, GA 30120. Tel. (404) 387-3747.

◊Hidden Jewel◊

Russell Cave

Unique Record of 8,000 Years of Human Habitation

Location Extreme northeast Alabama, 8 miles west of Bridgeport, Alabama, and 30 miles southwest of Chattanooga, Tennessee. Take U.S. 72 to Bridgeport, then Highway 75 north to the rural community of Mt. Carmel, then right onto Highway 98 and the entrance. Vehicles over 13 feet high must take Highway 74 or Highway 75 to Mt. Carmel from U.S. 72.

Russell Cave National Monument is open daily, except December 25, 8 A.M.–5 P.M.; in winter, until 4:30 P.M. For more information contact Superintendent, Russell Cave National Monument, Bridgeport, AL 35740. Tel. (205) 495-2672.

Frame of Reference Russell Cave was significant from at least 7000 B.C. to about A.D. 1650, beginning in the early Archaic period (7000–3500 B.C.) to the middle Mississippian cultural period (A.D. 1000–1700), which ended about the time of European settlement in North America.

Significance Evidence unearthed here suggests that nomadic hunters, then extended Stone Age families, occupied Russell Cave beginning 8,000 years ago. The layered floor of this limestone cave, near a water source but high above the flood plain, has yielded 2½ tons of artifacts. The rich finds of this cave distinguish it from the region's thousands of limestone caves formed by an ancient sea. The artifacts, as well as the prehistoric caveman skeletons unearthed here, have revealed a unique, detailed, and continuous record of human habitation in North America. Visitors reach Russell Cave entrance by an asphalt path and wooden staircase. You can walk inside the cave on a plank footpath.

The story discovered in this cavern, curving 270 feet into a limestone mountain, has given new and valuable insight into Stone Age life. Findings here have shed light on the evolution of Native North Americans. People were living in Russell Cave thousands of years before the dawn of civilization in the Middle East and ancient Egypt (5000–3500 B.C.).

About the Site The Russell Cave archaeologists have studied what was a cave shelter, about the size of a small auditorium. Retreating Ice Age glaciers formed it 11,000 years ago. The shelter stands 107 feet wide and 26 feet high at its mouth, which opens 32 feet up the mountainside. The cave entrance overlooks a small pond, the result of an ancient cavern collapse, that revealed the opening visitors now enter. Mist rises from the cool waters and drenches the surrounding, dense forest. Russell Cave is the centerpiece of a 310-acre wooded park 10 miles from the Tennessee River. It lies in a tributary valley called Doran's Cove.

A second, lower entrance in the mountain provides passage to a true, tubular cave of unknown reaches and low, tight passages. A usually complacent stream flows into the cave and exits miles away. With heavy rainfall, the stream quickly rises, overwhelming the cave and anyone unfortunate enough to be inside. No wonder ancient people preferred the higher cave shelter. Only experienced spelunkers can enter, with written permission from the park service.

A visitor center houses a museum with artifacts excavated from the cave. A small theater features a menu of four videos and a slide show explaining the cave's geological and biological stories. Recommended viewing includes the video *A Window in Time*. There's also a small gift shop. Visitors also can view a 1,000-year-old burial mound at the site, a 3/5-mile hiking trail, and a shelter for hands-on ranger talks (upon request).

Hot Tips This historic jewel is definitely hidden amid Alabama farmlands. Look at its isolation as a plus: there are no wax museums, no amusement rides, no souvenir shirts. In fact, the remote valley's pristine nature fuels the imagination. Allow two hours at the site.

Take a snack with you. The visitor center has a beverage machine and picnic tables. Food and accommodations are available in Bridgeport and nearby towns in Alabama and Tennessee, including Chattanooga.

When hiking to the cave, stay on the marked asphalt path to avoid sinkholes and other hazards. Moss makes the path slippery in places. Watch at least one of the videos before you enter the cave; otherwise the visit could be a hit-or-miss proposition. Ordering pamphlets in advance may help. A reprint from a 1956 *National Geographic Magazine*, "Life 8,000 Years Ago Uncovered in an Alabama Cave," is especially good.

The Best Stuff Hiking to this prehistoric shelter, you'll experience a time warp and shivers down your spine. Visitors walk where cave dwellers are known to have once walked. Inside the cave shelter you descend into an excavated pit near the site of 1950s archaeological digs. Here's what you'll find:

Layers of Time. In the pit, a large yardstick of time corresponds to the layers of the pit wall. The yardstick starts at the cave's original stone floor, which was made of limestone slabs dropped from the ceiling around the end of the Ice Age. Over time the fallen slabs formed a new floor, which rose higher and higher above flood level. The rising floor also was a result of human response to the accumulation of household debris: occupants brought in basketfuls of dirt to cover discarded bones and broken objects, and voilà!—spanking-clean, new floor! It's been estimated that an inch of dirt deposits represents a century of occupation.

By the time the cave was last occupied, as the Renaissance overtook Europe, the cave floor had moved 32 feet up the mountain. Archaeologists have read the floor layers like the pages of a book. The pages held rich deposits of points, fishhooks, bone needles, baskets, pump drills, jewelry, pottery, charcoal remains of ancient home fires, human bones, and the remains of an obviously well-loved dog. A push-button audio program in the pit tells about cave excavation.

Four-Thousand-Year-Old Face. Among the museum exhibits is the reconstruction of a face from a 4,000-year-old skull found in the cave. The skull belonged to a 40-something male. Earliest inhabitants simply buried the dead in the cave floor. Studies show that this ancient man suffered from malnutrition, arthritis, and severe tooth wear. Nine burials were found in the cave.

Then and Now Since 1961 the National Park Service has administered the monument as an archaeological site. Amateur archaeologists first ascertained the cave's importance in the early 1950s. They contacted the Smithsonian Institution and the National Geographic Society, which conducted excavations at the site. The society then bought the property from local farmers and donated it to the American people. The flurry of activity following discovery of the cave's riches ended 50 years ago. Most of the excavated treasures are in storage; others are displayed in various museums. Only a handful remain at the site. Portions of the cave remain deliberately untouched for future study and discovery.

Experts say the wooded Alabama landscape here looks about as it did at the end of the Ice Age.

◊Hidden Jewel◊

Cumberland Gap

Where Daniel Boone Blazed the Wilderness Road

Location At the point in the Appalachian Mountains where the states of Kentucky, Virginia, and Tennessee meet. Cumberland Gap is accessible from the east via U.S. 58, and from the west and south via U.S. 25E. The visitor center is ¼ mile south of Middlesboro Kentucky on U.S. 25E.

Cumberland Gap National Historical Park is open daily, 8 A.M.–dusk. The visitor center is open daily, except December 25, 8 A.M.–5 P.M. Shuttlebus tours to the Hensley Settlement ($) are scheduled daily, June through August, and on weekends, September through October. Reservations are recommended. Special programs and events are scheduled on summer and on fall weekends. For information contact Superintendent, Cumberland Gap National Historical Park, P.O. Box 1848, Middlesboro, KY 40965. Tel. (606) 248-2817.

Frame of Reference White men began traversing Cumberland Gap in the mid–18th century, around the time of the American Revolution, to the 1830s. The Gap, however, had long been a key pass for buffalo and a Native North American Warrior's Path before white men discovered it. The Wilderness Road was built through the Gap in 1775.

Significance This natural, **V**-shaped low spot in the towering chain of the Appalachian Mountains made possible the country's first "Oregon Trail." Through this doorway famous frontiersman Daniel Boone and 30 men hacked out the 208-mile-long Wilderness Road in less than three weeks. The road opened up what was then the West to pioneers seeking better lives. Until that time, the mountain barrier, hostile Native North Americans, and warring French had kept settlers bound to the East Coast. In 1795 the trail was widened to accommodate wagons and stagecoaches.

Although the turmoil of the American Revolution slowed migration, more than 300,000 settlers poured through Cumberland Gap before 1800. Abraham Lincoln's grandfather passed through the Gap on his way to Kentucky in 1782.

The Wilderness Road ended near present-day Lexington, Kentucky, at the Kentucky River. Here Boone and other settlers later built Fort Boonesborough. Until the time of the Wilderness Road, the Kentucky Bluegrass region was untamed and unsettled. Native North American tribes had agreed that the bountiful land would remain open hunting grounds. During the 1820s and 1830s the opening of more direct northern routes west, including the Erie Canal, eliminated the need for the Wilderness Road.

About the Site You can walk a short portion of the original Wilderness Road through Cumberland Gap. The Gap's name comes from the nearby Cumberland River, which an early explorer named in homage to King George's son, the Duke of Cumberland.

The original trail walk is part of a 70-mile network of trails through the 20,000-acre park, about 17½ miles long and averaging 1⅔ miles wide through three states. Permits are required for overnight hiking along longer trails. The park boasts many scenic vistas and campgrounds ($). At Pinnacle Overlook you'll gain breathtaking views of three states. If you climb the ⅘-mile trail up Tri-State Peak, you can stand in the three states at the Tri-State Marker.

The visitor center houses a small museum, gift shop, and video room. Here you can see two videos, one on the history of Cumberland Gap, the second on the Hensley Settlement. The Hensley Settlement, high atop nearby Brush Mountain, was a community of 12 scattered farmsteads that flourished for nearly five decades beginning in 1904. Sherman Hensley, who established the community, was the last to leave the isolated settlement of about 100 people in 1951. Today costumed interpreters work the three reconstructed farmsteads in warm months. Kids will enjoy visiting the one-room mountain schoolhouse and learning about the isolated mountaineers' strange social life.

Boone's Last Home

Daniel Boone's last home is located in Defiance, Missouri, 35 miles west of St. Louis. The stone home and surrounding grounds are open to the public. Boone built the house from 1799 to 1812 and died there in 1820. Many of the Boone family's personal belongings remain in the house. For more information contact Historic Daniel Boone Home and Boonesfield Village, Inc., 1868 Highway F, Defiance, MO 63341. Tel. (314) 987-2251.

The Gap will soon look much like pioneers saw it two centuries ago, thanks to new 4,600-foot-long twin tunnels through Cumberland Mountain. The tunnels take traffic around the Gap area. The historic 19th-century village of Cumberland Gap is nearby.

Hot Tips Begin your visit at the visitor center, where you can get maps and information. Picnic areas are near the campground on U.S. 58 in Virginia. The park is a wild area; never hike alone. Dress for the mountain's cooler climate, and watch for poisonous copperheads and timber rattlesnakes, as well as poisonous plants. Watch your footing.

Contact the park in advance for hiking and camping information. If you don't take the shuttlebus tour of Hensley Settlement, you will need a four-wheel-drive vehicle to negotiate the steep, primitive road to the site. Intrepid hikers can take a seven-mile trail loop to the site.

Food and accommodations are available in Middlesboro.

The Best Stuff The pristine nature of the park not only wows visitors but allows them to appreciate the legend of Daniel Boone. Boone, a contemporary of George Washington's during the French and Indian War, was already a famous hunter and woodsman when Judge Richard Henderson of North Carolina formed a plan to settle the dark and bloody ground of Kentucky. In 1774 Henderson formed the Transylvania Company and recruited Boone, who had already spent years exploring Kentucky, to blaze a trail through the mountains. Henderson planned to organize the colony of Transylvania, selling land he had purchased dubiously from Cherokees to settlers. The plan failed.

Boone, a natural leader with the courage, strength, and honesty admired on the frontier, chose 30 men for the task Henderson asked of him. The men axed trees, moved stumps, and filled in holes to blaze what pioneers later dubbed "the Wilderness Road." Boone's road ran from the Holston River at present-day Kingsport, Tennessee, to the Kentucky River. Men in Boone's party were paid $53 for their labor. Despite attacks by Native North Americans and other hardships, most of the crew stayed with Boone to settle Fort Boonesborough.

Native North Americans, eager to protect hunting land, attacked the fort. The most famous attack came in 1778, when 400 Native North Americans surrounded the small, rectangular fort. Forty Kentucky riflemen held them off.

During his explorations and settlement in the Bluegrass country, Native North Americans captured Boone several times. He always escaped. Native North Americans killed Boone's father and a son and captured a daughter. Boone rescued her. Such tales have fueled Boone's legendary stature.

Kids will enjoy their visit more if they are familiar with the story of Daniel Boone. Many books are available. Catherine E. Chambers's *Daniel Boone and the Wilderness Road* is good.

Then and Now Boone wasn't the first white man to find Cumberland Gap, which geologists think was formed by water erosion, nor was he the first to explore or settle Kentucky; historians just gave him better exposure. Credit for discovering the pass in 1750 goes to Dr. Thomas Walker of Virginia, who wrote a description of it. The French and Indian War postponed exploration. At the war's end hunters used the pass. But Boone was first to blaze a pioneer trail and mark a path through the Kentucky wilderness.

After the Wilderness Road heyday had passed and the Civil War began, both the North and South considered the gap strategic. The pass changed hands four times, each time with trees felled and camps built, but no battles happened there. Today you can see the sites of Civil War camps along Gap trails.

After the war the Gap lay in desolate waste. In the mid-1880s the discovery of coal and iron led to a brief industrial boom. A crumbling stone iron furnace remains as a reminder of the mines, railroads, furnaces, and factories of that bygone era. Congress established the Cumberland Gap National Park in 1940.

Elsewhere in the Area Dr. Thomas Walker State Historic Site is located near Barbourville, Kentucky. Fort Boonesborough State Park, which features Daniel Boone's reconstructed fort, is in Richmond, Kentucky. Both are northwest of Cumberland Gap.

◆Hidden Jewel◆

Natchez

America's First Urban Frontier

Location Southwestern Mississippi on the Mississippi River, 115 miles southwest of Jackson, Mississippi, and 120 miles northwest of New Orleans. From the north and west take U.S. 65. From the south take U.S. 61, and from the east take U.S. 84/98. Proceed to the historic waterfront. Melrose Mansion, temporary park headquarters, is located at 1 Melrose-Montebello Parkway.

Natchez National Historical Park is open daily, except December 25, 8:30 A.M.–5 P.M. Guided tours of Melrose Estate ($) are conducted daily between 9 A.M. and 4 P.M. For more information contact Superintendent, Natchez National Historical Park, P.O. Box 1208, Natchez, MS 39121. Tel. (601) 442-7047.

For information about Natchez contact the Natchez Convention and Visitors Bureau, P.O. Box 1485, Natchez, MS 39121-6345. Tel. (601) 446-6345 or 1-800-99 NATCHEZ.

Frame of Reference In the early to mid–19th century fortune-seekers raced to the lower Mississippi River valley to cultivate cotton, in high demand as the Industrial Revolution blossomed. Natchez reigned as symbolic capital of the South's slaveholding "Cotton Kingdom" in the 1840s and 1860s, until the

Grand Village of the Natchez

When French colonizers arrived in what is now Mississippi in the early 18th century, one group of Native North American Mound Builders still occupied their villages. These were the Natchez Indians.

Until French colonization and conflict drove the Natchez from their ancestral homeland, they had lived in the area for 500 years. By 1730 disease and warfare had virtually eradicated the Natchez. Much of what experts theorize about North America's prehistoric Mound Builders comes from European accounts of the Natchez Indians.

Natchez culture reached its height almost 500 years ago, in the mid-1500s. It was a rigid caste system. The Natchez's supreme deity was the sun; the high priest was called a Sun.

The Grand Village of the Natchez Indians preserves two large mounds—the Great Mound of the Sun's House and Temple Mound—and the sites of two ceremonial plazas. Visitors can view a reconstructed Natchez house and corn granary. The visitor center houses excavated artifacts and exhibits.

The Grand Village of the Natchez Indians is open daily, except Thanksgiving, December 25, and January 1, Monday through Saturday, 9 A.M.–5 P.M., and Sunday, 1:30 P.M.–5 P.M. Call the park for additional holiday closings. The 126-acre park is located within the city limits of Natchez. From U.S. 61 (Seargent S. Prentiss Drive), go south of the Natchez Regional Medical Center and turn east onto Jefferson Davis Boulevard. Proceed half a mile to the park entrance and visitor center.

For more information contact Grand Village of the Natchez, 400 Jefferson Davis Boulevard, Natchez, MS 39120. Tel. (601) 446-6502.

Civil War ended the burgeoning prosperity. The town was first settled as a French trading post in 1714.

Significance This Mississippi River port of cotton planters' vast estates was antebellum America's westernmost point of civilization, now called the Old West. Eli Whitney's 1793 cotton gin, northeastern textile looms, and foreign markets raised the demand for cotton to a fevered pitch. People of all stripe poured into the Deep South looking to plant the lucrative cotton seed. Cotton became America's number-one cash crop.

Natchez offered a prime river location, warm climate, cheap fertile land, well-established plantation system based on slavery, and business-minded elite. Natchez became King Cotton's throne. It was the commercial, cultural, and social center of the 19th-century slaveholding cotton belt.

As the cotton plantations spread west from South Carolina and Georgia into Mississippi, Alabama, Louisiana, and Arkansas, a ribbon of civilization developed along the fertile Mississippi Valley. It included other river towns like Vicksburg and Port Gibson.

This genteel frontier included magnificent estates with Greek Revival mansions, formal gardens, elegant furniture, and elaborate social events. Wealthy plantation owners, mainly sons of elite Southern families, often spent summers in Europe.

Today Natchez preserves the era when cotton was king. A walk among the antebellum mansions here is a trip back in time.

About the Site The Natchez National Historical Park, established in 1990, is still under development. The park, located within Natchez city limits, now comprises these three units:

◆Hidden Jewel◆
The Natchez Trace

The old Natchez Trace from Nashville, Tennessee, to Natchez, Mississippi, is alive and well. Today the 450-mile trace includes the Natchez Trace Parkway and three segments of walking and horseback riding trails.

Trace refers to a trail first created by buffalo or animal hooves. Native North Americans used the Natchez Trace long before white explorers, trappers, hunters, and settlers did.

Construction work continues at both ends of the parkway, a modern but restricted-traffic road, around Nashville and Natchez. The only visitor center now stands where the auto tour ends, at Tupelo, Mississippi.

Trail segment locations are in Tennessee, south of Franklin near the community of Leipers Fork (25 miles); north of Jackson, Mississippi (25 miles, currently under development); and near Port Gibson, Mississippi, at the Rocky Springs camping area (15 miles). All 70 miles of the trails run within parkway lands. Trail segments include parts of the original trace.

Natchez Trace Parkway highlights include frontier battlegrounds, a Chickasaw Indian village site, Indian mounds, and the site near Hohenwald, Tennessee, where Meriwether Lewis died of gunshot wounds (probably self-inflicted) in 1809. A monument marks his grave. You'll also find campgrounds, water stops, food, and accommodations.

For information on the Natchez Trace National Scenic Trail and the Natchez Trace Parkway contact Natchez Trace Parkway, R.R. 1, NT-143, Tupelo, MS 38801. Tel. (601) 856-7321. To order books or video guides about the trace, ask for a Natchez Trace Bookstore Order Form. Tel. (601) 680-4002.

- **Melrose Estate.** This 80-acre estate has a Greek Revival mansion, restored slave quarters, formal gardens, and grounds buildings. Melrose represents Natchez's zenith of power. The estate owners were a lawyer from Pennsylvania and his wife, who was of an influential Mississippi family. They owned huge plantations in Mississippi, Louisiana, and Arkansas.
- **William Johnson House Complex,** 210 State Street. This 1841 Greek Revival–style townhouse was the home of freed slave William Johnson. This prominent African American owned a barbershop, which became a news exchange center, 1,500 acres of land—and slaves. Johnson's diaries chronicle life in antebellum Natchez. The house is undergoing restoration.
- **Fort Rosalie Site,** 504 South Canal Street. The government is purchasing the site where the French in 1716 built a palisade known as Fort Rosalie on bluffs of the Mississippi River. The fort was to protect the trading post established in 1714. The French built a second fort in 1730 at the site after Natchez Indians destroyed the first one a year earlier. Nothing remains of the fort.

Tours of more than 50 antebellum homes and churches are available in historic Natchez. The city, located on a wide river expanse at a bend, preserves remnants of its French, Spanish, and British past. Tours are by bus, horse-drawn carriage, trolley, and riverboat.

Civil War Siege of Vicksburg

Vicksburg National Military Park and Cemetery in Vicksburg, 74 miles northeast of Natchez, protects the site of the Civil War siege of Vicksburg. After the surrender at Vicksburg on July 4, 1863, Union forces gained undisputed control of the Mississippi River. The adjacent U.S.S. *Cairo* Museum displays artifacts from the Union gunboat, the first in history to be sunk by an electrically detonated mine.

Vicksburg also has many fine antebellum houses, the Gray & Blue Naval Museum, and the Yesterday's Children Antique Doll and Toy Museum.

Vicksburg National Military Park Visitor Center is open daily, except December 25, 8 A.M.–5 P.M.; the tour road is open daily, 8 A.M.–5 P.M. with extended summer hours. The U.S.S. *Cairo* Museum is open daily, in winter, 8:30 A.M.–5 P.M., and from April through October, 9:30 A.M.–6 P.M.

For information contact Superintendent, Vicksburg NMP, 3210 Clay Street, Vicksburg, MS 39180. Tel. (601) 636-0583.

Hot Tips Allow half a day to see the park and other Natchez sites. Summer weather is hot and sticky. Buy antebellum home tickets at the Canal Street Depot at Canal and State streets. This is the starting point of city tours and horse-drawn carriage tours. A scenic riverwalk, Natchez Under-the-Hill, offers saloons, restaurants, and shops. Food and accommodations are available in Natchez.

The Best Stuff Amid the splendor of Melrose you'll find the story of slaves, with whose labor the kingdom of cotton thrived. At the Melrose mansion you can tour reconstructed slave quarters. The long wooden houses, with dingy whitewashed walls and rough plank floors, stood near the barnyard. Field hands and their families probably called them home. The larger dwelling contains exhibits and a room furnished as a slave cabin would have been in the 1860s.

Slave life varied from one time to another, one state to another, and one plantation to another. Slave codes, which dictated how slaves should be treated, were secondary to the master's attitude. Generally food and housing were minimal, workdays went from dawn to dusk, and punishment swiftly followed when the master's rules were broken. Whipping was the most common form of punishment.

When Congress banned the importation of slaves from Africa in 1808, slaveowning became a rich man's endeavor. Natchez's few hundred families might have paid $1,500 to $2,000 for a skilled slave. Natchez's busy slave market was the second largest in the South.

It's not surprising that most Southerners, most of whom were small farmers, did not own slaves. In 1860 the total number of slaveholders in the South was 383,637 out of 8 million people. Because slaveowners usually had families, however, about ¼ of the Southern population was touched directly by slavery. But the wealthy plantation-owning elite set the tone of the South's economic and social life.

Slavery became a Southern institution, ended only by the Emancipation Proclamation and the Civil War. As slavery became institutionalized, abolitionist efforts increased, as did the moral isolation of an entire region. Emancipation of slaves wiped out a $4 billion investment in human flesh and blood.

Then and Now In 1860, just before the outbreak of the Civil War, America produced 60 percent of the world's cotton crop. Most of that was grown in the lower Mississippi River Valley. From 1830 to 1860, King Cotton was the major export to foreign markets, accounting for half of all U.S. exports. But by 1860 British textile expansion had ebbed, and world demand for cotton declined.

After the Civil War the government seized cotton fields that escaped destruction as federal tax payment. Pundits intoned that the South lost the war because of its reliance on King Cotton and slavery. Not until 1879 would cotton production equal the record harvest of 1860.

Today America's expanded cotton belt relies on mechanization, modern farming methods, and government price supports. An increased use of synthetic fibers had cut into production, but consumer demand for natural fibers such as cotton is rising again.

Elsewhere in the Area Natchez Museum of African American History and Culture is at 307-A Market Street; Natchez Costume and Doll Museum, Magnolia Hall, is at 215 Pearl Street; Emerald Mound, one of the largest Indian ceremonial mound in North America, is located about 10 miles northeast of Natchez on the Natchez Trace Parkway. (The largest mound is Cahokia in Illinois.)

7
WEST SOUTH CENTRAL

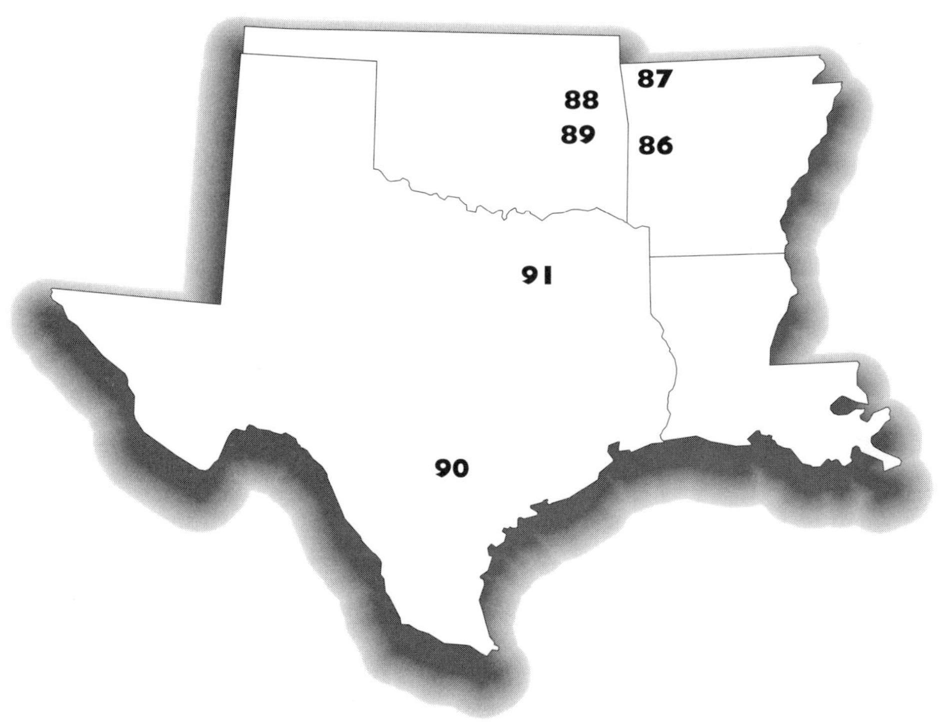

Key

Numbers correspond to site numbers on the map.

Arkansas
86. Fort Smith
87. Pea Ridge

Oklahoma
88. Tahlequah/ Sequoyah's Cabin
89. Fort Gibson
The Trail of Tears (see National Trails System Map on pages xv)

Texas
90. The Alamo/ The Missions of San Antonio
91. Dealey Plaza

Fort Smith

Law and Order on a Lawless Frontier

Location West central Arkansas at the border of Oklahoma, in downtown Fort Smith. From I-40 take U.S. 64 onto 2nd Street at the foot of the Arkansas River Bridge to enter park area. The visitor center temporarily is housed in the old maintenance facility on South 3rd Street in the park, near the parking lot entrance. Circle left around the visitor center to get to the parking lot.

Fort Smith National Historic Site ($) is open daily, except Thanksgiving, December 25, and January 1, 9 A.M.–5 P.M. For information contact Superintendent, Fort Smith National Historic Site, P.O. Box 1406, Fort Smith, AR, 72902. Tel. (501) 783-3961. The site is undergoing extensive renovations, scheduled to continue through 1999. Currently, the Old Barracks, which housed the federal courtroom, underground jail, and the visitor center, is closed. The attached second jail also is closed for renovation.

For information on the town's historic buildings, contact the Fort Smith Convention and Visitors Bureau, 2 North B Street, Fort Smith, AR 72901. Tel. 1-800-637-1477 or (501) 783-8888.

Frame of Reference Fort Smith's 80-year history spans most of the 19th century. The first Fort Smith was built in 1817. The second Fort Smith, most of which stands today, was built in 1838. The fort served as a military base until 1871. From 1872 to 1896, its abandoned barracks housed the legendary Federal Court of the Western District of Arkansas at the edge of Indian territory.

Significance Fort Smith, the Little Gibraltar on the Arkansas, is famous for its sequential roles as peacekeeper, protector, and law enforcer. For 80 years the fort stood watch on the border between Arkansas, then the edge of the United States, and the permanent Native North American territory, today's Oklahoma.

Fort Smith's second and most famous role, that of frontier law enforcer, began in 1872. The Native North American frontier had moved so far beyond the Arkansas state boundary by this time that the fort could no longer function as a supply depot. When the army moved out, the Federal Court of the Western District of Arkansas moved in. In the dignified courtroom in the fort's old barracks, Judge Isaac Parker, known as "the Hanging Judge," presided for 21 years.

The fort's infamous jail, dubbed "hell on the border" by inmates and critics, housed young, first-time offenders alongside hardened criminals. Seventy-nine criminals hanged until they died from the fort's gallows, which could accommodate six hangings at one time. Infamous outlaws, like the Dalton Brothers and Belle Star, faced justice here. The stories of their criminal careers and trials are legendary, but Judge Parker's 200 resourceful deputy marshals are just as colorful.

The fort first served as the military peacekeeper among warring Native North American tribes. Soldiers protected peaceful Native North Americans and settlers. Tribal fighting flared as a result of President Andrew Jackson's policy of Indian Removal, which forced Western tribes to share their lands with displaced Eastern tribes. The fort later served as a supply stop for the Native North American tribes on the Trail of Tears from 1830 to 1834. In the 1850s Fort Smith was a key depot servicing military posts that stood closer to the westward-moving frontier.

About the Site When renovations are complete visitors can tour two original buildings, the only survivors of the second Fort Smith's 29 structures. They are the 1838 commissary storehouse and the 1849 Old Barracks. The three-story sandstone barracks were converted into the federal courthouse.

Judge Parker's restored first-floor courtroom stands as it was in the Hanging Judge's days. Visitors can view the original "hell on the border" jail in the cellar beneath the Old Barracks. The 1888 jail, a large wing of the courthouse/barracks, is closed for renovation.

The reconstructed, whitewashed wooden gallows stands in its original location. A huge, 37-star garrison flag flutters from a 100-foot flagpole, exactly like the one that stood at the fort from 1867 to 1871. A concrete canopy protects the fort's original cistern.

At the western end of the park you'll find the ruins of the first Fort Smith on Belle Point along the Arkansas River. Only the stone foundations remain of the small, stockaded fort that housed only 130 men at most. The U.S. Park Service excavated the ruins in 1963. From this hill visitors have a lovely view of the confluence of the Arkansas and Poteau rivers.

The visitor center houses a limited exhibit area, bookstore, and small theater. Here you can see an 18-minute slide show, *Fort Smith, Peacekeeper of the Indian Territory*, on request. Ranger-guided tours are offered in season.

One block down Rogers Street stands the privately run Old Fort Museum($). Artifacts here include Judge Parker's leather chair and rope taken from the lifeless neck of outlaw Cherokee Bill. Other historic homes dot the downtown area. A restored Fort Smith trolley ($) offers inexpensive tours.

Hot Tips Allow two hours to visit Fort Smith. Add another hour if you visit the nearby museum. Self-guided walking tours are over a paved trail, which can be muddy. Watch carefully when crossing the railroad tracks to the site of the first fort. Watch children; traffic can be heavy on streets around the park. A town picnic site is located near the bridge. Food and accommodations are available in the town of Fort Smith.

Advance reading will enhance a visit to Fort Smith. Send for a free copy of *Frontier Ledger, Notes on the History of Fort Smith*. You'll learn about courageous deputy marshals, murderous bank robbers, "hell on the border," and Hanging Judge Parker's frontier philosophy. When you tour the fort, spin a few yarns for the kids. Attention-grabbers will help them enjoy this Old West survivor.

Clint Eastwood's *Hang 'Em High* (1968) is based on the story of Judge Parker at Fort Smith.

The Best Stuff The U. S. deputy marshals in the Wild West of 100 years ago had tough jobs. During Judge Parker's tenure, more than half of his 200 deputy marshals died violently in the line of duty.

After the Civil War the Indian territory became a haven for outlaws and criminal gangs. Confusion over judicial jurisdiction, easy victims, and vast spaces for hiding beckoned the likes of Belle Star, "Queen of the Bandits"; the train-robbing Dalton Gang; and the notorious murderer Cherokee Bill. The low-paid law enforcers, some of whom crossed the line to criminality themselves, embodied the romantic Old West traits of resourcefulness and independence.

Take Deputy Marshall Bass Reeves, an illiterate ex-slave. The six-foot Reeves once dressed as a beggar and walked 28 miles into Indian territory searching for two outlaw brothers. Beggar Bass went right up to the brothers' house and knocked on the door. He appealed to the outlaws' mother for a meal and a place to spend the night. She complied.

Reeves waited in bed for the partying brothers to return. During the night he handcuffed the men. Then he marched them all the way back to Fort Smith, their mother cursing Reeves the entire way. Exhibits tell of the marshals' exploits.

Pea Ridge: Civil War Battlefield Tells Stories of the Cherokee

Pea Ridge in northwest Arkansas is best known as a Civil War battlefield. Here the Union ended Confederate efforts to gain control of Missouri and the Missouri and Mississippi rivers.

But Pea Ridge also tells two stories of the Cherokee people: the Trail of Tears and the violent intratribal Civil War divisions that nearly destroyed the Cherokee Nation.

The isolated military park, named for the Ozark ridge where the battle raged, protects a stretch of the Trail of Tears. Visitors can walk the now-paved Telegraph Road, where in the 1830s thousands of people from the Cherokee and four other tribes walked on a forced exodus west. The battlefield is an important stop along the Trail of Tears auto tour.

Pea Ridge was the first Civil War battle in which Native North American troops participated. About 1,000 Cherokees fought in the Confederate ranks here. They helped defeat two companies of Union cavalry. Cherokee participation on both sides in the Civil War drove a wedge of division deeper into the soul of the tribe, already suffering internal strife after the Trail of Tears ordeal. The issue of slavery also was heated. Some wealthy Cherokees owned black slaves. After the Civil War ended the Cherokees emancipated 4,000 slaves.

Cherokee Principal Chief John Ross took a neutral stand in the Civil War, although he, too, was angry that the U.S. government had been delinquent on treaty payments. His critic, Stand Watie, a slaveowner, commanded a company of independent Cherokee militia. Watie organized several more Cherokee companies to fight against the hated federal government. Stand Watie became the only full-blooded Native

☛

Life was no picnic for criminals either. A good look at the dark, stuffy cellar with 29-by-55-foot cells for 100 men, one water source, and filthy toilet pits makes visitors understand what the appellation "hell on the border" meant.

Then and Now Fort Smith's judicial life began after the Civil War, when the abandoned barracks served as a hospital for both Union and Confederate troops. Fire had destroyed all of the fort's buildings except the barracks and commissary.

North American brigadier general in the Confederate Army.

After the Civil War more infighting, outlaws, and disease killed about 7,000 Cherokee people. The Cherokee Nation almost ceased to exist. The federal government divided and sold most Cherokee lands after the war.

Pea Ridge National Military Park ($) is located 10 miles north of Rogers, Arkansas, on Highway 62. It is open daily, except Thanksgiving, December 25, and January 1, 8 A.M.–5 P.M. Elkhorn Tavern, center of the fighting, is open daily, from May through October, 10 A.M.–4 P.M. For more information contact Pea Ridge National Military Park, P.O. Box 700, Pea Ridge, AR 72751-0700. Tel. (501) 451-8122.

▲

Judge Isaac Parker, despite his reputation, was a tireless, honest defender of justice. He also supported Native North American rights. For 21 years he toiled in his dignified courtroom, hearing 13,000 cases, always following his motto, "Do equal and exact justice."

As the Native North American population dwindled and the number of white settlers exploded, new courts arose to handle civil and criminal cases. In 1896 Congress ended the territorial authority of Judge Parker's court. Ten weeks later Judge Parker died of Bright's disease and 21 years of overworking. A legendary frontier era ended.

The gallows was dismantled and burned. Today a sign posted on the 12 steps to the reconstructed hanging platform reads "Please keep off the gallows. Respect it as an instrument of justice." Structures from the town's frontier days, when saloons and bordellos were the predominant businesses, survive and welcome visitors.

Elsewhere in the Area Fort Smith Trolley Museum ($) is at 100 South 4th Street; Miss Laura's ($), the only former bordello listed on the National Register of Historic Places, is at 1 North B Street; numerous historic homes are in the area; and the U.S. National Cemetery, site of Judge Isaac Parker's grave, is at 522 Garland at South 6th Street. Fort Chaffee is east of Fort Smith on Highway 22. Drive-through tours are available.

Tahlequah

Trail's End for the Cherokee

Location Northeastern Oklahoma, 66 miles southeast of Tulsa and 18 miles northeast of Muskogee. Take U.S. 62/10/82, which becomes Muskogee Avenue, into downtown. Follow signs to Historic Downtown Tahlequah.

Tahlequah, capital of the Cherokee Nation, offers a mix of publicly and privately operated sites. Viewing of buildings on self-guided downtown tours is possible any time. Days and hours of operation of sites vary; some are open seasonally.

For more information contact the Tourism Council, Tahlequah Area Chamber of Commerce, 123 East Delaware Street, Tahlequah, OK 74464. Tel. (918) 456-3742. The Cherokee Heritage Center ($), Tsa-La-Gi Ancient Village and outdoor *Trail of Tears Drama* ($), are open daily, May through Labor Day. For information contact Cherokee Heritage Center, P.O. Box 515, Tahlequah, OK 74465. Tel. (918) 456-6007.

Frame of Reference Tahlequah first came into prominence in the mid–19th century. Tahlequah became the capital of the Cherokee Nation in 1841, soon after the Cherokee who survived the Trail of Tears (1838–39) signed their constitution in 1839. The city remains tribal headquarters today.

Significance Tahlequah was the end of the Trail of Tears for the Cherokee. The town's name probably came from an old Cherokee town in Tennessee, Ta-lik-wa. The Trail of Tears resulted from the U.S. government's Indian Removal Policy, which forced 16,000 Cherokee and Native North Americans of four other tribes to relocate from their ancient homelands in the southeastern United States. The 6,000 Cherokee survivors of the journey,

Fort Gibson

Fort Gibson was the westernmost fort of a string of U.S. forts that once guarded the American frontier. The stockaded fort's sandstone buildings were a last stop on the 1,000-mile Trail of Tears in 1838–1839. The fort was established in 1824.

Next to the two-story barracks a granite monument reads "In honor of the men of the Seventh United States Infantry and their commander General Matthew Arbuckle who founded Fort Gibson April 21, 1824, and all the other soldiers of the War of 1812 who served and died in the Indian Territory."

Visitors can tour the fort's half-dozen surviving buildings. The former commissary houses a small visitor center and gift shop.

Fort Gibson Military Park Visitor Center is open from Monday through Saturday, 9 A.M.–5 P.M., and Sunday, 1 P.M.–5 P.M. To get there from U.S. 62, take Route 80 in the town of Fort Gibson to Route 80A (East Street). Follow curves left on East Street to Garrison Avenue past the Baptist Church. Park at the visitor center.

For information contact the Oklahoma Historical Society, 2100 North Lincoln Boulevard, Oklahoma City, OK 73105. Tel. (405) 521-2491.

which the Cherokee called *Nunahi-Duna-Tlo-Hilu-I*, "Trail Where They Cried," began a new life in the "permanent Indian territory," today's Oklahoma.

Tahlequah represents the history of the Cherokee, the second-largest tribe in America. (Navajo is the largest.) Here visitors can learn of a dramatic chapter in the story of America's frontier.

About the Site Tahlequah isn't a typical town. Downtown signs bear street names in the Cherokee language, written beneath the English version. The town's heart is Cherokee Capitol Square, a park-like setting for the 1867 Old Cherokee National Capitol. The red-brick, two-story capitol is the oldest government building in Oklahoma. It stands where the Cherokee Council first met under a shed in 1839 to draw up a constitution. Because of Sequoyah, a pioneering Cherokee who had developed a Cherokee alphabet by 1821, leaders were able to write this groundbreaking constitution.

The capitol building is open weekdays 8 A.M.–5 P.M. for self-guided tours.

A small Memorial Garden beside the capitol honors Principal Chief John Ross, Confederate Brigadier General Stand Watie, Cherokee war veterans, and the tribe's 169-year-old newspaper, the *Cherokee Advocate*. The newspaper, successor to the seminal *Cherokee Phoenix*, was Oklahoma's first legal newspaper.

Chief John Ross, ⅛ Cherokee, opposed removal and was the leading advocate of Cherokee independence. He became a beloved hero to the Cherokee. Other downtown sites include 1845 Cherokee Supreme Court building, 1874 Cherokee National Prison, and several historic homes.

The Trail of Tears

The forced journey of 16,000 Cherokee Indians from their ancestral homelands in North Carolina, Georgia, Tennessee, and Alabama in 1838 and 1839 has come to symbolize a dark era in American history. The Trail of Tears, which the Cherokee call *Nunahi-Duna-Tlo-Hilu-I*, or "Trail Where They Cried," was a culmination of white settlement, tenuous treaties, and the discovery of gold on Cherokee lands.

The trail was the result of the U.S. government's Indian Removal Policy. President Andrew Jackson designed the policy to obtain lands by treaty. His plan was to relocate Native North Americans from their ancestral homelands in the east to the permanent Indian territory in the West, today's Oklahoma. Jackson's plan included four other eastern Indian tribes, but it was especially cruel for the Cherokee. The tribe had gone along with the government's rules and white man's customs.

Although the Trail of Tears National Historic Trail sites are still evolving, you can follow the trail by car. Congress established the trail in 1987. The auto route follows highways through 10 states and is marked with Trail of Tears signs. Some trail sites are federally operated; others are maintained by state and local governments or private organizations. Many are on private land.

The Cherokee ceded their eastern lands to the U.S. government under the Treaty of New Echota. Only 20 Cherokee signed the treaty at a meeting in 1836 in New Echota, Georgia. None were elected officials of the Cherokee Nation. But the U.S. Senate ratified the treaty anyway—by one vote.

It wasn't until May 1838 that federal troops and state militia began to round up Cherokees into stockades, preparing for the journey to Indian territory. Families were separated. There was little time to

☛

Nearby sites related to the Cherokee and the Trail of Tears include these:

- **Cherokee Heritage Center.** Southeast of downtown Tahlequah, off U.S. 62. Follow signs. At this wooded, 44-acre park you will find the Cherokee National Museum (open year-round); an amphitheater for *Trail of Tears* drama (July and August); Tsa-La-Gi Ancient Village, a re-creation of an authentic 16th-century Cherokee settlement; Adams Corner Rural Village, a re-creation of a typical 19th-century community in the Indian territory (May through Labor Day); Trail of Tears Memorial Chapel; and a wooded park for picnicking and recreation.
- **Cherokee Nation Gift Shop.** U.S. 62 south, next to tribal headquarters. Cherokee art is sold here.
- **Cherokee National Headquarters and Tribal Complex.** This 800-acre complex includes government facilities and Sequoyah High School. Brief presentations are offered on tribal affairs. Call Cherokee Nation's Public Affairs Office for visit arrangements. Tel. (918) 456-0671, ext. 2550.
- **Fort Gibson.** Buildings of this 1824 stockaded fort, a Trail of Tears terminus, stand 17 miles southwest of Tahlequah in the town of Fort Gibson.

Hot Tips Because of the seasonal operation of many sites, it's best to visit Tahlequah in summer. You will need a map for your self-guided tour. It's best to obtain one in advance, but you can get one at the Cherokee Nation Gift Shop. Allow three hours for your visit, unless you plan to see the *Trail of Tears* drama. A step-on guide is offered free to bus tour groups. Call the Tahlequah Area Chamber of Commerce for reservations.

gather possessions. White looters ransacked Cherokee homes as soldiers led the Cherokee away.

The ill-equipped Cherokee began their journeys in the spring and summer of 1838. They followed four main routes, one almost entirely by water. Disease, exhaustion, and exposure claimed thousands of Cherokee lives, some say up to 4,000. Nearly 1/5 of the Cherokee population died on the Trail of Tears.

The Cherokee survivors reestablished the Cherokee Nation soon after their arrival in Oklahoma in 1839. Because Sequoyah's alphabet had made them a literate tribe, they wrote a constitution. They made Tahlequah, Oklahoma, the capital. It remains their tribal headquarters today.

To escape the government roundup, about 1,000 Cherokees hid in the mountains of North Carolina and Tennessee. They established their tribal government in 1868 in Cherokee, North Carolina. Their descendants are known as the Eastern Band of Cherokee Indians.

Outdoor dramas and museums at both the beginning and end of the Trail of Tears in Cherokee and Tahlequah tell the story of the Cherokee's forced march.

For more information on the Trail of Tears contact Long Distance Trails Group Office, Santa Fe, National Park Service, P.O. Box 728, Santa Fe, NM 87504-0728. Tel. (505) 988-6888. Also contact Trail of Tears Association, P.O. Box 2069, Cherokee, NC 28719. In Arkansas contact Trail of Tears Association, 1100 North University, Suite 133, Little Rock, AR 72207. Tel. (501) 666-9032. Charter memberships to the Trail of Tears Association are available through this address.

Check with local chambers of commerce and tourist bureaus for information about Trail of Tears sites on local property. Consult guidebooks and ask for permission where needed before entering private land.

▲

Food and accommodations are available in Tahlequah. The Cherokee Nation Restaurant offers inexpensive lunches. Cherokee foods are part of a buffet offered before the *Trail of Tears* drama at the Tas-La-Gi Buffet. For information contact the Cherokee Heritage Center.

The Best Stuff The Cherokee Heritage Center offers a memorable, hands-on experience of the Trail of Tears. Kids will enjoy learning how the Cherokee lived at the Tsa-La-Gi Ancient Village. Exhibits at the museum are educational and engaging, as is the *Trail of Tears* drama. The natural park setting itself helps re-create the land where the weary survivors of the trail began life anew.

Then and Now Tahlequah boasts that it is the "Fifty-fifth Best Small Town in America." The town hosts a growing retirement community. The descendants of the Cherokee who survived the Trail of Tears and other townsfolk go about their business as visitors descend on the town to learn of the Cherokee past. Oklahoma now has the largest Native American population of any state in the union.

Sequoyah's Cabin

Sequoyah's 1829 log home is located near Sallisaw, Oklahoma. Sequoyah spent 12 years developing the 86-character alphabet that quickly led to Indian literacy, the Cherokee Constitution, and the *Cherokee Advocate*. As a child, he had observed white settlers reading from books, what he called "talking leaves." Enduring ridicule and isolation, Sequoyah wrote with charcoal on manuscripts of bark. After he completed his invention, Sequoyah established a school in his log home. Within six months, every Cherokee who could speak the Cherokee language could read it.

Sequoyah received many honors from both the Cherokee and whites. One was having the name of the stately California redwood named after him.

For information on Sequoyah's home contact Oklahoma Tourism and Recreation, 2401 North Lincoln Boulevard, Oklahoma City, OK 73105. Tel. 1-800-652-6552 or (405) 521-2409.

Note The Cherokee Indian Reservation, home of descendants of the Eastern Band of Cherokee, lies in the Appalachian Mountains of western North Carolina. Here visitors also find a museum, ancient village, and a drama on the Trail of Tears, *Unto These Hills*.

Elsewhere in the Area The Cherokee Courthouse, Tahlonteeskee, is located in Gore, Oklahoma. The Five Civilized Tribes Museum stands just off U.S. 69 near Muskogee. The museum preserves history, art, and artifacts of the Choctaw, Chickasaw, Cherokee, Seminole, and Creek tribes who walked the Trail of Tears. Also visit Spiro Mounds Archaeological Park, off U.S. 59, three miles east of Spiro, Oklahoma. The park preserves 400-year-old mounds and the site where prehistoric Native North Americans lived A.D. 600 to A.D. 1450.

The Alamo

Legendary Cradle of Texas Liberty

Location Downtown San Antonio, Texas, in Alamo Plaza, bounded by Alamo, East Houston and East Crockett streets. The plaza is a few blocks north of the convention center. Follow signs.

The Alamo, the remains of Spanish Mission San Antonio de Valero, is open Monday through Saturday, 9 A.M.–5:30 P.M., and Sunday, 10 A.M.–5:30 P.M. The annual Pilgrimage to the Alamo takes place every April. The Daughters of the Republic of Texas operate the site. For more information contact The Alamo, P.O. Box 2599, San Antonio, TX 78299. Tel. (210) 225-1391.

San Antonio Missions National Historical Park, which includes four other 18th-century Spanish missions, is open daily, except December 25 and January 1, 8 A.M.–5 P.M., and during Daylight Savings Time, 9 A.M.–6 P.M. School presentations require reservations. For information contact Superintendent, San Antonio Missions National Historical Park, 2202 Roosevelt Avenue, San Antonio, TX 78210. Tel. (210) 229-5701.

For information on San Antonio historical sites contact San Antonio Convention and Visitors Bureau, P.O. Box 2277, San Antonio, TX 78298. Tel. 1-800-447-3372 or (210) 270-8700.

Frame of Reference During the first half of the 19th century, "Texas Fever" drew a steady stream of white settlers into the Mexican territory, and American sentiments for independence from Mexico heated to the boiling point. Americans in Texas began to demand statehood in 1832 and 1833. They rose to armed rebellion in 1835. The Battle of the Alamo took place from February 23 to March 6, 1836.

Significance At this fortified Spanish adobe mission, 189 Texas patriots held out for 12 days in pitched battle against Mexican dictator General Antonio López de Santa Anna and his army of 1,800 men.

After Mexico won independence from Spain in 1821 it claimed the territory of Texas as a province. The abandoned mission, which Franciscan friars began building around 1724, became a key Mexican fort. Spanish troops named it Pueblo del Alamo, "House of the Cottonwood," for the plentiful trees along the San Antonio River. Texans seized the fort and the town from the Mexicans in 1835 in the first battle of the Texas Revolution. In response Santa Anna, the self-styled "Napoleon of the West," led his army to San Antonio.

On day 13 of the Battle of the Alamo, the Mexican army breached the fort's north wall. Intense fighting raged all over the fort. As Mexicans overwhelmed the Alamo defenders in one area, the Texans dropped back to another area, fighting like demons. The battle ended with the annihilation of all the Texans. The dead included legendary frontiersmen, soldier, and Tennessee congressman Davy Crockett; Native North American fighter, slave smuggler, and Bowie knife inventor Jim Bowie; and fort commander Lieutenant Colonel William B. Travis.

Before the fort finally fell, the Alamo's volunteer soldiers may have wiped out a third of Santa Anna's army. (Some estimates are as low as 600.)

In the aftermath of the dramatically lopsided battle, Crockett, Bowie, Travis, and their fellow fighters were hailed as martyred heroes.

About the Site Although the Alamo was remote in 1836, with the closest town 76 miles away, Texas's most famous historic site now stands amid the towering buildings of downtown San Antonio. Visitors almost stumble upon it. Although its stature looms large in the minds of Texans, today's Alamo physically is a shadow of yesterday's fortress.

Two original stone-and-mortar buildings survive: the cross-shaped mission church, "the shrine," as Lieutenant Colonel Travis referred to it; and the Long Barrack. A connecting wall and stone patio also remain. The surviving buildings stand in a 4.2-acre park landscaped with native plants. The never-finished mission church, about 22 feet high and 60 feet wide, and its exhibits are devoted to the slain defenders. The Long Barrack, where the Texans may have made their valiant last stand, tells the Alamo story from Spanish times through the establishment of the Republic of Texas.

Among the treasures in the 191-foot-long, partially reconstructed barracks, you will find Crockett's beloved rifle Old Betsy. The museum also displays Rezin Bowie's hunting knife and Lieutenant Colonel Travis's gold ring.

The Alamo complex includes a video viewing area, where you can see a continuously running, 15-minute orientation video. Tours are self-guided. Guides give scheduled history talks. Since 1936 a second museum and gift shop have stood next to the chapel. A library was added in 1950.

The Missions of San Antonio

San Antonio boasts four other 18th-century Spanish missions: Mission Nuestra Senora de la Purisima Concepción; Mission San Jose y San Miguel de Aguayo, the oldest "Queen of Missions" with its famous Rose Window; Mission San Juan Capistrano; and Mission San Franciso de la Espada. The four missions are part of the San Antonio Missions National Historical Park.

The park's jewel is the restored Mission San Jose. Concepción is the oldest unrestored church in America, standing as it did when completed in 1755. The missions remain active centers of worship. A well-preserved portion of the Acequias (irrigation ditches) the Franciscans built is near Mission Espada. A marked auto tour, "The Missions Trail," connects the four missions over eight miles along the San Antonio River.

Spanish missions flourished in Texas between 1745 and 1775. Many survive. The Alamo is San Antonio's oldest mission.

The route connecting the four missions on the Missions Trail may be confusing. When the San Antonio River rises, the trail is rerouted. Check with park rangers at the Missions National Park to plan your auto tour.

In 1836 the Alamo's west wall extended 458 feet; its south and north walls, 161 feet. The fort's vacant interior, surrounded by barracks, a hospital, and other structures, was the fort's plaza. The city has absorbed most of the land where the complete fort stood.

In Alamo Plaza, a towering, white-marble Alamo cenotaph marks the site. The 1939 memorial by Italian sculptor Pompeo Coppini lists the names of the dead and depicts the heroes.

An IMAX Theater ($) faces the Alamo's rear entrance in Rivercenter Mall, at 803 East Commerce Street. Here you can see a body-shaking, 45-minute docudrama on the Alamo, *The Price of Freedom*. The theater is not part of the Alamo site.

Hot Tips Allow 1½ hours to visit the Alamo and museum. In summer expect a waiting line at the shrine's iron gate. The IMAX movie can give you needed information before your visit, but here's a warning: the movie's bloody violence, thundering speakers, and six-story movie screen may frighten young children.

Advance reading will enhance a visit. Call the Alamo Information Desk and order *The Alamo: Long Barracks Museum*, a publication compiled by the Daughters of the Republic of Texas. Pick up maps and information about San Antonio attractions and events at a Visitor Information Center, 317 Alamo Plaza.

Suggested pretrip movies include *Alamo: 13 Days to Glory* (1987), with James Arness and the late Raul Julia as Santa Anna. Also check out the *The Alamo* (1960), starring John Wayne.

Food and accommodations are available in San Antonio.

The Best Stuff You haven't seen the Alamo until you've beheld it at night. Floodlights bathe the venerable shrine in a surreal aura of immortality. The place seems a touchable myth in relief against San Antonio's twinkling backdrop. Plan to stop by in the evening.

But it's the riveting story of the 13-day siege that draws visitors from around the world to the Alamo. Looking at the famous humped silhouette of the shrine—which was added by the U.S. Army in 1850 and was not present at the 1836 battle—you can visualize Davy Crockett, out of ammunition, knocking Santa Anna's men aside their heads with the butt of Old Betsy. Hollywood may gloss over the Texans' character flaws, but most don't question Davy and the Texans died for what they believed.

Historians disagree on the facts surrounding the siege of 1836. Legend has it that when Santa Anna and his army arrived, garrison leader Travis knew the situation was hopeless. His letters for reinforcements had gone unanswered. With his sword, Travis drew a line in the dirt, telling his men "Those prepared to give their lives in freedom's cause come over to me."

Every man except one crossed the line. That man escaped over the fort wall. Jim Bowie, bedridden with pneumonia, had friends carry his cot across.

On March 6 Mexican bugles played Degüello, "No Mercy for the Defenders." The Alamo fighters twice repulsed Santa Anna's forces. On the third try, the Mexicans broke through the north wall. Popular accounts say all defenders were slain; Santa Anna had wounded survivors shot. But some claim a French mercenary survived by persuading Santa Anna that he had been forced to fight against his will. Santa Anna allowed women and children to live.

Texas won its independence seven weeks later on April 21, 1836, at the Battle of San Jacinto. Sam Houston, commander-in-chief of Texas forces, surprised Santa Anna's encampment. The battle took place just west of the San Jacinto River, near the city that now bears Houston's name. The Texans, yelling "Remember the Alamo," took only 18 minutes to subdue the Mexicans and take Santa Anna prisoner. The war was over.

Then and Now After Santa Anna's defeat, the Lone Star Republic drafted a constitution, elected Houston president, and voted for statehood. Politics over the expansion of slavery and the 1844 presidential campaign kept Texan statehood in abeyance. Texas didn't enter the Union until after the election to the presidency of "dark horse" southerner James K. Polk in 1845.

Four air force bases and an army base now call San Antonio home. Texas is America's third-most-populated state. The lone star on Texas's state flag commemorates its unique heritage.

Elsewhere in the Area Spanish Governor's Palace ($), at Military Plaza on Camaron Street, is a 1772, 10-room, adobe-walled structure that was the seat of the Spanish government when Americans established the first colonies in Texas. The River Walk, *Paseo del Rio*, winds several miles through midtown San Antonio. Museums, of both history and art, include Pioneer Hall, Cowboy Museum, Ripley's Believe It or Not, Plaza Theater of Wax, Buckhorn Hall of Horns Museum, Texas Star Trail (walking tour of 80 historic sites), Fort Sam Houston, and the Museum at Military Bases Complex.

You'll also find trolley tours, riverboat cruises, a number of historic buildings, and a variety of restaurants, shops, and cabarets. Also, the David Crockett Monument in Ozona, Texas, in Crockett County, about 200 miles northwest of San Antonio, bears a nostrum attributed to the Alamo hero, "Be sure you are right, then go ahead."

The San Jacinto Battleground State Historic Park is located in Deer Park, Texas, just east of Houston. A 570-foot concrete-and-limestone monument marks the site where Texans quickly defeated General Santa Anna's army in the final battle for Texas's independence. A museum and multi-image presentation tell the story. Battleship *Texas* resides here.

◆Hidden Jewel◆

Dealey Plaza

The Kennedy Assassination Site

Location The western edge of downtown Dallas, Texas, in Dealey Plaza at Houston and Elm streets. The Sixth Floor Museum is located at 411 Elm Street. From U.S. 35E, exit at Woodall Rodgers Freeway onto Griffin Street. Take a right onto Ross Avenue. Take Ross west until it turns into Houston Street. Park off Houston Street at the Visitors Center Museum Shop in the Dallas County Administration Building.

Dealey Plaza National Historic Landmark District, which includes a local park and private businesses, is accessible at all times.

The Sixth Floor Museum ($) is open daily, except December 25, 9 A.M.–6 P.M., with extended seasonal hours. For information on Dealey Plaza and The Sixth Floor Museum contact the Dallas County Historical Foundation, 411 Elm Street, Suite 120, Dallas, TX 75202-3301. Tel. (214) 653-6659.

Frame of Reference The early 1960s was a period of Civil Rights and labor unrest in America, as well as a time of increased U.S. confrontations with foreign powers. President John F. Kennedy was assassinated November 22, 1963.

Significance Here President Kennedy was fatally shot by an assassin's bullet as his open limousine eased west on Elm Street into Dealey Plaza. He was wounded in the head and neck. In the car with the nation's 35th president was his wife, Jackie, and Texas governor John Connally. The assassin, 24-year-old Lee Harvey Oswald, fired from the sixth floor of the Texas School Book Depository. The building was renamed the Dallas County Administration Building in 1981.

President and Mrs. Kennedy had come to Dallas as part of a scheduled, two-day Texas tour in preparation for Kennedy's 1964 reelection campaign. Governor Connally had greeted them. The 12:30 P.M. shooting seriously wounded Governor Connally. Mrs. Kennedy was uninjured.

The 46-year-old president was pronounced dead at 1 P.M. at Parkland Memorial Hospital, where he had been transported within minutes of the shooting. Mystery and theories of conspiracy surround the Kennedy Assassination to this day.

About the Site The Dealey Plaza National Historic Landmark District, which the National Park Service designated in 1993, includes several city blocks around the assassination site and the buildings that face Dealey Plaza.

The district also encompasses the 3.07-acre Dealey Plaza park with its famous grassy knoll. Conspiracy theorists speculate that a second gunman may have fired at Kennedy from this grassy knoll on Elm Street's north side. The district's centerpiece is the seven-story Dallas County Administration Building, which houses the Sixth Floor Museum. The discretely named museum fills the sixth floor of the old book depository where lawmen found Oswald's "assassin's nest."

The museum, through educational and historical exhibits, examines the life, death, and legacy of President Kennedy within the context of American history. The 9,000-square-foot exhibition features 400 photographs, six documentary films, 1960s artifacts, and the original window from which it is believed Oswald fired at Kennedy. The window is on loan to the museum. It had been removed and replaced by the owners who bought the building after the assassination.

Visitors can see a scale model of Dealey Plaza, which the FBI prepared for the Warren Commission during its investigations of Kennedy's death.

Behind protective glass at the corner window stands a reconstruction of Oswald's assassin's nest. The reconstruction is based on photographs taken soon after the shooting. Oswald had propped a cardboard box of readers on the windowsill to rest his firing arm on.

A row of museum windows faces south onto Elm Street. Visitors can see the route the Kennedy motorcade took through Dealey Plaza. One video presentation includes brief nonviolent portions of the famous 8-mm film taken by a bystander, Abraham Zapruder, at the time of the assassination. Visits to the museum are self-guided.

The Dealey Plaza National Historic Landmark District also includes a National Historical Landmark Plaque near the spot where Kennedy was shot, the triple underpass over Elm Street, the rail yards and switching tower, and a visitor center/museum shop behind the depository building. The John F. Kennedy Memorial Plaza sits adjacent to the district at Market and Commerce streets.

Hot Tips Allow 1½ hours to tour the Sixth Floor Museum. Purchase tickets at the Museum Shop in the Visitors Center. Audiocassette rentals for self-guided tours are also available. The tape is available in seven languages and in a special kids' version. However, this site is not for young children.

Prepare yourself for the strong emotional impact of the museum. Add another half hour for a walk through Dealey Plaza and the surrounding area. Watch for heavy traffic.

Exterior elevators carry visitors from the visitor center so that county business on the other floors of the building remains undisturbed.

Trolley tours($), food, and accommodations are available in Dallas.

The Best Stuff The Sixth Floor Museum gives an honest, well-balanced look at President Kennedy, Oswald, the turbulent 1960s, and the assassination—before and after. Everything here is worthy of your time and interest. The chilling re-creation of Oswald's assassin's nest is riveting. It will stick in your mind for years to come.

Glass walls now enclose the small area at the window where the rifle fire originated. Here, about a half-hour after the shooting, police found a barricade of pasteboard boxes of books, three spent bullet cartridges, and a paper bag near the white brick wall. You can compare the re-creation with displayed photographs taken upon discovery of the nest.

Investigators found fingerprints and palm prints on two boxes. The prints later were linked to Oswald, an order clerk who began work at the depository that October. Ten minutes later, investigators found a rifle stuffed between boxes near the sixth-floor staircase across the open floor from the corner window. The museum also re-creates this scene.

It's moving to walk the grassy knoll next to Elm Street, where the Kennedy limousine was about to move beneath the triple underpass when Oswald's shot rang out. Many investigations of the assassination have alluded to shots fired by a second gunman from this knoll. The second-gunman theory has fueled speculation of a conspiracy. Investigators, however, found no evidence on the knoll after the shooting.

Other Kennedy Sites

President Kennedy is buried in Arlington National Cemetery. His wife, Jackie, who died in 1994, is buried alongside him. An eternal flame burns at the gravesite. Kennedy's birthplace in Brookline, Massachusetts, is a National Historic Site open for tours. For information contact John F. Kennedy National Historic Site, 83 Beals Street, Brookline, MA 02146. Tel. (617) 566-7937.

The New Museum at the John F. Kennedy Library in Boston tells the Kennedy story. For information contact The Kennedy Library, Columbia Point, Boston, MA 02125. Tel (617) 929-4523.

Then and Now An exhibit in the Sixth Floor Museum titled "Who Did It?" confirms that 80 percent of Americans think that Kennedy was killed as the result of a conspiracy. Historical records of the assassination reveal these key events:

- President Kennedy was shot at 12:30 P.M. as his motorcade approached the second lamppost on Elm Street in front of the Book Depository. He was pronounced dead at 1 P.M.
- Oswald was seen in the depository 35 minutes before the shooting and two minutes afterward. At 1:18 P.M. police learned of the murder of a Dallas policeman near downtown. A witness who saw Oswald minutes after that shooting led officers to the Texas Theater, where they arrested Oswald at 1:50 P.M.
- On November 24, 1963, Jack Ruby shot and killed Oswald on live television as Oswald was being transferred from city to county jail. Ruby died of cancer before his second trial.
- A special national commission headed by Chief Justice Earl Warren investigated the assassination. In its 1964 report it concluded that Oswald had acted alone. The report was controversial. More official investigations followed. Some investigations pointed to a conspiracy; others did not. In 1988 the U.S. Justice Department officially closed the investigation.

For 26 years Dallas, its reputation sullied by the same media spotlight that gave President Kennedy status as a martyred leader, remained quiet about the assassination. A downtown memorial to Kennedy was dedicated in 1970, but questions about what to do with the Book Depository remained unanswered. Finally, in 1977 the county purchased the building from private owners. Officials in 1979 approved plans for a museum. Fund-raising got underway. The Sixth Floor Museum opened in February 1989. More than 420,000 visitors from around the world come here annually.

Elsewhere in the Area Fair Park on Robert P. Cullum Boulevard is home to seven museums and America's largest collection of art deco architecture. Old City Park, off Thornton Freeway, features a village of restored turn-of-the century buildings.

MOUNTAIN

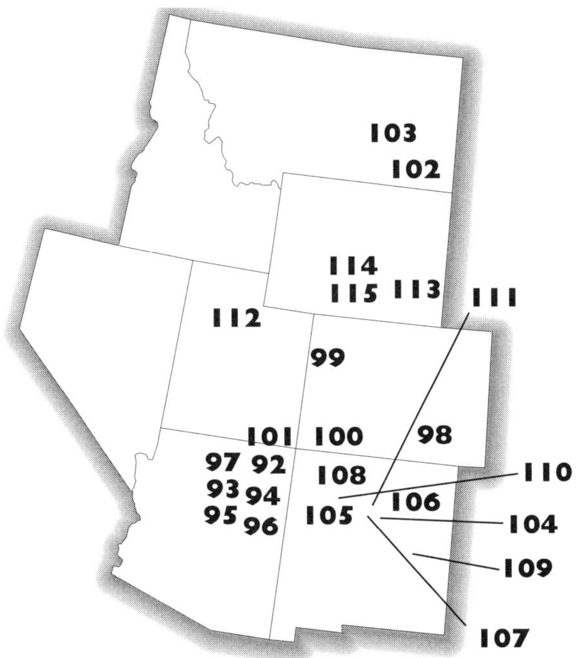

Key

Numbers correspond to site numbers on the map.

Arizona

92. Canyon de Chelly
93. Hopi Reservations
94. The Hubbell Trading Post
95. Wupatki
96. Walnut Canyon
97. Navajo

Colorado

98. Bent's Old Fort
99. Dinosaur Monument
100. Mesa Verde
101. Hovenweep

Montana

102. Little Bighorn Battlefield
103. Pompey's Pillar

New Mexico

104. Bandelier
105. Chaco Canyon
106. Fort Union
107. Santa Fe
108. Aztec
109. Pecos
110. Salmon Ruin
111. Petroglyph National Monument

Santa Fe Trail (see National Trails System Map on page xv)

Utah

Mormon Pioneer Trail (see National Trails System Map on page xv)

112. Promontory Summit

Wyoming

113. Fort Laramie
114. Best Wagon Ruts
115. Register Cliff

Canyon de Chelly

Spectacular Beauty, Unique History Lessons

Location Northeastern Arizona, 145 miles northeast of Flagstaff, Arizona, and 64 miles northwest of Gallup, New Mexico, on the Navajo Indian Reservation. From the north and south take U.S. 191 to Chinle, then Highway 7 three miles to the park entrance. Follow the signs. From the east and west take I-40 to U.S. 191 north, 90 miles to Chinle, to Highway 7 and the park.

Canyon de Chelly National Monument is open daily, from October through April, 8 A.M.–5 P.M. and from May through September, 8 A.M.–6 P.M. Special programs are offered in the summer, including nightly campfire programs in the amphitheater. For more information contact Superintendent, Canyon de Chelly National Monument, P.O. Box 588, Chinle, AZ 86503. Tel. (520) 674-5500.

Frame of Reference Native North Americans have continuously inhabited Canyon de Chelly for about 2,000 years. Evidence suggests occupation up to 7,000 years ago. The canyon's cliff dwellings date to the Anasazi, prehistoric Indians who lived in the Four Corners area almost 1,000 years ago (A.D. 1040–1275).

Glossary of Some Native North American Terms

Anasazi: The Navajo word for "ancient ones." The Anasazi generally flourished in the Four Corners region about 1,000 years ago. Their descendants are among some of the modern tribes of the Four Corners region.

Kiva: An underground ceremonial room; a pit-house circular in shape. Access to the kivas, which usually had wood-beamed roofs above ground, was by ladder. The Anasazi used kivas as community and ceremonial centers. (Modern kivas are sites for the most sacred ceremonies.) Steps from an anteroom provided access to Great Kivas. The Great Kivas were much larger and more elaborate than other southwestern kivas.

Pueblo: Spanish word for the multiroom dwellings of the Southwest. Prehistoric pueblos may be multistoried. Rooms share adjoining walls. Many open to a communal courtyard. Pueblos usually contain kivas. A pueblo can be a village unto itself. Think of them as apartment buildings or condominium complexes.

Significance Canyon de Chelly and two companion canyons offer spectacular vistas and unique lessons in southwestern Native North American history. This fertile cradle in the Arizona desert has curious land formations, colorful canyon walls, and numerous prehistoric ruins.

Canyon de Chelly is a record of human settlement in America.

About the Site Canyon de Chelly (pronounced "shey") is one of the most beautiful canyons in the Southwest. Bright red cliffs, swirls of sandstone formations, and lush stands of cottonwood on the canyon floor weave a rich tapestry of form and color. The modern Navajo ranchers still live in hogans and tend sheep along the Chinle Wash on the canyon floor.

A 2½-mile loop trail winds to the park's most spectacular cliff dwelling, the 900-year-old White House ruins. U.S. Army discoverers named the stone-and-mud dwelling for the white-plastered walls on the ruin's upper portion. Prehistoric Native North Americans lived in the White House for 200 years. The trail to the canyon floor is very steep, meandering 600 feet down a cliff.

You can only gaze up at the White House from below. Sheer canyon walls rise above the ruin, high on the cliff. The two other canyons in the 83,840-acre park offer similar views after long and strenuous hikes. Visitors can see ancient rock art in places. Prehistoric artists pecked drawings into the cliffs' canyon varnish, the dark patina created by bacteria on some moist canyon walls. Except for the White House Ruins Trail, hiking in the canyon requires a permit. Visitors must be accompanied by a park ranger or an authorized Navajo guide ($). Visitors can drive to the canyon bottom in a four-wheel-drive vehicle, permitted only with an authorized Navajo guide ($). Obtain permits and guide information at the visitor center.

Visiting Hopi Reservations

Some villages of the Hopi Indian Reservation in northeastern Arizona welcome visitors. Each village sets it own visitor policy. All prohibit photography. The 12 Hopi villages are located at the top of or at the foot of three mesas, aptly called the First, Second, and Third Mesas. Most Hopis live in or near the villages.

Orabi on the Third Mesa dates back 900 years to A.D. 1100. It is regarded as the oldest continuously inhabited settlement in the United States. Walpi on the First Mesa may be the most spectacular village. A Hopi guide is required. Cliff-edge houses dot its terraces; its beautiful views have remained essentially unchanged for centuries. Some villages allow visitors to view ancestral ruins and ancient ceremonies.

The Hopi Cultural Center Motel on Second Mesa offers rooms to the public. Tel. (520) 734-2401.

For more information contact Office of Public Relations, The Hopi Tribe, P.O. Box 123, Kykotsmovi, AZ 86039. Tel (520) 734-2441, ext. 341 or 360.

From two auto loops (one 34 miles, one 37 miles) along the rims of the canyons, pullouts allow spectacular views. Allow two hours for each canyon loop. Pick up guidebooks at the visitor center. Autos must stay on paved roads.

Horseback tours ($) are available, as are authorized Navajo-guided hiking tours. Rangers offer many warm-month activities. In summer months, rangers conduct special programs in the amphitheater next to the campground.

The visitor center houses a museum, bookstore, and area to view a 22-minute orientation video, *Canyon Voices*.

Hot Tips Allow up to a day for a visit to the White House ruins and a leisurely drive around the canyons' rims. Allow appropriate time for additional hikes. Take plenty of water. The trail into Canyon de Chelly becomes very narrow in places with sheer drop-offs. Allow 2½ hours for the loop and a walk across the sandy canyon floor to the ruins. Pit toilets are located near the ruins. Watch for slippery areas on the trails and ice in cold months. Do not enter any ruins. Ice and snow may close backcountry trails.

This is not a site for very young children. Younger children may be frightened, or not scared enough, of the steep hiking trails into the canyon. Kids can learn about the Anasazi and Navajo in a *Junior Ranger* activities sheet. Ask for it at the visitor center.

Food and accommodations are available in Chinle. Campsites are available free on a first-come, first-served basis at Cottonwood Campground and Spider Rock Campground year-round.

The historic Thunderbird Lodge, at the mouth of Canyon de Chelly, has food and accommodations. The lodge also offers Navajo-guided canyon tours ($$) in six-wheel-drive vehicles. For information contact Thunderbird Lodge, P.O. Box 548, Chinle, AZ 86503. Tel. 1-800-679-BIRD or (520) 674-5841.

The Hubbell Trading Post

Fifty miles south of Canyon de Chelly in northeastern Arizona you can wet your whistle on soda and days gone by at the 100-year-old Hubbell Trading Post. It's located in Ganado on the Navajo Reservation. The red-stone Trading Post is still open for business. Allow one hour.

The post and 160-acre homesite belonged to John Lorenzo Hubbell, the dean of the white traders to the Navajo. Hubbell provided for mutually beneficial contact among whites, Mexicans, and the Navajo. Hubbell began trading here in 1876, soon after the Navajo were confined to the reservation.

Today visitors can view the trading post bursting with foodstuffs; piles of Navajo rugs, pottery, and wood carvings; and Navajo, Zuni, and Hopi crafts. A self-guided tour also includes the ranch and barn filled with antique farm machinery. Pick up a guide for one dollar at the visitor center.

Rangers lead daily tours of the Hubbell home, with a limit of 15 people per tour. The home protects a priceless collection of handmade baskets, Navajo rugs scattered everywhere, books, and 143 ink drawings of Native North Americans on the walls.

Hubbell Trading Post National Historic Site is open daily, except Thanksgiving, December 25, and January 1, in summer, 8 A.M.–6 P.M., and the rest of the year, 8 A.M.–5 P.M. From Flagstaff, Arizona, or Gallop, New Mexico, take I-40 to U.S. 191 north at Chambers, Arizona. At Ganado, take U.S. 264 west to park entrance. Proceed carefully down the red-dirt road. For information contact Superintendent, Hubbell Trading Post National Historic Site, P.O. Box 150, Ganado, AZ 86505. Tel. (520) 755-3475.

The Best Stuff The Navajo here advise visitors to take in the silence and beauty, and the canyon will speak to you.

Then and Now Canyon de Chelly preserves the long history of the native southwestern people. Today, 40 to 50 Navajo families farm the canyon bottom and mesa tops. Modern Navajo claim 130 clans; there were four original clans. The Navajo consider Canyon de Chelly, strategically located amid four sacred mountains, a great holy place.

Elsewhere in the Area The Four Corners Monument ($) is 68 miles or 1½ hours, driving time away from Chinle. Here you can have your picture taken while standing in the four states that meet here—Arizona, Colorado, New Mexico, and Utah. It is located ¼ mile west of U.S. 160, 40 miles southwest of Cortez, Colorado. The site is open daily in summer, 7 A.M.–8 P.M., and the rest of the year, 8 A.M.–5 P.M. For information contact Navajo Parks and Recreation Department, P.O. Box 9000, Window Rock, AZ 86515. Tel. (520) 871-6647.

A musical drama, *Anasazi, the Ancient Ones* ($), is served up in summer months along with dinner in an outdoor amphitheater in Farmington, New Mexico—135 miles from Chinle. Dinner is at 6:30 P.M.; the performance begins at 8 P.M. For information contact the Farmington Convention and Visitors Bureau, 203 West Main, Farmington, NM 87401. Tel. 1-800-448-1240.

The Museum of Northern Arizona ($) is located three hours away in Flagstaff. This museum, dedicated to helping visitors understand and interpret the Colorado Plateau, has exhibits on geology, anthropology, biology, and fine arts including works by Hopi, Navajo, and Zuni artists. The museum is open daily, except Thanksgiving, December 25, and January 1, 9 A.M.–5 P.M. For information contact the Museum of Northern Arizona, Route 4, P.O. Box 720, Flagstaff, AZ 86001. Tel. (520) 774-5213.

Canyon de Chelly sheltered prehistoric American Indians for one thousand years and served as an ancestral stronghold for the Navajo Indians. *Fred Mang, Jr., National Park Service*

Bent's Old Fort

Southwest's Premier Frontier Trading Center

Location Southeastern Colorado, 8 miles east of La Junta and 15 miles west of Las Animas on Highway 194. From U.S. 50 at La Junta take Highway 194 north to park entrance. From Las Animas take Highway 194 from west end of town to site.

Bent's Old Fort National Historic Site ($ over 17) is open daily, except Thanksgiving, December 25, and January 1, in summer, 8 A.M.–5:30 P.M. and the rest of the year, 9 A.M.–4 P.M. Ranger tours and demonstrations are offered in warm months. Christmas Celebration is in December; Children's Day is in July. For information contact Bent's Old Fort National Historic Site, 35110 Highway 194 East, La Junta, CO 81050-9523. Tel. (719) 384-2596.

Frame of Reference During the 1830s and 1840s the southwestern frontier was opened for trade and the Santa Fe Trail (1821–80) was going through its heyday. The fort was built in 1833 and was abandoned in 1849.

Significance This adobe "Castle on the Plain" became perhaps the most important trade center and travel stop on the Santa Fe Trail. For 16 colorful years it dominated trade with the Southern Plains Indians. The personal attributes, business acumen, and political connections of its founders, Charles and William Bent and their partner Ceran St. Vrain, made the fort a key player in America's manifest destiny.

The fort, about ¼ of a city block in size, was headquarters for the partners' wildly successful trading venture, the Bent–St. Vrain Company. The fort's strategic location at a ford of the Arkansas River, between the Rocky Mountain fur-trapping country and Native North American hunting grounds, contributed greatly to its success.

The Bents named their adobe castle Fort William, but white traders called it Bent's Fort. Native North Americans called it Bent's Big Lodge. Later William built another fort on the Arkansas River. This became Bent's New Fort. This first fort became known as Bent's Old Fort.

Like the more enduring trading post Fort Union in the Great Northern Plains, Bent's Old Fort was an important cultural crossroads. The fort brought together Anglo Americans, mostly men but some visiting women; Mexicans; Native North Americans; African Americans; and Frenchmen to trade, replenish travel supplies, make repairs, and rest.

Among the famous people associated with the fort is Christopher "Kit" Carson. He was America's most famous frontiersman after Daniel Boone. Carson, whom St. Vrain mentored, was an admired guide, Native North American fighter, and hunter. He supplied the fort with buffalo meat. (Parents may recall the 1950s television show "Kit Carson" as well as the 1940 movie.) Nevada's capital, Carson City, takes its name from him.

During the Mexican War of 1846, the fort's strategic location made it a military staging point for U.S. invasions into Mexico. In 1849, after Charles Bent's murder in an Indian-Mexican uprising, William Bent abandoned the fort. Legend has it that a distraught William himself set the fire that destroyed the empty "castle."

About the Site The reconstructed adobe fort stands on a tract along the north bank of the Arkansas River. The fort is built of authentic materials, according to descriptions in diaries and contemporary drawings. Reproductions fill its sparse rooms. It stands on original foundations and has two circular bastions at opposite corners.

Visitors can wander around the open courtyard, where a huge fur press reigns opposite the fort's massive wooden doors. Your self-guided tour continues through a dozen rooms on two levels, including St. Vrain's quarters, the billiard room, kitchen, warehouses, dining room, laborers' quarters, and trappers and hunters' quarters. You'll quickly notice how the smaller and cruder quarters reveal social distinctions among staff.

The corner Council Room, neutral ground for Native North American peace councils, serves as a visitor entrance station. Costumed interpreters help you plan your visit. Visitors can watch a video on the fort, its cultural mix of visitors, and the Santa Fe Trail.

In the next-door Trade Room, where a warm fire knocks off seasonal chill, a gift shop functions as a trading post of yesteryear. Livestock and horses in a corral at the fort's rear give the atmosphere an authentic smell.

Dinosaur Monument

Young people who love dinosaurs may enjoy the 145-million-year-old dinosaur bones at Dinosaur National Monument on the northeast Utah/northwest Colorado border. The visitor center is two miles east of Dinosaur, Colorado. The Dinosaur Quarry is located seven miles north of Jensen, Utah.

Fossilized bones of dinosaurs, mostly stegosaurus and brontosaurus, lie exposed in a desert ridge, once the banks of an ancient river. Millions of years ago seas encroached into the area, depositing mud and sand. Then cataclysmic geological forces pushed back the sea, and sediments became rock. Eventually the bone-laden strata of sandstone rose to the surface. Erosion finally revealed the bones.

Today this exposed "bony" ridge functions as a back wall for a towering glass dinosaur quarry museum. This site in Colorado is the world's largest known deposit of fossilized dinosaur bones.

Archaeologists have excavated most of the dinosaur bones found here, including several nearly complete skeletons. You'll find these bones displayed in museums around the country. But the ancient bones remaining in this arid wilderness gallery still make a visit worthwhile.

The 190,962-acre park has beautiful rivers, mountain vistas, and abundant wildlife. Visitors can enjoy hiking, river running, fishing, and camping at two campgrounds. The visitor center offers exhibits and a short orientation slide program.

Dinosaur National Monument Quarry ($) is open daily, except Thanksgiving, December 25, and January 1, from October through May, 8 A.M.–4:30 P.M., and in summer, 8 A.M.–7 P.M. Visitor center headquarters are closed weekends in winter. Backcountry and canyon roads are closed all winter. A shuttle bus runs from the visitor center to the quarry in summer months. For information contact Superintendent, Dinosaur National Monument, 4545 Highway 40, Dinosaur, CO 81610. Tel (970) 374-3000. For current information on hours and activities call (801) 789-2115.

A low stone wall encloses a small cemetery near the fort entrance. Thirteen people who died at the fort or on the Santa Fe Trail are buried there.

Hot Tips Allow 1½ hours for your visit. A lengthy paved trail leads from the parking lot to the fort. If the walk is too difficult, arrange for transportation in the information center at the parking lot. The center also has exhibits. Fort grounds are gravel and dirt and can become extremely muddy after rain or snowfall. Food and accommodations are available in La Junta and Las Animas.

Young visitors may enjoy the activity book *Bent's Old Fort Adventure Guide for Kids*, created by Doug Rudig for the Bent's Old Fort Historical Association. Look for it in the Trading Room.

The Best Stuff This is where you can imagine what the Santa Fe Trail was like 160 years ago. The mud, the buckskin-clad interpreters, the fires in the adobe fireplaces—and the smell—all contribute to an authentic Western ambiance.

Then and Now In its heyday, Bent's Old Fort employed from 40 to 60 men of different cultures and different tongues. Some days a wagon train rolled in from Independence, Missouri, with tired and hungry travelers, goods for trade in Mexico, and news from "civilization."

The Big Lodge offered a taste of the good life in the middle of the harsh desert. Head cook Charlotte Green, a black slave brought from St. Louis, prepared fine and varied dishes served on pewter and fine linen. Ladies on the trail with their husbands stayed in a relatively fancy corner room upstairs. Usually the fort's resident physician used this room.

Here Susan Magoffin stayed for 10 days recuperating from illness and a miscarriage. Her 1846 diary is one of the best records of the fort's daily life. She wrote

> ***July 26, 1846***
> ***The outside exactly fills my idea of an ancient castle. . . . Inside is a large square; all around this and next to the wall are rooms, some 25 in number. They have dirt floors—which are sprinkled with water several times a day to prevent dust. . . . Some of these rooms are occupied by boarders as bed chambers. One is a dining room—another a kitchen—a little store, a blacksmith's shop, a barber's shop, an ice house, which receives perhaps more customers than any other.***

Today few farms stand at the fort's distant periphery. But the 400,000 visitors here annually see much the same thing Mrs. Magoffin saw.

Elsewhere in the Area The Kit Carson Museum in Las Animas, 8700 Highway 50, is a cluster of historic buildings including an adobe museum with artifacts and exhibits, an 1860 log stage station, the 1882 plank-and-dirt Las Animas City Jail, and the 1876 stone Bent County Jail. The museum is open daily in summer months only. For more information contact Pioneer Historical Society of Bent County, Colorado, P.O. Box 68, Las Animas, CO 81054.

Mesa Verde

Crown Jewel of Southwestern Archaeology

Location Southwestern Colorado, in the high Colorado plateau country west of the Rocky Mountains. The park entrance is nine miles west of Mancos, Colorado, and eight miles east of Cortez, Colorado, off U.S. 160. Look for signs.

Mesa Verde National Park ($; $5 per vehicle) Chief Ranger's Office and Chapin Mesa Archaeological Museum are open daily, in summer, 8 A.M.–6:30 P.M., and the rest of the year, 8 A.M.–5 P.M. Two sections of the park, Wetherill Mesa and Far View—which has a visitor center, restaurant, and lodging—are closed during winter months.

A third section, Chapin Mesa, is open year-round and offers the best-preserved cliff dwelling, Spruce Tree House. Guided tours of some ruins are available year-round, although most interpretive activities take place mid-June through Labor Day. Self-guided tours of many ruins ($) are limited to summer months. The Ruins Road auto tour loops on Chapin Mesa, open 8 A.M.–sunset. For more information contact Superintendent, Mesa Verde National Park, P.O. Box 8, Mesa Verde, CO 81330. Tel. (970) 529-4465.

Weather determines road conditions and may force some sites to close. Ice and snow may make it necessary to use snow tires or chains in order to negotiate the steep and winding road up the mesa. For weather information Tel. (970) 529-4465 or (970) 529-4475. Dial 1610 AM for radio information. Allow 45 minutes to drive from the park entrance up the mesa to the park headquarters and main parking lot.

Frame of Reference The Anasazi, or "ancient ones," built the first pithouse villages at Mesa Verde about 1,400 years ago (A.D. 550). Mesa Verde culture reached its peak 800 years ago (about A.D. 1200). By A.D. 1300, the cliff houses and villages here were mysteriously abandoned. Artifacts unearthed here suggest nomadic habitation began 11,000 years ago.

Significance Mesa Verde National Park protects the most extensive array of cliff dwellings in America. These include the Cliff Palace ruins, with 217 rooms and 12 kivas, the largest cliff dwelling in North America. Mesa Verde, Spanish for "green table," is considered the crown jewel of southwestern U.S. archaeology. The park is a World Heritage Site. This means it makes a unique contribution to the world's cultural history.

The park, a high mesa dissected by several deep sandstone canyons averaging 650 feet deep, preserves the physical remains of a vigorous agricultural civilization that flourished here for about 700 years. Experts theorize that the Anasazi of Mesa Verde are ancestors of Native North American tribes in northern Arizona and New Mexico.

A Family Guide to Ancient Ruins

Consider Safety, Kids' Ages, and Attention-Grabbers

The Four Corners region brims with dramatic prehistoric Native North American ruins and spectacular natural wonders: painted deserts, dormant volcanoes, a meteor crater, a petrified forest, Monument Valley, the Grand Canyon. . . . Let's face it, a visitor could spend months here and not see everything he or she would like to see.

Which ruins among the thousands in the Four Corners region promise the best visits for the whole family?

The answer basically depends on three factors: safety, children's ages, and the presence or absence of attention-grabbers at the site.

- ***Safety.*** Many of the ancient Native North American ruins are found in canyons, with steep cliffs and dangerous hiking paths. It may be unwise to take young children to these sites.
- ***Children's Ages.*** Age brings up two more considerations: time and physical exertion. Hikes to some ruins require long stretches of time. Younger children may not enjoy hours of walking. Strollers are dangerous or useless on some trails. Children under age eight probably won't appreciate any prehistoric or historic sites. They simply are too young to put the experience into a meaningful context.
- ***Attention-Grabbers.*** Will your children really be excited by gazing at crumbling mud ruins in a canyon wall? Obviously it depends in part on their age and maturity. But some sites have built-in attention-grabbers that evoke emotion. These include exciting up-close views; short, fun hikes with good vistas; or even a chance to climb up, over, around, and through prehistoric ruins. Look for sites that offer physical treats children will like—and remember.

Get advance information with physical descriptions of sites when planning visits. *InterPARK Messenger,* published by the National Park Service, provides good descriptions of Four Corners national parks, monuments, and historical areas. Ask for it when contacting sites. There's also a listing and brief description of national parks throughout America in *The Complete Guide to America's National Parks,* published by the National Park Foundation.

Here are guidelines to the major prehistoric Native American ruins in the Four Corners region. You decide which of the generally 1,000-year-old sites promise the safest, best-educational, and most-memorable visits for the whole family. Sites are coded according to the following key: three asterisks (***) means most desirable and one asterisk (*) means least desirable.

***__Wupatki__ ($; $4 per vehicle). This is 35 miles northeast of Flagstaff, Arizona. Here you can drive close to unexcavated ruins and actually walk in some rooms. There are wonderful views. The centerpiece is the Wupatki Ruin, an 85-room pueblo located a short distance behind the visitor center. Trails slope. You can't get up-close views of the ruins (no entrance), but you can actually enter an ancient amphitheater and a restored ball court with six-foot walls. There's also a mysterious blowhole. Ranger hikes are available seasonally. In the 35,000-acre park lie 2,600 prehistoric ruins, historic Navajo sites, and many spectacular natural features. Included are lava flows, views of the Painted Desert and Sunset Crater, and the remains of the youngest of 400 volcanoes in the Flagstaff area. There is a separate visitor center. Older kids will love the hike over frozen, black lava flows. Wupatki is open daily, except December 25, in winter, 8 A.M.–5 P.M. and in summer, 8 A.M.–6 P.M.

For information contact Superintendent, Wupatki National Monument, 2717 North Steves Boulevard, Suite 3, Flagstaff, AZ 86004. Tel. (520) 556-7040.

***__Walnut Canyon__ ($). Now here's a treat for older kids. It's mildly strenuous to descend and ascend 238 steps into the 440-foot canyon. The one-mile Island Trail Loop becomes narrow along steep cliffsides. You'll love entering some of the 25 ancient dwellings built into caves along the trail. Several are fully restored. Look for the soot of prehistoric fires on the ceilings and the 800-year-old fingerprints of the builders of the stone walls. The short canyon rim trail offers stunning views. You can see 75 additional ruins. For information contact Walnut Canyon National Monument, Walnut Canyon Road, Flagstaff, AZ 86004. Tel. (520) 526-3367.

***__Aztec__ ($). Everyone will love walking through the fully restored Great Kiva here. Park at the visitor center, easily reached by paved road. Walk an easy ¼-mile trail through the main pueblo ruin, where you can enter the restored Great Kiva. You need spend only two hours to take in the 27-acre site, including an orientation video, small museum, and bookstore. An on-site trading post offers snacks and gifts. Early settlers believed Aztecs from Mexico built the village. The name stuck. For information contact Superintendent, Aztec Ruins National Monument, P.O. Box 640, Aztec, NM 87410. Tel. (505) 334-6174.

***Pecos ($). This park is 25 miles southeast of Santa Fe, New Mexico, and can be incorporated with visits to Bandelier, Fort Union, and other Santa Fe Trail sites. You can spend less than two hours here to see the ruins of an ancient "city," a mighty, 600-room village, one of the largest 15th-century pueblos. You can enter a reconstructed kiva and see ancient walls of this 600-year-old community of 2,000 prehistoric people. The 1½-mile trail loop is easy to walk, though steep in one place. It's 7,000 feet above sea level.

In addition to the Native North American ruins, you'll find the remains of once-towering, adobe Spanish missions and an accompanying labyrinth of supportive rooms. The highlight of this exciting visit is the view of the entire valley from this small mesa. The lovely visitor center houses a museum, bookstore, and theater, where you can view an interesting 10-minute orientation movie. For information contact Pecos National Historical Park, P.O. Drawer 418, Pecos, NM 87552-0418. Tel. (505) 757-6414.

**Salmon Ruin ($). Located two miles west of Bloomfield, New Mexico, on U.S. 64, this 900-year-old, E-shaped pueblo was a Chaco outlier. The 177-room, two-story "apartment" ruin and Great Kiva are the centerpieces of a 22-acre park, which has a museum, gift shop, short hiking trail to the ruins, and the San Juan County Archaeological Research Center and Library (both are open to the public). The adjacent Heritage Park offers exhibits of traditional habitations of the many prehistoric and historic groups of the Four Corners Region. Visitors can enter structures and participate in hands-on activities.

For information contact San Juan County Archaeological Research Center and Library at the Salmon Ruin, P.O. Box 125, Bloomfield, NM 87413. Tel. (505) 632-2013.

**Petroglyph National Monument ($). Take I-40 west of downtown Albuquerque to Unser Boulevard and three miles north. This site has three easily accessible, short hiking trails to most of the 15,000 works of rock art along a 17-mile-long volcanic escarpment. Backcountry trails also offer views of five volcanic cones on the mesa top. This is the only national monument dedicated to ancient rock art. Most petroglyphs are about 600 years old, but some may date to 3,000 years ago. There are also 100 archaeological sites telling the story of 12,000 years of human habitation.

For more information contact Petroglyph National Monument, National Park Service, 4735 Unser Boulevard NW, Albuquerque, NM 87120. Tel. (505) 839-4429.

*Navajo ($). This is in northeast Arizona, 50 miles northeast of Tuba City. Two year-round trails requiring strenuous hiking down steep cliffs offer spectacular views of the Betatakin Ruin and the Aspen Forest Overlook. Ranger-guided hikes down a long, steep trail over rough terrain are conducted seasonally to Betatakin, a 125-room cliff dwelling. There is a limit of 25 people per tour.

Reserved permits are required for the self-guided (and extremely strenuous) hike to the Keet Seel Ruins in Tsegi Canyon. Permits are limited to 20 visitors per day. Neither site can be entered without a ranger. Sites have a nice picnic area, terrific orientation videos and slide show, bookstore, and gift shop. Camping and Navajo horse tours ($$$) are offered. For information contact Superintendent, Navajo National Monument, HC-71 Box 3, Tonalea, AZ 86044-9704. Tel. (520) 672-2366 or (520) 672-2367.

*Hovenweep Southeastern Utah and southwestern Colorado. The main ruins among the six groups of sites, the Tower Ruins and Hovenweep Castle, are 45 miles west of Cortez, Colorado. The extreme isolation of this park makes visiting here unattractive for families. Driving to the site is via 46 miles of paved and gravel roads through ranchlands. There are no amenities nearby, but a small visitor center has a beverage machine, restroom, and picnic tables.

A ½-mile trail loop takes you around one side of the canyon rim. Sleeping Ute Mountain towers 18 miles away. A two-hour trail loop going down a canyon past the Tower ruins is steep and often slick. Still, the nearly 1,000-year-old masonry ruins teetering on the cliff edges are magnificent. Allow half a day.

For information contact Area Manager, Hovenweep National Monument, McElmo Route, Cortez, CO 81321. Tel. (970) 749-0510.

Also check out the biggies:

***Bandelier (see listing).

***Mesa Verde. Top 10 Site (see listing).

**Canyon de Chelly (see listing).

**Chaco Canyon (see listing).

The drawback to these biggies is that they require half a day to see. Younger family members may get tired and antsy.

The park protects 4,000 prehistoric ruins. These include 600 sandstone canyon cliff dwellings, which are sometimes part of elaborate stone cities fashioned in large alcoves. The park also boasts amazing towers, a mysterious Sun Temple, rock art, and spectacular views of ruins from canyon rims. At several mesa points, visitors have far-reaching views of four states.

White cowboys "discovered" Mesa Verde ruins about 100 years ago. The government established the park in 1906. It became a World Heritage Site in 1978.

About the Site The 52,000-acre park is virtually a prehistoric ruins resort. The park's centerpiece is the ruins of dwellings, built of red sandstone and timber. But you'll also find a network of hiking trails, private guided bus tours($), private air transportation($), a visitor center/museum, theater, archaeological museum, bookstore, post office, park headquarters with chief ranger's office, amphitheater, restaurant, gas station, snack bars, lodge, and gift/crafts shops.

Some facilities are open in summer only, as are many hiking trails to the ruins. At Park Point along the entrance road, you can see a panoramic view of four states. At 8,671 feet, Park Point is the highest point on the mesa. Next to some ruins, you'll find the toe and hand holds that the Anasazi sculpted to reach their homes.

The park comprises three main areas: Chapin Mesa, open year-round; Wetherill Mesa; and Far View Sites Complex. The latter areas are open summer months only.

CHAPIN MESA

Ruins Road takes you through 700 years of Anasazi ruins along two six-mile loops—the Mesa Top Ruins Loop and the Cliff Palace Loop. This is a self-guided auto tour route. Signs mark stops along the road.

Chapin Mesa features year-round, one-hour ranger-guided tours to the Spruce Tree House ruins, which are located behind the Archaeological Museum. You can drive to the Balcony House ruins along the Cliff Palace Loop. Hiking to the ruins is allowed only in summer and early fall. Here is more information about each loop:

- Mesa Top Ruins Loop. You can walk to some mesa-top ruins—both pit houses and pueblos—and view cliff dwellings from canyon-rim vistas. Sites include Navajo Canyon Overlook, which offers an incredible view, but you may need binoculars to enjoy the 60 cliff ruins on the far canyon wall; pit houses, underground dwellings with surface roofs that are the earliest mesa housing; Square Tower House; Tribal Village Pueblo Sites; Sun Point Pueblo and Overlook; Oak Tree House; Fire Temple; and New Fire House and Sun Temple.
- Cliff Palace Loop. This loop includes Cliff Palace, the largest cliff dwelling in North America (circa A.D. 1209–1275); Cliff Canyon Overlook; House of Many Windows; Hemenway House Overlook; and Balcony House, which has seasonal ranger-guided tours.

WETHERILL MESA

The road to Wetherill Mesa (closed winters) is 12 miles one way from Far View Visitors Center, located 15 miles from the park entrance. From the parking lot, a free minitram takes you to the ruin trails. There's also a ½-mile nature trail.

Sites here include Step House, where you'll find the only reconstructed pit houses in the park; Long House, second-largest cliff dwelling in the park, also open for ranger-guided tours; pit house villages; pueblo villages; Badger House; Two Raven House; Nordenskiöld House (unexcavated); and overlooks to other ruins.

Far View Sites Complex

This cluster of villages (closed winters) is open only when road conditions are good. It is found about a mile south of the Far View Visitor Center. You can view six sites within walking distance of the parking area. Far View may have been the most densely populated area in Mesa Verde, with as many as 50 villages located in a ½-mile square.

Sleeping Ute Mountain

From Mesa Verde National Park, you can view Sleeping Ute Mountain, a well-known area landmark near Cortez. The great, rocky mountain looks like a man at rest with his chin and toes pointing skyward. His crossed arms mark the mountain's highest point. Legend has it that the Ute chief one day will rise up and reclaim his ancestral lands.

Sites here include Far View House, which has an especially large kiva; Pipe Shrine House; Far View Tower; Mummy Lake; Far View Ditch, an ancient man-made reservoir and collection ditch; Megalithic House; and Coyote Village.

Hot Tips Expect to spend at least half a day at each of the three major park areas. The minimum visit should be a ½-day tour of Chapin Mesa. You easily could spend a week here.

Food and restrooms are located in all three major park areas. Picnic sites are available on Chapin Mesa. Seasonal camping is offered at Morefield Campground ($) within the park boundaries. No reservations are required. Food and accommodations are available in Cortez and Durango, 36 miles east.

Seasonal commercial bus tours of Chapin Mesa leave from Far View Motor Lodge. For information contact ARAMARK Mesa Verde, P.O. Box 277, Mancos, CO 81328. Tel. (970) 529-4421.

Autos are restricted to paved roads and turnouts; hikers are restricted to trails. Length and weight restrictions are imposed on vehicles for Wetherill Mesa.

Get park information in advance. The park is immense, and you should plan your visit carefully, especially if children are included. Recommended reading includes *Mesa Verde: A Complete Guide* by Gian Mercurio and Maxymilian L. Peschel. Contact the park for purchasing information.

Browse for books on Mesa Verde via the Internet at http://www.mesaverde.org.

Pick up individual trail guides at Far View Visitor Center or at the chief ranger's office on Chapin Mesa.

Warning Park elevations vary from 6,000 to 8,500 feet. Hiking may be difficult for those with heart or respiratory problems. Hiking trails are steep and uneven and may include ladders. Young children or people with physical problems may have difficulty. Kids will enjoy the Junior Ranger Program. Check with park rangers.

The Best Stuff Just viewing the magnificent cliff dwellings from the canyon rims is worth the trip to Mesa Verde, but exploring the ancient ruins up close is even better.

At Balcony House visitors follow the park ranger down a 150-step staircase, up a 32-foot ladder, through a narrow, 12-foot-long tunnel, and up a 60-foot vertical cliff. The tours are strenuous. Guided tours take place in summer only; waits are at least an hour. The Long House guided tour has similar thrills.

No matter when you visit, you can hike with a ranger down into Spruce Canyon and walk up to the ruins of Spruce Tree House. You can peer through keyhole-shaped doors and see the rooms where Anasazi slept 800 years ago. Eyeball the mud plaster still intact on many walls, descend into a reconstructed kiva, and stand in the courtyard of the village, where the cliff dwellers conducted most daily activities. Black soot from ancient fires still colors the ceiling of the canyon alcove, up to 60 feet deep and 89 feet long. The small rooms of the house were up to eight layers deep and three stories high.

Then and Now Mesa Verde dwellings went through several major phases, from the building of the oldest pit houses on the mesa top to the best-known era, the Classic period of A.D. 1100 to 1300.

During this Classic period, the Anasazi built the huge masonry pueblos and the cliff dwellings that have made the park famous. During this period of advanced architecture, the Mesa Verde pottery, with its black geometric designs on a white background, and basket weaving became flourishing arts.

From the dwellings, artifacts, and burials that have been excavated in huge garbage heaps at the site, we have gained the scanty knowledge we have of these ancient people who farmed mesa tops. We think the average life span was 32 to 34 years. Men averaged five feet, five inches tall; women were five feet, one inch. The people conducted trade with neighbors.

Two hundred years before Spanish explorer Coronado crossed into what is now Colorado in 1541, the families of Mesa Verde had spent their last nights in the small stone rooms of their homes and had doused their last fires.

Elsewhere in the Area Ute Mountain Tribal Park is 22 miles south of Cortez; Crow Canyon Archaeological Center is in Cortez; Four Corner Area Monument is nearby; and Hovenweep National Monument is 40 miles west of Cortez.

Square Tower House is one of the ruins you'll find at Mesa Verde.
Jack Boucher, National Park Service

Little Bighorn Battlefield

Where Custer Made His Legendary Last Stand

Location South central Montana, on the Crow Indian reservation. Take I-90 (U.S. 87/212) to exit 510. Watch for signs. Take U.S. 212 one mile east to entrance.

The Little Bighorn Battlefield National Monument ($) is open daily, except Thanksgiving, December 25, and January 1, from Memorial Day through Labor Day, 8 A.M.–8 P.M., in winter months, 8 A.M.–4:30 P.M., and in fall and spring, 8 A.M.–6 P.M. One-hour guided bus tours ($) are available, as are a number of special programs. The Battlefield tour road may close earlier than the visitor center. Additional ranger talks and demonstrations are available in summer months. For more information contact Superintendent, Little Bighorn Battlefield National Monument, P.O. Box 39, Crow Agency, MT 59022. Tel. (406) 638-2621.

Frame of Reference The Battle of Little Bighorn took place on June 25 and 26, 1876, during the cavalry's final phase of killing or confining to reservations the few holdout tribes at the final phase of the Plains Indian wars (early 1860s to late 1870s), as white American expansion into the West resumed with renewed zeal, angering Native North Americans. White conflict with Native North Americans began with the first European settlements in North America and continued through the 1890s.

Significance On this grassy hillside in isolated Montana Territory, up to 2,000 Lakota (called Sioux by whites) and Cheyenne warriors killed Lieutenant Colonel George Armstrong Custer and all the men of the Seventh Cavalry battalion under his command. The Sioux and Cheyenne were holdout tribes. They refused to follow treaties and stay on reservations. Custer and his Seventh Cavalry were part of a military effort to bring the renegade tribes under control.

Because of no fewer than a dozen movies, four plays, a long list of books, and more than 900 different artworks—including one million copies of a poster that hung in saloons around the country at the turn of the century—the Battle of Little Bighorn is one of the most famous battles in U.S. history. The battle took place near Wyoming's Little Bighorn River, hence its name.

The two-day, multiphased battle is remembered as "Custer's Last Stand." But the lopsided confrontation also was the last great stand for the Plains Indians before their defeat.

After the battle the victorious warriors mutilated bodies of the fallen. Word of the carnage spread like a prairie wildfire. Custer, age 36, was glorified as a hero. The U.S. Army responded with all-out warfare on defiant Plains Indians.

The Little Bighorn Monument today memorializes one of the last armed efforts of the Northern Plains Indians to keep their ancestral lands and preserve their way of life.

About the Site The monument preserves two sites of fighting during the battle. The most significant is Custer Hill, where Custer and the surviving remnants of his battalion perished. The second is the nearby Reno-Benteen Battlefield. Here two cavalry leaders, Major Marcus A. Reno and Captain Frederick W. Benteen, led separate flanking actions in the battle. Native North American warriors held their men under siege for hours.

A 10-mile, self-guided auto trail takes visitors to significant battle sites. Monuments and markers tell of the battle that took place within a 5-mile stretch of the Little Bighorn Valley.

A granite monument erected in 1881 reigns atop Custer Hill. It lists the names of 220 soldiers, Native North American scouts, and civilians who died here. (Some are unknown.) Small, white-marble tombstones scattered over the hillside mark the first gravesites of Custer and his men. A black iron fence surrounds most of the tombstones.

The day after the battle, survivors among Reno and Benteen's men buried the men where they fell. They marked the graves with wooden stakes. In 1881 the men were reburied in a single grave at the crest of the hill where the stone monument now stands.

The visitor center at Custer Hill houses a small but interesting museum featuring the Custer Collection. There are also audiovisual programs on the Sioux War of 1876, a gift shop, and a theater. Here you can see an excellent 40-minute documentary, *Last Stand at Little Bighorn*, which tells of the battle, its causes, and its after-

Pompey's Pillar

If you're following Lewis and Clark's Voyage of Discovery (1803–06) through Montana, take an hour to visit Pompey's Pillar ($). Here you'll find the only physical evidence remaining of the historic exploration of the West. Captain William Clark inscribed his name and the date into the towering sandstone butte, which stood at the Yellowstone River he had been traveling.

Pompey's Pillar, a National Historic Landmark, is located just north of U.S. 94, 28 miles east of Billings, exit 23 at U.S. 312.

Today the ground upon which Clark stood as he etched his name has eroded away. Visitors must climb 114 wooden steps to see the signature. A locked, glass display case mounted into the side of the butte protects Clark's etching: "W. Clark, July 25, 1806."

Climb another 112 steps to the top to get a spectacular view of the Yellowstone Valley, which Clark wrote about in his journals as "a most extensive view in every direction. . . ." The view now encompasses hay fields, farms, an iron bridge, and paved highways.

Clark named the 150-foot-high butte "Pompy's Tower" after the baby son of Shoshone Squaw Sacakawea, and Baptiste Charbonneau, whom Clark called "Pomp." Sacakawea served as Lewis and Clark's interpreter. *Pomp* means "little chief" in the Shoshone language.

The Crow people called the ancient landmark "where the mountain lion lies." After the Lewis and Clark journals were published in 1814, the new name stuck.

The visitor center, with a small gift shop, is open Memorial Day weekend to September 30 only. The boardwalk to Clark's signature is open year-round. Park at the gate off-season. Access to the boardwalk is about a one-mile hike. Interpretive tours are offered in summer. Use insect spray in warm months. Stay on the boardwalk.

For more information contact Bureau of Land Management, Billings Resource Area, 810 East Main Street, Billings, MT 59105. Tel. (406) 657-6262.

math. A 28-minute film, *Brushing Away Time*, investigates archaeological discoveries made at the battlefield during the 1980s and 1990s.

Visitors can walk the Custer National Cemetery, proclaimed a national cemetary in 1879, where nearly 5,000 soldiers and their dependents are buried. Rangers also offer guided tours. At the visitor center, park rangers give regularly scheduled interpretative talks about the battle. Included is one from the Native North American point of view, offered by a descendant of Lakotas who fought here.

Hot Tips Allow half a day at the site. Start at the visitor center, where you can pick up a map and list of programs. You also can rent a CD-ROM or buy ($) an audio tour guide of the battlefield. The visitor center sits at the foot of Custer Hill and next to Custer National Cemetery. You can see both on foot. Stay on sidewalks. Walking on the battlefield is prohibited. Use of metal detectors, digging, and collecting relics or bones is illegal at the battlefield as well as on adjacent Native North American lands. Watch for rattlesnakes.

Your auto tour should begin at the Reno-Benteen Battlefield, where the battle action began. Follow the park tour road five miles to this site. A ½-mile loop trail takes you around the area Major Reno's forces occupied.

Dress for the plains' seasonal weather extremes. No picnicking or smoking is allowed at the site. Food is available near the park entrance. Food and accommodations are available at Billings, Montana, 65 miles northwest, and at Hardin, Montana, 18 miles north.

Many books and numerous movies tell of Custer, Sitting Bull, Crazy Horse, and the battle. The 1970 movie *Little Big Man*, starring Dustin Hoffman, offers the then-new viewpoint that Custer was not the shining hero of legend. A visit here reaffirms this theme.

The Best Stuff Most folks head first for Custer Hill. You can walk up an asphalt path past the iron fence enclosing 54 white-marble markers splayed in a small area of the grassy hillside. The name of each man who fell at that spot is etched in the two-foot headstone: "Arthur Reed, Civilian, Fell Here, June 25, 1876."

At the center, near the crest, one stone carries a black shield reading: "G. A. Custer, BVT Major General, Lieutenant Colonel, 7th U.S. Cav. Fell Here, June 2, 1876." Custer was awarded the rank of major general for his daring during the Civil War. After the war he returned to the rank of captain. He was promoted during the Indian wars to the rank of lieutenant colonel.

A small sign at the granite stones covering the grave warns visitors: "Mass Grave. Please Keep Off." In 1877 the officers' remains were removed to various cemeteries throughout the country. General Custer was buried at West Point. He graduated from there at the bottom of his class. Native North Americans removed bodies of their slain warriors soon after the battle.

A push-button audio program at the monument ends with these words: "This is hallowed ground. Men from two very different cultures died fighting for their beliefs."

The museum displays Custer's personal effects, including a trunk with his name in gold, his blue battle jacket and forage cap, a brush, and a pink soap bar.

Then and Now The military campaign of 1876 against the Sioux and Cheyenne began after the Native North Americans left reservations and resumed raids on settlements and travelers. These acts of defiance against the 1868 treaty signed at Fort Laramie followed the 1874 discovery of gold on Black Hills treaty lands by no one other than Custer himself. The Civil War hero was leading a search for a new fort site, but he also took along professional geologists. They found gold.

The Seventh Cavalry was part of three separate expeditions that were to converge on the Native North Americans concentrated in southeastern Montana. The Native North Americans had gathered around spiritual leader Sitting Bull, who had seen a vision of victory. It also was time for an annual festival gathering. Custer was eager to attack Native North Americans encamped at Little Bighorn, possibly because he had dreams of glory.

Custer hastily split the Seventh Cavalry into three groups. His plan was to have the 600 men of the Seventh Cavalry surround the Native North Americans and attack them before they could flee, which he thought they would do. Despite warnings from his Native North American scouts, however, Custer was unaware of the great number of Indians encamped in the Little Bighorn Valley—some reports say up to 7,000—of which 1,500 to 2,000 were warriors.

Two groups split off from Custer, one under the command of Major Reno, the other under Captain Benteen. Warriors outflanked both. Reno and Benteen were unaware of Custer's maneuvers. No one under Custer's command survived, so no one knows exactly what happened next. But what probably happened was that after disastrous initial fights, Custer and about 80 of his remaining men ran toward Custer Hill.

Near the crest about 2,000 Native North American warriors surrounded the 42 army men who had survived to that point. They killed every last cavalryman, including Custer. Custer's end of the three-pronged attack lasted about 1½ hours. In the end U.S. Cavalry deaths totaled 272; the Native North Americans lost 60 to 100 warriors.

The warriors fought with the fury of a people wronged, protecting their homes and families. The U.S. soldiers ferociously withstood the attack with such courage that even Sitting Bull later acknowledged their fortitude. But in the end, there were no victors, only survivors and lessons in history.

Recently the Park Service has been trying to balance the story of the greatly imbalanced battle. In 1991 President George Bush signed into law a name change for the site from Custer Battlefield National Monument to the present name. Lakota park interpreters were added to tell the other side of the story. The documentary shown at the visitor center paints Custer as a rash man out for personal glory.

Today the words of Black Elk, the legendary Sioux survivor of the battle, grace the side of the visitor center in large, wooden letters painted black: "Know the Power That Is Peace."

Elsewhere in the Area Two trading posts stand near the park entrance on U.S. 212. The Reno-Benteen Museum is on I-90 near the battlefield.

Bandelier

Enchanting Network of Anasazi Dwellings

Location North central New Mexico on the Pajarito Plateau, 46 miles west of Santa Fe. From Santa Fe take U.S. 285 north to Pojoaque, then go west on Route 502, then south on Route 4 to the park.

Bandelier National Monument ($) Visitor Center is open daily, except December 25 and January 1, in summer, 8 A.M.–6 P.M., and the rest of the year, 8 A.M.–4:30 P.M. Trails are open dawn to dusk. Ranger tours are offered in summer. For information contact Superintendent, Bandelier National Monument, Los Alamos, NM 87544. Weather conditions can make travel into the canyon treacherous. For 24-hour information, Tel. (505) 672-0343.

Frame of Reference The Four Corners area was occupied by the Anasazi, ancient ancestors of southwestern Native North Americans, about 1,000 years ago. Evidence found in Bandelier suggests transient occupation began 11,000 years ago, but building began in earnest 700 years ago, around A.D. 1300. Bandelier communities thrived for about 300 years. By A.D. 1600 the canyon and mesas were mysteriously abandoned.

More Historical, Natural Wonders

El Morro ($) in west central New Mexico, is a mesa rising 200 feet above the surrounding country, resembling a fortress (Spanish *morro*). Two self-guided trails (one ½ mile; one 2 miles) in the 881-acre park cover rough terrain. The visitor center has a 12-minute orientation video.

El Morro National Monument is open daily, except December 25 and January 1, in summer, 8 A.M.–7 P.M., and the rest of the year, 8 A.M.–5 P.M. For information contact Superintendent, El Morro National Monument, Route 2, P.O. Box 43, Ramah, NM 87321-9603. Tel. (505) 783-4226.

El Malpais is midway between Albuquerque and Gallup, New Mexico, south of I-40 in high desert lands. There's a visitor center in the town of Grants at 601 East Santa Fe Street. Of the park's 377,000 acres, 85 percent are wilderness. El Malpais, Spanish for "badlands," is best known for its lava flows, which are rough and can cause nasty accidents. There are abundant hiking trails, caves, craters, overlooks, canyons, sinkholes, and vast areas for wilderness exploration. All are self-guided. Permits are required for overnight, primitive camping.

For information contact El Malpais National Monument, P.O. Box 939, Grants, NM 87020. Tel. (505) 287-3407.

Significance In the spongelike volcanic cliffs of this spectacular canyon Anasazi families occupied natural caves. The sculpted caves give the pink-and-buff cliffs an enchanting Swiss-cheese appearance. Ancient people also built a vast and amazing network of multiroomed, mud-and-stone community dwellings (pueblos) and stone houses next to the tuff cliffs, along the canyon floor, and in villages on the surrounding plateau.

The Anasazi of Bandelier—named for Adolph Bandelier, who pioneered research into Four Corners ruins beginning in 1880—came here possibly after prolonged draught forced them from more northern Four Corners areas.

Thousands of Anasazi ruins remain in the park; only 50 have been excavated. Bandelier offers a provocative link to the ancient history of southwestern Native North Americans and helps tell the story of prehistoric America.

About the Site This 50-square-mile park has 70 miles of hiking trails to ancient ruins, natural wonders, and spectacular vistas. The park's 3 miles of paved road take you 600 feet down into the Frijoles Canyon, cut by the babbling Rito de los Frijoles (Bean Creek). Here a 1½-mile, self-guided Main Loop Trail takes visitors to the cave and cliff dwellings and to most of the excavated ruins.

Main Loop Trail. The 21 sites along the rough-and-tumble Main Loop Trail include the pueblo ruins of the Tyuonyi village, Big Kiva, and a series of cave dwellings. You can enter some of the caves by ladders. The loop also includes a cave kiva, a reconstructed talus (cliff stone) house, the multilevel Long House ruins—one of America's earliest "condominium" complexes—as well as prehistoric rock art.

An additional one-mile loop takes you to the Ceremonial Cave. Intrepid visitors reach the Ceremonial Cave by climbing four ladders, 140 feet up the canyon cliff. There you will see ruins of rooms sculpted into the cliff. Another ladder takes you down into a restored cliff kiva.

Backcountry Trails. Backcountry trails take visitors to the ruins of five villages on the high plateau, the pictograph-covered Painted Cave in Capulin Canyon, and postcard vistas. Trails include the three-mile Falls Trail, which leads to the upper and lower waterfalls of the canyon. Bean Creek eventually drops into the Rio Grande and falls in the southeastern corner of the park.

Tsankawi Village. The unexcavated ruins of the Tsankawi Village are located about 11 miles north of the park's main entrance on Route 4. A primitive 1½-mile trail loop takes you to the ruins. You can travel the remains of an ancient footpath to the village. At places the path becomes a deep groove up to 18 inches deep, worn over centuries into the soft stone by sandaled feet.

The park's rustic visitor center, once part of a privately owned lodge, houses a museum with excavated artifacts, a bookstore, and a theater. Here you can see an outstanding orientation video. The visitor center complex includes a snack bar with outdoor seating, a gift shop, and the Cottonwood Picnic Area.

Seventy percent of Bandelier is part of the national wilderness system. Cross-country ski trails operate in snowy months at the far edges of the park.

Hot Tips Park literature says that you can sample the park in as little as one hour. Don't believe it. Plan to spend half a day (more for backcountry hiking) to savor Bandelier's beauty and unique volcanic dwellings.

Warning The average elevation of the nearly 38,000-acre park is 7,000 feet. Hiking the steep and rocky trails can be difficult for visitors from lower elevations. Don't attempt the climb to the Ceremonial Cave if you have physical problems or fear heights. Stay on designated trails, and do not touch the ruins. Cold months may bring ice, snow, and slippery conditions.

Get trail guidebooks ($) and free overnight backpacking permits from the visitor center. Juniper Campground ($) connects to the canyon by the 1½-mile Frey Trail. Sites are available on a first-come, first-served basis for family camping. Food is available at the site. Food and accommodations are available in Santa Fe, Los Alamos, and White Rock, New Mexico.

From April through October parking space is scarce. You may have to wait an hour or more for a parking space in the limited parking lot.

Advance reading will enhance your visit. Recommended reading includes Patricia Barey's *Bandelier National Monument*. Contact the park. Also, Adolph Bandelier's groundbreaking novel, *The Delight Makers*, first published in the 1890s, is still in print.

The Best Stuff The Main Loop Trail winds up cliffs and around weird, spiked rock formations. It's like wandering through an amusement park maze. Climbing up the crude ladders made of ponderosa pine uprights and juniper crossbars to 850-year-old cave homes is terrific.

You can sit in the prehistoric cave rooms and contemplate the verdant canyon below. Look up and see blackened cave ceilings, the result not only of ancient domestic fires, but of an ancient method of sealing with flame. The Anasazi coated the ceiling with a "plaster" of ground stone and animal blood. Enter the caves only with ladders.

If you have the stamina to visit the Ceremonial Cave, wow, is it worth the climb! Frijoles Creek babbles 14 stories below you among green trees. In the cave you'll see where ancient ceremonial fires blackened the 40-foot arched ceiling.

Then and Now The Bandelier village network reached its peak population of hundreds in the 1400s. The population rose and fell with circumstances. The prosperous farmers may have sown the seeds of their demise.

The Anasazi may have overfarmed the dry mesa land. The social structure may have broken down; infighting may have occurred. Or maybe the canyon and plateau dwellers simply became restless. Whatever the reason, by the time Spanish explorers ventured this far north from Mexico, Bandelier was empty.

Unfortunately, not all of the park's 300,000 yearly visitors respect and protect this beautiful site. Modern names and initials scar cave walls. Reddish pictographs that once graced the living room walls of Long House have been defaced. Plexiglas protects a few survivors.

Elsewhere in the Area Historic Santa Fe, New Mexico, is 46 miles away.

Chaco Canyon

A 1,000-Year-Old Hub of Ancient Ones' Society

Location Northwest New Mexico, 150 miles northwest of Albuquerque, New Mexico, and 90 miles northeast of Gallop, New Mexico. From Gallop take I-40 east to Thoreau, then take U.S. 371 north. At the fork go right to Seven Lakes, then north on Highway 57 to the visitor center. Follow the signs. From Albuquerque take U.S. 25 north to Route 44 north to Nageezi. Watch for signs. Take Route 57 south into the park.

Chaco Culture National Historical Park ($) Visitor Center is open daily, from Memorial Day through Labor Day, 8 A.M.–6 P.M., and the rest of the year, 8 A.M.–5 P.M. Ranger-guided tours and evening campfire programs are offered in season. For more information contact Superintendent, Chaco Culture National Historical Park, P.O. Box 220, Nageezi, NM 87037. Tel. (505) 786-7014.

Note This park is isolated and primitive. The nearest town is 60 miles away, and there are no services in the park. Plan ahead. The last 20 to 26 miles of road leading to the park are dirt and gravel. Roads become slippery and often impassable during rain or snow. Check with the park about weather conditions before you visit.

Fort Union

Fort Union National Monument ($) preserves the adobe ruins of an important Santa Fe Trail stop. This sprawling fort, actually a third built on the site, stood at the trail's west end. The Defender of the Southwest commanded the intersection of the Mountain and Cimarron branches.

Fort Union, first constructed in 1851, was the largest U.S. military installation of the 19th-century southwestern frontier. It is located in northwestern New Mexico, 60 miles east of Santa Fe, just west of U.S. 25. Follow the signs.

A portion of the park preserves a stretch of clear Santa Fe Trail ruts. Fort Union's past also includes an important role in stopping a Confederate advance into the West. The visitor center houses exhibits.

The monument is open daily, except December 25 and January 1, 8 A.M.–5 P.M., with extended hours in summer. Living-history demonstrations are offered. For information contact Superintendent, Fort Union National Monument, P.O. Box 127, Watrous, NM 87753. Tel (505) 425-8025.

Frame of Reference The Anasazi (ancient ones) civilization flourished in the Southwest about 1,000 years ago. This was from the mid-800s to the early-1100s, hundreds of years before Columbus's voyage. The Anasazi culture dominated the region's society for 150 years before the people mysteriously began to leave. The canyon was abandoned by the end of the 12th century.

Significance The desert park protects what was the heart of a vast regional network of at least 150 ancient Native North American communities. The spectacular stone structures of this 10-mile-long, gray-and-tan canyon are unique in several ways: their massiveness, their distinct and intricate masonry, and the amount of planning and labor their construction must have demanded.

Two unusual features also distinguish the Chaco community from its ancient neighbors: the large number of Great Kivas found here—at least18—and the spectacular 400-mile network of engineered clay roads between Chaco's Great Houses and outlying villages, called *outliers*.

Some archaeologists, after studying the Great Houses and their many storage rooms opening to the prehistoric roads, theorize that Chaco was a great depository of food for the outliers. Chaco may have been one of the great "urban" population centers of prehistoric times in North America. Experts estimate a population of up to 5,000.

Chaco's Great Houses are multistoried villages in their own right. Experts have characterized them as ancient America's largest housing complexes, unrivaled in size until the 1800s, when high-rise apartments were built in New York City.

The Santa Fe Trail

America's most famous commercial highway, the Santa Fe Trail, covered about 1,000 miles through five states. For much of the 19th century, the trail was one of North America's busiest thoroughfares.

The trail began in several Missouri frontier towns, principally Independence. It followed routes first used by Native North Americans and then by white explorers and fur traders. The dusty trail wound its way through prairies, forests, and mountains of Missouri, Kansas, Oklahoma, Colorado, and New Mexico. Santa Fe, the capital of Mexican Territory, was the trail's end.

Today modern highways of the Santa Fe National Historic Trail parallel much of the original trail. Self-guided auto tour routes are marked with distinctive brown-and-gold signs. Adventure-seeking travelers can visit the trail's natural landmarks, stretches of wagon wheel ruts, and historic stops along the route.

The Santa Fe Trail, forged in hardship and steeped in legend, began in 1821 with Mexican Independence from Spain. Mexico then opened up trade with America, which Spain had declared illegal. Use of the trail ended in 1880 with the coming of the railroad into New Mexico.

History credits an American businessman, William Becknell, with blazing the Santa Fe Trail. Becknell and his party, anticipating the Mexican Revolution before leaving Missouri in 1821, arrived in a welcoming Santa Fe only months after Mexico had won independence.

Becknell's venture was speculative and dangerous but wildly profitable. The trail Becknell blazed sparked the lust for wealth of many back on the frontier.

From 1821 to 1880 thousands of wagon caravans loaded with trade goods poured into the Southwest. Entrepreneurs left with big profits. Emigrants, missionaries, adventurers, and gold-seekers also traveled the highway.

Freight wagons loaded with goods often pushed past Santa Fe to trading centers deep in Mexico. For about 60 years, the Santa Fe Trail linked Mexico to a

☛

The massiveness and complexity of Chaco's ruins are unsurpassed. Chaco represents the height of pre-Columbian pueblo civilization in North America.

Chaco became a national park in 1907 and a World Heritage Site in 1987, meaning that it makes a unique and significant contribution to the world's cultural and natural legacy.

About the Site The 32-square-mile park in the barren heart of the San Juan Basin contains 3,600 well-preserved ruins. These include the multiroomed Great Houses of Chaco and a multitude of small houses near the canyon wall. Earlier pit houses also dot the park.

Only 1 percent of the ruins have been excavated. Hiking paths lead to nine Great Houses, most excavated. Most sites are short walking distances from a paved, one-way road that loops through the canyon floor. Park at pullouts only. Visitors can reach other ruins via backcountry hiking trails (permit necessary).

All backcountry ruins are closed from a half an hour after sunset to a half an hour before sunrise.

A trail from the visitor center takes you through the unexcavated ruins of a Great House, Una Vida (Spanish for "one life"). Climb up a cliffside, look down on the ruins, and admire rock art over your head.

On the canyon rim you'll also see more rock art and sections of the wide, linear roads between the Great Houses and outliers. Sections of prehistoric stairs with carved handholds run vertically up the canyon cliffs at places. The sacred, 2,019-foot Fajada Butte dominates the canyon.

global trade network. Through rivers, canals, and other trails, St. Louis, New York, and even Europe received goods from Santa Fe and Mexico City.

When driving today's Santa Fe Trail, look for these National Park Service sites: Pecos National Historical Park and Fort Union National Monument, both in New Mexico; Bent's Old Fort National Historic Site in Colorado; and Fort Larned National Historic Site in Kansas. Fort Larned has a Santa Fe Trail Center. Each site has trail exhibits.

U.S. Forest Service sites include Comanche National Grassland in Colorado, Kiowa National Grassland in New Mexico, and Cimarron National Grassland in Kansas.

Much of the modern trail passes over private property. Some landowners protect sites and allow visitors. Respect owners' rights. Other trail sites are protected by state, county, and city parks. Local museums, chambers of commerce, tourist information centers, and guidebooks are sources of information. Marc Simmon's *Following the Santa Fe Trail: A Guide for Modern Travelers* is useful.

For information on the Santa Fe National Historic Trail contact these groups:

- **Long Distance Trails Group Office**—Santa Fe, National Park Service, Southwest Regional Office, P.O. Box 728, Santa Fe, NM 87504-0728. Tel. (505) 988-6888.
- **Santa Fe Trail Association,** Santa Fe Trail Center, R.R. 3, Larned, KS 67550. Tel. (316) 285-2054.
- **Kansas Division of Travel and Tourism,** 700 Southwest Harrison, Suite 1300, Topeka, KS 66603-3712. Tel. (913) 296-2009 or 1-800-252-6727. (Most of the trail winds through Kansas; ruts are plentiful.)

For information on the longest continuous stretch of Santa Fe Trail ruts, contact the Boot Hill Museum, Inc., Dodge City, KS, 67801. Watch for signs to the site. A 140-acre park, located a few miles from Dodge City, preserves these clear remains of the trail.

▲

The visitor center near Fajada Butte houses an excellent museum displaying some of the extraordinary artifacts excavated here. Chaco is known for its exquisitely crafted jewelry. A video center features three self-serve orientation videos. One on the Chaco Legacy is one hour; the other two are a half an hour each. A bookstore and wall map of Chaco in relief will help you plan your visit.

Hot Tips Plan to spend a full day touring the ruins along the auto route. Plan accordingly for backcountry hikes. Backcountry hiking requires a free hiking permit from the visitor center. Rangers don't want to close the park while you're still "out there."

Warning Chaco Canyon is 6,200 feet above sea level. Hiking here may be difficult for those from lower elevations or those with health problems. Roads to the park traverse an open cattle range: watch for animals on the road.

Biking is allowed on two roads leading to outlier ruins. One bike trail is three miles round-trip; the other is 23⅘ miles round-trip. Take plenty of water for biking and hiking in warm months. The desert terrain is rocky, uneven, and very steep in places. Wear hiking shoes and appropriate clothing.

Pick up free maps and individual guides to ruins for 25¢ at the visitor center. Recommended reading includes *Chaco: A Cultural Legacy* by Michele Strutin. No climbing is allowed on ruins or prehistoric stairways.

Camping is available at the Gallo Campground one mile from the visitor center on a first-come, first-served basis. Food is available at trading posts at Blanco, Nageezi, and Crownpoint.

Santa Fe: Trail's End

The historic city of Santa Fe was the enticing destination of the 19th-century Santa Fe Trail. It is America's oldest state capital and has come to symbolize the old Southwest.

Today's Santa Fe, meaning "holy faith" in Spanish, preserves tantalizing remnants of the area's Spanish, Pueblo Indian, and pioneer past, as well as appealing adobe architecture and colorful ambiance.

During the Santa Fe Trail's heyday in the 1830s the city's Main Plaza buzzed with activity. The arrival of a clattering trade caravan spawned a human tsunami of Mexican trappers, Indian craftsmen, Anglo traders, and New Mexican vendors. The governor of New Mexico may have watched the action from the adobe Palace of the Governors on the plaza's south side. Today the 400-year-old palace welcomes tourists from around the globe.

Pueblo craftspeople hawk their beautiful (and pricey) wares beneath the palace's timber overhangs. Built in 1609 to 1610, the Palace of the Governors is America's oldest state capitol, although New Mexico didn't become a state until 1912.

Modern Santa Fe is one of the largest art markets in the world. City blocks bulge with art galleries, shops, and restaurants. The city's emerald centerpiece is the grassy Main Plaza where the Santa Fe Trail caravans once arrived. Now, traditionally dressed Native North Americans, rhinestoned cowboys, 20-something snowboarders, and sandaled Yuppies share the narrow downtown streets with a permanent population of about 60,000.

Other important Santa Fe sites include these:

- **San Miguel Mission.** Tlaxcala Native North Americans built his adobe church in 1610. The church, with its five-foot-thick walls and ornate altar, remains active today. It is the oldest operating church in America.

Accommodations are available in Farmington, Gallop, and Albuquerque.

Take weather forecasts seriously. Rain quickly turns Chaco's dirt roads into treacherous seas of mud!

The Best Stuff Two Great Houses dominate the stone ruins at Chaco: Pueblo Bonito, dubbed "the Ruin of Ruins," and Chetro Ketl. Both were once massive, multistoried, intricate masonry pueblos with large courtyards, Great Kivas of 60-foot diameters, and large rooms. You can get a close look at these ruins by walking trails that wind through them. Here are the great sites:

- **Pueblo Bonito** (Spanish for "pretty village") is the most celebrated and most investigated site in Chaco. The **D**-shaped, four-story, terraced pueblo has 650 rooms, some with remnants of original mud plaster. It once contained 40 kivas, including two Great Kivas, and may have housed as many as 1,000 people.
- **Chetro Ketl** covers 3½ acres with its 500 rooms and 16 kivas, including one Great Kiva and a tower kiva. Most interesting are the two closely spaced, parallel walls that surround the open plaza of this pueblo. What was the use of this "moat"? Across the back of the massive walls' remains, you can see a groove at the second-story floor level where a balcony floor was secured. The canyon wall still shows holes where roof and floor beams of smaller structures stood. Archaeologists think it took 50 million pieces of sandstone and 26,000 trees for beams to build this extraordinary masonry Great House.
- **Best Bet** Take the 1½-mile backcountry trail up the canyon wall behind the Kin Kletso ruin if you have time. Drive to Kin Kletso and park there. From this trail, which is steep in places, you'll get an overview of both Pueblo Bonito and Chetro Ketl. The trail also affords a closer look at the prehistoric Jackson Stairway. Best of all, you can actually walk a section of a sunken prehistoric road.

- **The Old House.** This "puddle" adobe is a remnant of a pre-Spanish Native North American pueblo that predates Coronado's 1541 entry into New Mexico. It's called "the Oldest House in America." (A house in St. Augustine, Florida, makes the same claim.)
- **Cross of the Martyrs.** Climb the stairs to a towering white cross overlooking the city. Bronze plaques at the site tell of Santa Fe's heritage.
- **Santuario de Guadalupe.** This 200-year-old adobe mission is now a museum and performing arts center.

If you visit Santa Fe around the Christmas holidays, you'll experience the New Mexican tradition of *farolitos*. These sand-filled paper bags line the streets and buildings, bathing the city in twinkling lights and nostalgia.

Downtown parking is tight, but 15 city-owned parking lots dot the area. Walking is on sidewalks. Historic buildings have uneven floors.

For more information contact the Santa Fe Convention and Visitors Bureau, 201 West Marcy Street, Santa Fe, NM 87501-0909. Tel. (505) 984-6760 or 1-800-777-2489. Also contact the New Mexico State Department of Tourism, Santa Fe Welcome Center, Lamy Building, 491 Old Santa Fe Trail, Santa Fe, NM 87501.

Note Santa Fe's altitude is 7,000 feet. Travelers from lower elevations need about 48 hours to adjust to the thinner air.

▲

A Throne? Hike up the cliff at the unexcavated Una Vida behind the visitor center, and you'll find not only petroglyphs, but a partially carved stone "chair" overlooking the ruin. The huge chair looks like a prehistoric throne.

Then and Now Building activity began at Chaco Canyon about 2,500 years ago. It flourished in unprecedented grandeur for several hundred years, beginning in the C.E. 800s. For nearly seven centuries the structures stood undisturbed until a U.S. Army expedition, heading west from Santa Fe to quell Navajo raids against ranchers, discovered them in 1849.

Though the Navajo had long been familiar with them, white men were fascinated by these ancient ruins. Excavations and investigations through the years have yielded many clues but few certainties about their ancient builders. Archaeologists today are still unraveling the mysteries. Awed visitors can only guess at them.

The back wall of Pueblo Bonito in Chaco Canyon shows masonry styles developed during the prehistoric pueblo era. *George A. Grant, National Park Service*

Promontory Summit

Last Spike of the Transcontinental Railroad

Location Northern Utah, 32 miles west of Brigham City and 8 miles east of Great Salt Lake's northern tip. From the north take U.S. 84 south to exit 26 to Highway 83 past Thiokol Rocket Park (Lampo Junction). Turn right at the sign for Golden Spike. Follow brown signs to the visitor center. From the south take U.S. 84/15 to exit 368 onto Highway 13/83 west to Corrine. Continue on Highway 83. Turn left at brown Golden Spike sign at Thiokol/Lampo Junction, and continue following signs to the visitor center.

Golden Spike National Historic Site ($) is open daily, except Thanksgiving, December 25, and January 1, from Memorial Day weekend through Labor Day, 8 A.M.–6 P.M., and the rest of the year, 8 A.M.–4:30 P.M. The reconstructed steam locomotives *Jupiter* and *119* are on display and running from May 1 through May 14 and from September 3 through October 14, 9:30 A.M.–4 P.M., and May 25 through September 2, 10:30 A.M.–5 P.M. Special steam demonstrations are available seasonally; special events take place year-round.

For more information contact Ranger Division, Golden Spike National Historic Site, P.O. Box 897, Brigham City, UT 84302-0897. Tel. (801) 471-2209.

Frame of Reference The Transcontinental Railroad culminated America's 19th-century railroad-building era. The first railroads were laid in the 1830s. The idea of the transcontinental railroad came about in 1832. The great wave of railroad building occurred in the 1850s. In 1863 the Central Pacific and Union Pacific railroads both broke ground on an East/West linkup project. On May 10, 1869, the first transcontinental railroad was completed and the Golden Spike driven.

Significance Here, at a stark pass in the Promontory Mountains of Utah, dignitaries of the Central Pacific and the Union Pacific railroads drove four ceremonial spikes—including the famous Golden Spike—into a polished laurelwood tie. Their gesture symbolized the completion of the 1,776-mile transcontinental railroad. Congress chose Promontory Summit as the linkup site because it was equidistant between the ends of Union Pacific tracks in the West and Central Pacific tracks in the East.

It took four years, thousands of men, and hundreds of millions of dollars to build the historic, cross-country link that brought a quick end to the pioneer era and transformed America.

At the Golden Spike ceremony, a railroad worker drove in the final four iron spikes that actually connected the railroads. As he hammered them into a regular pine tie, newly strung telegraph lines signaled his taps across the nation: D-O-N-E. The time was 12:47 P.M.

America's first transcontinental railroad became the final catalyst for the settling of the West. Trips that had taken pioneers five to six months to complete by wagon now required only six to seven days. The transcontinental railroad's two rails, a mere four feet, eight inches apart, literally and figuratively bound the nation. In traversing the last barriers of wilderness, it cemented economic, political, and social ties among states, changing America forever.

About the Site A self-guided auto tour of the park takes visitors over nine miles of one-way, gravel roads along the original transcontinental railroad grades. Numbered spike markers along the tour route explain the site and the building of the railroad. In addition, a 1½-mile self-guided walking trail, the Big Fill Walk, takes you to the sites of two man-made railroad wonders: Big Fill and Big Trestle.

Union Pacific workers built the Big Trestle, wood scaffolding to support rails, across a deep ravine at the site. Central Pacific workers constructed the Big Fill, a bridge of rock and gravel to support tracks, in the same ravine.

Why the same ravine? Because both railroad companies were locked in a race to lay rail beds, believing that the one with the longer beds eventually would have the rights to more track. The race reached absurd heights. The companies laid parallel beds, some almost within site of each other. Congress ended the wasteful race by declaring that the rails would meet at Promontory Summit. The Central Pacific tore down Big Trestle soon after the Golden Spike ceremony.

The Mormon Pioneer Trail

From 1846 to 1869 about 70,000 Mormons came to the Valley of the Great Salt Lake by way of what is known as the Mormon Pioneer Trail. The 1,300-mile-long trail over desert, mountains, and rivers began in Nauvoo, Illinois, last home to the persecuted, peripatetic Mormons. Led by Joseph Smith, who founded the Church of Jesus Christ of Latter-Day Saints in 1830, they headed to Utah to practice their religion in peace.

Modern-day travelers can follow much of the historic Mormon Trail on marked auto routes. Much of the trail lies on privately owned land, but federal, state, and local governments also own significant portions. You can see long stretches of the original trail in several of the five states the trail covered, especially Wyoming. Here stretches of trail ruts, created by wagon wheels, are clearly visible.

A 60-foot monument commemorates the Mormon Trail pioneers near Salt Lake City, Utah, about 70 miles southeast of Golden Spike Park. The monument stands in This Is the Place state park.

For more information on the Mormon Trail contact these organizations:

- **National Park Service,** Long Distance Trails Office, 324 South State Street, Suite 250, P.O. Box 45155, Salt Lake City, UT 84145-0155. Tel. (801) 539-4093.
- **Iowa Mormon Trails Association,** 100 East Railroad, P.O. Box 283, Afton, IA 50830-0283.
- **Utah Division of Parks and Recreation,** 1636 West North Temple, Salt Lake City, UT 84116.
- **Bureau of Land Management, Historic Trails Office,** 1701 East E Street, Casper, WY 82601.

Bureaus of tourism in individual states also offer information. If you want to visit trail sites on private land, you must obtain the landowner's permission.

Years later, the railroads agreed to make Ogden, Utah, the railroad switch site instead of Promontory. Today only the trestle's rock fill abutments remain. The Big Fill remains much the same.

The original transcontinental tracks were torn out in 1942 and donated as scrap metal for the World War II effort. The remote park today has 1.7 miles of "transcontinental" track relaid on the 1860s railroad grades. In addition to drill holes, rock-lined culverts, stack rocks, and cuts and fills, highlights include these:

- **"Ten Miles in One Day" sign.** In the great railroad race to Promontory, the Central Pacific established a record that has never been broken. One thousand Central Pacific men laid one mile of track per hour. By day's end, they had advanced their rails 10 miles and 56 feet to this marker.

  On flat land work teams, often headed by ex-army officers, could lay two to five miles of track per day. Laborers laid 2,500 wooden ties per mile, then placed two pairs of 30-foot, 560-pound rails per minute on top. "Spikers" hammered 10 spikes per rail, using three blows per spike.
- **Chinaman's Arch.** The Central Pacific crews were mainly Chinese men looking to make money then return home. Lured by the gold rush and then railroad jobs, Chinese laborers flocked to America. The laborers, called "coolies," were willing to take taxing, dangerous jobs that others would not. The Central Pacific imported 11,000 Chinese men, who became the backbone of the railroad workforce. The Union Pacific employed a large number of Irish immigrants and ex–Civil War soldiers.
- **Ceremony Reenactments.** Visitors can relive the climactic "Weddin' of the Rails" at 11:30 A.M. and 1:30 P.M., daily, April through October, at the very spot where the railroad was completed. A 3:30 P.M. locomotive demonstration is added in the summer months. Authentic replicas of the two steam engines that drew special ceremonial trains to Promontory rumble toward each other. They pull up to the one-rail gap left in the track where the railroad was completed 130 years ago. A Golden Spike ceremony is reenacted May 11 through October 12 on Friday, Saturday, and Sunday.

  The visitor center houses a museum, bookstore, and theater where you can see an orientation slide show and films. Park rangers give interpretative talks here, as well as seasonal trackside talks under tents.

Hot Tips Pick up a guide for the Promontory Trail ($1) at the visitor center. Allow three hours for your visit if you take both the auto and walking tours.

Warning Keep close watch on children during the steam locomotives' running. Stand at least 15 feet away from the track to avoid the scalding steam from the locomotives. Do not put coins or objects on the tracks. Kids will love this re-creation.

The closest gas stations, stores, and repair garages are 26 miles from the park. Food and accommodations are available in Brigham City, Tremonton, and Ogden. The visitor center has picnic tables and vending machines.

Children will enjoy the *Golden Spike Jr. Engineer Workbook* as they tour the site. Ask for it at the visitor center.

The Best Stuff The highlight of the visit is the mega-sensory tête-à-tête of *Jupiter* and *119*. No one's likely to forget this attention-grabber, with the big engines' billowing steam, screeching iron wheels, and body-shaking rumbles.

Long after their glorious moment in 1869, both steam engines were sold for scrap. A California firm has lovingly re-created them over a four-year period using photographs and an 1870 design engineer's handbook. The engines were christened in 1979 with water from the Atlantic and Pacific oceans.

The hazards of building the railroads through unforgiving deserts, rivers, and especially the Sierra Nevada meant loss of lives. Living conditions could be horrible. Makeshift encampments, like the one at Promontory, were hotbeds of gambling, alcohol abuse, prostitution, and violence. Workers dubbed them "Hell on Wheels."

Then and Now Details of the Golden Spike ceremony are sketchy and unreliable. The ceremony was hastily arranged. Delays and mishaps plagued it, and reporters were unsure of the ceremony site. In fact, no reporters actually attended the ceremony at Promontory Summit. They were at Promontory Point, 37 miles south. That place appeared on their maps.

Inaccurate accounts of the ceremony could explain the belief that only one Golden Spike joined the transcontinental rails. Of the four ceremonial spikes, the most famous is the Golden Spike driven by Leland Stanford, a Central Pacific principal—along with three other Sacramento, California, store owners. A second spike made from gold came from the proprietor of the *San Franciso News Letter*. A silver spike came from the state of Nevada. The Arizona Territory presented a spike made from gold, silver, and iron.

Engraved on Stanford's 5⅝-inch Golden Spike, now residing in the Stanford University Museum in Palo Alto, California, are the words "May God continue the unity of our Country as this Railroad unites the two great Oceans of the world." The Stanford museum also protects Nevada's silver spike and the silver-plated maul used to drive the ceremonial spikes. Arizona's spike is part of the Smithsonian's transportation museum. The second golden spike's fate is unknown. The 7½-foot laurelwood tie was burned in a railroad office fire.

After the first transcontinental railroad was completed, other railroads came together for transcontinental routes. By the turn of the century nine trunk lines and their connections made travel from sea to sea routine. The American frontier collapsed.

The death knell for the Promontory section of the railroad came in 1904, when the Southern Pacific, heir of the Central Pacific, finished a 103-mile-long track across the middle of the Great Salt Lake. Traffic dwindled over the "Promontory Branch." In 1942 the tracks here were removed. In 1956 the last railroad-related building at Promontory burned down.

Elsewhere in the Area You can drive a 90-mile section of the original Central Pacific railroad grade. The Transcontinental Railroad National Backcountry Byway begins at the western end of Golden Spike park and ends in Lucin, Utah. The grade runs through desert land; it is remote and undeveloped. High clearance vehicles of no more than 30 feet are recommended. For information contact Bureau of Land Management, Salt Lake Field Office, 2370 South 2300 West, Salt Lake City, UT 84119. Tel. (801) 977-4300.

Fort Laramie

Ellis Island of the West

Location Southeastern Wyoming, about 30 miles northeast of Wheatland, 3 miles southwest of the town of Fort Laramie. From U.S. 26, follow signs to Highway 160 south to the park entrance.

Laramie National Historic Site ($) is open daily, except Thanksgiving, December 25, and January 1, 8 A.M.–4:30 P.M., with extended hours from mid-May to late September. Interpretive programs and guided tours are available in summer. For information contact Superintendent, Fort Laramie National Historic Site, P.O. Box 86, Fort Laramie, WY 82212. Tel. (307) 837-2221.

Frame of Reference Fort Laramie was occupied in the mid- to late 1800s, a period of accelerated westward expansion in America. The fort began in 1834 as a small, garrisoned fur-trading post, Fort William. This fort moved to the present site and was renamed Fort John. The American Fur Company bought Fort John in 1836, then sold it in 1849 to the U.S. Army, which named it Fort Laramie. The army abandoned the fort in 1890.

What Is Manifest Destiny?

In 1845 John Louis O'Sullivan, editor of the *United States Magazine and Democratic Review,* coined the term *manifest destiny* for the American spirit of western expansion. He wrote "Our manifest destiny is to overspread the continents allotted by Providence for the free development of our yearly multiplying millions."

Ever since, the words *manifest destiny* have been used to describe the ideal that drew 19th-century settlers to the West.

Significance Fort Laramie and the fur-trading post that preceded it reigned for 50 years as one of the most important outposts in the 19th-century West. The "Grand Old Post" stood on a unique stretch of Wyoming Territory where the Oregon, California, and Mormon trails converged. All the forces of manifest destiny—God, gold, land, freedom—lay beyond Fort Laramie. Today the fort embodies the West of yesterday.

In its heyday between 1849 and 1859 the fort, called the "Ellis Island of the West," welcomed more than 350,000 saints and sinners: fur traders, pioneers seeking land or religious freedom, gold-seekers, Pony Express riders, Overland Stage travelers to Black Hills gold country, and soldiers engaged in the Plains Indian wars. A trickle then a flood of people from the East and Midwest came to this North Platt Valley crossroads. Fort Laramie provided rest, supplies, and protection.

Fort Laramie was the last stop before the arduous Rocky Mountain passage. Eventually it evolved into a sizable Western town of about 60 structures. The fort had no palisades. Wood was too scarce and expensive in the long, arid shadow of the mountains.

In its last 40 years, Fort Laramie was a site of important treaty negotiations between the U.S. government and the Plains Indians. It also served as a main point of departure for military advances against the Native North Americans when treaties inevitably broke down.

About the Site The partially restored fort stands in a bend of the Laramie River near its junction with the North Platte River. Of the 60 original buildings, 22 remain. These include the cavalry barracks, post trader's store, captain's quarters, commissary storehouse, surgeon's quarters, bachelors' quarters, and guardhouses. The structures were built in phases with the distinctive architecture of different times. About a dozen have been restored to their 19th-century appearance. Fort Laramie is named for French fur trader Jacques La Ramie, who worked in the tributaries of the North Platte.

Sites at the 833-acre park range from foundations to broken adobe or lime grout walls reaching to the sky and to the pristinely restored Victorian homes of Officers Row. A visitor center, housing a small museum and gift shop, occupies a portion of the old commissary building. You can walk the site of the original Fort John on the riverbank.

During the summer the Sutler's Store is open for business. It offers reproduction items like those the civilian post trader sold to soldiers and travelers. Visitors can quench their thirst at the next-door Enlisted Men's Bar with a cold sarsaparilla.

Near the fort the ghostly ruins of the Cheyenne-Deadwood Stagecoach Stop caress the sky like unfinished sculptures. Two miles above the fort the original 1875 iron Army Bridge spans the North Platte. The army built the bridge to accommodate traffic from Cheyenne, Wyoming, to the gold-rich lands north of Fort Laramie. You can park at the bow-string arch bridge and walk across it.

Hot Tips Allow half a day for your visit. Fort Laramie covers a lot of ground and offers many activities. Parents of young children should pick and choose buildings and events to visit. Dress for the weather extremes found in the plains. Walking trails can be dusty or muddy.

Start your self-guided tour at the visitor center (Stop 1) located at the fort's rear. Pick up a map with a numbered guide to sites. Snacks are available in the Enlisted Men's Bar (Stop 17). Picnic tables are at the site. Food and campgrounds can be found in the nearby communities of Ft. Laramie, Guernsey, and Lingle.

Dial AM 1610 on your car radio for park information.

The Best Stuff Two restored and furnished buildings, the bachelor officer's quarters—affectionately called "Old Bedlam"—and the cavalry barracks, are the most fun to tour. Kids will also enjoy going inside the old guardhouse where soldiers were confined for seemingly small infractions.

The white, two-story Old Bedlam has wide front porches on both levels. It is Wyoming's oldest standing building. It earned its nickname from the boisterous sounds of its occupants, bachelor officers, who passed time with alcohol and poker. From behind glass barriers, you can look into bedrooms and see fur rugs, three double beds per room, and names of officers scrawled above the fireplaces. At the nearby cavalry barracks visitors can view mess halls, offices, and long dorm rooms lined with green iron beds.

Then and Now Fort Laramie is noted for its dual role of peacemaker and base of attack against the Plains Indians. In 1851 government officials and chiefs came together at the fort and negotiated the famous Treaty of Fort Laramie. The uneasy period of peace that followed was shattered by a cow.

In 1854 a Sioux Indian supposedly killed a cow belonging to emigrant Mormons. A scouting party under 2nd Lieutenant John Grattan left Fort Laramie to arrest the cow-slayer. When the soldiers arrived at a nearby Sioux village, a fight ensued. Sioux killed Grattan and his 29 men. The incident became known as the Grattan Massacre.

A second Fort Laramie Treaty was signed in 1868. The fort hosted a huge meeting between the army and 10,000 Plains Indians, who camped at the site. The later discovery of gold in the Black Hills dashed this treaty. Fortune-seeking whites swarmed into the gold fields; Native North Americans fiercely retaliated. The army's harsh actions against Native North Americans resumed full force.

When the Plains Indians at last were successfully confined to reservations, the last army garrison left Fort Laramie in 1890. The frontier had ended. The government auctioned off Fort Laramie. Homesteaders, whom the fort's soldiers had helped protect, bought

The Best Wagon Ruts and Register Cliff

Two of the most enduring symbols of the Oregon Trail await you near the tiny town of Guernsey, Wyoming, sometimes called "the hub of the Oregon Trail." The first is the Oregon Trail Ruts State Historic Site, which protects deep ruts carved into the sandstone hillsides by thousands of covered wagons and carts. The second is Register Cliff, where emigrants etched their names into the towering bluff that protected their Plains campsites.

Guernsey, modern-day home of a Wyoming National Guard post, straddles U.S. 26 along the North Platte River about 11 miles west of Fort Laramie and 98 miles north of Cheyenne.

The Oregon Trail Ruts site, on the North Platte River 1½ miles southeast of Guernsey, is a national monument. Register Cliff State Historic Site rises above the North Platte just east of the ruts, 3.8 miles southeast of the town. Follow signs from U.S. 26 to the sites. A concrete plaque next to the river at Register Cliff marks the site of a Pony Express Station from 1860 to 1861. You can get maps and information at the Guernsey Visitor Center at 90 South Wyoming Street, one block south of U.S. 26.

At the Wagon Ruts site, you can walk right up to the wagon carvings and touch them. The ruts dip several feet below the grayish sandstone outcropping above the North Platte banks. Of the 300 miles of visible wagon ruts along the 2,170-mile Oregon Trail, these are probably the most riveting. The tracks, slightly wider than the iron-rimmed wagon wheels that passed here, run 40 to 50 yards over the rugged hill. The rock between the ruts is slightly lower than the ridge, beaten down by thousands of oxen hooves. Except for a large historic plaque, a scraggly pine growing where the wagons must have traveled, a red-

☛

the buildings. Settlers opened up businesses. The cavalry barracks became a popular hotel with a bar and dance hall.

Old Bedlam, however, was not sold. The last post trader, John Hunton, held on to the once-rocking bachelor quarters until his death in 1928, although he sold parts of it as scrap.

The state of Wyoming bought the site in 1937. The federal government acquired it in 1938 and began a massive stabilization and restoration program.

Elsewhere in the Area

Grattan Massacre Monument is ½ mile south of Lingle, 10 miles east of Laramie; Oregon Trail Ruts and Register Cliff of the Oregon Trail are near Guernsey, 13 miles west. On U.S. 26 west of Guernsey, a rest stop named Olinger's Overlook of the North Platte Valley displays a kiosk and information markers pointing to 10 important historical sites in the valley.

and-white grain silo, a farm in the distance, and the sound of trucks on U.S. 26, this is what the wagonmasters saw exactly at this place 150 years ago.

Watch for roaming cattle at Register Cliff, rising 150 feet in an area now posted as open range. Pioneers camped at the base of the beige-colored outcropping after a day's travel from Fort Laramie and etched their names into nature's "motel register." To find the names of fur traders and Oregon Trail emigrants, walk toward the river. A chain-link fence protects these names, like that of "W. D. Smith 1849." A fence also protects a small burial ground at the foot of the cliff.

Another famous Oregon Trail site in Wyoming is Independence Rock State Historic Site, about 50 miles southwest of Casper, off Highway 220. Here thousands of pioneers also carved their names in stone.

For information about these and other Oregon Trail sites in Wyoming contact the Wyoming Division of Tourism, I-25 at College Drive, Cheyenne, WY 82002. Tel. (307) 777-7777.

PACIFIC

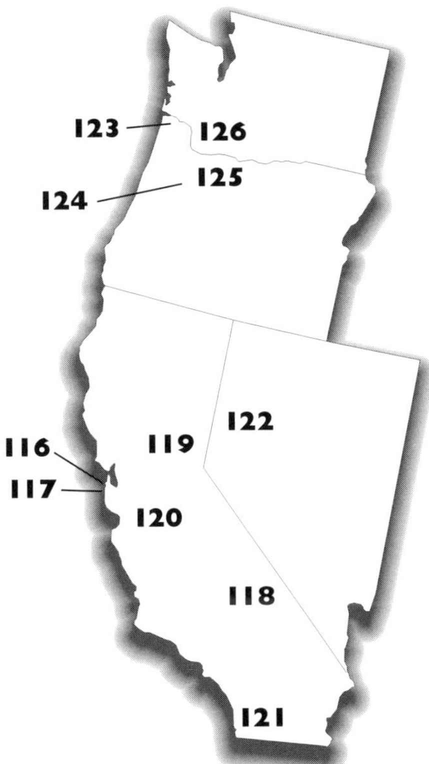

Key

Numbers correspond to site numbers on the map.

California

116. Alcatraz
117. Fort Point, Maritime Museum, and Hyde Street Pier
118. Manzanar
119. Marshall Gold Discovery Site
120. Old Town Sacramento
121. San Diego

Nevada

122. Virginia City

Oregon

123. Fort Clatsop and Astoria's Unique Column

Lewis and Clark Trail (see National Trails System Map on pages xv)

124. Oregon City and Oregon's Oregon Trail
125. Mount Hood

Oregon Trail (see National Trails System Map on page xv)

Washington

126. Fort Vancouver

Alcatraz

Infamous Federal Penitentiary, "the Rock"

Location San Francisco Bay, 1¼ miles from the bustling city waterfront. Part of the Golden Gate National Recreation Area (a Top 10 Site). Visitors can reach Alcatraz only by ferry. The Red and White Fleet is the official concessionaire to the federal park. Regularly scheduled ferries depart from Pier 41, end of Stockton Street at Fisherman's Wharf. Pier 41 can be reached via the Embarcadero, which traverses much of San Francisco's waterfront. Limited parking is available on the street and at public decks and lots nearby. It's advisable to take public transportation to the waterfront.

Alcatraz Island ($) is a unit of the Golden Gate National Recreation Area. Visitor centers are open daily, except Thanksgiving, December 25, and January 1, 10 A.M.–5 P.M. The last Alcatraz ferry ($) departs at 2:15 P.M. and leaves the island at 4:30 P.M. For Alcatraz information contact Superintendent, Fort Mason, Building 201, San Francisco, CA 94123. Tel. (415) 556-0560 or (415) 705-1042.

> "You are entitled to food, clothing, shelter, and medical attention. Anything else you get is a privilege."
>
> —*Number 5, Alcatraz Prison Rules and Regulations, 1934*

Make ferry reservations at least one day in advance for individuals and groups of less than fifteen people. For reservations call (415) 546-2700. For reservations for groups of 15 or more, call (415) 546-2653. Ticket price can include rental of the cellhouse audio tour. An additional two dollars is charged for telephone reservations. You can also make reservations in person at the Pier 41 ticket window.

Frame of Reference From the early 1930s years of Prohibition and the Great Depression to the Civil Rights era of the early 1960s, Alcatraz Island served as the site for a federal penitentiary (1932–63). The island was home to a U.S. Army fort built in 1853 and abandoned in 1907. It was used as barracks, then a military prison until the 1930s. Native North Americans first visited the island 15,000 years ago.

Significance Alcatraz is best known as the "Rock," the maximum-security, minimum-privilege federal penitentiary that was the last stop for the rottenest of the rotten apples. The U.S. Department of Justice opened the prison in an effort to stem a tidal wave of crime spawned during Prohibition and the Great Depression. The FBI wanted a big stick to lord over criminals; it wanted to send a message.

Alcatraz, which Spanish explorers named in the 18th century for either the pelicans or cormorants who live there, was the Justice Department's superprison. Exactly 1,545 troublemakers and escape risks did time on Alcatraz during its 29 years as a federal prison. But it was the famous inmates, like Al "Scarface" Capone, George "Machine Gun" Kelly, and Robert Stroud, "Birdman of Alcatraz," that gave the Rock its mystique.

The Rock's isolation, restriction of visitors, extreme security, and 14 daredevil—but futile—escape attempts cemented its reputation. A string of movies and television shows have augmented Alcatraz's infamy and allure.

U.S. Attorney General Robert Kennedy closed the prison following public protests over the prison's deteriorating condition and spiraling costs.

About the Site Visits to Alcatraz are self-guided. The island's most famous building, the three-tiered cellhouse, is the only building open for tours. When built in 1912 it was the world's largest reinforced concrete building. Most of the buildings that remain on the 22-acre island are closed due to disrepair. Many have been destroyed.

The renovated, 336-cell cellhouse covers the island pinnacle where the former fort citadel stood. One restored guard tower remains of the half dozen that watched the island during the penitentiary era. The 84-foot concrete lighthouse replaced one built in 1854; it was the first lighthouse on the West Coast. A 1940 welded-steel water tank dominates the skyline.

Whence California's Name?

History tells two versions of how America's most populated state got its name. One is that *California* comes from the Spanish words *ocaliento forto,* "hot furnace," referring to the deserts of southern California.

The second theory refers to the legend of Calafia that may have inspired Spanish explorers and their benefactors. The legend comes from a 16th-century adventure book, *The Deeds of Esplandian,* by Spanish writer Ordoñez de Montalvo. Montalvo described a fabled island lying "to the right of the Indies" called Calafia. Here, he wrote, gold and pearls were abundant.

Hernando Cortés, conqueror of Mexico, may have named the land he explored in 1534 and 1535 "California," believing it to be the place Montalvo had described.

Among the closed buildings are the former barracks (later civilian apartments), the post exchange/officer's club, and several operational buildings. Some buildings are nothing but charred hulls. Protesting Native North Americans burned out these buildings and destroyed others during a 19-month occupation in 1969 to 1971. Piles of rubble dot the island.

During the island's prison era, corrections officers and their families occupied apartments and homes on the island. Alcatraz was called "the little town with the big prison." Most residences are now gone. Grass grows through sidewalk cracks; ivy and wildflowers flourish along the aging concrete walls. Visitors can glimpse traces of ornamental gardens planted by the Alcatraz children in the 1950s.

The ground-floor, brick casemates of the large, four-story barracks house a small museum, bookstore, and theater. Here on four screens visitors can see a 13-minute movie, *Secrets of Alcatraz*. Several hiking trails afford great views of San Francisco and the bay.

Hot Tips Allow three hours for your visit. Plan to spend two hours on the island; ferry trips are 20 minutes each way. Ferry boarding lines are usually long. Wear comfortable shoes, and take a jacket.

Be prepared to walk up a ¼-mile steep concrete walk to the cellhouse at the top of the Rock. Watch for cracks and broken concrete. Do not enter off-limits buildings; they are dangerous.

Guidebooks are one dollar at kiosks near the landing dock. Line up for the audiocassette tour at the Cellhouse Tour entrance. Do not stop the tape once you have begun the tour; tapes automatically rewind.

Food and restrooms are located at Pier 41, on the ferry, and on the island dock. Little water is available on the island; take your own. No alcohol or pets are allowed. Food and accommodations are available in San Francisco. Restaurants and shops abound near the waterfront area.

Check your local video store for the 1996 movie *The Rock* with Sean Connery and Nicolas Cage or the 1995 movie *Murder in the First* with Kevin Bacon, Christian Slater, and Gary Oldman before your visit.

The Best Stuff In the cellhouse you can imagine what life behind bars was like for America's really bad guys. (The prisoners were all male. Women were not considered "incorrigible" until 1969, after Alcatraz closed.) You can wander among the cellblocks and go down cell rows with names like Broadway and Michigan Avenue. Enter a small cell with pale lime walls; look through the bars. With the help of an award-winning audio program, you're in "Hellcatraz."

The massive cellhouse was home to about 250 men at one time, each serving an average 8 to 10 years. Corrections officers opened cell doors electronically and had no keys for safety reasons. Armed officers patrolled from high, caged gun galleries located at each end of the four cell rows.

The audio tour takes you to the barber shop, hospital, library, and dining hall (called "the gas chamber" for the tear gas canisters on the ceiling that could be opened if there was trouble).

Cellblock D was the isolation wing, the prison inside the prison, called the "Treatment Unit." The most intractable prisoners landed here, in the prison's 42 most-loathed cells. One inmate spent 13 years here, with no privileges. Cells 9 through 14 have solid doors behind a set of bars. These were the solitary confinement cells, the "Hole." Prisoners here lived in total darkness.

THE FAMOUS ESCAPE ATTEMPTS

The tour's best moments center on a 1946 escape attempt. Six inmates attempted to "blast out" of the prison with weapons seized from captured correctional officers. Tens of thousands of people lined the bay shore as U.S. Marines bombarded the cellhouse with rifle grenades. Visitors today can see patched holes in the roof of Corridor E where the grenades broke through. Blast marks remain on the floor.

You can also follow the movements of the most famous escape, engineered by inmate Frank Morris in 1962. Visitors witness the patched holes where Morris and two brothers chipped out of their cells, then climbed through the utility connections and onto the roof. The escapees slipped from the cellhouse into the bay. Lawmen found makeshift equipment used in the escape floating in the water. They believed the men drowned. The escape is immortalized in a book and the 1979 movie *Escape from Alcatraz*, starring Clint Eastwood.

Then and Now Although ex-inmates told newspapers of psychological torment and inhumane treatment at Alcatraz, reports also document tasty food, a state-of-the-art facility, and no hint of the overcrowding plaguing today's prisons.

Most everything that was ever taken to the Rock remains. Empty tanks and old machinery sit around the dock. Much of it—fencing, machinery bits, and bricks—rests in the jumble of boulders at the foot of its steep cliffs, which the army blasted from its mounded slopes in the 1800s.

The largest western gull populations in California call Alcatraz home. Birds, plants, and tidepool life also thrive here.

The site became a federal park in 1970 and opened for tours in 1973. Now one million people annually tour the empty prison where visitors once were unwelcome.

Elsewhere in the Area See Fort Point listing.

Fort Point

The Fort Sumter of the West Coast

Location San Francisco, California, beneath the south end of the Golden Gate Bridge. Part of the Golden Gate National Recreation Area (a Top 10 Site). In San Francisco take U.S. 101 to the Lincoln Boulevard exit. Go north on Lincoln to Long Avenue and take a left toward the San Francisco Bay. Continue on Marine Drive past the Golden Gate Recreational Area Headquarters to the fort parking lot.

Fort Point National Historic Site is open Wednesday through Sunday, except Thanksgiving, December 25, and January 1, 10 A.M.–5 P.M.; Sutler's Store closes at 4:30 P.M. Ranger-guided tours and special programs are available. For information contact Fort Point National Historic Site, P.O. Box 29333, Presidio of San Franciso, CA 94129. Tel. (415) 556-1693.

Fort Point is part of the 70,000-acre Golden Gate National Recreation Area, which encompasses 22 natural and historic sites including Alcatraz; the Presidio, the 1,480-acre U.S. Army base/urban park; Fort Mason, now a cultural and recreation center; Muir Woods, one of the Bay Area's last uncut stands of old-growth redwood; and the San Francisco Maritime National Historical Park. For information contact Superintendent, Golden Gate National Recreation Area, Building 201, Fort Mason, San Francisco, CA 94123. Tel. (415) 556-0560.

Maritime Museum and Hyde Street Pier

Aquatic Park, between Fort Mason and Fisherman's Wharf on the bayfront, is home to the San Francisco Maritime Museum National Historical Park. The park includes a Maritime Store and the Hyde Street Pier ($). Here a fleet of historic ships representing the development of America's Pacific Coast is moored.

The pier's historic vessels include the 1890 side-wheel ferry *Eureka*, the 1907 tug *Hercules*, the 1891 scow schooner *Alma*, the 1914 paddle tug *Eppleton Hall*, the 1895 lumber-carrying schooner *C. A. Thayer*, and the 1886 square-rigged Cape Horn sailing vessel *Balclutha*. The liberty ship S. S. *Jeremiah O'Brien* rests at Pier 3 in Fort Mason, and the World War II submarine U.S.S. *Pampanito* resides at Pier 45. Climb aboard for hands-on, ranger-led programs. Fort Mason houses the National Maritime Museum Library.

The Hyde Street Pier is open daily, from May 16 through September 15, 10 A.M.–6 P.M., and from September 16 through May 15, 9:30 A.M.–5 P.M. Tickets are sold at the pier entrance. Tel. (415) 556-6435. The Maritime Museum is open 10 A.M.–5 P.M. Tel. (415) 556-3002.

In Aquatic Park you also can buy tickets for the famous Hyde Street Cable Car at the cable car turnaround.

Frame of Reference Fort Point was occupied from the mid–19th century, after the Mexican War and during the California gold rush, to the mid–20th century. The U.S. Army completed Fort Point in 1861. The fort was abandoned in 1943. The fort location was the site of a Spanish adobe fort, Castillo de San Joaquin, from 1793 to 1853.

Significance After the United States' defeat of Mexico and the discovery of gold in California, the San Francisco Bay became the most valuable commercial site in North America. Fort Point was built to protect this prize. The U.S. Army planned Fort Point as one of three massive, pre–Civil War coastal fortifications and a series of smaller batteries in the Golden Gate area. Remnants of one fort remain on Alcatraz Island. A third fort, at Lime Point on the opposite side of the bay, was never finished.

Fort Point was built much like Fort Sumter, the famous fort in Charleston Harbor, South Carolina, where the Civil War began. Like its East Coast sister fort, it is built mainly of brick. Fort Point's brick was specially made in a brickyard just south of the fort. The "Pride of the Pacific" is the only brick fort west of the Mississippi River and is the only fort of the period with casemates (arched gun rooms) on the West Coast.

During the fort's heyday in 1865, 475 soldiers were stationed here. Their job was to defend San Francisco against a Confederate attack that never materialized. No shots were ever fired in anger from the fort or against it. In fact, no enemy vessel ever tried to pass

Manzanar: Remote Remains of World War II Internment Camp

At the foot of the Sierra Nevada in eastern California lies Manzanar National Historic Site. Here in the Owens Valley, the U.S. government interned 10,000 Japanese Americans during World War II. The Manzanar War Relocation Center was one of 10 such relocation camps created by Executive Order No. 9066 on February 19, 1942.

Today, with tenacity, you can visit the camp's remains. The site is located 10 miles north of Lone Pine and 5 miles south of Independence on U.S. 395. Roads into the camp are overgrown, with deep gullies and soft sand in places. Hikers should wear sturdy shoes and bring drinking water.

Established as a historic site in March 1992, Manzanar is not yet developed as a park. Federal, state, and local agencies are working on a long-range protection plan and a visitor-use plan. As of publication, this site has no facilities, campsites, or personnel. The 550-acre site includes the camp's living area, once enclosed by barbed wire and guard towers, and various administrative facilities.

Visible remains include the large, wooden camp auditorium, the stonework shells of the pagodalike police post and sentry house, and parts of the administrative buildings. Visitors can see concrete foundations and sections of water and sewer systems. When the camp closed in 1945 most buildings were sold at auction and removed from the site.

The Eastern California Museum in Independence houses exhibits on Manzanar's history. The orchard-growing village of Manzanar, which gave the site its name, thrived from 1910 to 1935. Native North Americans lived there for centuries.

For information contact Manzanar Information, c/o Superintendent, Death Valley National Monument, Death Valley, CA 92328. Tel. (760) 878-2932.

the formidable guns of Fort Point, called the "Gibraltar of the West Coast." The garrison's imposing presence gave notice that San Francisco, the most important West Coast city, rivaling New York in the East, would be protected at all costs.

Today this sentry at the Golden Gate symbolizes 200 years of San Francisco's commercial and military significance.

About the Site The Golden Gate Bridge arches over the three-tiered, semirectangular fort. The fort's walls, five to seven feet thick, nestle right up to the famous red bridge's southern support. It occupies a point of land 100 by 150 yards jutting into San Francisco Bay. Waves lap at the fort's foundation, merely feet from the water.

Visitors enter through studded wooded doors of the fort's only entrance, the once heavily guarded sally port. Tours, either ranger-guided or self-guided, take you through the concrete parade area, up sets of original stairs, and through most of the fort's 90 casemates. Some of the rooms are restored, and a few, such as the kitchen and surgeon's office, are furnished.

Several rooms contain exhibits, including "Women at War" and "Ready and Forward," the story of African American soldiers. All of the fort's artillery had been dismounted by 1900, but today you can see where the fort's 102 massive cannons were mounted. Cannon embrasures (openings) face the bay and ocean on the west, north, and east. Now bricks and concrete blocks close the embrasures. Iron bars across them are rusted out. Three tiers of rifle slits cover the southern land face.

On the fort's top, called the "barbette tier," stands the 1864 Fort Point lighthouse. The 27-foot wooden lighthouse replaced the original built in the 1850s, one of the first on the West Coast. Use of the light, 83 feet from the ground, was discontinued in 1934 because the new Golden Gate Bridge partially hid it from ships. A row of cannons once faced the Golden Gate, as did as two flanking bastions. Only the cannon mounts remain.

The first floor houses the Sutler's Store, so named for the civilian or "sutler" appointed as official supplier to soldiers; a theater, where you can view a 17-minute orientation film; and cannons, including a rare San Martin made in Peru in 1684. The Mexican cannon was a prize of the Mexican War. A group of independence fighters, including John Charles Fremont and Kit Carson, took it from the abandoned Castillo de San Joaquin in 1844.

Hot Tips Arrive early. Parking is very limited, and the Golden Gate National Recreation Area is America's most-visited park. In addition to the Fort Point parking lot, you also can park off Lincoln Street in the Presidio. Walking paths also connect Fort Point to the Golden Gate Bridge, which buzzes with pedestrians and bikers, as well as 96 million cars each year.

Allow two hours for your visit. Take snacks. Only hot beverages are offered in Sutler's Store. There are outside, portable toilets only. Concrete floors, the sally port, and stairs can be slippery when wet. The 62 steps to the fort top are steep. You can rent audiocassette tours ($) at Sutler's Store. Print guides sell for one dollar.

Food and accommodations are available in San Francisco. Consider lunch or dinner at Fisherman's Wharf or Pier 39, where restaurants and shops abound.

The Fort Point web site address is http://www.nps.gov/fppo. The Golden Gate National Recreation Area address is http://www.nps.gov/goga.

The Best Stuff The U.S. Army planned Fort Point as the most formidable deterrence America could build against naval attack. Today the sturdy fortress remains a unique marvel of pre–Civil War design and craftsmanship. To build the fort workers laid slabs of granite imported from China atop concrete footings secured to bedrock.

Fort construction required millions of bricks. To form the interlocking patterns of the arched casemates laborers erected temporary wooden forms. Masons laid the brick atop the forms in the intricate patterns. When workers removed the wooden forms, they smoothed out the arches to a fine finish.

You will find more examples of the masons' skills in the three freestanding granite stairways inside the fort. The spiral stairs are made of handcut stone, each step weighing about 1,000 pounds. The weight of each stone bears down on the one below it, keeping the steps in place without a central support column. You can climb the well-worn stairs, which were built to stand even if the fort around them was demolished. Modern steel beams support the stairs today.

The 1,500-foot granite seawall enclosing the tip of Fort Point was completed in 1869. It has withstood waves for 130 years. Although reinforced with granite boulders, the seawall remains a masterpiece of engineering.

Visitors who have seen the ruins of Fort Sumter can now see about what that famous fort looked like before its Civil War bombardment.

Then and Now Spanish colonizers first recognized the fort's strategic military site at the narrowest point of San Francisco Bay's only entrance. They called the 100-foot-high promontory "Punta del Cantil Blanco," or "White Cliff Point." When the U.S. Army decided to build a fort, engineers tore down the old Spanish castillo. They cut down the cliff until it stood only 15 feet above the bay. This allowed placement of the lowest gun tier near the water, as military technology of the day dictated.

The fort's official name was Fort Winfield Scott, named after an army hero. But soldiers called it Fort Point. The name stuck. As the United States secured control of California, the army built a gauntlet of forts and gun batteries to protect the Golden Gate.

Enemy attacks never came, and by the end of World War II all guns were dismounted. The Golden Gate National Recreation Area preserves the batteries and fort sites today. Visitors can walk a 9.1-mile coastal trail to view the empty concrete batteries and forts. For information contact the Golden Gate National Recreation Area. Ask for the *Map and Guide to the Seacoast Fortifications of the Golden Gate*. The cost is $1.50.

Elsewhere in the Area Muir Woods is 12 miles north of the Golden Gate Bridge, reached by U.S. 101 and Highway 1.

Marshall Gold Discovery Site

Where the Rush to California Was Ignited

Location Northern California, in Coloma, 40 miles east of Sacramento, in the foothills of the Sierra Nevada. From Sacramento and the east take U.S. 50 to Placerville, then Highway 49 north 10 miles to Coloma and the park. Or take U.S. 80 to Auburn, then Highway 49 south 12 miles to Coloma. Highway 49, the scenic Mother Lode Highway, is a paved roller coaster ride through the mountains.

Marshall Gold Discovery State Historic Park ($) is open daily, except Thanksgiving, December 25, and January 1, 10 A.M.–sunset. Gold Discovery Day is celebrated every January 24; Gold Rush Days are in October. The celebration features the U.S. National Gold Panning Championships. There are special events and programs. For information contact Marshall Gold Discovery State Historic Park, P.O. Box 265, 310 Back Street, Coloma, CA 95613. Tel. (916) 622-3470 or (916) 622-6198.

For information on California Gold Rush State Parks contact Department of Parks and Recreation, State of California, The Resources Agency, P.O. Box 942896, Sacramento, CA 94296-0001. A detailed guide is available for two dollars. Other gold rush sites in the state are privately owned and operated.

The California Trail

Gold-seeking forty-niners rushed to California via three major routes: by ship around Cape Horn, through the Isthmus of Panama, and over land across the Plains.

The overland route became the most traveled trail to the West. The 5,600-mile trail began at Independence, Missouri, with lesser jumping-off points in St. Joseph, Missouri, and Council Bluffs, Iowa. Modern-day travelers can follow the trail by car via the California National Historic Trail.

From its starting point to Wyoming the trail generally follows the paths of other famous trails: Oregon, Mormon, and Pony Express. Known mainly as the chief road of travel for the gold-seekers of 1849, the trail also served as an important overland route for settlers in the Pacific Northwest.

At the end of the California Trail stood Sutter's Fort, an enormous, enclosed bustling village of settlers and shops on the Sacramento River. Swiss homesteader John Sutter built the fort in 1843 at present-day Sacramento.

Although Sutter named his fiefdom New Helvetia, settlers called it simply Sutter's Fort, after its founder. Here thousands of gold-seekers bought supplies to take into the foothills of the Sierra Nevada to find their fortune. Eventually miners overran Sutter's settlement as well as his sawmill where gold first was first found.

The National Park Service and other groups are currently at work planning the California National Historic Trail. For more information contact these groups:

- **Oregon-California Trail Association,** P.O. Box 1019, Independence, MO, 64051-0519. Tel. (816) 252-2276.
- **National Park Service Long-Distance Trails Office,** SLC, 324 South State Street, P.O. Box 45155, Salt Lake City, UT 84145-0155. Tel. (801) 539-4094.

Frame of Reference Gold was mined here beginning in the mid–19th century, around the time the 1849 California gold rush began, until World War II, when U.S. gold mining was halted by executive order. Most California gold had been mined, however, by the turn of the century. Gold was discovered in Coloma on January 24, 1848.

Significance Here, on a rocky bank of the American River, James Wilson Marshall made the first significant discovery of gold from California's Mother Lode. He found the gold in the tailrace of John Sutter's sawmill, which he operated. Marshall's discovery ignited an unprecedented, worldwide migration that we know as the California gold rush. Almost overnight the gold rush transformed California, a neglected, 300-year-old Spanish province, into a thriving state with a booming network of businesses, industry, and transportation. America as a whole was changed forever, too.

Today visitors can pan for gold at a designated site along the river where Marshall found the world's most famous flakes of gold. Finders keepers.

Within months Marshall's discovery had been broadcast in San Francisco, in Congress, and around the globe. In 1849 a tidal wave of gold-seekers, called "forty-niners," descended on Coloma. The settlement quickly became a giant campground, the first arrivals sleeping on the valley floor. Then Coloma metamorphosed into a sea of tents, made largely from the white can-

Exploring the Mother Lode

California's Mother Lode no longer draws hordes of fortune-seeking miners, but her natural beauty, abundant recreational areas, and historic gold rush buildings remain a lure. You can explore the Mother Lode country via Highway 49, California's "Golden Chain."

The Mother Lode is the name given to California's rich vein of gold-bearing rock. The vein, which stretched nearly 120 miles along the western side of the Sierra Nevada, was the main source of gold from the gold rush days to the turn of the century.

Mother Lode width averaged from a few hundred feet to a mile or more wide. Other deposits ran parallel to the Mother Lode, as well as to the north of it, making California's total gold-bearing system 300 hundred miles long and 30 miles wide. The Mother Lode runs like blood vessels through nine counties from Sierra City in the north to Mariposa in the south.

In addition to hiking, fishing, and winter sports, Mother Lode country offers plenty of old mining sights. California has preserved six gold rush towns as state parks.

Perhaps the best preserved is Columbia in Tuolumne County. This was one of the richest mining towns. The gravel beds surrounding the Columbia yielded $87 million in gold. The mining town of Bodie, in the high mountains west of Yosemite National Park, may be the most interesting. The once-rich-and-wild town stands almost as it was when abandoned at the beginning of World War II, a genuine ghost town.

Hangtown's Gold Bug Park and Mine, 10 miles south of Coloma in Placerville (formerly Hangtown), has the only mine you can actually enter. The privately operated mine is open seasonally at 549 Main Street. Tel. (916) 642-5232.

The Empire Mine, largest gold mine in the Mother Lode, is located about 40 miles north of Coloma at the Empire Mine State Historic Park in Grass Valley. The main shaft is illuminated for 150 feet at the mine that was the longest continuously operated gold mine in America. It closed in 1956.

For information on California's Golden Chain Highway contact The Golden Chain Council of the Mother Lode, Inc., P.O. Box 7046, Auburn, CA 95604.

vas sails of ships in San Francisco Bay. Soon a town sprang up, complete with homes, shops, and saloons to service the argonauts.

Within two years California became America's 31st state. Gold fever continued to spread. Immigrants from all points of the compass sailed into San Francisco hoping to get rich quick. San Francisco bloomed into a bustling commercial port. Worldwide inflation followed the influx of many millions of dollars worth of gold on the market.

Coloma, "Queen of the Mines," continued to grow as fortune-seeking men, most young and single, poured upon the gold discovery site. By February 1849 its population was 50,000. From Coloma throngs spread up the river canyons panning for nuggets. Then they trudged into the mountains, where deep-earth mining tapped rich veins of gold until there was no more.

Today the mining-era remnants of Coloma, named for the Cullomah Native North Americans who first lived here, symbolize the California gold rush.

About the Site The park encompasses about 70 percent of today's Coloma, population 300. The 1½-mile Monument Loop hiking trail takes visitors to the surviving handful of public buildings, shops, and homes—including James Marshall's cabin—built during gold rush years. The loop also takes in the actual spot where Marshall discovered gold, now marked by a cobblestone monument; a full-size, working replica of Sutter's sawmill; and a 7-mile- long mining ditch.

Old Town Sacramento

After the discovery of gold by James Marshall in 1848 Sacramento was the main trading center for the gold miners. At a site near the confluence of the Sacramento and American rivers, John Sutter, who built the sawmill where Marshall found gold, built Sutter's Fort in 1839. A settlement grew and then flourished as opportunity-seeking businessmen set up shop.

With the arrival of Sam Brannan, who went on to become the first businessman to ship fruit to the East Coast and California's first millionaire, a city bloomed. Brannan's store became the cornerstone of the waterfront city that became California's capital in 1854.

Today a historic district on the Sacramento riverfront, Old Sacramento, preserves the gold-rush-era settlement. The 27-acre district on the east bank of the Sacramento River protects 53 19th-century buildings. Several dozen of these buildings played key roles in the history of Sacramento and California.

Visitors can enjoy riverboat cruises, horse-drawn carriage tours, and steam train rides on summer weekends.

Among Old Sacramento's historic sites are these:

- **Big Four Building,** I Street, was where much of the transcontinental railroad was planned.
- **B. F. Hastings Building,** J and 2nd streets, was used as the western terminus for the Pony Express and was home to California's first Supreme Court.
- **Pony Express Monument,** 2nd and J streets, commemorates the 1,966-mile return mail run in 1860 from Sacramento to St. Joseph, Missouri, in less than 10 days. The bronze statue depicts rider Sam Hamilton on his horse.
- **The State Railroad Museum** is at 2nd and I streets.

Buildings on a town tour include a schoolhouse, gun shop, tinsmith shop, blacksmith shop, county jail ruins, two stone Chinese stores—the Man Lee and the Wah Hop—that catered to the large number of Chinese miners, and St. John's Church, now used for weddings. Living-history demonstrations take place at most sites. Other attractions include these:

- **Marshall Monument and Gravesite.** An 1889 bronze-colored 41-foot metal statue of James Marshall stands atop Gold Hill at Marshall's gravesite. Marshall points to the river site where he discovered gold.
- **Gold-Panning Site.** You can pan for gold at the Pleasant Flat area on the river's east side. To reach the site drive or walk across the Mt. Murphy Road Bridge and go to the parking lot. Use only pans and hands. No dogs are allowed. Keep your gold, but please return sand, rocks, and anything else you find to the river.
- **Mining Exhibit.** An outdoor display of mining equipment, from the early and simple to the late and complex, stands adjacent to the visitor center. Demonstrations are available.
- **Monroe Ridge Trail.** A scenic three-mile hiking trail, with spectacular views of the Coloma Valley, begins at Marshall Monument. The trail is named in memory of the pioneer

The park, mostly held by private owners, offers year-round events. It hosts one of the largest jazz festivals in the world. Allow three hours for your visit. Wear sturdy shoes. Streets are cobblestone, and sidewalks are uneven planks.

The attractions, museums, and 120 shops of Old Sacramento generally are open daily, 10 A.M.–5 P.M. Restaurants may close later. The site can be reached by car or on foot from downtown Sacramento. From all directions take I-5 to the J Street exit and follow the signs. There's limited on-street parking with strict time restrictions, and as well as nearby parking lots and decks.

Visitor Information Center in the Fratt Building at 1101 2nd Street, has maps and lists of events. Maps are also available at sidewalk kiosks.

For more information contact Sacramento Convention and Visitors Bureau, 1421 K Street, Sacramento, CA 95814. Tel. (916) 442-7644. The Old Sacramento web site address is www.old-sacramento.com.

Other Sacramento sites not to be missed include Sutter's Fort State Historical Park, California State Indian Museum, Towne Ford Museum, Governor's Mansion, and Leland Stanford Mansion.

▲

San Diego
Where California Began

Three hundred years before the 1849 gold rush, explorers sailed California's coast, claiming the land for Spain. Among the explorers was Juan Rodríguez Cabrillo. Where he landed, modern-day San Diego, is considered the birthplace of California.

Only 50 years after Columbus landed in the New World, Cabrillo's expedition explored the entire length of the California coast. He landed at the place he named San Miguel, now San Diego, on September 28, 1542. His epic voyage gave Spain its first detailed knowledge of the mysterious West Coast land. Though other Spanish explorers followed, renaming sites first named by Cabrillo, his achievements were unchallenged.

Today a monument in San Diego commemorates Cabrillo's discovery of California. Visitors to San

☛

Monroe family, which traces its origins to former slave Nancy Gooch. Gooch's descendants worked in Coloma, carved out a prosperous life, and owned the land where the gold discovery park now stands. They sold it to California in the 1940s.

Pioneer Cemetery and Winery Tour. Walk through the 1849 cemetery where 600 pioneers are buried. A second cemetery behind St. John's Church contains 80 to 100 hundred graves, 25 of which are unknown. Visitors can view ruins of the Coloma Winery and Vineyard House.

A visitor center houses a museum; exhibits; bookstore; and theater, where you can view an orientation video, *Coloma Gold*, on request.

Hot Tips Plan to spend half a day at the site. Eat lunch at one of three large picnic sites. Restrooms have no soap dispensers. Dress for the weather and wear sturdy shoes. Part of the Monument Tour paved trail is steep and sometimes slippery.

Watch children near the river, which has a swift current and drops. Use caution crossing Highway 49 to the sawmill and discovery site. Adjacent parking is available. Food is available seasonally in historic Coloma and year-round in nearby towns. Accommodations are available in Auburn, Placerville, South Lake Tahoe, and Sacramento.

The Best Stuff The spine-tingling possibility of getting rich quick still lingers in Coloma. So go ahead, pan for gold! Make it a fam-

Diego will find other important sites related to the birthplace of California. Foremost is the 1769 Spanish Mission San Diego de Alcala, symbolizing the birthplace of San Diego.

Cabrillo National Monument ($) is located within the San Diego city limits at the southern end of Point Loma. The monument marks the site of Cabrillo's first landing in California. From downtown take Rosecrans Street, turn right on Canon Street, then turn left onto Catalina Boulevard. Proceed through the Naval Ocean System Center gates to the end of the point. City buses make several trips daily to the monument. The monument is open daily, 9 A.M.–5:15 P.M., with extended summer hours.

For information contact Superintendent, Cabrillo National Monument, P.O. Box 6670, San Diego, CA 92166. Tel. (619) 557-5450.

Other San Diego historic sites include these:

- **San Diego de Alcala,** located on Presidio Hill. Other Spanish missions are located in the area.
- **Old Town San Diego.** Get a taste of early California life at Old Town San Diego State Historic Park. Here among the colorful shops, restaurants, and gardens, you'll find the park's centerpiece: the 1829 elegant adobe home, La Casa de Estudillo. Tel. (619) 220-5422.
- **Balboa Park,** southeast of Old Town. Ornate historic buildings grace the 1,400-acre park, home to the famous San Diego Zoo.
- **San Juan Capistrano.** Called the jewel of the California missions, the 1776 San Juan Capistrano Mission is also famous for the legendary swallows that return yearly on March 19th, St. Joseph's Day. Although encroaching development has scared off most of the birds, some still come back nearly on schedule. Efforts to lure the birds back to Capistrano are ongoing. Meanwhile the famous mission still entices flocks of visitors with is splendid gilded altar.

For more information on the mission contact Mission San Juan Capistrano, P.O. Box 697, San Juan Capistrano, CA 92693. Tel. (714) 248-2049.

For information on San Diego historic sites contact the San Diego Visitor Information Center, 2688 East Mission Bay Drive, San Diego, CA 92109. Tel. (619) 276-8200.

▲

ily affair. First, ask for a pamphlet titled *Panning for GOLD in Coloma* at the visitor center bookstore. The pamphlet gives step-by-step instructions. Second, bring your own panning equipment or buy a pan at the bookstore. Special panning kits include a how-to video and a bag of "pay-dirt" sand, guaranteed to contain four grains of gold. You also can rent kits at mining supply stores in Coloma and pan in nearby troughs. Third, proceed to the appropriate panning site. Finally, have fun.

If you find bits of gold in the river, it will be what's called "placer gold," found on the earth's surface. Placer gold usually drifts in water from the gold-laden mountains, hiding in sand and eddies.

Then and Now When Coloma had yielded her gold, the miners moved on. Coloma gradually lost its luster and its people. Only the patient Chinese remained to pan the river. In 1857 the El Dorado county seat was moved to Placerville.

Boomtowns of restless young men mushroomed around other California mines. Women were rare, but whiskey was plentiful. The mining towns were hotbeds of instability, lawlessness, and violence. The men and the towns came and went.

By 1851 the California gold rush had passed. Gold production, however, continued until the end of the century, when the last nuggets of gold were mined

Tracing Nevada's Big Rush

The California gold rush petered out by 1851. Years passed before prospectors again found wildly rich gold veins. But these, such as that at Pike's Peak in Colorado, paled in comparison to the gold—and silver—found in 1859 in Nevada.

Visitors today can savor the preserved mines and towns where a second gold rush began on the other side of the Sierra Nevada. From California's Mother Lode, move on to Nevada's Comstock Lode in Virginia City territory.

Two miners discovered gold a mile up the side of Mount Davidson, at the Carson River near Gold Hill, Nevada. A third miner, Henry T. P. Comstock, "Old Pancake," talked his way into a share by claiming the find was on his property. He gave the giant vein his name. Within 20 years the deep shafts of the Comstock Lode had yielded $300 million worth of gold and silver.

Nearby, miner James Finney, called "Old Virginny" after his birthplace of Virginia, struck another lucrative vein. Finney christened with whiskey the tent-and-dugout town that grew around the vein "Old Virginny Town," in honor of himself. Meanwhile, miners digging for gold found a troublesome blue mud stuck to their shovels and picks. It turned out to be silver. And a lot of it.

The town that gold and silver built evolved into glistening Virginia City, the most important settlement between Denver and San Francisco. In 1861 Nevada became a territory. It became a state in 1864.

Nevada's boom days of 140 years ago are alive and well in Virginia City. The city and surrounding Comstock Historic District protect the Comstock mines and the towns of Gold Hill and Silver City. Little has changed in what was once the richest place on earth. Virginia City visitors can walk boardwalks in front of historic shops and tour gold rush mansions, mines, and saloons.

Other Virginia City sites include the Fourth Ward School Museum, Julia C. Bullette Red Light Museum, 1860 Mackay Mansion Museum, Virginia and Truckee Railroad (35-minute steam ride), Virginia City Trolley, Way It Was Museum (Comstock mining artifacts), Nevada Gambling Museum, Mark Twain Museum of Memories, Piper's Opera House, and Wild West Museum.

For more information contact Virginia City Chamber of Commerce, P.O. Box 464, Virginia City, NV 89440. Tel. (702) 847-0311.

from deep within the earth. Some of the old mining towns hung on and thrive today. Others are ghost towns, attracting only the curious.

Some experts say that the forty-niners' get-rich-quick mentality made a dark, indelible mark on the American psyche that has never gone away and that the gold rush permanently corrupted the nation's work ethic.

Elsewhere in the Area Donner Memorial State Park is on I-80 west of Truckee.

Fort Clatsop

End of the Voyage for Lewis and Clark

Location Coastal Oregon, on the banks of a Columbia River tributary, 6 miles southwest of Astoria and 91 miles northwest of Portland. From the north and south take U.S. 101/26 to Business 101 at Astoria. Follow signs three miles to the park entrance. From the east take U.S. 30, the Lewis and Clark auto tour route, to U.S. 101 to Business 101 south. Follow signs to the park entrance.

The Salt Works unit of the park is located in the resort town of Seaside, 15 miles southwest of Fort Clatsop. From U.S. 101 take Avenue G toward the beach. Turn left on South Beach Drive and go five blocks. Turn right on Lewis and Clark Way, a dead end. Park on the street. The Salt Works in on the left inside an iron fence.

Fort Clatsop National Memorial ($) is open daily, except December 25, in summer, 8 A.M.–6 P.M., and the rest of the year, 8 A.M.–5 P.M. There are special events and seasonal interpretive programs. For information contact Superintendent, Fort Clatsop National Memorial, Route 3, P.O. Box 604-FC, Astoria, OR 97103. Tel. (503) 861-2471.

Frame of Reference Lewis and Clark's "Voyage of Discovery" took place in the early 19th century (1804–1806). The expedition encamped at Fort Clatsop for three months of the winter of 1805 to 1806. They began building the fort on December 8, 1805, and had shelter by Christmas Eve. The expedition left the fort on March 23, 1806, on return to St. Louis.

Significance Here where the Columbia, the "Big River of the West," empties into the Pacific Ocean, the weary, 33-person Lewis and Clark party spent a soggy but important winter in their handhewn garrison, Fort Clatsop. The expedition had completed half of its 28-month, 8,000-mile round trip to the West Coast. The Voyage of Discovery, undertaken at the behest of President Thomas Jefferson, was mostly by water.

Jefferson had just finished negotiating the Louisiana Purchase from France for $15 million. He wanted to know about the vast country he had bought. He chose Meriwether Lewis to lead the exploratory expedition into this unknown wilderness. Lewis, in turn, selected his admired friend William Clark as co-commander.

Lewis and Clark, both exceptional frontiersmen and writers, kept meticulous journals, which included descriptions of people, wildlife, plants, and terrain, as well as maps. They collected specimens of many animals and plant life previously unknown. These famous journals added 1,000 new words to the American vocabulary while expanding knowledge of the unknown West as Jefferson had wanted.

At Fort Clatsop, named for the local Clatsop Indians, Lewis and Clark reworked their journals. The captains reflected on their experiences and revised their return route. They also established friendly relations with area Native North Americans, paving the way for emigrants.

The Voyage of Discovery team built Fort Clatsop on the Netul River, a Columbia tributary, near present-day Astoria. (The river's name is now Lewis and Clark River.) Astoria is named for John Jacob Astor, the New York financier who built a fur-trading-fort, Fort Astoria, on the Columbia in 1811. Astoria was America's first permanent settlement west of the Rocky Mountains.

About the Site Fort Clatsop today is an exact replica of the 50-foot-square, log stockade with a slanted roof that the expedition built. It stands amid a forest of towering Sitka spruce and Douglas fir. The Astoria community, following Clark's sketches, reconstructed the fort in 1955. Two rows of seven connected rooms, each with central fireplaces, line a 20-by-48-foot parade ground. There a historically accurate American flag flies atop a log pole.

Mud and moss fill the spaces between the logs, just as they did in 1805. A thick mat of moss grows on the fort roof, a result of near-constant rainfall, which Lewis and Clark complained about in their journals. Of the 106 days the corps spent at Fort Clatsop, only 12 were without rain.

One mile of wood-chip trails takes visitors from the visitor center to the fort, through a forest of moss-covered, colossal conifers, to a canoe launch, and then back through the 125-acre park. The canoe launch

Astoria's Unique Column

From the top of 600-foot Coxcomb Hill east of Astoria's downtown, an ornately inscribed, 125-foot reinforced concrete column reigns over a postcard panorama. Called "the Astoria Column," this unique tower, dedicated in 1926, commemorates the westward sweep of discovery and migration. Visitors can climb 164 steps to the top.

The Astoria Column is the only monument of its kind in the world. Patterned after the nearly- 2,000-year-old Trojan Column in Rome, it is the only large piece of memorial architecture of reinforced concrete with a pictorial frieze in the sgraffito technique. This technique, used by Italian-born artist Attilio Pusterla on the column, involves images etched on the surface.

Pusterla inscribed 14 scenes that scroll around the column. The scenes illustrate important events in Astoria's history, beginning with Captain Robert Gray's discovery of the Columbia River in 1792 and ending with the coming of settlers and the railroad.

Visitors take a spiral staircase inside the column to a small viewing platform at the top. When weather cooperates, you can see the Columbia River mouth, the Pacific Ocean, and, to the far east, the peak of Mount St. Helen.

The city of Astoria owns the column, built with money from the Astor family and the Great Northern Railroad. Fund-raising efforts are underway for artwork restoration.

To reach the column take U.S. 30 or U.S. 101 into town. Both become Marine Drive. From Marine Drive on the waterfront, take 16th Street to the top of the ridge, then turn right and proceed on 15th Street. Follow the signs.

For information on the Astoria area contact Astoria Warrenton Area Chamber of Commerce, 111 West Marine Drive, P.O. Box 176, Astoria, OR 97103. Tel. (503) 328-6311 or 1-800-875-6807. Ask for the *Explorers Guide*.

marks the place where the Lewis and Clark expedition probably landed. Markers by the trail point out native trees and plants first identified in the captains' journals.

The spacious visitor center houses a museum, bookstore, and large theater. Among museum artifacts are a knife and file believed to have belonged to John Shields, a private in the expedition party. The theater offers a 17-minute orientation slide show and an excellent 32-minute film, *We Proceeded On: The Expedition of Lewis and Clark, 1804–06*. The visitor center lobby has a video viewing area offering a selection of four videos about life at Fort Clatsop. There's also a guide to park fauna.

The Salt Works

The Salt Works in Seaside sits at the place where five men from Fort Clatsop boiled seawater to produce salt. The monument is a reconstruction of the rock oven with five brass kettles of saltwater on top and a marker. In December 1805 the men boiled 1,400 gallons of seawater over two months, producing 3½ bushels of salt to season food, trade, and take on their return trip. They built the salt camp where the sea had a high salt content and wood and game were plentiful.

Because there are few parking spaces near the Salt Works, it's wise to park in downtown Seaside and walk to the site.

Hot Tips Allow two hours to visit the fort and 20 minutes to visit the Salt Works. Dress for wet weather, and wear sturdy shoes. Keep children away from

The Lewis and Clark Trail

Modern-day explorers can follow Lewis and Clark's epic Voyage of Discovery on the Lewis and Clark National Historic Trail. You can trace the unique American journey of 1804 to 1806 by boat, on foot, or by car.

The Lewis and Clark Trail loops for 8,000 miles over northwestern America, touching 11 states. It took the 33 to 45 people 28 months to make the journey.

President Thomas Jefferson, who commissioned the voyage, hoped to find a northwest passage to the Pacific Ocean. Congress approved $2,500 for the voyage's expenses.

After a year of study and preparation, the "Corps of Discovery" departed from a fort at the confluence of the Mississippi and Missouri rivers near St. Louis. They left at 4 P.M. on May 14, 1804. During Meriwether Lewis and William Clark's first winter at Fort Mandan, near present-day Bismarck, North Dakota, a French fur trapper, Toussaint Charbonneau, and his Shoshone wife, Sakakawea, joined the party as interpreters and guides. A replica of Fort Mandan stands near the original winter encampment site, now under water.

The voyagers, mostly military men, endured swift rivers, hot deserts, harsh storms, attacking animals, bitter mountain snow, lack of food, and, once, hostile Native North Americans. But they proceeded on. Only one man didn't return to St. Louis when the voyage ended at noon on September 23, 1806. He died of what was probably a ruptured appendix.

Captains Lewis and Clark demonstrated great management skills and resourcefulness. Along the way the captains befriended Native North Americans, exchanging gifts and handing out Jefferson's Peace Medal. These diplomatic deeds helped pave the way for settlers.

A few physical reminders of the journey remain along their route, such as Clark's self-inscribed name

☛

the water. Use caution at the canoe launch site, which is slippery. Wood chips on the trail can be slick.

The site has no beverages or snacks. Picnic tables are available. Ask about the *Junior Explorer Program* for kids ages 9 through 12. It makes touring the park more fun.

Camping is available at nearby Fort Stevens. Food and accommodations are available in Astoria and Warrenton.

Several good children's books about Lewis and Clark are in bookstores. Check out Sanna Kiesling's *The Lewis and Clark Expedition*. *The Journals of Lewis and Clark* is the best introduction to Fort Clatsop. It's especially interesting to read of the Killamuck, Chinnooks, and Clatsop Indians, who no longer survive. Also read about the party's diet: *wappato* roots, spoiled elk meat, fish, and Clark's favorite, dog meat.

on Pompey's Pillar in Montana. Today rivers, plants, colleges, monuments, museums, parks, and towns along the trail are named for Lewis and Clark.

The Voyage of Discovery stands as America's true epic journey and one of the greatest explorations in world history.

For more information about the Lewis and Clark Trail contact these groups:

- National Park Service, Lewis and Clark National Historic Trail, 700 Rayovac Drive, Suite 100, Madison, WI 53711. Tel. (608) 264-5610.
- Lewis and Clark Trail Heritage Foundation, Inc., P.O. Box 3434, Great Falls, MT 59403. Tel. (406) 453-7091.
- Lewis and Clark Interpretive Association, P.O. Box 2848, Great Falls, MT 59403. This organization has information on the summer Lewis and Clark Festival in Great Falls. ▲

The Best Stuff For history buffs who've traveled the Lewis and Clark Trail, whether by car or literature-fed imagination, this rustic fort in the enchanted forest cements the journey, just as it did for the Corps of Discovery.

Running your eyes over the handhewn cots, tables, chairs, and especially the writing desk in Lewis and Clark's personal quarters, you feel you've dropped in on America's greatest epic in progress.

Lewis and Clark's living quarters are on the right, next to the corner room of guide/interpreter Toussaint Charbonneau, his Shoshone wife, Sakakawea, and their infant son, Baptiste.

Check out the enlisted men's quarters left of the wooden gate. The soldiers spent a lot of time in their flea-riddled bunks, sick with colds and stomach pains. A big tree stump served as a table. When the expedition party arrived in 1805 they had trouble finding a clearing in the thick forest. To build Fort Clatsop, they felled several towering trees. Rather than removing the giant stumps, they simply designed the fort to accommodate the stumps as furniture.

Then and Now Lewis and Clark saw trees more than 300 feet tall with 40-foot circumferences at the base. Now after years of logging, later growths reach only 100 feet. Park rangers say some of the giant Sitka spruce in the park are true survivors; they may have witnessed Fort Clatsop's original construction.

Northwest Oregon's coastal weather is unchanged: rain, rain, and more rain. A coat of lush green moss eerily engulfs nearly everything in sight: trees, rocks, even mailbox posts. Rainfall averages nearly 63 inches annually. Temperatures are mild year-round.

Just right of the canoe landing site neat rows of pilings stand watch in the river. The pilings are part of an active logging operation. Trucks drop newly cut logs into the river, and they collect against the pilings. Boats then harvest them. Other estuary pilings are the remains of 39 turn-of-the-century salmon canneries or boat facilities.

Elsewhere in the Area Columbia River Maritime Museum is at 1792 Marine Drive; the Heritage Museum is at 16th and Exchange; the Astoria Walking Tour of 74 historic buildings is nearby; the Shot in Astoria driving tour takes visitors to the sites of numerous movie filmings; Old Firestation Museum is at 30th and Marine Drive; and the Flavel House, a Victorian mansion, is at 8th and Duane.

Fort Stevens State Park and Fort Stevens Historical Area are located as far west as you can go in Oregon. At Ecola State Park west of Fort Clatsop the 7½-mile Tillamook Trail traces the route Clark took over "Clark's Mountain" to see a beached whale. The 1896 Battery Russell, used through World War II, and the I-25 Monument, site of a Japanese submarine attack, are located southwest of Fort Clatsop.

In Washington, just north of the Columbia, spreads Fort Canby State Park. Here, where the expedition first camped before moving to the protected Fort Clatsop site, you'll find a museum dedicated to Lewis and Clark. Another museum located at nearby Fort Columbia is open seasonally.

America's tallest fir tree stands alongside U.S. 26. Watch for signs.

For an additional treat take the Columbia River Estuary Driving Tour. Ask a park ranger for a guide or contact CREST, 750 Commercial Street, Room 214, Astoria, OR 97103. Tel. (503) 325-0435.

Fort Clatsop National Memorial features Lewis and Clark's reconstructed fort on the Netul River Pacific and features special events and seasonal interpretive programs. *William S. Keller, National Park Service*

•Hidden Jewel•

Oregon City

End of the Oregon Trail

Location Northwest Oregon, at the northern edge of the Willamette Valley, 20 miles south of Portland, Oregon. From Portland and the south take U.S. 205 to exit 10. Follow signs to the End of the Oregon Trail Interpretive Center at 1726 Washington Street near U.S. 205.

The End of the Oregon Trail Interpretive Center is open in summer, Monday through Saturday, 9 A.M.–6 P.M., and Sunday, 10 A.M.–5 P.M. Shows ($) are scheduled weekdays every 45 minutes beginning at 9:15 A.M., with the last show at 4:45 P.M., and Sunday show times begin at 10 A.M., with the last show at 4 P.M. Winter hours are Monday through Saturday, 9 A.M.–5 P.M., and Sunday, 11 A.M.–5 P.M. Weekday show times begin at 9:30 A.M., with the last show at 4 P.M., and Sunday show times begin at 11:30 A.M., with the last show at 4 P.M. A summer outdoor theater production, *Oregon Fever* ($), is presented most evenings. It will reopen in the summer of 1998.

For information contact End of the Oregon Trail Interpretive Center, 1726 Washington Street, Oregon City, OR 97045. Tel. (503) 657-9336. For information and tickets to Oregon Fever, call (503) 657-0988.

Oregon's Oregon Trail

The Oregon Trail in Oregon winds 547 miles from the state's eastern border to Oregon City. You can follow the general direction of the trail by car on marked highways. The trail crosses private, state, and federal lands, but all of the 50 trail interpretive sites are accessible on established roads. (Please respect landowners' property.)

In the 1800s weary Oregon Trail emigrants had two choices for the final leg of their journey to Oregon City, which they called "the gates of Eden." Choice one was found about 80 miles northeast of their destination; emigrants could take a treacherous water route along the Columbia River. This route took them past Fort Vancouver and a chance for rest and supplies. Then they continued south on the Willamette River.

In 1845, when trail migration had gone from a trickle to a torrent, an enterprising Oregon man had an idea that became choice two. Sam Barlow decided to build a road over the south shoulder of towering **Mount Hood** to make a more direct route to Oregon City. With the official blessing of the Oregon Provisional Government and $4,000 from a friend, Barlow had the road built in the summer of 1846. He opened his Mount Hood Toll Road in time for the fall wagon-train traffic.

☛

Frame of Reference The Oregon Trail years were 1841 through 1860. The peak year of Oregon Trail migration was 1850. Oregon City was founded in 1844.

Significance Located at the falls of the Willamette (Wil–LAM–it) River, Oregon City was the official end of the Oregon Trail. Today numerous historic sites in the city and the privately operated End of the Trail Interpretive Center commemorate the mass migration of pioneers along the Oregon Trail.

Pioneers suffering "Oregon fever" came to Oregon City because that was where they could file claims for free land. Oregon City first functioned as the seat of the provisional government, then as capital of the Oregon Territory. The settlement, founded in 1829 in the fertile Willamette Valley, also had grass for animals, fresh water, plentiful fish at the falls, and businesses to replenish supplies.

Dr. John McLoughlin, commander of the Hudson's Bay Company's Fort Vancouver 25 miles north, founded Oregon City when he built three houses here. McLoughlin hoped his city would push British influence farther south. Then England could lay further claim to the vast Northwest Territory that Great Britain and the United States jointly held.

Oregon City was incorporated in 1844, making it the first true city west of the Mississippi River.

Meanwhile McLoughlin, a Canadian doctor, sold supplies, extended credit, and heartily encouraged American emigrants. In 1845, as Fort Vancouver's influence declined, McLoughlin's superiors forced him to retire. He bought Oregon City from the Hudson's Bay Company for $20,000. He built businesses—many dependent on the thunderous Willamette Falls (the "Niagara Falls of the Northwest")—served as mayor, and donated land for schools and churches. He continued to support the American pioneers, whom he came to believe had the right to the land. He took U.S. citizenship in 1851 and became known as "the Father of Oregon."

Trail enthusiasts now can trace the road, which the emigrants dubbed "the Barlow Road," at Mount Hood. The 11,245-foot Cascade Summit is about one hour east of Oregon City. The self-guided tour takes tenacity, but you can see remnants of the original road on hills, toll gate replicas, and ruts cut when wagons careened downhill. Plan your visit when Mount Hood snows have receded and roads are open. Tours begin at Laurel Hill.

To negotiate Laurel Hill's steep slopes, emigrants sometimes unloaded their wagons, took their goods to the bottom of the hill, and then lowered the wagon on ropes slipped around trees. Or they set the brakes on the wagons' back wheels, chained trees to the wagons for anchors, and made their way down the hillside chutes. As the wagons shimmied down the hill, the wheels spewed out gravel, eroding the passage. Eventually the chutes became impassable and emigrants found new ones. Evidence of these hillside chutes remains today.

A useful guide to this last stretch of Oregon Trail is Jim Tompkins's *Discovering Laurel Hill and the Barlow Road*. Buy the booklet from the interpretive center or the Oregon Trail Foundation, Inc., P.O. Box 511, Oregon City, OR 97045. Tel. (503) 557-1151. For more information contact these organizations:

- **Oregon Tourism Division,** 775 Summer Street NE, Salem, OR 97310. Tel. (503) 986-0000 or 1-800-547-7842.
- **Mt. Hood Visitor Information Center,** 65000 East Highway 26, Welches, OR 97067. Tel. (503) 622-4822.

▲

Oregon City was the Pacific Northwest's center of culture, business, and government even before Congress declared the Oregon Territory in 1848. The city is a city of firsts in the American West. Oregon City can boast America's first city jail, first newspaper (the *Spectator*), first Protestant Church, first hotel west of the Rockies (the Main Street House), first fire department on the West Coast, first navigation locks in the Pacific Northwest, and first long-distance transmissions of electricity, thanks to the falls.

Oregon City was the beginning of Oregon.

About the Site The End of the Oregon Trail Interpretive Center comprises three buildings that look like three wagons, each 50 feet high.

A guided tour "show" begins at Wagon #1, the Missouri Center. Visitors enter an Independence, Missouri, store—McCoy & Noland, Provisioners—and take a seat. A chatty trail guide, with the help of an audiovisual show, lists what you'll need to get safely out to Oregon Country, including a sturdy wagon, a team of oxen, 600 pounds of bacon, 20 pounds of sugar, coffee, bullets, and much more.

Wagon #2 houses the Cascade Theater. Here a fabulous 22-minute multimedia event, *Oregon!*, tells about the Oregon Trail through the diaries of four travelers.

You reach Oregon in Wagon #3. The museum and exhibits are free. There's also a gift shop and information table here.

The Oregon Trail

About 400,000 emigrants traveled the 2,170-mile Oregon Trail from Missouri to Oregon in the early 19th century. Oregon Trail pioneers were called *emigrants* because they were leaving the United States for unsettled territories.

Today you can follow in the emigrants' footsteps, exploring on foot and by auto the 125 historic sites and 300 miles of wagon ruts along the Oregon Trail corridor. Much of the original trail today is interstate highway.

The Oregon Trail years began about 1840. The trail's peak year was 1850. By 1860, when the Civil War erupted, an estimated 300,000 emigrants had traveled the trail. The completion of the transcontinental railroad in 1869 wrote the final chapter of the trail's pioneer migration.

Oregon Trail pioneers left everything they knew and loved in the East to seek free land and better lives in the West. They made their way to the edge of the frontier in Missouri. There they readied for their overland journey. At jumping-off points like Independence, they repaired their prairie schooners or bought new ones, learned to drive a team of oxen, and bought supplies. By the time they were ready to pull out, their wagons were filled to capacity, so emigrants mostly walked.

Wagon caravans, usually headed by seasoned trail masters, followed paths forged by Native North Americans and mountain men. Trail maps were courtesy of John Charles Fremont, "the Pathfinder," who had explored the region in the early 1840s. In 1842 Fremont mapped the Oregon Trail. Reports of his explorations, some with famous frontiersman Christopher "Kit" Carson, were published in 1845. Fremont's work heightened interest in the West.

The Oregon Trail held hardship and death. An estimated 6 to 10 percent of emigrants—maybe 20,000 people—died en route to the Pacific Northwest. That translates to one grave every 80 yards of the way. Most Oregon Trail graves are unmarked. Disease, especially cholera, caused most deaths; accidents were a close second. Most accidental deaths were from gunshot wounds.

☛

The Interpretive Center occupies Abernathy Green, 8½ grassy acres that served as the main arrival area for Oregon Trail emigrants.

You can buy tickets for regularly scheduled shows at a booth near the parking lot. The museum store sells tickets when the booth is closed.

HISTORIC OREGON CITY

Oregon City sits on three basalt terraces formed by the withdrawal of an ancient sea toward the Pacific. The low riverfront area preserves the city's first business area. Here you can stroll along one of the American West's first Main Streets. All historic buildings have descriptive plaques.

At this level, one mile south of downtown above the Willamette Falls, sits the old riverboat settlement of Canemah. Visitors can take a walking tour of the Canemah Historic District. You can see houses built in the 1850s, 1860s, and 1870s. The falls area is the site of the country's first public amusement park, built in 1882.

A few hundred feet above, Oregon City's second level protects the residential district known as the McLoughlin Neighborhood. Here you'll find the 1845 home of Dr. John McLoughlin and the next-door home of Dr. Forbes Barclay. Stone steps and the Municipal Elevator at the end of 7th Street connect the terraces.

The most famous tale of hardship and tragedy on the Oregon Trail involved the 81-person party led by George Donner, an Illinois farmer, in 1846. The Donner Party was a textbook study of mistakes. The group started out too late to avoid mountain snows. They took risky shortcuts. They ditched precious supplies. In the last mountain pass before their destination, Sacramento, a major snowfall trapped the desperate pioneers. Stranded and starving, some ate the flesh of the dead. Only 47 survivors made it to California.

The Oregon Trail branched into several segments along portions of its final half, but the route through the Rocky Mountains was South Pass in Wyoming. Some of the clearest stretches of wagon ruts along the trail remain in Wyoming.

Emigrant diaries vividly describe natural land formations along the trail and made places such as Chimney Rock, Scotts Bluff, Register Cliff, and Independence Rock famous. Travelers today enjoy these landmarks with the conveniences of restrooms, restaurants, and motels.

For maps and information on the Oregon Trail contact these groups:

- **National Park Service,** Long-Distance Trails Office, 324 South State Street, Salt Lake City, UT 84145-0155. Tel. (801) 539-4093.
- **Oregon-California Trails Association,** 524 South Osage Street, P.O. Box 1019, Independence, MO 64501-0519. Tel. (816) 252-2276.
- **Oregon Trail Coordinating Council,** 222 Northwest Davis, Suite 309, Portland, OR 97205. Tel. (503) 228-7245.

You also can contact the Bureau of Land Management in individual states, as well as state departments of tourism. Some private companies offer overnight wagon-train treks along portions of the trail.

▲

The McLoughlin House National Historic Site ($) is open daily, except in January, on all major holidays, and Monday, from Tuesday through Saturday, 10 A.M.–4 P.M., and Sunday, 1 P.M.–4 P.M. It is located in McLoughlin Park between 7th and 8th streets, at 713

Center Street. The Barclay House is at 719 Center Street. For information contact Curator, McLoughlin House National Historic Site, 713 Center Street, Oregon City, OR 97045. Tel. (503) 656-5146.

The city's third level, 200 feet above the second, stretches south and east toward Mount Hood and the Cascade Mountains. It includes the early settlement of Elyville along Molalla Avenue. Historic homes here are not open to the public.

Hot Tips Allow 1½ hours at the Interpretive Center. Plan on a ½ day visit to include the McLoughlin House, the Barclay House, and downtown sites.

The Oregon City Trolley offers free tours from the Interpretive Center to the Clackamas County Historical Museum. Call (503) 656-1629 for information. The Interpretive Center web site address is http://www.teleport.com./~eotic.

Food and accommodations are available in Oregon City and Portland. Snacks and gourmet coffee can be purchased at a snack wagon at the Interpretive Center.

Arrive at least 15 minutes before your scheduled tour time. The Interpretive Center theaters have benches without back rests. If this presents a problem for you, head for the back row and lean against the wall. You'll be sitting for 45 minutes.

The Best Stuff The multimedia presentation *Oregon!* is fabulous. Stories of four real-life individuals who traveled the Oregon Trail 140 years ago unfold on a wall-size screen. You're surrounded by blood-stirring sounds of commissioned musical scores and ballads. Lights flash to create prairie storms; winds blow through speakers behind you. By the time the 22-minute show is over, you'll feel as if you've been walking for days on a 2000-mile journey.

The costumed guide is terrific as he readies you for the trail in "Missouri." Using plenty of Oregon Trail props—including a genuine buffalo chip—he delivers a lot of infotainment.

Then and Now Just as Independence, Missouri, the Oregon Trail head, now stands in the long shadow of Kansas City, Oregon City sits in the shadow of Portland, Oregon's largest city. The National Park Service identified Oregon City as the official end of the Oregon Trail in August 1981.

Elsewhere in the Area Clackamas County Museum of History is at 211 Tumwater Drive. In Portland, the Oregon History Center is at 1200 Southwest Park; the Pittock Mansion is at 3229 Northwest Pittock Drive; Oregon Maritime Center and Museum is at 113 Southwest Front Avenue; and Cowboys Then and Now Museum is at 729 Northeast Oregon.

On the other side of the state at Baker City, the Oregon Trail Regional Museum also has Oregon Trail exhibits.

Fort Vancouver

Hub of the 19th-Century Pacific Northwest

Location Southwest Washington State at the Oregon border. The fort stands across the Columbia River from Portland, Oregon, and 137 miles south of Tacoma, Washington. From the north and south take U.S. 5 to the Mill Plain Boulevard exit. Follow signs to the visitor center on East Evergreen Boulevard. From the west take U.S. 26 to U.S. 5; from the east take U.S. 84 to U.S. 5.

Fort Vancouver National Historic Site ($) is open daily, except Thanksgiving, December 24 and 25, and January 1, from September 22 through May 9, 9 A.M.–4 P.M., and from May 10 through September 21, 9 A.M.–5 P.M. Interpretive programs and special events include Queen Victoria's Birthday on May 18 and Trappers' Brigade Encampment, July 19 and 20. For information contact Superintendent, Fort Vancouver National Historic Site, 612 East Reserve Street, Vancouver, WA 98601-3897. Tel. (360) 696-7655.

For information on Officers' Row, contact the Vancouver/Clark County Visitors and Convention Bureau, 404 East 15th Street, Suite 11, Vancouver, WA 98663. Tel. (360) 642-2400 or 1-800-451-2542.

Frame of Reference In the mid–19th century, England and the United States were locked in a struggle for control of the fur-rich Pacific Northwest. The English established Fort Vancouver in 1825 as headquarters for its Hudson's Bay Company. The fort's fur-trading heyday was the 1830s and 1840s.

In 1849 the fur company vacated the fort. The U.S. Army established Camp Vancouver, later renamed Vancouver Barracks, at the site. Vancouver Barracks remains active today. Fire and decay destroyed the original Fort Vancouver by 1866.

Significance For more than three critical decades Fort Vancouver served as the center of the Hudson's Bay Company operations in the Pacific Northwest. At this fort, physically isolated but bustling with activity, England ruled the region's lucrative fur trade. Fort Vancouver, named in honor of British sea explorer Captain George Vancouver, anchored British claim to the Pacific Northwest region.

Under the command of Dr. John McLoughlin, the fort's "Chief Factor," the post served as the British company's regional supply depot and administrative center. It headed five fur-trading posts and 23 forts in present-day British Columbia, Washington, and Oregon.

The British gave McLoughlin, a Canadian physician, a mandate to establish British territorial supremacy and thwart America's westward expansion. He ignored it. McLoughlin warmly supplied Oregon Trail settlers and extended them credit. His deeds earned him the ire of his superiors—he was forced to retire—but the love of Americans. McLoughlin moved south and founded Oregon City.

Until the huge Oregon Trail migration in the 1840s and 1850s, Fort Vancouver and the Hudson's Bay Company reigned supreme. The fort introduced white civilization into the Northwest and helped develop the region. Throngs of American settlers, however, loosened England's grip on the land.

In 1846 a treaty between the United States and England established the 49th Parallel at the southern boundary of Canada. Fort Vancouver was stranded deep within American soil. The Hudson's Bay Company soon relinquished the fort to the U.S. Army. The Hudson's Bay Company continued trade in the area through the 1850s but moved out in 1860.

The U.S. Army's new Camp Vancouver was the first U.S. military post in Oregon Territory. Other firsts include the first orchards in the Northwest and the region's first theatrical performance, produced by naval officers. Also Chief Factor McLoughlin is considered the grandfather of the famous Washington State apple industry.

About the Site Fort Vancouver is a work in progress. Reconstruction began in 1966. About a dozen bare wood buildings and a 15-foot-high Douglas fir stockade have been completed. The stockade encloses the buildings and a grassy rectangle about the size of two football fields. Asphalt slabs outline sites of another dozen buildings slated for future reconstruction.

Visitors can tour Chief Factor's house, the blacksmith shop, Native North American trade shop/dispensary, wash house, kitchen, fur-shipping room, and a bastion and necessaries (outhouses). A corner building serves as headquarters for the fort's ongoing archaeological studies. Visitors can watch as researchers identify and label some of the one million artifacts unearthed at the 65-acre park.

A nearby English garden symbolizes the many gardens and fields of self-sufficient Fort Vancouver's heyday. At that time a laborer's village of up to 750 people surrounded the fort palisades. Nothing remains of the village nor the perimeter fence that enclosed it and 2,500 British acres. Vancouver Barracks occupy the area today.

The park visitor center houses a fine museum, gift shop, and theater where you can watch a 15-minute orientation video. The video is part of a series titled *Landmarks of the Oregon Country*. In summer the fort is alive with costumed interpreters; building tours are self-guided. The rest of the year visits are by guided tour only.

OFFICERS' ROW

Across the street from the Fort Vancouver Visitor Center stands the Officers' Row National Historic District. The district preserves a stately row of 21 Victorian homes built for army officers stationed at Camp Vancouver. The city of Vancouver owns the unique site. It is the only entire row of historical officers' homes preserved in the nation. The row also is the Pacific Northwest's first neighborhood.

The ornate houses, built between 1850 and 1906, were home to generals and their families. Military notables such as General Ulysses S. Grant, General George Marshall, and General Omar Bradley lived and worked here.

Today condominiums and offices fill most of the homes, but several are open to the public. These include the 1850 Grant House—formerly the commanding officer's home, then the officer's club, and now a restaurant—and the Marshall House. Both have gift shops. Officers' Row overlooks tree-lined Vancouver Central Park on the high banks of the Columbia River.

Hot Tips Allow two hours for the fort tour, museum, and video. Add additional time if you include Officers' Row. Dress for the weather. Ground in the fort is uneven and may be muddy. Parking lots are located at the visitor center and the fort, situated down a long hill behind the visitor center. Food and accommodations are available in Vancouver and Portland.

The Best Stuff Park rangers say kids enjoy the dispensary and fur warehouse the most. Older visitors may find the elegant Chief Factor's House, with its large dining hall, plush Victorian parlor, and front-door grapevine, fascinating. When costumed interpreters crank up fires in the blacksmith's shop, the bakery, and the Chief Factor's kitchen, it's a hands-on treat.

Historic furnishings are exceptionally detailed and interesting. The tour will give you a good idea of what it was like to be hospitalized at the fort in the 1840s, what officers ate with their pewter tableware, and how a beaver pelt was readied for shipment to England to be made into hats, coat trims, and mufflers for the wealthy.

Then and Now In 1818, less than two decades after Lewis and Clark came through, England and the United States agreed to a joint occupation of the Oregon Territory until a boundary could be decided. But seven years later the Hudson's Bay Company boldly moved its northwest headquarters here from Fort George in coastal Astoria.

Fort Vancouver drove out fur-trapping competition in the Northwest with its "fur brigades" of 20 to 50 trappers, sometimes including families. The brigades would trap an area until there were no pelt-bearing animals left. Records show that in 1843 alone Fort Vancouver handled 61,118 whole pelts, mostly beaver.

By the time the British withdrew from the region, the short-lived fur trade was declining anyway. European and American high society had forsaken beaver hats for silk ones. Other American fur-trading posts, such as John Astor's American Fur Company in North Dakota and Bent's Old Fort in southern Colorado also ran aground.

Today four-lane Highway 14, the Lewis and Clark Highway, runs between the reconstructed fort and the Columbia River. The huge Interstate Bridge, built in 1917, spans the Columbia, only a stone's throw from Fort Vancouver's parade ground.

Washington, once part of the Oregon Territory, separated from Oregon in March 1853.

Elsewhere in the Area Pearson Air Park Museum is located next to Fort Vancouver. The city of Vancouver has many historic buildings, homes, and parks. Dr. John McLoughlin's house is located in Oregon City, 20 miles south of Portland.

The site of the first sawmill in the Northwest, built in 1847 to serve Hudson's Bay Company, stands on Highway 14, six miles east of I-5. Old Apple Tree Park, near the east intersection of U.S. 5 and Highway 14 on Columbia Way, honors McLoughlin. The park's cornerstone is the Old Apple Tree, planted in 1826 under McLoughlin's direction. The tree still bears fruit.

Appendix I

TOP TEN SITES

(in alphabetical order)

Dayton Aviation Trail, Ohio

Edison's Laboratory, New Jersey

Freedom Trail, Massachusetts

Gettysburg, Pennsylvania

Golden Gate National Recreation Area, California. Listed under Fort Point, a 70,000-acre site of 22 natural and historic sites including Fort Point; Alcatraz; the Presidio, the 1,480-acre U.S. Army base/urban park; Fort Mason, now a cultural and recreation center; Muir Woods, one of the Bay Area's last uncut stands of old-growth redwood; and the San Francisco Maritime National Historical Park.

Independence National Historical Park, Pennsylvania

Jamestown, Williamsburg, and Yorktown, Virginia

Lincoln Heritage Trail, includes sites in Kentucky, Indiana, and Illinois

Martin Luther King Jr. National Historic Site, Georgia

Mesa Verde, Colorado

Appendix II

◆ Top Ten Hidden Jewels ◆

(in alphabetical order)

Crazy Horse Memorial, South Dakota

Cumberland Gap, Kentucky

Dealey Plaza Including The Sixth Floor Museum, Texas

Knife River Indian Villages, North Dakota

Moundville, Alabama

Natchez/Natchez Trace, Mississippi

Oregon City, Oregon

Russell Cave, Alabama

Seneca Falls and the Women's Rights National Historical Park, New York

Washington's Crossing, New Jersey and Pennsylvania

Bibliography

Bahne, Charles. *The Complete Guide to Boston's Freedom Trail*. Cambridge, MA: Newtowne Publishing, 1993.

Barey, Patricia. *Bandelier National Monument*. Tucson, AZ: Southwest Parks and Monuments Association, 1990.

Bergon, Frank. *Journals of Lewis and Clark*. Toronto: Penguin Books, 1989.

Bollinger, Mark J., and Landrum, Brenda G., editors. *The Story of Andersonville Prison and American Prisoners of War*. Atlanta, GA: Eastern National Park and Monument Association, 1993.

Briggs, Rose T. *Plymouth Rock: History and Significance*. Boston, MA: Nimrod Press, 1968.

Brown, Willard D. *The Story of Buckman Tavern*. Lexington, MA: Lexington Historical Society, 1989.

Carlson, John B. "Hopewell: Prehistoric America's Golden Age," *Early Man* magazine. Evanston, IL: Northwestern Archaeological Program, 1979.

Carruth, Garton. *The Encyclopedia of American Facts & Dates*. New York: Harper & Row, Publishers, 1987.

Catton, Bruce, and American Heritage editors. *The Battle of Gettysburg*. Mahwah, NJ: Troll Associates, 1993.

Cook, Dorothy Meade. *Heart Bags & Hand Shakes: The Story of the Cook Collection*. Lake Ann, MI: National Woodlands Publishing Co., 1994.

Daughters of the Republic of Texas. *The Alamo: Long Barracks Museum*. Dallas, TX: Taylor Publishing Co., 1986.

Davis, Kenneth C. *Don't Know Much About History*. New York: Avon Books, 1995.

Delgadod, James P. *Alcatraz: Island of Change*. San Francisco, CA: Golden Gate Parks Association, 1991.

Dillinger, William C. *The Gold Discovery: James Marshall and the California Gold Rush*. Santa Barbara, CA: California Parks and Recreation, 1990.

Dublin, Thomas. *Lowell: The Story of an Industrial City*. Washington, D.C.: National Park Service, 1992.

Dykeman, Wilma. *With Fire and Sword: The Battle of Kings Mountain 1780.* Washington, D.C.: National Park Service, 1978.

Foulke, Patricia, and Foulke, Robert. *Colonial America.* Old Saybrook, CT: Globe Pequot Press, 1995.

Gardner, Mark. *Little Bighorn Battlefield National Monument.* Tucson, AZ: Southwest Parks and Monuments Association, 1996.

Glotzhober, Robert C., and Lepper, Bradley T. *Serpent Mound, Ohio's Enigmatic Effigy Mound.* Columbus, OH: Ohio Historical Society, 1994.

Griffin, Lynne, and McCann, Kelly. *The Book of Women.* Holbrook, MA: Bob Adams, Inc., 1992.

Hakim, Rita. *Martin Luther King Jr. and the March Toward Freedom.* Brookfield, CT: The Millbrook Press, 1991.

Hamblin, Colin B. *Ellis Island.* Santa Barbara, CA: Companion Press, 1994.

Houk, Rose. *Golden Spike.* Tucson, AZ: Southwest Parks and Monument Association, 1990.

Johnston, Norma. *Remember the Ladies: The First Women's Rights Convention.* New York: Scholastic, Inc., 1995.

Knight, James E. *Boston Tea Party* . Mahwah, NJ: Troll Associates, 1982.

Lekson, Stephen H., Windes, Thomas C., Stein, John R., and Judge, W. James. "Chaco Canyon Community," *Scientific American*, July 1988.

Lepper, Bradley T. *People of the Mounds: Ohio's Hopewell Culture.* Columbus, OH: Ohio Historical Society, 1995.

Marsh, Dorothy. *Life at Russell Cave.* New York: Eastern National Park & Monument Association, 1980.

Mercurio, Gian, and Peschel, Maxymilian L. *Mesa Verde: a Complete Guide.* Cortez, CO: Lonewolf Publishing, 1995.

Meyers, L. F. *History, Battles and Fall of the Alamo.* San Antonio, TX: Daughters of the Republic of Texas, 1896.

Miller, Carl. "Life 8,000 Years Ago Uncovered in an Alabama Cave." Washington, D.C.: National Geographic Magazine, 1956.

Mink, Claudia Gellman. *Cahokia: City of the Sun.* Collinsville, IL: Cahokia Mounds Museum Society, 1992.

O'Brien, William Patrick. *Independence Square, a Convenient Guide to the Past for Today's Pioneers.* AMERIFAX, 1985.

Oliva, Leo E. *Fort Scott, Courage and Conflict on the Border.* Topeka, KS: Kansas State Historical Society, 1996.

Peckham, Alford S. *Lexington: Gateway to Freedom*. Lexington, MA: Lexington Chamber of Commerce, 1992.

Price, William H. *Civil War Handbook*. Fairfax, VA: L. B. Prince Co., Inc., 1961.

Reid, Russell. *Sakakawea: The Bird Woman*. Bismarck, ND: State Historical Society of North Dakota, 1986.

Richards, Norman. *The Story of Old Ironsides (Cornerstones of Freedom)*. Chicago: Childrens Press, 1967.

Rudig, Doug. *Bent's Old Fort Adventure Guide for Kids*. La Junta, CO: Bent's Old Fort National Historical Association, 1984.

Salts, Bobbi. *Discover Mount Rushmore*. Scottsdale, AZ: American Educational Press, 1995.

Sewall, Marcia. *The Pilgrims of Plimoth*. New York: Aladdin Paperbacks, 1986.

Smelser, Marshall, and Gundersen, Joan R. *American History at a Glance*. New York: Harper Perennial, 1978.

St. Louis Regional Commerce & Growth Association. *Mounds to Mansions: Historical Sites of the St. Louis Region*. St. Louis, MO: St. Louis Regional Commerce & Growth Association, 1976.

Stratton, Elaine. *St. Louis and the River: A "Lite" History*. St. Louis, MO: Swiss Village Book Store, 1988.

Strutin, Michele. *Chaco: A Cultural Legacy*. Tucson, AZ: Southwest Parks & Monuments Association, 1994.

Sullivan, Noelle, and Vrooman, Nicholas Peterson. *M-e' E'cci Aashi Awadi: The Knife River Indian Villages*. Medora, ND: Theodore Roosevelt Nature and History Association, 1995.

Time-Life Books, editors. *The American Indians* series. Alexandria, VA: Time-Life Books, 1994.

Tindall, George Brown, and Shi, David E. *America: A Narrative History*. New York: W. W. Norton & Co., 1996.

Utley, Robert M. *Little Bighorn Battlefield: A History and Guide to the Battle of the Little Bighorn*. Washington, D.C.: National Park Service, 1994.

Walthall, John A. *Moundville: An Introduction to the Archaeology of a Mississippian Chiefdom*. Tuscaloosa, AL: Alabama Museum of Natural History, 1994.

Whipple, S. Lawrence. *The Hancock-Clarke House*. Lexington, MA: Lexington Historical Society, 1984.

Zinsser, William. *American Places*. New York: Harper Perennial, 1992.

Acknowledgments

My loving and heartfelt thanks go to my husband, Barry Ahrendt, whose support on many levels makes all the difference in the world. I also thank my teenage daughters, Katie and Georgianna, who took time from their busy lives to visit historic sites with me and share their views.

For their encouragement and support, I am grateful to my family, especially my brother Ed, and to my friends, particularly Lenore Henry. Thanks also to Dr. Bart Wendell and to my fellow travelers on the Lewis and Clark Trail, Fran and Dick Ungemach.

Last, but not least, my sincere appreciation goes to the small army of park rangers and volunteers at historic sites across America who cheerfully endured my barrage of questions and greatly helped illuminate this book.

Index